AMERICAN
GAY

Worlds of Desire: The Chicago Series on Sexuality, Gender, and Culture
Edited by Gilbert Herdt

American

G·A·Y

STEPHEN O. MURRAY

THE UNIVERSITY OF CHICAGO PRESS
Chicago and London

Stephen O. Murray is the author of six books, including *Latin American Male Homosexualities* and *Oceanic Homosexualities*.

The University of Chicago Press, Chicago 60637
The University of Chicago Press, Ltd., London
©1996 by The University of Chicago
All rights reserved. Published 1996
Printed in the United States of America

05 04 03 02 01 00 99 98 97 96   5 4 3 2 1

ISBN (cloth): 0-226-55191-1
ISBN (paper): 0-226-55193-8

Library of Congress Cataloging-in-Publication Data

Murray, Stephen O.
    American gay / Stephen O. Murray.
      p.   cm.—(Worlds of desire)
    Includes bibliographical references and index.
    ISBN 0-226-55191-1 (cloth).—ISBN 0-226-55193-8 (paper)
    1. Gays—North America.   2. Homosexuality—North
America.
  I. Title. II. Series.
  HQ76.3.N67M87   1996
  306.76′6′097—dc20
                                   95-49388
                                    CIP

To the memory of friends who helped shape this book and who should have been around to read it—

PHILIP W. BLUMSTEIN

JOEL I. BRODSKY

GREGORY BURGARD

JOSEPH J. HAYES

R. LAUD HUMPHREYS

MARTIN P. LEVINE

TEDE MATTHEWS

KENNETH W. PAYNE

JESSE O. SAWYER

ROSENDO CHAUES TABTAB

—and to the appallingly large number of other gay intellectuals AIDS prevented me from knowing better

Contents

CONTENTS

CONTENTS

Illustrations

Introduction

This book is my attempt to make sense of my own society—one that continues to imperil me for being gay—and to see whether the theories put forth to explain modern society and modern homosexuality make any sense of the changing lesbigay [1] lives I have seen in the northernmost two countries of North America.[2] From the time I was an undergraduate and throughout my foreshortened adult life, I have compared Anglo North American ways of conceiving and managing homosexuality with those of other cultures. Although the panicked mobilization against homosexuals in the United States seems approached only by that in Canada and the British Isles,[3] neither in my fairly extensive physical travels nor in my more extensive reading about other times and places have I found any utopia for sexual nonconformists. However, coming from romantic traditions, I believe that anything that does not affirm existing social arrangements makes alternative ones more likely— at the very least, by opening cognitive space in which imagination and hope can live. I don't like how either my natal society or the scholarly disciplines in which I have been involved [4] denigrate and marginalize homosexuality and those for whom open avowal of homosexual orientation is a defining part of self (i.e., an *identity*). Insofar as I seek to understand the way things are, it is

1. "Lesbigay" may be read as either 'lesbian and gay' or as 'lesbian, bisexual, and gay'.

2. My experiences of the emerging gay organization of the next two countries (Mexico and Guatemala) are the focus of Murray 1995a,b.

3. Australia in recent years stands in the way of linking this particular animus to "English-speaking," and Noye (1997) notes that in Africa former French colonies have more punitive sodomy laws than former British colonies, despite the contrast between the Code Napoléon with no sodomy proscription and the punitive British laws still in force at the time colonies achieved independence.

4. Particularly anthropology (Weston 1993b), but see also Murray 1989a, 1990b on sociology.

1

not to forgive, but to push to do better: to form a better society and to formulate better theory.

Much of the homosexual behavior in Anglo North America, and even more of it in Latin America, is not between persons who consider themselves to be "homosexuals." Most homosexual behavior occurs outside the often simplistic roles recognized (by labels) in a society. This is true even where, as in contemporary cities in the Americas, people know and use multiple labels for self-reference.

Although to understand North American homosexualities, one needs to know that there are other arrangements of the often conflated analytical categories of sexuality, sex, and gender in other places,[5] the present volume does not attempt further to refine cross-cultural typology, nor to consider multiple instances of each type.[6] Instead, it focuses on the gender-to-gay transformation, on what has happened since that transition occurred in North America, and on the complexity (especially racial/ethnic) of contemporary North American lesbigay communities.[7]

What is distinctive about the "modern" (gay/egalitarian) cultural conception and social organization of homosexuality—the type of central interest in this volume—is the combination of (1) a consciousness of group distinctiveness, (2) separate institutions and culture (de-assimilation) based on the *possibilities* of (3) egalitarian (not gender-role-bound or involving the submission of the young) and of (4) exclusive (not bisexual) same-sex relations.[8]

5. See Murray 1994b. Even in much feminist discourse, *gender* is often a codeword for "sex," neither a distinct level of analysis (with more than one kind of gendering per sex), nor a continuous variable.

6. This is how I organized material from a geographical arc extending from Madagascar to the Bering Sea in Murray 1992a. The introduction to that volume lays out the typology.

7. The appendix to chapter 6 focuses on theorizing about a widely attested traditional gender-defined role previously called *berdache* (a term rejected by some contemporary lesbigay native people and anthropologists in favor of *two-spirited*). The rapidly expanding literature debates continuity between this role and contemporary lesbigay Indians and whether (homo)-sexuality was a criterial feature or a strong correlation. Roscoe 1987 provides a comprehensive review of the primary literature; Roscoe 1995b takes on the question of calling such persons from the Native American past *gay;* and Roscoe 1988b collects contemporary lesbigay Native voices.

8. Adam 1979; also see Plummer 1981, 1992. On the process of diffusion/development of the modern/gay type elsewhere, see Murray 1992a:353–96, 1992b, 1995a, c, 1996; Carrier 1995; Murray and Roscoe 1997. Lesbian communities are less fully developed on all four characteristics. I attribute this to lesser numbers of those committed to and defining themselves as "lesbian" (in contrast to gay men), to discrimination against women (especially against women unaccompanied by men in "public"), and to primary socialization (which remains primarily women's work, though eradicating "sissy" traits is more shared than most other childrearing tasks are).

It is both arrogant and ignorant to suppose that no one ever noticed a pattern of same-sex sexuality (one's own or others') or that there were no congregations of those seeking such pleasures before the term *homosexual* was coined in 1869,[9] or before it diffused to societies beyond northwest Europe and Anglo North America more recently. Similarly, there have been some exclusively homosexual individuals and some egalitarian homosexual relationships throughout recorded history. What is distinctive is the dovetailing of these not themselves unprecedented characteristics and their importance for larger congeries than tricks, pairs, or small cliques of same-sex lovers.

The first two chapters discuss the mass basis, political mobilization, and cultural florescence based on consciousness of shared homosexuality. Since the whole book challenges received notions about society and the place in it of homosexual behavior, and of people defining themselves as homosexual (lesbian, gay, queer),[10] and because several friends have suggested that my writing (in particular, my 1984 book, which was an earlier draft of part 1) approaches being theoretically nihilistic,[11] it may be apposite to note that my own initial conception of homosexuality (not least my own, once I recognized it) grew from believing in the utopian oppositional role in which Herbert Marcuse cast *homosexuals* in *Eros and Civilization* (1955).[12] In the Frankfurt School–Hegelian/Freudian Marxism lens through which I first thought about homosexuality (abetted by Dennis Altman's 1971 book, *Homosexual: Oppression and Liberation*, published just barely in time to be available to me in my own coming out), negation of negation is not just affirmation, but is the *only* imaginable affirmation in an increasingly formally rational, substantively irrational, dystopian world.

Long before the shattering of linearity and totality by deconstructionists and the vogue of Mikhail Bakhtin and poststructuralists, Herbert Marcuse and Theodor Adorno advocated and exemplified multiple, partial approaches

9. On self-conceptions see Murray 1988b; Mott and Assunção 1988; Dall'Orto 1988; on recognized cruising grounds see Murray and Gerard 1983; Rocke 1988; Ruggiero 1985.

10. Generally, I endeavor to use terms that people use to describe themselves. I use "moral entrepreneur" and "creationist" knowing that those so labeled might not recognize themselves in these labels.

11. Gerard (1988:497) suggested that I was a closet Weberian. I thought that my comparativism was *explicitly* Weberian. Moreover, I think that my bases in the urban, multi-ethnic symbolic interactionism of Frank Miyamoto and Tamotsu Shibutani and the social psychology of resistance and reproduction of domination of Adam (1978c) are obvious. Resistance has recently been a favorite topic for anthropological discourse, e.g., Scott 1985, 1990.

12. Homosexuality, for Marcuse (and for Harry Hay, see Roscoe 1996), presented a welcome possibility of challenge to the ontological structure of technological society and reproduction of competitive, aggressive men and commodified women, not a certainty of a new consciousness, let alone successful collective action to overthrow the existing technological society.

3

to understanding social phenomena. My book approaches modern North American homosexualities from a number of perspectives, encompassing at least some variety of experiences, kinds of data, and levels of analysis. I try to quantify what can be quantified and to listen closely to native voices to understand variety within categories and to understand others' experiences of being gay, lesbian (etc.) in twentieth-century North America.

The chapters in part 1 move forward through time (at varying speeds!), focusing on some of the surprises thrown up by history to and after incipient lesbigay "liberation." I find various sociological theoretical perspectives either wrong or inadequate for understanding North American lesbigay history, society, and culture. Since the late 1970s I have conceived of lesbigay people as a quasi-ethnic group, stressing our challenges to the venerable stigmatization of "homosexuals" and our voluntary de-assimilation from the dominant society, its gender and relationship norms, and its institutions. Chapters 3–5 discuss instances of lesbians[13] and gay men trying to reincorporate themselves into conventional morality by joining in denigrating various conceptions of unruly types who must be controlled (and/or rejected) by right-thinking, "respectable" homosexuals. There is a long-running or recurrent split between those who demand that gay people (including lesbians) be accepted as we are, in all our diversity,[14] and those who believe that what makes many straight people uncomfortable can and should be suppressed, so that only homosexuals who are otherwise entirely "respectable"[15] should exist—or at least that only conventional ones should ever appear in public.

Coming from the aforementioned romantic tradition of celebrating differences (in particular, the special genius of particular peoples resisting domination), in this book as elsewhere I stress how lesbigay people differ, both from the dominant society and from each other. I don't think that "we're the same except for what we do in bed." I think that we—at least the many of us who grew up estranged (sexually or otherwise) from the dominant

13. Chapter 3 focuses on "the New Man." I do not attempt to explain the contemporaneous "New Woman" of lesbian feminism nor the greater reliance on gender idioms (especially *butch/ femme*) among women than among men after the first flush of liberation rhetoric. See Zimmerman 1990:120–60; Faderman 1991b:204–52, 1992; Taylor and Whittier 1992; Weston 1993a.

14. A relatively early statement of this: "Just as blacks have come to recognize that no matter what their income, neighborhood, diction, or hue, they will remain 'niggers' so long as white society clings to its racial clichés, so every homosexual who has even one foot out of the closet knows that no matter what he says or how he acts, he will continue to be branded a 'queer' or a 'faggot' by straight society" (Mount 1972:10). For a more recent one, see Tucker (1988).

15. Specifically, conforming to the gender and conventional dress of their natal sex, church-going, involved in long-term monogamous couples, and not visibly involved in S&M or in indecorous protest of the status quo.

culture—see the world differently from those who unquestioningly fit into it. Moreover, what we do in bed is not very different from what straight people do—so that both halves of the claim are wrong.[16] While maintaining this, I am well aware of what I consider some individuals' compensatory hyperconformity. I am also aware that a few people never realized (or experienced) homosexuality as a basis for social condemnation, and that many individuals ("queer" as well as "closeted") don't want to be "defined" by their sexuality. In common with some of my friends whom I quote in chapter 8, I consider *gay* a state of mind, not of body, so that homosexual apologists for the socio-political status quo are not *gay* (or *lesbian*), i.e., those with gay(/lesbian) identity are only a minority of those who engage in homosexual behavior.

The chapters in part 2 try to make sense of *homosexual role* and of *gay community* and to examine how same-sex couples are like and unlike male–female couples. Each of these chapters includes a short appendix about some more specific aspect of the topic (a supposed "third gender" role, the formal rationality of having a "type," and "gay ghetto" costs and rewards).

The chapters in part 3 examine racial/ethnic differences in identification as *gay/lesbian/queer:* differences in timing and support in the rites of passage of coming out and moving to a city with a prominent gay community in chapter 9, external, allegedly "professional" models of gay African Americans before 1980 in chapter 10, representations since then of their own lesbigay and African American experiences in chapter 11. Chapters 12 and 13 discuss the bits of both kinds of representation of Mexican American and Asian/Pacific homosexualities that are available. I examine generational as well as geographic and racial/ethnic differences in conception of *gay community* (and *queer community*) in chapter 8, generational differences in migration and earning in the second half of chapter 9.

SOME CAUTIONS

Categories select some similarities and ignore some differences in what is categorized. This is no less true for the ethnic than for the sexual identity categories used herein, or for other categories such as *woman* or *capitalism.*[17]

---

16. This applies more to gay men than to lesbians, although there is probably as much diversity in sexual styles within the categories *gay, lesbian,* and *straight* as there is between them.

17. Thought requires categories—whereas categories do not require thought, and often enough, afford a comfortable substitute for it. Intellectuals hoping to think categories all the way through and/or to transvalue them and/or to call attention to their history(/historicity) tend to forget that most people are unconcerned about historically sound, consistent, or logical assign-

In my view, an enduring lesson of structuralism is that thought (not just categorization) operates by contrast(s). One can only understand what something is by differentiating it from what it is not.

Having briefly outlined what I am doing in this book, I feel the need also to discuss briefly some of what I am not doing (with a bit about why).

1. *Idealism.* Throughout the book, I recurrently argue—against the fantasies intellectuals have of their own importance—that while ideas matter (especially conceiving possible alternatives to social orders masked as "natural" ones), they don't matter all that much.

I believe that writing, and other kinds of representation, reflect rather than invent. The mirrors of "representation" are selectively placed and often distorting, so that inventorying representations is not a very good way to infer what typically goes on in any social world (alas!).[18] As an undergraduate, I wrote what I still think was a very good term paper on research (notably the Payne Fund studies) that attempted to blame Hollywood movies for changes in American sexual mores after World War I. Later attempts to blame violence against women on "pornography" (including films without women) seem to me to repeat the pattern of seeking to smash the mirrors—while denying that they could be reflecting anything already "out there" in the world. I would not deny that representations may channel desires. In my long-ago paper, I argued that if Hollywood taught people how to kiss, it is remarkable that tongues ever got involved, since even long kissing scenes do not show the tongues in action. Some will dismiss this as naive realism. Perhaps it is. But that anyone else sees or interprets texts or films in the way various scholars in "cultural studies" (including "queer theory") see or interpret them seems to me to require demonstration, i.e., empirical study of reception by whatever the actual audience is or was, and empirical evidence that such seeing and interpreting has any effect on what people do. I think it unlikely that North American homosexualities are going to change as a result of this book, just as I also think it unlikely that nineteenth-century psychiatric discourse invented homosexual self-consciousness, increased the repetition of homosexual acts, or invented homosexual selves.[19]

2. *Language.* Although I feel that in some sense I "went native" while

---

ment of phenomena to categories. Even category-generating intellectuals use some categories unreflectingly (in their technical work and, certainly, in their everyday life).

18. Even apart from genre conventions. The late John Boswell suggested the "cum shot" in hardcore films as an example of the danger of too-direct inference from cultural product to general patterns of conduct (specifically, inferring that 20th-century men always ejaculated outside their sexual partners).

19. I discuss this instance in more detail in chapter 1.

studying ethno- and sociolinguists,[20] I have not incorporated my work on gay language use in this volume,[21] except for that on the native understanding of *gay community*. Although I am uncomfortable with the recent trend in American anthropology against knowing or studying languages other than English,[22] I am also aware that overestimation of the extent to which language determines perception (constructs reality) continues.[23] Without a word for it or any awareness of role models, lesbians and gay men recurrently seek love they have not seen represented, have not heard spoken. In 1925, F. O. Matthiesen wrote Russell Cheney,

> Of course, this life of ours is entirely new—neither of us knows of a parallel case. We stand in the middle of an uncharted, uninhabited country. That there have been other unions like ours is obvious, but we are unable to draw on their experience. (29 January letter reproduced in Hyde 1978:71)

Still, in the 1960s Paul Monette

> had no choice but to keep on looking in the wrong places for the thing I'd never seen: two men in love and laughing. For that was the image in my head, though I'd never read it in any book or seen it in any movie. (1992:178)

Representations may help people find how and where to fulfill desires; they do not create them. Naming neither creates nor fulfills them; though, I shall argue, the crystallization and valorization of a name and the articulation of shared experience are important to political mobilization and to community-building.

3. *Speaking Of and From (not speaking for)*. I know from the inside what it is like to be an Anglo gay male, but know that not all gay-identified white North American men share my experiences or my views. The places with extensive, institutionally elaborated gay communities in which I have lived, Toronto and San Francisco, are my primary field sites. In challenging generalizations from New York, I hope that I am not just replacing New York ethnocentrism with San Francisco ethnocentrism. I might mention that I grew up in a rural Midwestern small town[24] and have lived more of my life

20. My dissertation research (revised as Murray 1994c) was a study of the "tribe" of anthropological linguists.

21. E.g., Murray 1979a, 1981, 1983c, 1995c,d.

22. See Murray 1994c:473–78.

23. I believe that language channels thought and provides pre-existing categories, but that it is possible to think against categorization schemes, and even to formulate thoughts that are not in the rut of a particular language. That is, I lean to the Edward Sapir and Dorothy Lee versions of the "Sapir-Whorf[-Lee] hypothesis," stressing creativity and rejecting determinism (see Murray 1994c:190–202; Basso 1976).

24. In comparision to which the Minot, North Dakota discussed by J. Kramer (1995) is a metropolis filled with openly gay people (i.e., one would have seemed an astonishingly high number), as is "Southern Town" described by Whittier (1995).

there and in small U.S. cities than in Toronto and San Francisco. I have not forgotten what life is like for a gay (or proto-gay) man outside major metropolises, and have spent a considerable amount of time and energy exploring how gay (and proto-gay) life is thought and lived in such places as Guatemala, Japan, Kenya, Mexico, Pakistan, Peru, Taiwan, and Thailand. I claim "on-the-ground" comparative perspective supplementing "armchair" ethnology. I also have interrogated people from other places as opportunities have arisen. Nonetheless, the ground I consider most often in this book is San Francisco, where I have lived since 1978,[25] and which is at least symbolically a central site of modern/"gay" homosexuality in North America.[26]

4. *Systematics, Not History of Theory.* Being a sometime historian of social science discourse, I have not entirely curtailed my penchant for correcting the placing of some social theorists, and use the past tense for what people wrote rather than treating all writings as eternally present.[27] I think that a genuinely historicist history of social science research on "homosexuals" would be very interesting, but I have not undertaken that project herein.

I think that useful materials for current comparative and/or historical systematics can be extracted from research that was done by people who failed to realize that what they were observing had changed and was changing. As in many other regards, Chauncey (1994) is exemplary in his use of Henry (1941) and others. It seems to me that now-neglected research from before the gay liberation era[28] can tell us much of interest about how things used to be. It also seems to me that a history of the (quite separated) lesbian and gay 1970s needs doing. Both lesbian-feminism and clone life seem almost as remote from how we live and think now as is, say, the interwar Berlin scene Christopher Isherwood recorded. Descriptive studies done during the 1970s[29] seem forgotten, and their authors—dismissed as naive "essential-

25. That the data in chapters 10 and 13 also derive mostly from San Francisco has nothing to do with my living there. For my initial view, see Murray 1979e. On some other major U.S. cities, see Herdt 1992. D'Augelli and Hart 1987 is a rare study of rural gay life.

26. D'Emilio (1992:74) suggested that "for gay men and for lesbians, San Francisco has become akin to what Rome is for Catholics: a lot of us live there and many more make the pilgrimage." Myslik (1995:19) cut this back to San Francisco being something of what Jerusalem is for Jews: "most of us live somewhere else, fewer of us makes pilgrimages than in the past, our political power has moved elsewhere, but the cultural and emotional significance of the place cannot be overestimated."

27. My understanding of the distinction between systematics and history of theory derives from the first chapter of Merton 1968.

28. E.g., Leznoff 1954; Sawyer 1965; Hoffman 1968; Soneschein 1968; Sweet 1968; Warren 1972, 1974; and Weinberg and Williams 1974.

29. E.g., Cotton 1975; Moses 1978; Ponse 1978; Wolf 1979; Ettore 1980; S. Krieger 1983 on lesbians; Harry and Devall 1978b on gay men.

ists"[30]—have been lost to the lesbigay studies that have emerged with (mostly groundless) pretensions of being "theoretical." Particularly the women who wrote about 1970s lesbian groupings have vanished from collective memory. Some of the men who studied gay men then already had academic positions. Some are still alive and doing research.[31] Insofar as their works have not also been erased from collective memory, straw versions are pilloried.

At a number of junctures in this book, I point out research that needs doing. Before turning to sociological "grand theory," however, I want to urge would-be historians of the emergence of "modern homosexuality" to try to extract historical data from the surveys and ethnographies of lesbian and gay networks and communities before AIDS.

5. *Other kinds of diversity.* Part 3 of this volume focuses on racial/ethnic diversity. In North America, as elsewhere, "religion" is inextricably bound up with "ethnicity," but I don't see any Catholic vs. Protestant vs. Jewish conflict in the gay community (or Metropolitan Community Church vs. Dignity vs. Integrity, etc.). Suspicion of working through organized religion—*any* organized religion—exists, but generally (it seems to me) there is an "I think your efforts are doomed, but go ahead and try" attitude. Those who claim a distinctive "gay spirituality" are very ecumenical and willing to see it manifest both inside and outside the Judeo-Christian tradition.[32] Thus, I don't see that religious diversity among lesbigays matters to what I'm discussing.

Class does, and I write about it, although I am well aware that from a Marxist perspective I am a typical American sociologist more interested in stratification than in classical class analysis.

Finally, I am well aware of considerable diversity within the categories *black* and *white*, *Latino* and *Asian/Pacific*, though I use these rough distinctions and cross-cut them more by looking at relative income, generation, and geographical location than at differences in (ancestral) "national" origin for any but the second pair of "ethnicities" (in chapters 12 and 13).

30. This is a mythical beast that espouses the claim that all people who have engaged in homosexual behavior across time and space are identical.
31. I assume that most of the women are also alive. The ones I know were discouraged, particularly by negative responses from some of the same lesbians who most loudly decry "lesbian invisibility"; who do not themselves study lesbians, directly or very often; and who attack anyone who writes anything other than what they imagine they would write if they were to do research on lesbians. Gay men also criticize research on gay men, but "How dare someone study us who is not gay and can't possibly understand us?" seems much rarer: gay men have cooperated with researchers regardless of researchers' sex or (announced) sexual orientation. It seems obvious to me that collaboration combining insider and outsider perspectives is preferable. As with many things that seem obvious to me, this apparently is not obvious to others. See Hong 1994; Hong and Murray 1995; Murray 1993.
32. See Thompson 1987, 1994; Roscoe 1995a.

1

De-assimilation

One

Social Theory and the Anomalous Development of Gay Resistance

In all societies, individuals have some ideas about what they have in common with those nearest them, and know that others differ from them. Reports of social arrangements at variance with European ones during the Age of Discovery stimulated more grandiose programs for scientific comparison of societies. The Industrial Revolution and the French Revolution augmented and channeled this stimulus. Among those trying to make sense of those revolutions and their place as part of a process of social evolution were the three architects of sociology's "grand tradition": Karl Marx (1818–1883), Émile Durkheim (1858–1917), and Max Weber (1864–1919). None of them had professional training in sociology; nor did their precursors, such as Plato, Aristotle, Machiavelli, Vico, Hobbes, Locke, Montesquieu, and Rousseau, in theorizing about social order and structure.

Professional sociology often seems to resemble Bonaventure's God with its center nowhere and its periphery everywhere. There are sociologies of religion, sports, medicine, etc.[1] Yet there is a center, where the main concern is world-historical changes in systems of domination. This concern directly elaborates—and often incants—the intellectual patrimony of the Marx–Durkheim–Weber trinity.[2] Those who inhabit this center endeavor to explain how one system (e.g., capitalism) functions at a particular time and how one system arises from another (e.g., capitalism from feudalism). To those at the discipline's center, chronicling the lifeways of "queers" seems to be a dubious enterprise that is very unlikely to contribute to the building of a unified Theory of Society moving through world-historical processes to

1. J. Turner (1989) presents a particularly despairing view of the disintegration of sociology. Cf. Collins 1986 and Huber 1995.
2. See Nisbet 1966.

the happy futures envisioned by Marx, Durkheim, and the most influential American synthesizer of the European "grand theory," Talcott Parsons (1902–1979). Indeed, description of how people actually live has often struck those concerned with abstract, general theories of Society to be a diversion from the path to Important Knowledge. And, when the people described are homosexual, those doing research are suspected of motives such as voyeuristic titillation or special pleading.

If sociology's center has not held, as indicated by the profusion in recent years of antagonistic approaches, this is less a result of the trickling of sociologists' interests into queer byways than of the failure of classical theory to account for the contemporary social world, let alone to predict future changes. For instance, abolition of private ownership of the means of production in much of Europe and Asia resulted neither in the withering away of the state, nor in the elimination of inequality, nor in the elimination of the alienation that Marx saw as an inevitable result of capitalist production. More generally, the increasing division of labor and (according to Durkheim) consequent interdependence in and between states has not led to a meritocracy in which the family, ethnic, racial, and religious connections of individuals have ceased to matter—either to individuals or to the life chances of categories of persons. Groups intermediate between the state and atomized masses, based on primordial loyalties (e.g., to neighbors, coreligionists, work associates, or those bearing the same stigma), which conservatives from Louis de Bonald (1764–1850) to Robert Nisbet (born 1913) feared were being smashed, have demonstrated a remarkable tenacity, confounding the predictions and hopes of the French Enlightenment tradition, most influentially expressed within academic sociology by Parsons. At the same time, the increase in impersonal rules has not made the social world more comprehensible to its inhabitants.[3]

The macrohistorical processes projected by Marx and Durkheim from their consideration of European history have not been repeated elsewhere as predicted,[4] nor have subsequent events even in Europe followed their scenarios. Ready working-class involvement (and the enthusiastic support of various socialist parties) in the First World War showed international

3. Weber carefully distinguished formally rational procedures from any substantive rationality of outcomes and called the increase of impersonality the "disenchantment of the world."

4. In a remarkably Anglocentric presidential address to the American Sociological Association, James Coleman (1993) reiterated the universality and inevitability of the erosion of primordial institutions, following upon changes in the mode of production. He did not consider the family basis and frequently rural location of industrial development since World War II in Japan, Taiwan, Korea, Singapore, Hong Kong, and increasingly in Southeast Asia. The notion of Asian stasis and irrelevance dies hard (A. L. March 1974).

working-class solidarity to be a hope or an illusion rather than a description or prediction. The history of the Soviet Union (and other Marxist states) revealed the failure of a series of supposedly essential features of socialist states to result from the revolution and its abolition of private ownership of the means of production. The Soviet Union also proved that a number of "essential" features of capitalism are compatible with at least "socialism in one country"—even when the one country was extremely large and had a still larger empire.

Working-class heterogeneity is one explanation of the proletariat's failure to act out the historical part in which Marx cast it. Writing from the vantage point of racially homogeneous European states, all the builders of "the grand tradition" failed to take account of ethnic diversity.[5] Weber and Durkheim, if not Marx, lived to witness the breakup of the Hapsburg and Ottoman empires, indicating that unification—as exemplified by Germany and Italy a generation earlier—was not an inevitable world-historical trend.[6] While Durkheim undoubtedly would be gratified by the economic interdependence of the Common Market, he would be quite amazed by Basque and Breton separatist movements in *la patrie*.[7] Similarly, Marx would have been taken aback by the economic dominance of Great Russians throughout the history of the USSR, and by the Islamic rumblings along the southern rim of what should have been a classless society in which no oppressed creatures should have required the "opiate" of religion. Communism in the Soviet Union and Yugoslavia muted manifestations of ethnic hatreds.[8] Yet, after three generations of tutelage, the socialist "New Man" was a failure: ancient hatreds have exploded anew, in horrifying violence. Religion, ethnicity, family, and region have also all reemerged as the bases for mobilization in post-Maoist China.[9]

Even the builders of American sociological traditions—focusing on smaller social units over briefer periods of time—expected race, ethnicity, gender, etc. to wane in importance. The seminal work of W. I. Thomas and Florian Znaniecki (1927 [1913–18]) on Polish peasants immigrating to

5. See Nisbet 1966.

6. Although he found "ethnicity" a vague concept and believed that only negative actions stemmed from racial/ethnic consciousness, Weber (1978:393) was acutely aware that "political artifacts develop a sense of affinity akin to that of blood relationship" and stressed that "tribal consciousness is primarily formed by common political experiences and not by common descent" (p. 394). He was less certain about the progress inherent in European history than were Marx and Durkheim.

7. See Beer 1980; Nielson 1980.

8. Communist insurgents and regimes nonetheless appealed to nationalism with regularity, in Europe as well as in China, Vietnam, Cuba, and, most horrifyingly of all, Cambodia. See Verdery 1991 for an especially insightful analysis (of Romanian communist nationalism).

9. See Luo 1991; E. Friedman 1993; Siu 1993.

the United States exemplified Durkheim's conception of the necessary breakdown of traditional peasant society with accompanying "temporary" individual pathology. However, they expected both individual and social "disorganization" to disappear with integration into the modern world of, say, Chicago, and for the importance of ethnic subcultures to wane as contact with the dominant WASP American society reduced differences. They variously termed this process *assimilation, acculturation, accommodation.* Viewing conflict as a product of individual attitudes and values rather than of structured inequalities, sociologists expected conflicts to diminish as contact dissolved both the stereotypes and the cultural differences which produced them. Both the methodological streams from the sociology department at the University of Chicago counted on increasing contact to dissolve intergroup hostility.[10]

While interwar University of Chicago sociology students described seemingly every subculture extant in Chicago except the homosexual one,[11] anthropologists trained by Franz Boas (1858–1942) salvaged reminiscences of American Indian tribal cultures one at a time. Oddly enough, Boas, who constantly stressed differences among Amerindian cultures and strove to distinguish cultural phenomena from race, did not credit any distinctness of Jews.[12] Like Thomas and Park, Boas believed that differences of immigrant groups—including his own—would disappear in American society, the famed melting pot.[13] When anthropologists turned from enumerating cultural traits to examining the process of acculturation,[14] they treated cultures—and particularly the values posited as characteristic of them—as obstacles to "modernization." Anthropologists' view of this paralleled sociologists' earlier treatment of cultural diversity in American cities as obstacles to "assimilation." The desired and predicted end for both processes was approximate replication of middle-class WASP lifeways, still regarded as

10. I.e., quantitative (survey) analysis and interpretive case studies. Compare Stouffer et al. 1949 with Blumer 1973.

11. Deborah Goleman Wolf (personal communication, 1982) reported that a group of Herbert Blumer's students, including her mother, did an ethnography of the Chicago homosexual subculture around 1930 as a class project, but the results were not published and probably are lost. Nels Anderson (1923:137, 144) noted in passing that homosexuality was common among hoboes; Reckless (1926:202) noted the clustering of "perversion" in areas of "commercialized vice"; Saul Alinsky visited and briefly described Diamond Lil's, a homosexual taxi-dance hall (a 3-page account along with a pink envelope from it are in the Ernest Burgess papers at the Department of Special Collections, University of Chicago Libraries), and Richard Herrell has also found notes on and correspondence with hustlers in the Burgess papers.

12. Opler 1967.

13. In Boas's view (1912), even physical changes occurred rapidly.

14. Redfield, Linton, and Herskovits 1936; see Murray 1988b.

the highest possible human development—even by those who condemned nineteenth-century Social Darwinism (and other variants of unilinear social evolution).

Contrary to confident predictions, differences have not disappeared. Indeed, contact often exacerbates hostility, and thus reinforces rather than eliminates stereotyping.[15] Nor have particularistic identifications ceased. On the contrary, some groups written off in the generation of Durkheim and Weber (e.g., Basques, Bretons, Catalans, Slovenians) have reemerged. Others, notably those based on sex and on sexual preference—inconceivable to the fathers of sociology—have appeared, and have become more salient bases for mobilization than class. Ascribed characteristics (such as race, gender, and possibly sexual orientation) have taken on an importance quite out of keeping with the confident expectations of those in the grand tradition that these need not be considered, because their significance would decline and eventually disappear. As Shirley Lindenbaum (1995:277) remarked, "the more global our relations and flows of commerce, money, and people, the more rather than less we cling to place, neighborhood, nation, region, ethnic grouping, or religious belief as a specific marker of identity."

Groups based on characteristics which classical theory regarded as already anachronistic a century ago have not merely "assumed political functions comparable to those of a subordinate class; they have in important respects become more effective than social classes in mobilizing their forces in pursuit of collective ends," as Parkin (1978:622) wrote. If this be "rebellion" rather than the "revolution" awaited by Marxists, then "rebellion" is what recent history discloses, not the incipient fulfilling of the messianic expectations still pinned on the shrinking class that was supposed to be "universal." Insofar as sociology aims to analyze actual history rather than to explain the tarrying of the messiah, it must endeavor to explain the continued strength and/or emergence of social movements based on consciousness of shared ascribed characteristics.[16] Even before recent explosions of violence in formerly communist states, Parkin (1978:626) noted, "Whereas the modern proletariat appears to have a purely theoretical capacity to reconstitute the social order in its own image, ethnic groups have frequently displayed a more than abstract commitment to dissolving the boundaries of the nation state and redrawing them anew." At least in the United States (as Lenin feared), organized labor has so completely shirked its mission to transform society in

15. Gumperz 1982a,b; Murray 1991a.

16. There may be considerable redefinition and negotiation of the markers of these characteristics (and, therefore, of how many people are within whatever category). See J. Jackson 1995 on "Indian" in Colombia for an example notable for care in not treating novelty as inauthenticity.

the image of the universal proletarian class that gay organizations have garnered more political clout in some jurisdictions than organized labor now has—even in so traditionally a labor stronghold as San Francisco.[17] The emergence of a group consciousness and subsequent mobilization of a "people" who could not seriously have been designated a "group" three decades ago contrasts markedly with the erosion of class consciousness and the increasing impotence of organized labor. I do not regard this invidious contrast as any cause for celebration (not least because I recognize its tenuousness), but it should stimulate theoretical reconsideration of who are the agents in the drama of human history, circa the late twentieth century.[18]

Not just Marxist theory, but subsequent social theory has ill prepared us to understand the quite unpredicted emergence and successes, however limited, of racial and ethnic, women's and gay movements. While Jürgen Habermas has strayed far from anything identifiable as Marxist orthodoxy, he yet continues to posit an abstract universality (the utopia he terms "undistorted communication") as the *telos* of human history (evolution). In my view, this notion is as remote from reality as the self-actualization of the "universal class." If history is a process, not an incoherent set of events, then it resembles a list of conflicts, some based on class, some not only rationalized/ legitimated but *based on* factors other than class, rather than an approximation to the ultimate harmony Marx and Durkheim saw coming or that Habermas still sees coming (admittedly, by different steps).

Concurrently, the technology of surveillance and domination has increased. Michel Foucault, the prophet of this last process, remained as transfixed as were Marx, Weber, and Durkheim by the consolidation of monarchic states with rulers allied to the rising bourgeoisie in opposition to dispersed feudal interests. For Foucault, as for the fathers of sociology, the rise to dominance of capitalists is the dystopian hinge of human history. While Christians celebrate the Incarnation as the pivot of human history and Marx anticipated a grander Second Coming by the proletariat, Foucault expected nothing more than a consolidation of the consequences of capitalism's incarnation (the Great Divide between traditional and modern societies, which the French tend to conflate with what they ethnocentrically refer to as "la Revolution"). Like Weber, but unlike Marx and Durkheim, who believed utopia

17. See T. Weinberg 1978b, Murray 1979e.

18. New Social Movements are not all based on particularist identity politics (see A. P. Cohen 1985; Touraine 1985; Epstein 1987; Melucci 1989; chapter 5 below), though antiwar, antinuclear, and "green" movement participation often leads to some self-redefinition ("activist" for previously "non-political" conformists—as the previous self may retrospectively be drawn).

18

was near, Foucault expected *dys*topia: the expansion of already ubiquitous surveillance and subliminal control (including anticipatory self-control). Instead of following Marcuse (1955) in regarding homosexuality as an at least implicit criticism of the dominant social system based on competition, instinctual renunciation, etc., Foucault (1980) treated homosexuality as a conceptual entity invented by nineteenth-century medical science to control the thing (in this case, a species of homosexuals) it had created out of more-or-less random (in this case homosexual) behavior. By showing the complicity of early sexologists in defining themselves by their homosexual behavior, we can address Foucault's conspiracy theory of the emergence of one group based on characteristics other than class. Whether particularistic identities and the movements defined around them are foisted by devious would-be governors pursuing the venerable strategy of divide and conquer, or instead constitute emergent challenges to social arrangements from below, is in my view the most important question confronting contemporary social theory and social history. One possible avenue to revitalizing social theory so that it bears some relationship to contemporary reality and to the history which has produced it is to study those unexpected—indeed, anomalous—developments.

Foucault did not live to elaborate his passing suggestions about the creation of a species "homosexuality" in late nineteenth century medical discourse,[19] nor to search earlier forensic or medical discourses for other species, such as *sodomites* and *catamites*. His self-proclaimed disciples have only too rarely looked before that time, or at very much of the world, in trumpeting "the social construction of homosexuality," as is argued below. Opposition to domination is a mysterious emanation from unknowable springs for Foucault,[20] who lacked any confidence in a universal class's self-realization or the realization of the transcendent, undistorted communication Habermas envisages.

Like Marxist theory, classical bourgeois social theory—including the two major American theoretical perspectives descended from Durkheim and from W. I. Thomas, functionalism and symbolic interactionism respectively—ill prepared anyone to understand the emergence and limited successes of racial and ethnic, women's and gay movements. I believe that the emergence of new peoples, including my own, challenges the bases of re-

19. Foucault 1980:43. Hocquenghem (1978:37) presented the creation of "a new disease, homosexuality" in 1869 as an example of the psychiatric mania for classification discussed by Foucault (1961). In his introduction to the English translation of Hocquenghem's book (pp. 20–21), Jeffrey Weeks referred to both of these Foucault books.

20. One might read Foucault as regarding opposition to be impossible, not just mysterious.

ceived theory. However, these theories may provide some limited organization and illumination of empirical phenomena—provided we jettison the baggage of inevitable progress to a single "moral community." The messiah proletariat is not going to come, and the organic solidarity of specialized, interdependent occupational groups Durkheim foresaw as the means to salvation from normlessness (anomie) and heartless industrial capitalism is also not arising to transcend persisting differences.[21]

FUNCTIONALISM

The structuralist-functionalist tradition[22] included some recognition that moral consensus requires targets: specifically the spectacle of derogation (or stronger punishment) of negative role models. Natives of other cultures can tolerate blatant specimens of inadequate masculine socialization as a butt for (among other things) jokes, because such persons serve as a horrible warning of what boys must avoid becoming.[23] Possibly, the public punishment of "sodomites" served the same "function" in Inca and Aztec empires and in medieval Europe.[24] Somewhat similarly, Wikan (1977, 1982) suggested that the "function" of homosexual prostitutes in the Arabian city of Sohar, Oman, is to preserve women's virtue (honor) by providing an alternative receptacle for ejaculate.

To encourage heterosexuality and to deter exploration of and identification with homosexuality, many societies reward those who engage in homosexual behavior without appearing gender-deviant to remain invisible so as not to confuse the line between normal men and devalued queens, *berdache*, *mahu*, *khanith*, *faggots*, etc. Masculine gay men and feminine lesbians have been and continue to be rewarded for not announcing homosexual desires and behavior publicly—or even recognizing it in themselves.[25] Just as homosexuality without gender nonconformity is rewarded for remaining invisible, other empirically common counterexamples to the stereotypical misery

21. Given the concern throughout Durkheim's work with the increasing extent and obdurateness of anomie, "hoped" is probably more accurate than "foresaw."

22. For a systematic overview of the theoretical perspective, see Moore 1978.

23. Devereux 1937; Levy 1973.

24. "Civilization" outdid "barbarians" in producing terrifying warnings against sexual nonconformity. Even if less than "genocidal," the scale of pogroms in early modern Europe disrupted rather than reinforced hierarchical systems, so that the inquisitions had to be curbed— before inquiry into the character and behavior of the members of the ruling class got out of control: see Goodich 1979; M. E. Perry 1980; van der Meer 1984; Murray 1988a; Rocke 1988.

25. See Hencken 1984, discussed in chapter 6.

and derangement of necessarily fleeting encounters before the *fag* becomes too old to attract sexual partners must be suppressed. Therefore, obstacles to same-sex couples are built and maintained. Enduring same-sex couples must be invisible to "impressionable young people" who might find homosexuality (or ambisexuality) attractive if homosexuality appears to be a possibility rather than a sin or sickness.[26]

Representation of happy older lesbians and gay men in enduring relationships are particularly corrosive to heterosexist monopoly. "You'll be doomed to a lonely unhappy old age, and one that begins much earlier" is the second line of defense against commitment to homosexuality used to deter any who see that not everyone involved in homosexuality is gender-deviant. Representations of gay men with AIDS in the news media perpetuate the image of gay men necessarily cut off from humanity, dying alone and miserable, in contrast to pictures of children with AIDS *en famille*.[27] These conventional images shape and reinforce perceptions, despite having no relation to the reality portrayed. In fact, the mobilization of networks and volunteers has characterized the gay community's response to AIDS, in contrast to rejection by their families and neighbors of many children with AIDS. The price of representing gay men or lesbians in the 1950s and 1960s was that they had to seem miserable, and had either to commit suicide or be murdered by the end of American novels, plays, and movies then.

By the 1970s, popular media portrayed inevitable isolation and loneliness rather than death as the lot of "homosexuals." Death staged a major comeback in representations in the 1980s and 1990s, with AIDS equated with homosexuality (as is discussed further in chapter 4) and interpreted by some as "God's punishment" ("the wages of sin"). These misrepresentations keep homosexuality an unthinkable choice and thus preserve civilization, according

26. Works such as Berger 1981, Wolf 1984a, or Vacha 1985 that demonstrate the fallaciousness of widely credited views of older lesbians and gay men are important in undercutting this stigmatization, as was the work of Evelyn Hooker (1957) and others in showing that psychopathology is not a necessary concomitant of homosexual object choice. Those most committed to the "naturalness" of heterosexuality seem the least confident that it could survive in competition in any "free market." Especially in the United States, those most vigorous in extolling the "free market" are generally also the champions of government regulation of markets of ideas and images and are vociferous opponents of empirical research that shows that reality does not conform to their postulates, especially about sex, gender, and the family.

27. See Gilman 1988:259–62, 268, 270. The lack of physical contact between Tom Hanks and Antonio Banderas in the film *Philadelphia* contrasts markedly with Denzel Washington returning to his literally "touching" family. Such gay characters as appear in mass entertainment must be quarantined from each other within the frame, just as two men holding hands or dancing together are defined as instances of *public sex*, while a man and a woman kissing are not.

to those legislatively proscribing any representation of homosexuality without concurrent condemnation as dangerous "advocacy" or "promotion." [28]

To define the moral unit "us" of a society, others must be beyond the moral pale. Durkheim (1895) wrote of "normal" rates of deviance/crime that are necessary to provide occasions for exemplary punishments to affirm the moral order by publicly fixing the line between acceptable and unacceptable behavior. Durkheim's intellectual heirs have been concerned with boundary maintenance both between [29] and within groups. [30]

Of course, to serve an exemplary role as a moral counterexample, a deviant (of whatever sort) must be generally recognized as such. Prior to the Kinsey findings, when it was assumed a homosexual was a rara avis—*the* village queer and the single *mahu* per Tahitian village—and that each one could be readily recognized by everyone, because of their obvious gender nonconformity, homosexuality seemed consistent enough with a moral consensus model of society, i.e., "normal deviance" rather than subversive challenges of the moral order:

> The only material found in a system for marking boundaries, is the behavior of the participants; and the kinds of behavior which best perform this function are often deviant. . . . They mark the outside limits of the areas within which the norm has jurisdiction, and in this way assert how much diversity and variability can be contained within the system. . . . Thus, deviance cannot be dismissed simply as behavior which disrupts stability in society, but may itself be, in controlled quantities, an important condition of *preserving* stability. (Erikson 1962:13–15)

Mimicking Durkheim's attempt to mold the civic morality of the Third Republic, Parsons (and his students such as Robert Bellah) viewed the United States as a single moral community with shared values which could be appealed to, as the Swedish economist Gunnar Myrdal did when he examined American race relations in *The American Dilemma* (1944). Such a conception had no place for conflicting countercommunities based on such particularistic characteristics as ethnicity, religion, or sexual preference. They instead supposed an inexorable world-historical trend toward universality, rationality, and the transcendence of social organization based on ascribed features. [31]

28. See Crimp 1988:257–66; Watney 1987:66–67, 113; Weeks 1991:143: apparently homosexuality is irresistible if shown without moralistic condemnation.

29. Barth 1969.

30. Douglas 1966; Erikson 1962, 1966; Kitsuse 1962; Bergesen 1978; Gorman 1980.

31. In the paragraph of his major theoretical synthesis that he devoted to "ethnic subdivisions," Parsons (1951:188) suggested that ethnics "perform an important scapegoat function as

History does not come with guarantees, however. Northern Europe has developed a caste-like status of immigrants from former colonies and from southern Europe (the *Gastarbeiter*). Social practice (and, laggardly, social theory) challenged assimilation even as a goal, let alone a description. No more than Marxism did the Parsonian synthesis anticipate the emergence of a gay community replicating the capitalist institutions of the dominant society and organizing itself as a pressure group in the arena of electoral politics. The likewise unanticipated upheavals of the 1960s, following almost immediately upon the proclamation of "the end of ideology," [32] shattered the Parsonian synthesis, so that by the 1970s, when the institutional elaboration and political organization of gay men (and to a lesser extent, lesbians) occurred, the Parsonian paradigm for which such untoward facts were anomalous had crumbled. [33]

The study that showed how "deviance" could reinforce rather than challenge the "moral order" was Albert Reiss's "The social integration of 'queers' and 'peers'" (1961). [34] For masculine young *peers*, [35] behavior defined masculinity. In their view, insertees were *queer*. Peers' participation did not

---

targets for displaced aggression," while (not very compatibly) "for the members of a given ethnic group it may be suggested that they constitute a focus of security beyond the family which is in some respects less dysfunctional for the society than community solidarity would be." With race riots and a mass civil rights movement engulfing American cities during the middle 1960s, Parsons (1967:455) appealed to a single societal community with particular values that should include Negroes, as it had Catholic and Jewish European immigrants. In his view, religion, not economic factors, had been the fundamental obstacle for earlier inclusion in the American societal community; and he confusingly extended this to southern white supremacists (p. 460) while not acknowledging, let alone explaining, northern racisms.

32. D. Bell 1960.

33. See chapter 8. The revival of Parsons in neo-functionalism has carefully avoided discussion of homosexuality and emergent gay communities. Neo-functionalists seem to have forgotten the racial upheavals of the 1960s in the United States, which were similarly unanticipated by sociologists, even those still working on racial topics in the 1950s (as E. Hughes 1963 noted). The failure of Parsons (1960) to attend to the imminent racial conflict in the U.S.—in a book supposedly focused on "process" as well as "structure"—is particularly striking. He eventually addressed it in his value-focused way in Parsons 1967, where he also backed off from expecting assimilation to inclusion and overinterpreted the defeat of Barry Goldwater in the 1964 presidential election as a final rejection of reactionary forces and of mobilization against nonwhites.

34. In analyzing the early "homosexual community" in Montreal, Leznoff (1954; Leznoff and Westley 1956) did not discuss the functions of society served, but only the psychological functions for those involved: specifically, reduction of anxiety by providing a context in which homosexuality was taken for granted as normal. That pioneer functionalist study has more in common with Hooker's work on how individuals manage to adapt than with explanations of how such adaptations fit with, reproduce, or challenge a social order. Reiss, à la Durkheim, was more concerned with functions for the society.

35. Surely the vernacular term was *trade*.

challenge their masculine status, so long as they gave nothing more than their cocks (and possibly an occasional beating), i.e., so long as they "never took it." What they might take that was consistent with the role was money or possessions of queers. If taken without the consent of the queer, this was a tribute to the ingenuity and/or masculine prowess of the peer. Within this ideology of masculinity, theft enhanced masculine status. No one perceived prostitution as masculinizing, but, apparently, the insertors evaded this stigmatizing definition along with that of queer.[36]

Such a system could persist only with the collusion of those willing to enact the role of the queer, specifically by not challenging the valuation and self-image of those whose behavior was that of homosexual prostitution. So long as both parties believed in the dominance of the masculine actor and the submission (and, optimally, feminization) of the queer, "deviant" acts validated both peers' masculinity(/heterosexuality) and the deprecation of homosexuality. Queers kneeling to worship the symbols of trade's masculinity protected their fantasies and their sexual partners' masculine self-conceptions.

Beyond the financial rewards, sexual release, and the reassurance of masculinity, peers saw the dangers of succumbing to any temptations toward passivity. Most presumably "learned" they weren't *queer*—and didn't have to be to get off with men. Reiss's study did not assess the degree of "role distance" of those enacting the queer role versus the degree of self-hatred; but to whatever extent those playing the queer role credited its truth (and justice), their "deviant" conduct reinforced the moral order in general, and the superiority of heterosexual males in particular.[37]

In researching *Tearoom Trade* (1975), Laud Humphreys showed how far men could venture into homosexuality—beyond adolescence and even beyond exclusively insertor behavior—without considering themselves implicated as *queers* either by themselves or by their partners. Well-publicized tearoom (public lavatory) arrests (e.g., Supreme Court nominee Judge G. Harold Carswell) provide additional illustrations of Humphreys' findings that those involved in such settings who deny they are homosex "share highly conservative social and political views, surrounding

36. Wescott (1990 [1937]:9) remarked on "commercialization of one's sex [being] more respectable than the free gift of it," after mentioning a sailor who, having "manifested some enthusiasm, begged Jack not to tell any of his colleagues, who would not respect him if they knew." On "trade" neutralization of homosexual conduct, see John Rechy (1961; and in Leyland 1978:260) and Gore Vidal (in Leyland 1978:291, 273, 275).

37. On role distance see chapter 6. On the apparent acceptance of inferior status see Rath and Sircar 1960 on castes in India, and Adam 1978a:113–14, 1978b more generally.

themselves with an aura of respectability that I call 'the breastplate of righteousness.' "[38]

Thus (contra Marcuse 1955, alas), not only was homosexuality compatible with the existing moral order; so were homosexuals, for it was not just trade who "compensated" for suspect sexual behavior with hyperconformity in espousing traditional social values, especially about sex and gender. The complement of a Congressman mouthing Moral Majority slogans against "the sexual revolution" when not mouthing something more tangible in public lavatories is a transsexual acting out the "housewife" role anachronistic for those *born* female.[39] Converts exhibit greater zeal than those born to and able to take a status for granted. Freud's late metapsychological work (e.g., 1939) outlined a role for guilt in enhancing social conformity that universalizes the role Durkheim assigned "normal deviance" in upholding the moral order. Talcott Parsons added the metapsychology of the late Freud to his synthesis when he lowered his sights from the societal level to describing individual behavior maintaining a moral order. The stratification of sexual encounters (with the "masculine principle" on top in every sense), along with the "consent" to stigmatization of those seeking "real men" as partners, was perfectly consistent with the Parsonian vision.[40]

Parsons and Bales (1955) delineated complementary roles necessary to the functioning of small groups, of which they saw the family as a special case. The husband oriented toward the world outside the family exemplifies the *instrumental* role; the wife oriented inward to the family the *affective* role (also referred to as *expressive*, or as a *social-emotional specialist*). Blumstein and Schwartz's rich and mammoth comparative study (1983) of married, nonmarried cohabiting, gay male, and lesbian couples (discussed further in chapter 7) followed the functionalist tradition into a social world in which such stratification is mostly obsolete—although both lesbians and gay men

38. Humphreys 1971:76; also see Gagnon and Simon 1973:164. Tearooms also remain places in which heterosexually identified men in other countries have homosexual sex (see Bennett, Chapman, and Bray 1989; Gray 1988; Desroches 1990; Murray 1997).

39. Kando 1974.

40. More recently, for older (19–25-year-old) bodybuilders renting their bodies to gay men, Klein (1989:24) concluded that "the nature of this relationship, despite its symbiotic qualities, is negative. This is sufficient to create a distance, which in this context is adaptive. Among their own, each side denigrates the other." Besides being older than the hustlers studied by Reiss, the bodybuilders studied by Klein live in a time in which homosexuality is more openly discussed and the assumption that anyone who engages in homosexual behavior is *gay* is stronger. Another factor making compartmentalization more difficult is that, due to steroid use, the bodybuilders "couldn't get it up" (p. 23). Klein reported that their heterosexual behavior was to perform cunnilingus, but did not report whether they were orally or anally receptive with gay clients.

in their sample remained sensitive to conceptions of themselves or their partners fitting into the opposite sex's traditional gender role. Blumstein and
Schwartz substituted a polarity "work-centered/relationship-centered" for
"instrumental/affective." They contended that for a relationship to endure,
at least one partner must focus on keeping the relationship going well. Blumstein and Schwartz did not try to sort out whether relationships work better
when both partners are relationship-centered, or whether there is some advantage to one partner being oriented outward from the relationship to the
work world. That is, they did not try to sort out whether the roles are genuinely complementary, or merely differ.[41]

Their preference for asking about values rather than asking about behavior, and their preservation of the one-dimensional conception of power, are
also squarely in the functionalist tradition.[42] They do not appear to have
attempted to get at which partner establishes the agenda and limits for the
couple's decision-making (e.g., about what kinds of non-monogamy to consider). Viewing sex as a scarce resource within relationships, Blumstein and
Schwartz found that the relationship-centered partner initiates sex and the
powerful one refuses. They seem to have forgotten their own finding that
the powerful one tends to be the work-centered partner with greater income/
assets.[43] Such turning away from structured inequality has been characteristic of functionalists.

SYMBOLIC INTERACTIONISM

Most sociological research on homosexuality before the late 1970s, however,
was done within another, indigenously American tradition that unsuccessfully
rivaled functionalism for dominance in postwar American sociology: symbolic
interactionism.[44] "Classical" University of Chicago sociology research—in
which the perspective of symbolic interaction was first formed—examined
"unconventional careers" (e.g., typical patterns of taxi-hall dancer, jack-
roller, or hobo experiences) in the same way as higher prestige careers

41. Moreover, their data seem to indicate that durable relationships require roughly equivalent success in the outside world, even for partners who are not work-centered.

42. Blumstein and Schwartz 1983. See also Kollock, Blumstein, and Schwartz 1985. Cf.
Lukes 1974; Murray and Nardi 1979.

43. Except among lesbians, who are too busy being egalitarian for either partner to take
sexual initiative—which Blumstein and Schwartz consider one reason for lower rates of genital
sexuality among lesbian couples than among married or cohabiting heterosexual couples or gay
male couples.

44. For a historical overview of the theoretical perspective, see Fisher and Strauss 1978.

(e.g., medical ones). Chicago sociologists wrote about subcultures built by practically every imaginable social category in Chicago, *except* homosexuals (see n. 11).

As already noted, like Durkheim, the founders of the Chicago School of sociology (Albion Small, W. I. Thomas, Robert Park, Ernest Burgess) believed that the all-too-visible social pathology they saw around them would first fade, then gradually disappear (a process to be accelerated by sociological knowledge), as a modern moral order was consolidated to incorporate those uprooted by all those -*ations*—especially immigration and urbanization, both in turn products of the capitalization of agriculture and the spread of industrialization and capitalism. The modern society envisioned from Chicago was more ethnically diverse than was the *Gesellschaft* conceived by European theorists. Still, Chicago sociologists believed that the knocking together of those with different cultural backgrounds would break down, or at least wear off the rough edges of culturally distinctive differences.[45]

Moreover, symbolic interactionists have done little better than functionalists in treating the process of (sub)culture formation and replication diachronically. Despite having a processual theory, symbolic interactionists drift toward treating cultures as reified, static, homogeneous, and closed systems characteristic of a discrete, easily definable population segment that possesses a uniform body of knowledge, an identical set of "cultural elements," and a uniformly shared set of values.[46] A typically or generally shared definition of a situation (the quarry of symbolic interactionist investigation) is little more dynamic than the shared values that functionalists posit.

Too many symbolic interactionists describe symbols; too few analyze actual interaction in which cultural traditions are produced and reproduced at varying rates among those with a shared identification but divergent networks, and therefore irregular communication.[47] Thus, for instance, a slogan or a fashion from the Castro area of San Francisco, where many self-identified gay men are in daily communication with each other, may be carried back to a closeted network of gay men in rural Montana by one traveler months before someone else who lives in suburban San Francisco, unequivocally identifies himself as gay, but has few gay friends learns of it by reading *The Advocate* and tells a visiting straight friend from Dallas about it. The fashion

45. Sciulli (1988:80) concurs with Lyman (1984, 1988) that Herbert Blumer, the central symbolic interactionist advocate (in my view, a theoretical nihilist), questioned the predictions of unilinear assimilation of minority groups in the U.S.

46. E.g., Fine and Kleinman 1979:2.

47. See Fine and Kleinman 1983.

might flourish in Montana without ever having taken root in San Francisco. (Innovation may flow into the metropolis from the hinterlands, as well.) The friend from Dallas may diffuse it among his gay friends in Austin, who were not interested in what they'd seen in *The Advocate,* and so on. "Both personnel and information flow across the boundaries of subcultural systems, entering and exiting at irregular intervals," as Fine and Kleinman (1979:6) wrote, adding that "many cultural items never transmitted by the mass media are known throughout an extensive network . . . across distant places," while most persons in all the places remain unaware of them. Even "after an original spread through the mass media, additional diffusions will occur through interpersonal channels" as well (p. 9). Personal networks overlap but are never identical, and rarely even approach being closed. In addition to the indeterminacy resulting from network openness, processual knowledge is also made more difficult by the (sub)cultural transmission occurring without face-to-face/effective interaction (as for the suburban *Advocate* reader in the example).[48]

Although their model of identification with a group and the development and transmission of group culture is incomplete, symbolic interactionists deserve credit for trying to account for the actual transmission of social order decades before functionalists, and for at least attempting to consider identity and (sub)culture as formed situationally in dialectical processes consisting of more than the mechanical internalization of norms.[49]

The Chicago model of socialization (of which Herbert Blumer was the prophet, and notes on lectures by George Herbert Mead the scripture) held that an identity (i.e., a self) is an internalization of the view of significant others. If a *behavior* (say, a boy playing with girls) is interpreted by others as instancing a *category* (say, *sissy*), they will treat the boy as if he is that kind of person. By recognizing their conception of what he is, the boy will learn what

---

48. Fine and Kleinman (1979:5) and Shibutani (1955:566) rightly distinguish "communication" from "interaction." At other points (e.g., Fine and Kleinman 1979:14; Omark 1978: 273), symbolic interactionists forget this distinction. An individual is not necessarily in direct contact even with his/her "reference group." It may be (although prototypically is not) widely dispersed geographically. The members of this "group" may be unknown to each other as well. "Group" may be misleading in "reference group," which is a set of persons valued by a particular individual, not a particular set of persons valued by others, even by the other members of that same reference group.

49. However, popular dramaturgical notions like "scripts" (Gagnon and Simon 1973; Simon and Gagnon 1986) continue to beg questions about who writes the scripts, where "actors" find the scripts or the stages on which to rehearse and enact them. Rather than a "theory," *script* is a metaphor—an overly conscious, even cognized one. It usefully suggests greater variability (as well as greater elaboration of conduct) than does "norm."

he is. If he finds this entity credible (and important), his behavior will become a stable pattern *(conduct)* and a defining feature of self.[50]

According to symbolic interactionist theory, the self is largely or entirely a product of social definition.[51] What transforms behavior into conduct is labeling by others (or the conception that others are labeling one, or are likely to do so). In the social system of peers and queers discussed above, the homosexual behavior of the peers does not become homosexual conduct (or *identity*), because neither the peers nor the queers who know about the behavior so label them. Unless the police chance upon them in the act, no *queer* or *homosexual* label is applied—and the peers go merrily, but not gaily, on their way.

But what of the queers? Who labeled them? Within encounters with the peers, the peers of course do, but most encounters began with someone already set in the queer role, so explanation must look back before the particular occasion to locate the manufacture of the queer. Unfortunately for the theory, most people with homosexual, gay, or lesbian self-identities report never having been labeled. In his pioneer study of 182 men who considered themselves homosexual, Dank (1971:191) found "no cases in which the subject had come out in the context of being arrested on a charge involving homosexuality or being fired from a job because of homosexual behavior. . . . 4.5 percent of the sample came out in the context of public exposure."[52]

Although labeling theory posits labeling by agents of the state (policemen, judges) in official records, those who would rescue the theory might extend "labeling" from official acts to internalization of everyday epithets. Such a tack does not, however, salvage the theory, for even in this broader sense, labeling does not account for the data that have been gathered. Longitudinal

50. The accuracy of gauging how others view one is highly variable, and symbolic interactionists tend to be vague in distinguishing how others see one from how one thinks others see him/her.

51. Focused on a more homogenous, rural, and stable society, Mead emphasized primary socialization and the construction of an "I." Contemporary social interactionists are more concerned with the construction of a "me" in adolescent and adult socialization to multiple roles. Mead wrote about both, and may even have gone too far (all the way?) in writing "There are all sorts of different selves answering to all sorts of different social reactions" (1934:142). Shibutani (1955, 1961:129–30) took symbolic interactionism into a modern world in which an individual participates in diverse and often geographically separate social worlds.

52. On the parallel inapplicability of labeling theory for women, see Wolf 1979:33–39. Labeling sometimes crystallizes changed self-recognition, as in right-wing former Congressman Robert Bauman (in Marcus 1992:360–62) explaining that he "wasn't gay until 1983" when his marriage was annulled by the Roman Catholic Church.

studies, such as Green's (1986),[53] found that more than half the children whose effeminacy had been sufficiently noticed to have been included in an initial sample of markedly effeminate boys grew up to be heterosexual. Childhood effeminacy, then, is clearly not a sufficient cause (or even an adequate predictor) of adult homosexuality. Whether a sample is drawn on the basis of the alleged cause (those labeled "sissy," "queer," etc.) or the expected effect (adult homosexuality), the relationship occurs in no more than half the cases. Even proponents of childhood effeminacy as an explanation of homosexuality,[54] drawing on data in which retrospective bias is rife (i.e., remembering and reporting from the past what fits with current self-conception and forgetting what is discordant), do not find more than half of those with the effect reporting the supposed cause. Childhood effeminacy, therefore, is also not a necessary cause of adult homosexuality, nor a reliable early marker.[55] As is discussed in chapter 6, a phase of gender variance at the time of coming out may indicate deep, submerged desires less than social expectations. Even in the late 1980s, the social equation of homosexuality and effeminacy still led some male youths coming out to think that in order to "be gay" (and/or to attract men) they had to wear makeup and dress flamboyantly.[56]

That homosexual conduct generally occurs without ever being labeled by others should suffice to discredit "labeling theory," but—greater embarrassment to it—some men report coming out, and, in some cases, joining gay organizations, before ever having any homosexual encounters. That is, identity *(secondary deviance)* sometimes precedes behavior *(primary deviance)*. Within symbolic interactionist theory, there is no particular reason that an individual would objectify him/herself with a stigmatized label that no one had applied in interaction. However, many gay men and lesbians recall a kind of self-labeling. They report having felt "different" and estranged from what they were expected to want, wondering if others existed somewhere who felt similarly estranged, or wondering if their feelings meant that they were queer. How persons who were never labeled *queer* and were not gender-deviant (within whatever cultural expectations of gender existed where they

53. See Sedgwick's analysis (1991) of the cultural assumptions in longitudinal studies of boys judged very effeminate.

54. Harry 1982; Whitam 1977, 1980, 1983; Saghir and Robins 1973.

55. If half the "sissy boys" (in contrast to 4% of all boys) grow up gay, a significant statistical relationship exists. Unfortunately, the prospective studies did not follow hypermasculine homosocial boys to see if they also disproportionately grew up gay (see De Cecco 1987).

56. Herdt and Boxer 1993:126; Tremble, Schneider, and Appathurai 1989:261, 263. The lesbian parallel should slow Lacanian interpretation of gender-variant dressing as a quest for the phallus.

grew up) identified themselves as *homosexual* without(/before) any sexual experience is not easily explained by symbolic interactionist theory—or by any other theory, either. Such self-objectification/cognition as someone preferring the bodies and/or company of persons of the same sex clearly preceded the coining of the term *homosexual*. Some men apparently thought of themselves as *sodomites* without accepting the dominant Christian culture's meaning for the term (in particular, heresy).[57] The use of women's names by British *mollies* and their continental sisters in early modern Europe suggests an objectification of gender-crossing or -mixing, as well.[58]

More recently, two of the thirty men interviewed by Thomas Weinberg (1978a, 1983) labeled themselves before engaging in homosexual activity. In my study of folk models of *gay community* reported in chapter 8, five of 62 men in 1981, six of 90 in 1988, and six of 79 in my 1993 follow-up reported having come out at an age less than that at which they reported having their first homosexual experience, and long before knowing of—let alone interacting with—gay others. Troiden and Goode (1980) do not appear to have asked their respondents their age at first homosexual experience. Thus, no indicator of "primary deviance" occurs in their progression (listing mean ages for each) of "thought might be gay" (17.1), "feelings labeled gay" (19.7), "self labeled gay" (21.3), "association with two or more gay friends" (21.8), "first homosexual love relationship" (23.9). Harry (1982b) examined a number of recollections about adolescence to explain adult gay identity, including being a good student, fist fights, interest in girls, interest in the arts, cross-gender interests, lonerhood, etc., but not homosexual activity. Cass (1978) also avoided placing homosexual behavior at any of the six stages of "homosexual identity formation" she posited.[59]

For lesbians, Ponse (1978:125) listed a series of elements in the process of identity formation that reverses the primary–secondary deviance order:

> The first element is that the individual has a subjective sense of being different from heterosexual persons and identifies this difference as feelings of sexual-emotional attraction to her own sex. Second, an understanding of the homo-

---

57. Murray 1988a. Francisco Correa Netto provided a notable Portuguese example of resistance to what we now call heteronormativity (Mott and Assunção 1988). The 15th- and 16th-century Italian conceptions and resistances described by Ruggiero (1985), Rocke (1988), and Dall'Orto (1988) also deserve note. On earlier sexual conceptions of English women's intimate relationships, see Donoghue 1994.

58. Although usually contrasting with *catamite*, *sodomite* became somewhat generic. There were other terms in English for the masculine penetrators, including *mascularii* (ca. 1194; Johansson 1984:6) and *buggeranto* (ca. 1703; T. King 1994:44).

59. The stages are identity confusion, comparison, tolerance, acceptance, pride, synthesis—with no necessary progression from one to the next.

sexual or lesbian significance of these feelings is acquired. Third, the individual accepts these feelings and their implications for identity, i.e., the person comes out or accepts the identity of lesbian. Fourth, the individual seeks a community of like persons. Fifth, the individual becomes involved in a sexual-emotional lesbian relationship.

Ponse did not report how many of her informants' recollections exhibited this order, or how many included each (or any) feature, nor did she justify the order as either an analyst's or members' ideal type of the "normal" sequence. She called it a "series" rather than a "set" of features, and, although the first three obviously can be ordered in only one way, Ponse termed her series "atemporal." She presented examples in which the fifth feature is last, and asserted "feelings of sexual-emotional attraction to the same sex are more important than behavior, whether or not these feelings have been acted upon" (p. 124) and that it is "not the case that sexual activities or inclinations [are] requisite for lesbian identity" (p. 181).[60] The second feature in the list is crucial, but unexplained.

Wolf (1979) similarly deemphasized homosexual behavior as a factor—let alone the causal factor—in lesbian identification. In her view, sex is at the end of what Cronin (1974:270–71) termed "romantic drift." Schaefer (1976) reported lesbian identity formation preceding entrée to German lesbian institutions, but following sexual experience with women. Kahn (1991: 52) also found homosexual experience coinciding with lesbian identity for 93.3% of her Cincinnati sample. Riddle and Morin (1977) reported mean ages (cf. Troiden and Goode's statistics for men above) of 13.8 for awareness of homosexual feelings, 19.9 for same-sex sexual experience, 22.8 for first same-sex relationship, 23.2 for considering self "homosexual," and 29.7 for acquiring a "positive gay identity." Official labeling was so rare among those studied by Ponse, by Wolf, by Ettore (1980), and by Moses (1978) that they did not even mention it as a possible causal variable.[61] As Warren and Johnson noted, "Most homosexuals live out their lives without their sexual activity ever being made a public issue. And yet, it is evident that the vast majority of the members of the gay community possess the 'attributes' of 'secondary deviance'" (1972:76).

Rather than those with a gay identity being a subset of those engaged in some homosexual behavior, the sets intersect, with most of those with gay identity within the intersection and most of those with some homosexual behavior not in the intersection, as in Figure 1.1. *Homosexual (gay, lesbian,*

60. See A. Rich 1980, Zita 1981, and B. Martin 1988.
61. Contrast Schneider 1987, in which 10% of lesbian workers reported having lost an earlier job because of sexual orientation, with the 22% in Levine and Leonard 1984.

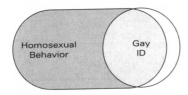

Fig. 1.1 Gay Identity in Relation to Homosexual Behavior

queer, etc.) is a "master status"[62] for some, but only for a minority even of those engaged in recurrent homosexual behavior.

Even symbolic interactionists with no commitment to labeling theory assert that "subcultural identification is possible only if the individual has the opportunity to interact with others who identify with the population segment and gain cultural information from them" (Fine and Kleinman 1979: 14).[63] This is just not the case. Lee (1978b) reported that those who eventually "went public" generally formed a gay identity before having any extended association with the gay subculture.

Essex Special Creationists

A group of sociologists at the University of Essex during the late 1970s developed a variant brand of neo-Marxist and Foucault-influenced symbolic interactionism.[64] They mostly ignored labeling of individuals.[65] Instead, they

62. E. Hughes 1945.

63. See Gagnon and Simon 1973:144–45; Dank 1971:182–83; and Omark 1978 for application to gay identity and interaction with gay-identified men. Mead (1934:140) wrote that "it is impossible to conceive of a self arising outside of social experience," although he also noted that "the body can be there and can operate in a very intelligent fashion without there being a self involved in the experience" (p. 136). I would apply the latter to much homosexual behavior not conceived as *homosexual*—or even as *sex* (Abramson 1992:119; Bolton 1992b:126).

64. See Weeks 1981, 1985, 1991; Plummer 1981b, 1989, 1992, 1995; Hart and Richardson 1981. Mary McIntosh also was (and is) at Essex. Her influential 1968 paper (discussed in detail in chapter 6) was overtly functionalist, though it has rarely been read that way. Weeks (1991: 157–69) now seeks to minimize the influence of Foucault, but examination of his charter-for-constructionism chapter in Plummer's 1981b collection shows that he cited Foucault considerably more than anyone else (15 times in contrast to 5 citations of Gagnon and Simon, 3 of McIntosh, and 2 of Plummer). He discussed Foucault more than anyone else (albeit not entirely uncritically). See also his preface to the foundational creationist text, Hocquenghem (1978). Rereading Weeks 1981 also reminded me how devoid it is of knowledge about typifications of homosexuality other than in "modern" medical literature, and of consideration even of earlier (than late 19th century) medical discourse or other kinds of "self" discourse.

65. See also Jeffreys 1985; Faderman 1978, 1981. More recently, Faderman (1991b:59–60) acknowledged that male homosexual subculture preceded medical discourse and that sexologists

developed a phylogeny based on labeling for ontogeny to recapitulate. On the individual level, its proponents worry that *gay* or *lesbian* is a reification of complex experience.[66] This group fails to acknowledge that not just sexually devalued selves are reifications: *all* social categories (folk and scientific, and especially those applied across time and space) force the flux of reality into schemata, overlooking or ignoring some perceivable differences.[67] As C. Wright Mills wrote (1968:230), "All concepts are 'caricatures.' They invite attention to selected features of some object." Unlike creationist critics of the concept *homosexual* as if it is uniquely imprecise, Kinsey, Pomeroy, and Martin noted (1948:639), "Not all things are black nor all things white. It is a fundamental of taxonomy that nature rarely deals with discrete categories." Not just taxonomies of sexualities simplify. All taxonomies simplify.

Just as every language uses only a few of the many contrasts of sounds humans can produce, so any society includes only a limited number of overtly labeled roles. Not all societies use sexual behavior to define roles, but in North America roles defined at least in part by sexual behavior exist.[68]

---

may have been only the midwives rather than the fathers of a lesbian subculture (while continuing to deny the possibility that working-class or nonwhite women could build any sort of women's culture).

66. For all the invocation of the diversity of human desires and social roles, the social constructionist (SC) canon through the 1980s was extremely ethnocentric (confined to consideration of Canada, the Netherlands, the United Kingdom, and the United States in the last hundred or so years). The palpable eagerness of many SC adherents to change the contemporary understanding of homosexuality—specifically, to deconstruct it into human ambisexual potentiality— perhaps accounts for a lack of interest in very different times and places. Weeks's longing (1985) for an imagined past time without labels complemented the Reaganite/Thatcherite longing for an illusory time of "traditional morality" including no public mention of homosexuality. One of the most extreme advocates of special creation of "the homosexual" by 19th-century medical discourse, David Halperin (1990:53), refreshingly disavowed what I see as Weeks's subtext, writing, "I offer no comfort to those who aspire to liberate us from our current pleasures in favor of some more free-wheeling, polymorphous sexuality" (cf. Weeks 1991:84). The work on ancient Greece by Halperin (1990) and Winkler (1990) expanded the horizons of SC to a society other than their own and to a much earlier time, while Plummer (1995) eagerly grasped at indications of "post-gay, post-lesbian" people.

67. Goodenough 1990:598–99. On recurrent ("natural") solutions, see Berlin 1992; Berlin and Kay 1991.

68. See chapter 6. The type discussed in the medical discourse that is supposed by some to have invented the *homosexual* was a gender-deviant *Uranian*. Weeks et al. obscure the discontinuity between this type and "the modern homosexual." In New York interwar vernacular discussed by Chauncey (1994), *queer* supplanted *fairy* before 1920. Chauncey (1982:119) noted that "*sexual inversion*, the term used in most of the nineteenth century [medical literature], had a much broader meaning than our present term *homosexuality*, which denotes solely the sex of the person one sexually desires. Sexual inversion, rather, connoted a total reversal of one's sex[/gender] role." Chauncey dated the change to "the turn of the century" (p. 116). In the

These are posited on the assumption that features such as gender identity, sex roles, gender roles, sexual object choice, and sexual identity covary straightforwardly. Just to take these five features, if we consider that each might take on three values (masculine, feminine, neither/both), there are 3 possible sets of features. English does not contain 243 terms for sexual orientation. There are not even 32 (the number of possible combinations if each feature is considered dichotomous). Outside the ivory tower, there are at most six role categories: heterosexual, bisexual, homosexual, transvestite, heterosexual transvestite, and transsexual. For many members of the culture the last four are conflated, and for some others the last five, leaving only two categories *(wrong* vs. *right, queer* vs. *normal,* or *gay* vs. *boring).*

Because Essex theorists decrying the falsely essentialist, misleadingly ontological status of homosexual identities acted as if such reduction of the flux of experience is unique to homosexual categorization, it is necessary to stress that *all* folk categorization schemata use only a few criterial features to sort phenomena. Some color schemata only distinguish "dark" or "light,"[69] but even an elaborated color lexicon like that in English does not have a distinct term for each gradation of wavelength. Or take anthropology's favorite domain, kinship:

> The total number of different relationships which can be distinguished is very large and reaches at least many hundred. No language possesses different terms for all of these, or even any considerable portion of them. . . . In grouping phenomena and concepts into words, too many vocables would be difficult to learn, overprecise, a strain in both speaking and listening, and a waste and disadvantage in most situations of living. . . . If, on the other hand, it tried to operate with only five or six terms, it is obvious that those would necessarily be so inclusive as to be very inexact. It happens, therefore, that almost all languages have unconsciously settled on a kinship roster of between 12 and 60 vocables. (Kroeber 1909:175, 171)

Just as English has a single kinship term *brother-in-law* for sister's husband as well as spouse's brother and does not distinguish *cousins* by maternal or paternal lines, there is no term or any distinct role expectation for a biological male with a male gender identity, a male sexual identity, heterosexual object choice, and female gender role. In the dominant culture there is not even a distinction between a person with homosexual object choice and homosexual identity and a person with only the former. Gayspeak has "closet case" for

---

general culture, I am not convinced that distinction between male homosexuality and effeminacy or that the "modern" object-choice definition is generally credited even now. It is not just elsewhere that the gendered meaning continues to seep back into *gay* (cf. Murray 1995d, 1994b).

69. Berlin and Kay 1969, 1991.

that, but what about a male with homosexual identity but heterosexual object choice (to parallel "political lesbian")?

I find something very suspicious about deploring the reification of behavior into homosexual categories without likewise deploring other social categorization schemata.[70] I have not seen these writers arguing that someone who is, say, genealogically one-quarter white should not consider himself *black,* or that because of the complication of interracial sexual behavior throughout history, classifying people as black or white violates empirical diversity. For a time, *quadroon* and *octoroon* were tenaciously maintained distinctions. It should be noticed that these very precise racial identifications were not the basis for collective action, as the crude black/white dichotomy has been. Similarly, consciousness of relative strata within the working class is a bar to class consciousness, and therefore to collective action, yet I have never seen Jeffrey Weeks decry the loss of nuance involved in speaking of the "working class." Though it is obvious to those with a longer historical perspective than Weeks has that forms of capitalism and urbanization existed before the Industrial Revolution, I have yet to see any work from Weeks et al. deconstructing "capitalism" as an arbitrary melange of features with no essential reality. Similarly, social constructionists have not been eager to deconstruct the conceptualization of male and female homosexuality as "the same thing," although this combination is unusual (uniquely "modern") in time and space.[71] It is especially inconceivable in the cultures in which adults masculinized their young sexual partners.[72]

Not since German(-speaking) Jewish professionals in the late nineteenth

70. See Murray 1981, 1983a, 1988c. I would readily grant that Plummer (1975), Weeks (1985), et al. have extended deconstruction to "sexuality" and "heterosexuality," though I consider Weeks's statement that "there was little evidence of male homosexual identity" before the late 19th century (1985:92) disingenuous in (typically) neglecting to address whether "identity" (not just "homosexual identity") is much attested before then by whatever standards he uses. Plummer (1995:93) similarly begs the question of the historicity of identity in general. Cf. T. King 1994. See Murray 1988c on the slovenliness and bad faith of Weeks's historical methods; and McIntosh 1968, Murray 1988a, and Trumbach 1977 et seq. on the dating of consciousness of a gender-deviant type distinct from the *sodomite.* Perhaps because the first sociologist I heard advocating the dissolution of the *gay* category, at the first American Sociological Association meeting I ever attended (in Montreal in 1974), was Edward Sagarin (who was hiding his earlier homophile activities as "Donald Webster Cory"), suspicions of closetry (personal stigma disavowal) rise easily when I hear complaints about being reduced to a gay or lesbian "reification."

71. Weeks (1991 [1981]:14) does note it, and Halperin (1990:24) wrote: "No category of homosexuality, defined in such a way to contain men and women alike, is indigenous to the ancient world." I would extend this to the rest of the world before the twentieth century in North America and northwestern Europe.

72. See Adam 1985; Herdt 1984; Murray 1991b, 1992a:3–150.

and early twentieth centuries tried to convince themselves that they were assimilated has there been a people with a set of intellectuals so bent on denying the existence of their own people, attacking any attempts to discover tradition, and deriding any affirmations of identity and pride in the identity.[73] "If we only avoid calling attention to our difference, hatred of us will go away—and those of us who aren't obvious are fully accepted" were delusions for Jews in German-speaking Europe, and is, I am convinced, also for neo-closetry. Special creationism is the ideology provided by intellectuals eager to deny lesbigay identity at a time when the Christian Right has sought to suppress the increased visibility of "alternative lifestyles," homosexuality in particular. Every story has its time, as Plummer (1995) repeatedly insists, and the time of deconstruction has been the time of Reagan and Thatcher, even if the British and North American anti-gay theorists have been less politically reactionary than such continental prophets of deconstructionism and quiescence as Martin Heidegger and Paul de Man.

The Foucaultian component of Essex deconstructionism dominated gay/lesbian studies in North America and northwestern Europe during the 1980s. Non–social scientists such as Lillian Faderman, Sheila Jeffreys, David Halperin, and Arno Schmitt made the late nineteenth century unique creation of "the homosexual" an axiom rather than a hypothesis,[74] and set criteria for establishing homosexual roles that would exclude everyone everywhere.[75] The ardent anti-essentialism of Halperin and Schmitt is particularly unsocial.[76] Since it treats *the homosexual* as the singular and unprecedented product of medical discourse, a more accurate label for the perspective is *special creationism*.

A More Flexible, More Social Constructionism

In 1988, in a huge and learned book, *The Construction of Homosexuality,* New York University criminologist David Greenberg provided a version of con-

---

73. Analysis of other traditions as "constructed" come from outside analysts (e.g., Handler 1984), not insiders distancing themselves from non-intellectuals proud of their identity and unconcerned about the historicity of what they regard as "traditional." See J. Jackson 1989, 1995.

74. Although I think disingenuously, Weeks (1991:4) referred to this as a "hypothesis." Discourse-centered scholars tend not to conceive of intracultural variability. Their training obviously encourages categorical rather than statistical thinking. Even descriptive statistics seem totally alien to them.

75. My favorite is Schmitt's (1992:10) argument against any Arab conception of homosexual persons because Arabic verbs for *fucking* "have no forms of reciprocity." Murray (1995c) and Murray and Roscoe (1996) consider other absurdities in his argument. Donoghue (1994:19, 43–44, 56, 215, 267, 276 n. 41) seriously challenges Faderman's claims that women having sex with women was unconceived in 18th-century England.

76. At least they focus on earlier times and on places other than their birthplaces.

structionism that remedied the two most spectacular failures of most Foucault epigones. Greenberg examined medical conceptions of homosexuality from earlier than the late nineteenth century, and organizations of homosexuality other than the "modern" egalitarian *(gay)* one. For all his admirably Weberian seriousness about systematic comparison of different social arrangements, Greenberg still shares with Weeks a more than nostalgic longing for totalizing Marxist and Freudian theories.

Unlike Weeks and other neo-neo-Marxist creationists, Greenberg realized that capitalism appeared before the 1869 coining of the word *homosexual,* and even before the Industrial Revolution. He placed the emergence of networks of sodomites in southern Europe with the decline of feudalism, and sensibly follows northwestward the recognition of male–male cruising and attempts to repress them. Although there is some documentation of male–male intercourse (officially labeled *sodomy*) outside the major cities of premodern Europe,[77] mobilization to *suppress* such outrageous behavior occurred in major cities (Florence, Seville, Amsterdam, London). The increasingly affluent merchant class used the sins and excesses of the aristocracy in making alliances with monarchs, whose attempts to centralize state power necessarily opposed them to aristocrats. Aristocrats' sexual looseness was horrifying enough to pious bourgeois Christians, but they seem to have been even more scandalized by the mingling of their social "betters" with the attractive youths from "the lower orders."[78] Whether pederasty became less frequent and/or transvestitism became more frequent,[79] by the late seventeenth century bourgeois moral entrepreneurs noticed/attacked aristocratic pederasty less than effeminacy (in all classes).[80] I think that monarchs had an

77. See Gerard 1981, 1982; Goodich 1979:89–123; Murray and Gerard 1981.

78. T. King 1994:41. This was still operative in the late 19th century. Oscar Wilde's "feasting with panthers" (i.e., lower-class boys) was especially outrageous to the English middle class.

79. Before his conversion to constructionist orthodoxy, Trumbach (1977) argued that there was a continuous subculture, and that McIntosh (1968) and others confused its accidental exposures by prosecution with its origin. Dynes (1981 and personal communications) argues that both Bray (1982) and Trumbach overstate the case for pederasty's eclipse in Hanoverian (Georgian) England (cf. Crompton 1985; Greenberg 1990:98–100). I still find very persuasive Trumbach's (1977) suggestion that publicity of effeminacy camouflaged non–gender-stratified homosexualities—in many times and places (including the early 20th century New York recalled by Chauncey 1994:83–103). I think that cultural beliefs about women's lack of sexual interests similarly camouflaged woman–woman sexual relations.

80. Greenberg 1988:310, 332–35. Courts across Europe considered people to *be* sodomites, not just to have committed acts of sodomy, even as the content of the category *sodomite* shifted from a man playing the insertive role with younger men or boys to an effeminate man who was sexually receptive (Murray 1988a; Trumbach 1985, 1988, 1989). I am unaware of any evidence that such effeminacy was "constructed" by juridical surveillance and prosecution.

interest in promoting foppishness rather than martial accomplishment among the aristocracy, and that bourgeois contempt for such demeanor and behavior further reduced the likelihood of the old nobility launching rebellions. Louis XIV made the most systematic effort to tame the nobility and have them compete in refinement at court rather than compete to rule the country.[81]

Greenberg (1988:328–29) noted that in England after the rise and fall of the Puritan Revolution, "clubs and taverns known as molly-houses, where men with homosexual interests could socialize, served as more sheltered meeting spots [than coffeehouses], particularly for the middle and lower classes." The molly house was an urban phenomenon, and so was the Society for the Reformation of Manners (founded in 1690), which targeted them and conduct that the Puritan regime had for a time suppressed: "The reforming societies were mainly concerned with illegal drinking establishments, bawdy houses, Sabbath breaking, swearing, and to some extent the theater, but in London they also instigated prosecutions on sodomy charges" (p. 329).[82] Greenberg noted that "members came primarily from the lower middle classes—artisans, apprentices, retailers" (p. 329), but did not press a class or status explanation for such crusades.[83] In the Netherlands, Calvinist merchants supported the start of a campaign against "sodomites" around a Catholic baron in Utrecht. The excesses of lower middle class zealots eventually disrupted trade and led the Protestant upper middle class to stop the widening accusations.[84]

It would be absurd to contend that medical discourse in any sense "constructed" either the traditional pederastic sodomite or the more modern molly. Aside from the lack of a medical discourse about either, physicians'

81. See Oresko 1988. The class analysis in this paragraph is mine. For an excellent analysis of English bourgeois differentiation of the proper/plain virile self from both aristocrats and the class-mixed mollies, see T. King 1994.

82. A discourse satirizing and castigating gender deviance existed a century earlier, recorded in the work of Phillip Stubbes, Thomas Adams, and later in Ben Jonson's 1616 play *Epicoene* and the 1620 pamphlet *Haec-Vir* (see Partridge 1958:161–77; Wright 1935:465–507). Like Queer Nation or Stonewall, the ink spilled on the mollies has led to vastly overestimating their importance in schematic just-so stories mistaken by some for histories.

83. Lower middle class status anxiety is relatively constant, as Kent Gerard reminded me. Thus, explaining the timing of moral crusades from it is implausible. Greenberg contends that the lower middle class members "were distressed by the crudity and uninhibited sexual manners of the urban poor and resented the profligate display of the wealthy" (p. 329). The former seems more plausible to me than the latter, because people generally compare themselves to those who are close to their status. On the other hand, upper-class behavior likely was a concern of those leaders who were themselves upper-class.

84. See Gerard 1981; van der Meer 1984.

status was not particularly high around 1700. "Medical authority" was as impotent in society as its treatments were ineffective for individual patients.[85]

A conceptual bifurcation between homosexual and heterosexual individuals existed, in that heterosexual interests and behavior were advanced as a defense against being "that kind of person," i.e., a "sodomite." Many accused sodomites and mollies had wives, children, and mistresses, yet "I can't be like that" had sufficient plausibility at least to be put forth as a defense.[86] This shows that there was a conception of "kind of person," not random acts of sodomy (as the nominalization *sodomite* should show).

Greenberg (1988: 346, 383) attributed absence of evidence of homosexual subcultures in seventeenth- and eighteenth-century North American colonies to the lack of large cities. With nineteenth-century urban growth, there is evidence of homosexual networks.[87]

According to Greenberg, nineteenth-century industrial capitalism needed especially disciplined workers. Ironically, at the same time industrialists sought to be unregulated by governments, they wanted workers' lives to be regulated.[88] He *assumes* that parents' attempts to produce the characters needed for anticipated occupations are at least moderately successful (p. 358), leaving vague how either they or he knows what these characters are or how to produce them: "On this assumption, early nineteenth-century middle-class parents would have begun raising their male children in ways that fostered self-assertiveness and competitiveness," and "the competitiveness instilled in boys through parental upbringing, as well as through direct participation in a competitive market economy, would have tended to discourage the acceptance of emotionally intimate relationships between men" (pp. 358–59). The conclusion that having sex with strangers "cannot plausibly be linked to capitalism; rather, it was an adaptation to the difficulty of sustaining ongoing relationships under conditions of severe repression" (n. 62) is interesting, but, both on the frontier and in the Eastern cities, the nineteenth century in North America seems to me to have been a time of considerable male adhesiveness, most notably celebrated by Walt Whitman,

85. I think that medical creationists have failed to recognize that the high status of physicians is even newer than medical discourse about intermediate-sex "Uranians." See Starr 1982.

86. Greenberg 1988: 337.

87. See Burnham 1973; M. Lynch 1985; C. Hughes 1893, 1907; Rosse 1892: 802, 806.

88. Rather than industrialists, it seems to me that it was middle-class women who sought to curb lower-class, "dangerous," often non-WASP men from drinking and lower-class women from renting out their bodies. Some financial support for these campaigns came from industrial capitalists. Agency in such matters—who dunnit?—tends to be as vague in Marxist as in functionalist theorizing. Greenberg (1993: 475–76) distinguishes a shift from industrialists to middle-class women in what became a crusade against immigrant male pleasures ("whoring" as well as drinking and homosocial conviviality).

and also of considerable female solidarity.[89] That "a high premium had to be placed on sexual restraint and on the preservation of the nuclear family" (p. 373) is also not obvious. It *was* placed, but did it *have* to be? This seems to me to commit the normative fallacy (equating *is* with *ought*) in a particularly functionalist manner (something exists, so let's figure out what its function is).

The threat of lesbians to late nineteenth century American society (capitalism?) that Greenberg (p. 387) found plausible in Faderman (1981) is odd, since she argued that lesbians weren't then conceived. Moreover, Greenberg (1988:88) decimated the cross-cultural relationship Werner (1979) claimed between natalism and repression of homosexuality that might otherwise have been useful to his argument about the production of workers for industrial capitalism. I also find it puzzling that small warrior societies can include some gender deviants and large capitalist ones cannot, and that women passing as men and/or becoming financially independent "did not threaten male identity as such" (p. 390).[90] How does one know what does or doesn't threaten male identity at a societal level? Was it really harder for nineteenth-century Anglo schoolboys living in boarding schools, or child coal miners working with their fathers, to de-identify with their mothers than, say, for Pueblo or Tahitian boys?

From already Freud-drenched consideration of the character that industrial capitalism "requires," Greenberg slid into a long discussion of the medical discourse about homosexuality (pp. 400–33). He correlated this medical discourse to "reform capitalism" and to the bureaucratization of modern states. State bans on child labor and mandates on schooling (prominent reforms) "reduced opportunities for sexual connection across generational lines," he wrote (p. 399). This would be useful for explaining a shift from age-stratified to gender-stratified homosexuality, except that this shift had already occurred much earlier with the (adult) mollies in England and somewhat earlier with drag balls in U.S. cities. Moreover, considerable age-stratified homosexuality among students flourished in boarding schools on

89. See Kinsey, Pomeroy, and Martin 1948:457, 631; M. Lynch 1985; Rotundo 1989; Faderman 1981. In England, "it was widely assumed in Victorian society that strong relationships between men were normal" (Weeks 1977:34). David Greenberg (personal communication, 1 Nov. 1994) suggests that the celebration might indicate the beginning of no longer being able to take homosocial conviviality for granted.

90. "Continued male rule required that male effeminacy be repudiated," Greenberg (1988: 388) wrote. I would think the demonstration that women can function independently (i.e., without men) would be more of a threat. Patriarchal military dictatorships in Latin America and patriarchal Arab states seem untroubled by flamboyant, phallus-worshipping gender deviants, who seem to me to reassure other men of their masculinity; so why must bureaucratic bourgeois states be incompatible with a few queens?

both sides of the Atlantic, and teacher–pupil relationships (i.e., transgenerational ones) were also not unknown.[91]

I must confess that it is also unclear to me why it was useful to bureaucracy(/ies) to explain homosexuality as caused by congenital gender anomaly. I guess that it afforded reformers with opportunities to display compassion. Only if gender deviance were infectious rather than congenital would it require surveillance and quarantine (making jobs for their keepers). Experts, homophile as well as medical, certainly were ready (eager) to be called upon to distinguish congenital gender deviants from those who *chose* to give themselves over to vice. Physicians and social workers expanded the market for caring for pathetic pathics, and some new bureaucracies developed. But, rather than medical discourse creating homosexuals, it seems to me that the inversion (intermediate sex, congenital invert, urning/Uranian) theory was fomented by men who felt that the category applied to them. It seems to me that many of its propounders intended the category to protect themselves and their friends from criminal prosecutions.[92] Even after World War II, the early homophile movement continued to seek medical authorization for compassion for a medical condition to supplant punishment for crimes. That medical treatment was frequently harsher and more invasive than prison regimens should not blind us to the complicity of Magnus Hirschfeld, his Scientific Humanitarian Committee (founded in 1897), and subsequent homophile organizations elsewhere in molding the to-be-pitied intermediate sex, increasing condemnations of those they labeled "pseudo-homosexuals" (in contrast to "congenital inverts") and even cooperating with forensic winnowing of "vice" from "genuine" (i.e., inborn) "disease." Along with other legacies of the age of reform that have been useful to reactionaries, there were unanticipated negative consequences for *homosexuals* of the attempt to inspire humanitarian compassion for gender deviates.

91. Some evidence that the sexual division of labor sharpened in 19th-century America or was especially sharp in comparative perspective would also be in order (p. 356). Greenberg (especially his 1990 article) has been more careful than Trumbach, Bray, et al. about inferring changes in rates of behavior (age-stratified homosexuality in this instance) from shifts of emphasis in discourse and to recognize that age-stratified homosexuality did not cease when the "mollies" were written about. I think that knowing something about the (lack of) empirical basis for "crime waves" (Fishman 1973) provides a useful inoculation against uncritical acceptance of printed discourse as demonstrating social changes, so that criminologists are unlikely to be susceptible to discourse creationism. Wolf (1979), Chauncey (1994), and Morris (1994: 17, 38) show that at least an occasional nonsociologist can recognize the simultaneity of divergent categorization schemata.

92. See Greenberg 1988: 408–10. Consequences often differ from intentions, but creationists claim that psychiatrists were dominating (inventing) inverts, not that invert psychiatrists, lawyers, and scientists were labeling themselves out of juridical range.

After reviewing medical conceptions of homosexuality and before considering lesbigay rights organizations and the more recent attempts to reverse the increasing visibility of lesbigay communities and individuals, Greenberg (1988:434–54) interposed a wide-ranging discussion of bureaucracy. Several readers, even some sociologists, have expressed confusion about why this chapter is there. The standard social constructionist path is directly from medical discourse to the counterdiscourse of gay organization, and some readers have been alarmed that Greenberg not only minimized the effect of medical discourse but then wandered off into considering bureaucracy. They have failed to see the pattern in Greenberg's book. As he pressed forward to and through "the construction of modern homosexuality," he always characterized the organization of society, then the organization of homosexuality and of attempts to suppress or repress homosexuality. Thus, "The decline of feudalism" preceded discussion of sodomite networks and attempts to curb them. "Competitive" (industrial) capitalism preceded discussion of the triumph of repression over applying laissez-faire to the masses. "Reform capitalism" preceded discussion of medicalization. And "bureaucracy" preceded discussion of post–World War II struggles for and against protection of lesbigay rights. Greenberg's chapter on bureaucracy is longer and more comparative (within a chapter) than earlier ones, but nonetheless focused on another ideal type of society. The socialization requirement for bureaucratic societies Greenberg advanced—"suppression of affective emotional responses toward males" (p. 447)—seems little different from the one he claimed for industrial capitalism. Given that impersonality is the defining attribute of bureaucracy, it has more credibility here, but I think that compartmentalization of roles is more common than characters (compleat bureaucrats) who are impersonal everywhere they go all the time. In particular, I do not think that fag-bashers generally come from the ranks of those being socialized for bureaucratic careers.[93]

Greenberg (1988) recognized the complexity of societies and of social changes. He did not press simple causal relations between the structure of the economy, the organization of homosexuality, and mobilization to sup-

93. Rather than displays of affection between men, I think that what bothers them is the link between affection and imagined sex, i.e., they are suppressing or repressing thoughts about the basis of their own homoaffectionality by dramatizing the difference between themselves and "fags." I quite agree with Greenberg's interpretation (1988:448) of San Miguel and Millham 1976 that "the greater the resemblance of the supposed homosexual to the subject, the greater the threat" as a basis for greater hatred of gender non-variant homosexual men, further substantiated by Laner and Laner 1979, and illustrated by the McCarthy era equation of communist and homosexual invisible subversion discussed by Bérubé 1990:265–70, Chauncey 1993, and D'Emilio 1992:57–73.

press whatever homosexuality is visible. He made psychological inferences about what is needed by particular kinds of society; he was certain that parents correctly recognize what will be needed; and he assumed that they efficiently manufacture the requisite characters. The first, I find unconvincing, the second even more so, and the third a leap of Freudo-Marxist faith.

Nonetheless, his book is a serious attempt to compare social constructions and constructors across vast expanses of time and space, and a refreshing break from dogmatic contrasts of "the modern homosexual" with a supposed flux of acts devoid of conceptions of recurring sexual desire and conduct everywhere in the world before the diffusion of medical categories. Greenberg (1988) avoided the ethnocentric absurdities of medical creationist dogma. He acknowledged that specialized—even exclusively—homosexual types existed before the 1860s and that "the world was neither conceptually nor behaviorally polymorphous perverse prior to the Industrial Revolution" (p. 485). He recognizes similarities between organization and repression of homosexuality in capitalist and communist states. He recognizes that classifications and proscriptions from earlier social formations persist and even reemerge, so that "ideas about homosexuality circulating at any given moment need not at all correspond in any direct, simple way to its gross social structure" (p. 494).[94] He criticizes Foucault's idealism and exaggerated sense of sudden breaks (pp. 489, 494, 498). In the mass of evidence about homosexualities and moral entrepreneurs that Greenberg supplies, he does not convincingly specify "just what aspects of social life are relevant" (his goal announced on p. 19)—alas. Nonetheless, in complicating the picture and abandoning simplistic claims about medical discourse (or a simplistic, essentialized "capitalism") creating social reality, he has moved from special creationism to sometimes-plausible social psychological constructings. Since so much of his historical explanation rides on very general typifications of families at different times, testing and refining his model will require much closer examination of changes in families—an already booming scholarly industry.

RESISTANCE TO STIGMA

When you are no longer the only one, the tide of history turns.
Paul Monette (1992:25)

Having followed one line of development of symbolic interactionist theory into recent quasi-Marxist explanations of the category *the homosexual*, I want

94. In contrast, Weeks (1977:4) denied inertia and insisted that ideologies must serve current "social functions."

to veer back in time to follow another line of development to the categories *queer* and *gay*.

Earlier, I mentioned Laud Humphreys's pioneer ethnography (1970, 1975) of non–gay-identified men who have sex with men in public, though secluded, places. From correlating denial of men's homosexuality with social and political ultraconservatism, Humphreys (1972) moved on to analyze the then young gay liberation movement, which was composed increasingly of those who had never been labeled, yet openly proclaimed their gayness, adopted various idioms of that era's youth counterculture, and sought coalitions with other groups challenging the status quo. Humphreys did not attempt to fit the emergence of the gay liberation movement into the functionalist or labeling or creationist frameworks discussed above. Instead, he built on Erving Goffman's rambling but suggestive book, *Stigma* (1963). Goffman, who specified his major and enduring concern in the title of his first book, *The Presentation of the Self in Everyday Life* (1959), explored (not particularly systematically) how individuals manage potentially discrediting information. He started with the assumption that in a large-scale, mobile society, no one is quite what he or she seems to be, since everyone has something(s) to hide. "Deviance" thus involves not a few deviants, but everyone (albeit to varying extents, depending on the social standards for the gravity of what they have to hide). For Goffman, everyone who is not already discredited is (to some degree) discreditable.[95]

The discreditable must cope with anxiety about being found out; the discredited with anxiety about being rejected on the basis, which they themselves may consider legitimate, that they are "that kind of person" (whatever is the kind that doesn't deserve to be treated as valid/whole human beings). For Goffman, feeling oneself discredited does not require labeling by anyone else; nor for that matter do such feelings require any objective basis (such as "primary deviance"). Since people apply labels selectively to themselves, being frozen in the naming glare of some representative of Society (parent, teacher, law enforcement personnel) is far from the only path to a sense of spoiled identity.[96]

95. The discreditable bear the additional burden of believing that their acceptance by others is based on others' ignorance that they are the kind of person they reject instead of the kind of person they simulate being (Goffman 1963:42): the "You wouldn't like me if you really knew what I am" complex. "Success in passing may exacerbate a subjective sense of isolation" and alienation, as Ponse (1978:62) observed. "If one must obscure or deny the true self in order to maintain a relationship, then the implication is that the true self is unacceptable" (p. 74). Moreover, fear of guilt by association leads closeted people not to associate with those who value lesbian and gay identities.

96. More interested in the vulnerabilities of the discreditable than in those of the discredited, Goffman assumed (just as functionalists do) that everyone shares credence in the validity

Traveling the short distance from "secondary deviance" to "spoiled identity" might not seem much of a conceptual advance, but Goffman's extension of the management of discrediting information from exotic "deviants" to everyone led him to glimpse another way of being in the world: accepting that one is indeed an instance of a discredited category, and challenging the legitimacy of that category's opprobrium. That is, instead of trying to deny a category ("I'm not one of them" or "I'm not like them") or living in disgrace ("We deserve it" or "We brought it on ourselves," etc.), some may decide "There's nothing wrong with the way we are, and therefore there's no need to deny what I am" (e.g., gay and proud, or queer and arrogant).[97]

Voluntary organizations—especially, voluntary organizations devoted to raising the status of some category of people—have long been a distinctive feature of the American scene. Goffman glimpsed the possibility of organizing to challenge the very stigma that is the only common feature of a group. Humphreys provided an exemplar in his case study of a movement committed to transvaluing the condemnation of homosexuality into its affirmation and celebration. "Normalization" of deviance can be a group strategy (as Leznoff and Westley 1956 had suggested), but it required a group (what Weeks et al. would deconstruct back into polymorphous flux) in frequent communication about common experiences of injustice. Organization of a movement, in Humphreys's view,[98] could not precede realizing (1) that the present treatment of one's kind is intolerable, (2) that others share this view that present reality is intolerable, and (3) that change is possible through group action. After a protest movement emerges, these conceptions seem so obvious that we are tempted to forget they were once widely unrecognized, e.g., when the sinfulness or sickness that was homosexuality was perceived to be inevitable and just.[99]

How did such perceptions change? Intellectuals like to believe that the

---

of the norms. On self-labeling in general, see Rotenberg 1974. On self-hatred (internalization of stigma), see Adam 1978c. I read Leznoff 1954 and Leznoff and Westley 1956:257, 263 (see also Chauncey 1994; Kennedy and Davis 1993) as evidence that norms were less shared during the 1950s than many later have supposed. Self-hatred is not missing on the other side of the gay liberation watershed, either (alas!).

97. Kitsuse (1980:9) added "tertiary deviance," i.e., the transformation of a stigmatized category into a positive self-concept, to the edifice of labeling theory (viz., Kitsuse 1962). On lesbian egalitarian utopianism see Ponse 1978:99–100; most of Wolf 1979; Faderman 1991b:216–19; and Zimmerman 1990:119–63.

98. Following Miyamoto 1964 and Toch 1965.

99. On the importance of subjective transformation of consciousness and increasing confidence in the possibility of successful resistance to previously accepted stigmatization by U.S. blacks, see McAdam 1982. On the more general centrality of the perception of a possible alternative, see Adam 1978c:123–24.

Truth will make men free (and possibly women as well), that books change the world. By thus revealing Truth, *An American Dilemma* (building on *Uncle Tom's Cabin*) set blacks free, and *Sexual Behavior in the Human Male* normalized homosexuality.[100] Such a view is very flattering to that stigmatized minority in America: intellectuals. However, in social history "In the beginning was the word" is, at most, a hypothesis. I suspect that historians have overstated the importance of supposedly "epoch-making" books. *An American Dilemma* indeed synthesized research about the position of "Negroes" in the United States at the time, but it was Myrdal's moral argument wrapped in the flag of the special mission of the United States to redeem the world that legitimated *Brown v. Board of Education* and other desegregation milestones.[101] Kinsey presented genuinely new data about unconventional sexual behavior, but despite his personal sympathy (even fascination) with homosexuals, insofar as his data bore at all on identity (which was not very far), he relativized homosexuality out of existence as a basis for identity. I think that Sagarin (1969:82–83), Altman (1971:114–15), D'Emilio (1983: 33–37) Humphreys (1972:59–60), Levin (1981:20), and Licata (1981:167) all overstate the importance of the first Kinsey report as a stimulus to homophile organization. Gagnon (1975:132) is right that the *reaction* to the first Kinsey report made sexuality a topic of open discussion even in respectable mass-circulation media. And D'Emilio (1983:37) is probably right that "by revealing that millions of Americans exhibited a strong erotic interest in their own sex,[102] the reports implicitly encouraged those still struggling in isolation against their sexual preference to accept their sexual inclinations" (p. 37). Revealing to individuals that they were not one of a kind was (and is) a vital step to group consciousness, which is a prerequisite to group action: a conceivable group precedes conceivable change of stigmatization. However, I fail to see how Kinsey's behavioral data contributed at all to this second step. The burgeoning postwar market for homoerotic paperback pulp fiction (male and female) and male physique magazines did more to show a widespread interest in glimpses of commonalty than Kinsey's behavioral statistics did. Kinsey himself cautioned the homophile movement not to press a case for being an oppressed minority.[103] The vision of even gradualist change pushed by minority organizations would seem to me to have come from re-

---

100. Or *The Well of Loneliness* is responsible for 1950s butch/femme roles (Faderman 1991b:173).

101. Southern 1981.

102. This is a rather peculiar formulation of the Kinsey study, which counted sexual outlets and avoided consideration of erotic interest!

103. D'Emilio 1983:83–84.

formist organizations such as the Anti-Defamation League of B'nai B'rith, the National Association for the Advancement of Colored People (NAACP), and the Urban League. Their gradual successes are more plausible factors in conceiving change as possible.[104] The black and student movements were important not just as examples, but because many of those who would participate in the early gay liberation organizations had direct experience in them (especially between 1963 and 1966).[105]

Along with ideas from the books of Myrdal and Kinsey and analogies from black struggles, important social changes were under way at the time the American homophile movement emerged (see below). Just prior to publication of the first Kinsey report was a major war, the effects of which included the massive mobilization of men into the single-sex environment of the armed forces and unprecedented recruitment of women into the wage-earning workforce. The former moved many men from small towns, through cities, and in many cases overseas; the latter moved some women out of the house and away from expectations about what constituted "women's work."[106] Both were isolated from the opposite sex to extents unusual for adults, and were freed from many constraints on same-sex bonding that previously had been taken for granted. Work on reference groups by the social scientists employed to study morale[107] may inadvertently have facilitated tolerance. A wartime task force report commissioned by the Surgeon General, and declassified decades later, recommended, "'particularly for soldiers overseas, homosexual relationships should be tolerated' as long as they were private, consensual and didn't disrupt the unit" (Bérubé 1981:20). Moreover, "The tension of living in the all-male world of the military, the comradeship that came with fighting a common enemy and the loneliness of being away from home in strange cities looking for companionship all helped to create a kind of 'gay ambiance'" (p. 20). This ambiance was particularly evident in large disembarkation cities such as New York, San Francisco, and

104. As was noted by Humphreys 1972:60–62; Yearwood and Weinberg 1979; Bérubé 1981; Marotta 1981:14; Licata 1981:173.

105. The extent of prior involvement of lesbian activists in such a women's movement as existed before the 1970s also deserves study.

106. In the recollections of women-loving women who were adults during World War II in Buffalo, N.Y., "jobs for lesbians were not a result of the war. They and their friends had been working since their teens. . . . In their minds the important effect of the war was to give more independence to all women, thereby making lesbians more like other women and less easy to identify" (Kennedy and Davis 1993:38; cf. Faderman 1991b:122; Schneider 1984). Rather than during the war, it was later, when defense jobs disappeared (especially for women), that joining the armed services became more attractive to gay working-class women (Kennedy and Davis 1993:77).

107. E.g., Stouffer et al. 1949.

Los Angeles. The wartime influx of young and available military personnel [108] was an impetus not only to homosexual behavior, but to the development of proto–gay bars. Being stationed overseas helped many to realize that American sanctions against homosexual behavior were not universal and inevitable.[109] The social disorganization and impoverishment in war zones clearly enhanced the sexual availability of the local populaces (of both sexes). A lesser legal concern with homosexual behavior long predated World War II, both in the Pacific societies and in the European nations governed by the Code Napoléon. Even after the war, expatriates marveled at the greater freedom from legal persecution in France and Italy, as early issues of *ONE* as well as the works of James Baldwin, Gore Vidal, and others attested.[110]

Once it was clear that the war was going to be won, official obliviousness ended. Sweeping purges of homosexuals, who were no longer essential to the war effort, provided the kind of official labeling that supposedly produces "secondary deviance." Less than honorably discharged personnel likely hesitated to return to small hometowns,[111] but others who had not been detected and who sought the freedom of the port cities also had reason not to go home to try to fit into postwar Middletowns and Plainvilles.

For some gay men and women, the war years simply strengthened a way of living they had previously chosen. People who had already come to a self-definition as homosexual or lesbian found greater opportunities during the war to meet others like themselves. At the same time, those who experienced strong same-sex attraction but felt inhibited from acting upon it suddenly possessed relatively more freedom to enter into homosexual relationships. . . . Although the military cast a wide net in order to meet its manpower needs, it preferred men who were young, single or with few dependents: a population group likely to include a disproportionate number of gay men. . . . Because the war removed large numbers of men and women from familial—and familiar—environ-

108. Discernible in John Horne Burns's *The Gallery,* Donald Vining's diaries, Christopher Isherwood's memoirs.

109. Larry Ross (personal communication, 1982) suggested that the World War I mobilization was the real introduction of rural Americans to alternative social and legal arrangements. World War II mobilized more men (and far more women). However, they dispersed across much of the globe through various ports, whereas all the World War I doughboys went to or through New York en route to France (see Chauncey 1994:142–45). Henry and Gross (1938:602) document interwar migration to a New York they thought of as "the capital of the American homosexual world."

110. E.g., Cheever (1991 [1957]:76). Many upper-class American lesbians, of whom Gertrude Stein and Natalie Barney are famous exemplars, had long been more comfortable in Paris (see Faderman 1991b:177), less for what it gave them than for what it didn't take away (as Stein put it).

111. Bérubé (1981:23), Licata (1981:166), and Faderman (1991b:126) suggested this. Plausible as it is, there is no systematic evidence for it.

ments, it freed homosexual eroticism from some of the structural restraints that made it appear marginal and isolated. (D'Emilio 1983: 24, 38)

Hundreds of thousands of young men and women were given their first taste of freedom from parental supervision and from the social norms of their home towns. (Licata 1981: 166)

Men freed from restraints by the possibility of death in combat found it difficult to revert to circumscribed behavior when they returned to civilian status. (Levin 1981: 19)

Castells (1983: 141) also repeated the unsubstantiated connection between dishonorable discharge and tarrying in San Francisco without adducing any even anecdotal evidence. Unfortunately, the relation of these plausible features of homosexual experience of World War II to the postwar homophile movement is entirely conjectural. C. Williams and Weinberg (1971), in the major study that interprets less than honorable discharges as a demonstration of labeling theory, cannot provide any test of whether such "labeled" men were likely to join homophile organizations—because they drew their sample of men less than honorably discharged for homosexuality from homophile organizations.

Of the nine men who served in World War II interviewed by Vacha (1985: 159), the only dishonorably discharged one did not join a homophile organization. He did remain in Los Angeles. One honorably discharged man and one who had not been in the military mentioned being early Mattachine members. Of the early Mattachine members Marcus (1992) interviewed, both of those who had been servicemen had been honorably discharged. Kehoe (1988: 19) does not report whether the one discharged lesbian of the twenty-seven in her study with military service later became politically involved.

Nor is there evidence that World War II increased the rate of permanent migration of homosexually inclined men and women to major cities. Migration does not seem to have been of interest to M. Weinberg and Williams (1974) in their lengthy questionnaire (from which they extracted the data in C. Williams and Weinberg 1971). None of the nine about whom information is available in Tobin and Wicker (1972) and Adair and Adair (1978) were discharged for homosexual reasons, and none grew up in rural settings.[112] D'Emilio (1983: 78, 87–90) adds three more early leaders who lived in major cities before the war, and suggests urban migration via military service for two lesbians (pp. 29–31) without specifying where they lived immediately before joining the war effort. All six men who served in World War II in my

112. The least urban place was Tulsa.

sample of gay San Francisco men received honorable discharge.[113] Three of these six belonged to homophile groups in the 1960s, and one organized a Mattachine chapter. From this small sample I would not be comfortable drawing any inferences about rank-and-file homosexuals within the 1940s war machine, nor about the rank and file in the 1950s homophile movement. Nevertheless, these data indicate that familiarity with homosexuality during World War II military service did not galvanize the leadership;[114] it did not provide their first exposure to homosexuality or to urban freedom by military service. Both former Mattachine members in Vacha 1985 were born in New York, and most of the gay men in his sample were either born in cities or had moved to them before military service (seven, in contrast to two men of rural origin who remained in cities after discharge and one who returned to the hinterlands). All six of those early activists interviewed in the first section of Marcus 1992 who mentioned where they grew up started in rural America.[115] The two veterans did not mention where they lived before joining the military.[116] I hope that the posited interrelation of military service, conditions of discharge, homophile organization membership, and metropolitan immigration will be tested with data being compiled in many local gay history projects. Figure 1.2 shows Bérubé's model, and how I would amend it.

Of course, postwar metropolitan location is not sufficient to account for membership. Many more stayed in cities than joined homophile organizations. I question whether there is any necessary relationship, either. That is, I am dubious that those dishonorably discharged were more likely than those honorably discharged to join homophile organizations (hence the question mark between the two).[117] My model contains a guess (the path with a negative sign) that those who grew up in metropolitan areas were less likely than those who did not to evade labeling. We would expect that practically all those who were members of early homophile organizations lived in metro-

113. The sample is described in chapter 8.

114. One must not assume that the characteristics of leaders are the same as those of followers. Status defense explanations of right-wing movements have come to grief by prematurely assuming equivalence (see Wallis 1977; Brym 1980; Hamilton 1982; Wood and Hughes 1984).

115. The only city mentioned was Galveston.

116. Morris Foote, the other man identified as a World War II veteran in Marcus 1992: 314–16, returned to Idaho and did not become involved in gay organizations until the late 1970s. Longtime Los Angeles activist Morris Kight lived in northern New Mexico until 1958 (Nardi, Sanders, and Marmor 1994:20).

117. From Schneider's data (1987:481) that lesbians who had lost a job after their sexual identity was revealed or discovered (10% of her sample) were much less likely to come out at work, one might generalize that labeling increases secretiveness more often than it politicizes people.

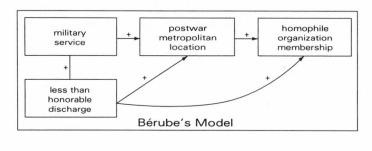

Bérube's Model

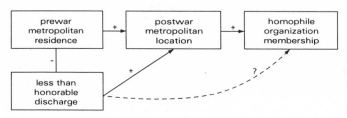

Fig. 1.2 Two Models of Postwar Homophile Organization Members' Social Backgrounds (Amended model in Murray 1984:26)

politan areas, and most seem to have lived in them before their military service (if any). I think it unlikely that we will be able to estimate how many dishonorably discharged homosexuals grew up in the countryside and small cities, nor how many of these returned to them after the war. It might still be possible to estimate what proportion of the veterans in homophile organizations were discharged less than honorably, and whether they grew up in urban environs, although such data have yet to be collated.

Rather than the disruption of social life occasioned by either world war as a source for coalescence of homosexually inclined individuals in North American cities, I would suggest that the long-term trend from farming and manufacturing to service occupations provided slots for men and women who were relatively detached or seeking to be autonomous from their families. At least in the eastern United States, the service sector began to grow in the 1830s with the railroad system.[118] Banks and corporate headquarters provided occupational slots for "ribbon clerks." In the twentieth century, the growing welfare state required new kinds of white-collar and pink-collar employees at the same time that blue-collar jobs (handling ocean freight and manufacturing) became increasingly scarce. The growth and florescence of San Francisco gay culture in particular occurred simultaneously with the

118. Beniger 1986.

rapid growth of San Francisco's downtown office space and the virtual end of manufacturing and handling ocean freight in San Francisco. The shift of jobs to the service sector is a long-term trend which gained momentum in the 1950s and still continues. Not one historical event (World War II), but a long-term process of social change seems to me to have facilitated gay and lesbian urban congregation and organization.

This has been a rather lengthy excursion into conjectural history away from the idealist explanations offered by analysts of the postwar emergence of homophile organizations. I think that conceiving the existing reality as intolerable and changeable was necessary for the formation of a social movement. Undoubtedly the Kinsey data and the example of the Negro reform movement encouraged the early homophile movement. I also think that the homophile movement was important in preparing the way for later changes, although the possibility that it did not affect anything should not be dismissed out of hand. The formation of a critical mass of people who viewed themselves as defined to some extent by homosexual desires was the central precondition for change, and was itself disproportionately facilitated by even tiny[119] organizations challenging the legitimacy of the dominant society's picture of *homosexuals.*

Although we are not sure of exactly what number constitutes the threshold, we can be confident that

> arrival at certain critical levels of size enables a social subsystem to create and support institutions which structure, envelop, protect, and foster its subculture. These institutions (e.g., dress styles, newspapers, associations) establish sources of authority and points of congregation and delimit social boundaries. In addition to the simple fact of the numbers themselves, they make possible and encourage keeping social ties within the group. (Fischer 1975:1325–26, 1329)[120]

Especially for groups that receive no media attention, social networks are a vital basis for social movement mobilization.[121] During the McCarthy era witch hunts, favorable publicity for the homophile movement was inconceivable. D'Emilio (1983) shows that the early Mattachine Society and Daugh-

---

119. According to Schur (1965:97), in the early 1960s only 2% of homosexuals were even aware of the existence of homophile organizations.

120. See also Fischer 1976:35–38, 1982:202–8. Two of the conditions Weber (1978:305) identified as increasing the likely success of class-conscious organization were the existence of a large number of persons in the same situation and their geographic concentration. There seems to be less residential concentration in Amsterdam and Bangkok, the Gay Meccas of Europe and Asia, than in North American gay ghettoes. Migrants may be more dispersed, but their number is important.

121. Snow, Zurcher, and Ekland-Olson 1980.

ters of Bilitis drew their members from preexisting social networks.[122] As is documented in chapter 8, men who migrated to San Francisco (and presumably also to other metropolises) before 1960 mostly lacked ties to these networks. They moved as individuals and did not know gay San Franciscans who could show them around or help them get established.

As the famous experiments of Solomon Asch (1958) show, one person perceiving him/herself to be the only one opposed to the view of others is unlikely to express dissent. Realizing that even one other person also opposes the consensus greatly increases the likelihood of enunciating contrary views. Two is perhaps the most critical number, enabling the first alliance, but two people cannot create a full range of alternative institutions. Fischer (1975)[123] stressed the importance of absolute numbers in arguing that the greater the concentration of people, the higher the rate of unconventionality, the greater the subcultural variety, the more intense the subcultures in conflict and competition with others, and, therefore, the greater the likelihood of collective action on behalf of the subculture.[124] He marshaled evidence from a variety of countries showing that city size "increases or at least maintains the cohesion and identity of ethnic subcultures—in spite of all the disorganizing aspects of urbanization, such as migration, economic change, and [the ready availability of] alternative subcultures" (p. 133). New subcultural institutions are possible with increases and concentrations of persons identifying with some particular oppositional characteristic. Moreover, "tolerance of sexual nonconformity," including homosexuality, is "strongly related to the size of the city in which respondents live"—though "it is much more

122. In 1953, "David L. Freeman" (the pseudonym used by Chuck Rowland as corresponding secretary of the Mattachine Foundation) asserted that "most homosexuals in this country, as a matter of fact, do participate in the homosexual culture and also in the dominant heterosexual culture and in any other culture from which they sprang or in which their lives involve them" (p. 10). He explained that "not all cultural groups are aware of their existence as such, and until the development of the Mattachine movement there was little consciousness of the existence of our homosexual culture," and that only a small minority of the small minority "who admit (at least to themselves) that they are indeed homosexual" recognize the existence of a "homosexual culture" (pp. 8–9). See also his interview in Marcus 1992:33–34; Wescott 1990 [1949]:248–49; Chauncey 1994; and Kennedy and Davis 1993 on pre-political homosexual consciousnesses.

123. Cf. Castells 1983:138.

124. In comparing social movements, Oliver and Marwell (1988) showed that the positive effect on collective action of the size of a population with grievances increases both with group heterogeneity and with overlapping social circles, even though a lower proportion (and even when fewer individuals) may be mobilized than within smaller populations: "Paradoxically, when groups are heterogeneous, fewer contributors may be needed to provide a good to larger groups" (p. 1; see also V. Taylor 1989:766–68 on exclusiveness and high commitment in small social movements).

strongly related to the size of city lived in when the respondent was age sixteen."[125]

The formation of a critical mass of people viewing themselves as defined to some extent by homosexual desires was the central precondition for change. It was facilitated quite out of proportion to the size of the organizations that challenged the legitimacy of the dominant society's policing of homosexual sociation.[126] Other facilitating circumstances included wartime homosociality, whether or not the war sped urban migration for those who became involved in the homosexual subculture (and even if official labeling was not part of their experience). Another, material change abetting the postwar expansion of public settings for meeting others interested in homosexuality was the introduction of penicillin and the concomitant reduction of anxiety about venereal diseases.[127]

Cultural factors that were important include the American tradition of printing dissident views and (some) valuing of freedom of expression. This is a value missing everywhere else in the Western Hemisphere—not that the value was sufficient in itself for extension to the homophile press without fight in the courts. Also important to the development of American gay movement(s) is the tradition of voluntary associations derived from the religious pluralism of the United States. The welfare state's takeover of insurance against disaster (the "safety net" function of the family) is an important prerequisite for the development of communities in industrialized societies, including the U.S., wherein the provision of health care remains a chaos of private and public responsibilities.[128]

Ostensibly Marxist historiographers of the homophile movement (D'Emilio 1983; Adam 1978a, 1987) have been oddly reticent about detailing the class origins of the early homophile leaders or rank and file. Licata (1981: 171), D'Emilio (1983:102–3), and Faderman (1991b:179–81, 190) alluded to a split along class lines within the Daughters of Bilitis between the middle-

---

125. See Stephan and McMullin 1982:411. Higher percentages of men in metropolitan regions are willing to identify themselves as gay to interviewers; or, gay men are more concentrated in metropolitan regions, whether this is due to migration or to greater visibility of homosexuality as a lifestyle (Laumann et al. 1994:304–9).

126. The early homophile movement focused on dealing with the depredations of local police (see Kight in Nardi, Sanders, and Marmor 1994:22). As is elaborated below, San Francisco homophile activists focused on churches and local elections earlier than did homophiles elsewhere. Little mobilization against the federal government occurred, except in the federal city. Federal policy, particularly purging federal employees, is (in effect) a local issue in Washington, D.C.

127. Levin 1981:20.

128. See Murray 1987b:199–21, 1992b, 1995a,b for contrasts.

class reformers (who were the ones who wrote the accounts of the organization's history and have been interviewed repeatedly by historians) preoccupied with respectability, and the original blue-collar members who wanted a secret, exclusively lesbian social organization rather than one focused on research and the education of straight publics (while enforcing gender conformity on lesbian advocates). Whether a similar split along class lines occurred in male homophile organizations (or for that matter between the politicos and the dance organizers of the early gay movement) has not been remarked.[129] No one seems to deny that cross-class sexual relations are more common among men than among women.[130]

Historians of the homophile era also have failed to address the extent to which early organizers were "free floating intellectuals"[131] or whether any early activists were members of the putatively universal class. Gay socialist scholars, who should be resistant to the "Great Man" theory of history, searching the 1950s for heroes have, as Levin noted (1981:21), exaggerated the importance to the early movement of Harry Hay, a bona fide Communist party organizer; so perhaps it is apposite to mention that his father was a manager of mines in West Africa and Chile.[132] More data on class origins and political commitments of leaders and led may be available, but to my knowledge no one has analyzed them.

In regard to women, Kennedy and Davis (1993:138) insist that "lesbian homophile organizations grew out of a working-class lesbian tradition," stressing in particular Buffalo butches' rebelliousness and the conviction that "a distinct kind of people deserved a better life" (p. 150). However, if there was any continuity of personnel, Kennedy and Davis neglected to mention

129. D'Emilio (1983) seems to me to have a double standard, criticizing the male homophile movement of the mid-to-late 1950s for accommodation, but not the Daughters of Bilitis leaders, who were at least as preoccupied with respectability, conventional gender appearance, and scientific legitimation as the Mattachine leaders were (see memories of Gittings and Lahusen, Shelley, and Winter in Marcus 1992:118–25, 133–35, 176, 182; confirmed by D. Martin and Lyon 1972:66). This is particularly noticeable in his account of the high dropout rate of DOB and failure to consider that its leaders' self-righteous moralism and dress code may have driven most women away (D'Emilio 1983:106, 228–30, 113, 125, 171). He seems to me to have an extremely Leninist view of a vanguard leadership mobilizing rather than representing the interests of the masses (see especially pp. 5, 210), although gay and lesbian consciousness, militancy, and self-acceptance emerged against the leadership of Cory and Call, Lyon and Martin, not from their analysis and organizational control.

130. Faderman 1991b:106, 178, 242; Kennedy and Davis 1993:4, 43–44.

131. See Brym 1980; Pinard and Hamilton 1988.

132. Timmons (1990) provided a biography of Hay. Roscoe (1996) explicated and collected Hay's writings.

it. Besides romanticizing working-class butches, they overestimated the atomism of middle-class women-loving women.[133]

If our theories are inadequate to explain the emergence of the postwar homophile movement, the disarray is even more evident in explaining the emergence of the gay liberation movement for, I think, two reasons: (1) New York provincialism, and (2) uncritical acceptance of a rhetoric of radical discontinuity across the watershed of 1969. That the concentration of publishers in New York reinforces local narcissism and enables recountings of local events to achieve wide currency is an interesting social fact, but is an obstacle to understanding general features of gay liberation movements. Memoirs of New York combatants provide interesting descriptive detail,[134] and hypotheses about processes *can* be generated from descriptions of events (mostly infighting) in the gay movement of one city. But any processes posited on such a basis cannot be tested with the very events purportedly being generalized (as Marotta 1981 does). The external validity of such claims depends upon testing the ability of the explanations to account for other data from other places.

The temptation to proclaim a sudden and total break with earlier work is not confined to those describing the gay "revolution," but is endemic to historians of political and scientific revolutions.[135] Except for Altman (1971), the book-length studies dealing with what the authors hope are general processes of gay movements [136] reveal continuities and parallels between homophile and gay liberation movements.[137] It is, predictably, the studies in the

133. They periodically mention the private-party circuit of such women. See Adelman 1986:116–17 for an example of a professional woman recalling 1950s parties and her development of a "community identity."

134. E.g., A. Bell 1971; Kantrowitz 1977; Tobin and Wicker 1972; Teal 1971—and the bases of Marotta 1981 and Duberman 1993.

135. See Tocqueville 1856; Murray 1980a, 1993.

136. Humphreys 1972; Wolf 1979; Marotta 1981; D'Emilio 1983; Adam 1987.

137. During the Reagan-Bush era with its becalmed reform movements, analysts of social movements rediscovered continuities between small, committed "liberal" groups and larger (even mass) "radical" movements that typically reject the coterie leaders but grow on the organizational base of the peripheral movement when political opportunities exist (compare McAdam 1982, Gitlin 1987, or V. Taylor 1989 with Adam 1987, D'Emilio 1983, or V. Taylor and Whittier 1992). I do not think the homophile movement fits Taylor's (1989) model of a movement "in abeyance," as she does (p. 772), because it was growing, not losing members, and, what is more important, because it did not shrink after earlier success (like the exodus from the women's movement followed attainment of suffrage). Despite the existence of earlier homophile movements, the American movement in the 1950s was discontinuous in personnel with pre–World War II European law reform movements, and, indeed, seemingly unaware of the precedents. Timmons (1990:163) reports that Christopher Isherwood contributed money but not his

small groups laboratory tradition (e.g., Chesebro 1981) that generalize from the microcosms of consciousness-raising groups to match the ahistorical views of some gay liberationists that they built a movement ex nihilo, or in direct conflict with closeted and/or "straight-identified" reformers.

In an era marked by exceptional generational conflict,[138] this penchant for rejecting elders' ways was probably an important part of the differentiation of the movement, but it also leads to serious distortion of the historical record. As NAACP was a model for the homophile movement, the Student Nonviolent Coordinating Committee (SNCC) was a model for the gay movement (among others). All these movements were marked by recurrent conflict between those (Marotta's term is "reformer") seeking tangible improvements in the lot of homosexuals and those ("revolutionaries") who believed in symbolic challenges but condemned any actual advances as "merely symbolic" and as indications of cooptation by "the system" (whether "the system" was conceived to be sexism, capitalism, gerontocracy, or some combination of these and other evils). Unless "the system" is totally overthrown, any tangible improvements endanger commitment to chiliastic movements. Better in this view to heighten "contradictions" and force action. Not exactly following this split between accepting or rejecting concrete gains was a split between those committed to building coalitions with other pressure groups and those who insisted on a single-issue focus to avoid further subordinating gay needs to virtuosi of the oppressèder-than-thou type.

The coalition/single issue split is still very much with us, especially in gay AIDS activism organizations, and is a good candidate for a universal feature. It plagued Mattachine earlier, and is, if anything, exacerbated for lesbians committed to both the women's movement and the gay movement. Conflict between "reformers" and those who regard themselves as "revolutionaries" is also common. What is unique to New York is the apparent brief triumph of the "revolutionaries"—if, perhaps, revolutionary rhetoric is mistaken for revolutionary action.[139]

---

name to the Mattachine Foundation in the spring of 1952. Isherwood had known Hirschfeld and the work of the prewar German movement but may not have communicated any of that history to Mattachine members. The December 1994 *ONE* newsletter mentioned a picture of a man who became an early ONE member with Hirschfeld during the 1920s.

138. In academic disciplines, between the Old and New Lefts, between the Old and New Rights, between preservationists and conservationists, within the black civil rights movement, within the women's movement, as well as between the homophile and gay movements.

139. Reflecting back on gay liberation groups in New York ca. 1969–70, Joel Brodsky (in my first conversation with him, on 18 July 1985) told me that the single-issue/coalition dichotomy differentiated the Gay Activists' Alliance (GAA) from the Gay Liberation Front (GLF), but that reform vs. revolution had nothing to do with what anyone actually did. He also

In general, as Miyamoto (1964:403) wrote,

> When large groups engage in intergroup conflict, a spectrum of attitudes will exist in each group, ranging from accommodationist to oppositionist. . . . As group tension increases, power will tend to shift from the accommodationist group to the protest [group], and as group tension declines, the reverse will be true, unless the protest group once in control is able to entrench itself by intimidation tactics.

In the instance he was describing, a revolt within one of the Japanese American concentration camps during World War II, "as the period of hostility extended, the intensity of feelings . . . showed a noticeable deflation and the leaders encountered progressively greater difficulty in sustaining popular opposition" (p. 400). Often, mass revolutionary zeal burns out quickly, even while a dedicated nucleus escalates the standards of radicalism for ever-smaller schismatic sects.

Looking at shared features, rather than the local news of yesteryear in New York City, we can begin with one shared even by New York: resistance. "As group tension develops it remains in latent form until some critical event occurs that serves to crystallize opinions and transform the tension to a manifest form," in Miyamoto's (1964:396) general formulation. One can predict that group dissatisfactions will explode, but it is impossible to predict what specific instance will lead to collective action—such science of collective behavior as exists does not have the analytical precision of inorganic chemistry.

Suttles (1972:51) contended that external aggression sometimes rapidly precipitates social atoms into a group. The mostly white and middle-class denizens of the Stonewall Inn[140] unexpectedly fought back when the New York police raided it in 1969, and those eager to channel the spontaneous anger into an organization came out of the woodwork in the subsequent evenings' demonstrations.[141] The first event gave a label to a whole generation,

---

stressed that GLF included many effeminists (followers of a cult of male effeminacy) scorned by GAA. He felt that Marotta recycled GAA definitions of their opposition to GLF from that era.

140. Contrary to the romantic myth, men familiar with the milieu then (e.g., Wilson 1994; Joel Brodsky) insist that the Stonewall clientele was middle-class white men and that very few drag queens or dykes or nonwhites were ever allowed admittance (except for Puerto Rican go-go dancers employed there). Duberman (1993) reluctantly demythologizes the multiethnicity and significant inclusion of women and drag queens in the Stonewall's clientele. A real (and earlier) example of drag queens fighting back was the series of 1966 demonstrations demanding service from Compton's cafeteria in San Francisco.

141. The 1968 confrontations at Columbia University (four years after the extensively televised Berkeley Free Speech demonstrations) surely must have afforded even those New Yorkers who were not there a glimpse of violent resistance as well as a vocabulary of oppression (the reality of which long preceded it).

but similar events occurred elsewhere, and earlier.[142] Even for New York City raids that summer, the Stonewall raid was probably less important than the raid on and protest against the raid on the Snake Pit bar later in the same summer.[143] Far more dramatic gay barricades were thrown up when the police invaded Montreal gay territory in 1977 (and led directly to the newly elected Parti Québecois pushing through inclusion of sexual orientation in the province's human rights code). In St. Louis in 1969, by mass arrests of Halloween masqueraders in the vicinity of gay bars,

> police accomplished what a number of others had failed to do, giving St. Louis homosexuals the melodrama necessary for "getting it together." The men in blue served as villains for the production and heroic Mandrake [the incipient local organization] had rescued the hapless heroines, thus demonstrating beyond doubt, that change was conceivable. (Humphreys 1972:90)

Shortly after I quoted Suttles (1972:13) that "it is in their 'foreign relations' that communities come into existence" and noted that only during the 1970s "have there been gay Torontonians willing to undertake foreign policy in the public glare,"[144] police raids on gay baths there provoked gay counterinsurgency.[145]

The precipitating incident in San Francisco in 1965 did not involve a riot, and involved the outrage of some prominent straight people who learned something about the intolerable reality of police harassment.[146] This lesson occurred at a New Year's Ball at California Hall in San Francisco,

142. The earliest demonstration against official harassment of homosexuality of which I am aware was in 1512, when a group of Florentine youths demanded that the government release men recently jailed for sodomy (Rocke 1988:31). An ongoing organization, the Compagnacci, contested the repression led by Savonarola.

"ECHO [East Coast Homophile] groups took to the streets in 1965 in public demonstrations at the Civil Service Commission, Department of State, White House, and Independence Hall in Philadelphia, attracting the attention of national news media" (Adam 1987:72). The Independence Day demonstrations at Independence Hall occurred annually thereafter (Kay Lahusen in Marcus 1992:123), and Barbara Gittings told me (in 1976) that in the spring of 1965 the Janus Society picketed a Philadelphia restaurant that would not serve those who "looked like homosexuals."

143. Wilson (1994) argues this explicitly. Those not mesmerized by the image of "Stonewall" as the pivot of the history of gay resistance can see this recoverable in various early memoirs and even in Duberman 1993.

144. Murray 1979b:174; see also Lee 1978a, 1979b.

145. Fleming 1983.

146. According to D'Emilio (1983:87–89, 182–84), the largest San Francisco raid occurred at the Tay-Bush Inn in August of 1961: 89 men and 14 women were arrested (and another 139 allegedly slipped away). Within a few months, all the bars mentioned in 1959 testimony about police payoffs ("gayola") were shut down one way or another. In New York State (with the election of Nelson Rockefeller governor in 1958), a parallel campaign against police corruption led to repression of gay bars in New York State at the same time (Kennedy and Davis 1993:75, 145–47).

organized by six homophile organizations, including the Daughters of Bilitis, to raise funds for the newly formed Council on Religion and the Homosexual. Prior to the ball, members of the council had arranged to meet with the police to see that the ball would go smoothly and to be sure the police were aware it was a "respectable" event. Yet, on the night of the ball, the police pursued a policy of deliberate harassment by taking photographs of each person entering California Hall, by parking a paddy wagon and several police cars outside the entrance to the building, and by entering the hall themselves. During the evening, three attorneys and a [straight] woman council-member were arrested for "obstructing an officer in the course of his duties" as they argued with the police at the entry to the hall. . . . The outrage felt by heterosexuals who had attended the ball, including clergymen and their wives, at this show of harassment led to a politicalization and a strengthening of their commitment to fight for the rights of the homophile community, once they themselves had experienced similar repressive actions at first hand. (Wolf 1979:55; see the accounts of those arrested in Marcus 1992:140–45, 152–62)

The ministers provided a legitimacy to the charges of police harassment that the word of "perverts" lacked. At the trial, the Judge Leo Friedman directed a verdict of acquittal and ordered the photographs (and negatives) taken by the police destroyed. This defeat lead the San Francisco Police to appoint a liaison and to end vice squad ("Sex Detail") harassment of lesbigay events.[147]

I have recounted this event at some length, because it shows that the more famous events following the New York City police raid on the Stonewall Inn are not the basis for a unique pattern of the process of gay-movement crystallization. Even though they occurred before the time Marotta's focus narrows to New York machinations, he neglected the San Francisco events— not only the New Year's Ball, but also picketing in the spring of 1969 by the Committee for Homosexual Freedom (CHF) of San Francisco businesses that fired gay employees (States Line Steamship Company and Tower Records),[148] of the San Francisco Federal Building in protest of federal discrimination, and of the *San Francisco Examiner* in protest of its columnist Robert Patterson's "Dreary Revels of S. F. 'Gay' Clubs"; or of the Society for Individual Rights (SIR) holding candidate nights, picketing and boycotting of Macy's California (for prosecuting restroom sex cases), holding dances, and

147. On the 30th anniversary of the California Hall affair, police invaded an AIDS benefit for alleged violations of alcohol control laws. Fire and alcohol codes continue to be selectively enforced against lesbigay gathering places.

148. After a few weeks of picketing and boycott, Tower Records reinstated Frank Denaro with back pay, an apology, and a pledge never again to discriminate against gay people. States Line did not reinstate Gale Whittington. Bill Walker explained the personal relationships involved, reinforced my view that no particular attention was paid to the "Stonewall riots" in San Francisco at the time, and directed me to the Charles Thorpe collection in the Gay and Lesbian Historical Society of Northern California of CHF flyers, newsletters, and press clippings.

(in April 1966, at 83 6th Street) establishing a gay community center—that prefigured New York events;[149] as well as those such as Black Cat diva José Sarria's 1961 supervisorial campaign, the gay part in George Christopher's mayoral campaign (the same year) and in later campaigns (notably Jack Morrison's 1965 election to the Board of Supervisors, Dianne Feinstein's 1969 election as president of the Board of Supervisors, and Richard Hongisto's 1971 election as sheriff) that prefigured lesbigay electoral organization also achieved in Chicago, Washington, Minneapolis, and Houston sooner than in New York. With the heritage of a general strike and the ongoing war between Governor Ronald Reagan and Berkeley students, San Franciscans had no need of New York examples of demonstrating or of organizing. "The worm has turned" was already being proclaimed in San Francisco before Stonewall.[150] Similarly, in Los Angeles (where homophile resistance began in 1950), a raid during the first hours of 1967 on the Black Cat and other Silver Lake bars led to the formation of an organization called Personal Rights in Defense and Education (PRIDE) that organized a protest march, and, when the march was not covered in the news media, began publication of a weekly newspaper, *The Advocate*. The next year (still a year before "Stonewall"), the Los Angeles Gay and Lesbian Community Services Center began.

Castells, who is at least somewhat aware of earlier events in San Francisco (although he did not mention any of the 1969 picketings in San Francisco), asserted (1983:142), "The single event that marked the development of a gay liberation movement in San Francisco, as it did in the rest of the country, was the Stonewall Revolt." Unfortunately, Castells did not provide any evidence of its salience in San Francisco, ca. 1969. The "radical" *CHF Newsletter* did not mention the event, while the "News Notes" of the August 1969

149. D'Emilio (1983, 1992) ignored these actions, except for the New Year's Ball, though he did discuss the rapid growth of SIR membership, its connection to gay bars and bargoers, and Leo Laurence's break with SIR (1983:190–91, 230–31). D'Emilio asserted that, once bar raids ceased, the Tavern Guild was content and no longer opposed oppression (1983:205). Although the organization and its members have never been sufficiently revolutionary for D'Emilio's preferences, historical evidence should be brought to bear on this assertion. Marcus (1992) followed the pattern of ignoring what occurred in California after 1965 other than newsmen getting jobs with San Francisco newspapers (in chapters primarily focused on their earlier lives). Adam (1987:72, 79) briefly mentioned some San Francisco organizing and actions. For a contemporary account that was readily available see Berlandt 1970:52–55.

150. This is the title of an article by Aubrey Bailey in the 20 May 1969 *CHF Newsletter* (p. 2). The easy passage of a resolution condemning "firing, taking economic sanctions and other oppressive action against any persons for reasons of sexual preference" at the business meeting at the 1969 annual meeting of the American Sociological Association on 3 September in San Francisco (reported in the *Vector*, the *CHF Newsletter*, and the *Advocate*) was immediately used to legitimate action against employment discrimination against lesbians and gay men (the main CHF focus).

Vector (the "reformist" SIR's monthly magazine) devoted more space to the publication of a book called *The Feminized Male* than to noting that "reactions are still being felt over the 'homosexual riots' that occurred in New York City's 'Village' in June and July" and that patrons became involved in a 'protest.'" To put it mildly, the "Sheridan Square riots" (as they were then called)[151] were not regarded as epochal in San Francisco in 1969. There was a "gay-in" at Speedway Meadows in Golden Gate Park the last Sunday in June of 1970. A flyer for it from "the Gay Celebration Front," advocating "freakin fag revolution," referred to "Christopher Street Liberation Day." There were commemorative marches in New York, Chicago, and Los Angeles in 1970,[152] but not until 1972 in San Francisco.[153] I would suggest that New York's position as the media center of the United States better explains why an occurrence there became a generalized symbol than any uniqueness or intrinsic importance of the occurrence itself.[154] Visibility in mass media of Stonewall coverage would also have to be demonstrated to make of "Stonewall" a stimulus for migration to gay centers (in general, or to Manhattan in particular). Considering that he discusses this process prior to 1969, Castells (1983:155) cannot really mean to suggest that mass media coverage of "Stonewall" inaugurated gay migration to larger cities with incipient "gay ghettoes."

For the widely fantasized drag queen vanguard of fighting back against the police, the August 1966 fracas at Compton's in San Francisco was both earlier and more certainly a drag queen action than the reaction to New York City police's raiding the mostly drag queen–less Stonewall Inn in 1969. Even

151. September 1969 *Los Angeles Advocate*, p. 3. Alongside a reprinting (from [a supplement to] the *New York Mattachine Society Newsletter*) of Dick Leitsch's report entitled "Police Raid on N.Y. Club Sets Off First Gay Riot," the *Advocate* ran an article entitled "N.Y. Gays: Will the Spark Die?" which condemned "extremists of various sorts [who] have been trying to capitalize on their own causes by leading the new revolutionaries down their own paths."

152. Coverage in the *Los Angeles Advocate* 4,11, pp. 1, 12.

153. As slight as were the direct effects of the actual events called "the Stonewall rebellion," as a symbol its importance is undeniable (like the Boston Tea Party and Paul Revere's Ride). It is also an interesting instance of the relatively rapid creation and transmission of a subcultural symbol, even, eventually, to where gay movements were more developed and successful (San Francisco and Amsterdam).

154. Not that immediate mass media coverage was extensive. GAA members' memoirs (e.g. Bell 1971; Kantrowitz 1977) were published, instead of memoirs of earlier and/or more successful lesbigay activists elsewhere. Even the Los Angeles–based filmmaker Arthur Dong's 1995 PBS program on the background of gay rights controversies, *Out Rage '69*, all but ignored everything except what enhances the Stonewall myth. Like other misrepresenters of the history of lesbigay political protest, Dong altogether omitted the early de-assimilationist Los Angeles Mattachine Society of Harry Hay (cf. Roscoe 1996). As Edmund White (1980:260) noted, New York City is the "media capital of the country and through its hands moves all the hype fed to the rest of America."

consciousness-raising, often credited to New York "Redstockings," may have been prefigured by Sudsofloppen in San Francisco.[155] Appearances to the contrary notwithstanding, establishing priority is not my concern,[156] nor is separating independent invention from diffusion. My concern is with adducing a general process from unique events—a task which requires systematic comparison rather than the assuming that what happens in New York City has been or will be repeated everywhere else.

Is, then, reacting to police raids a necessary catalyst of liberation movements? Not for the London or Vancouver GLF,[157] but after the myth of Stonewall was elevated to being a universal drama, the GLF model could diffuse without a reprise of the catalytic events (police raids).[158] Diffusion of both reformist and confrontationalist movements occurred throughout the English-speaking world (and beyond) during the early 1970s.[159] Generally, a sense of grievance leads to social movement participation, but a shock effect may mobilize those with low dissatisfaction more than those who already were highly dissatisfied before a particularly shocking event,[160] as mistreatment of persons with AIDS mobilized some gay men previously content with gay men's status more than it did many already involved in gay causes. Similarly, the impalement of a fearful illegal immigrant fleeing the 1969 New York police raid on the Snake Pit galvanized more heretofore quiescent gay men

155. Wolf 1979:61.

156. For election of open lesbigay candidates to state legislatures, one might note that Elaine Noble had been elected to the Massachusetts House of Representatives two years before Harvey Milk was defeated in 1976, and that California's first openly lesbigay legislator, Sheila Kuehl, was not elected until 1994. Milk's martyrdom (memorialized by Shilts's 1982 hagiography, along with an award-winning film and an opera—all from the perspective of his particular San Francisco gay political faction) has led to overestimating the extent and success of his leadership and forgetting his general conservatism (except in insisting—albeit only after his mother was dead—on the necessity for tearing off closet doors) and lack of interest in building coalitions with Latinos and African Americans. "Stonewall" is not the only myth in gay political history by any means!

157. Weeks 1977:18; Adam 1987:83–85.

158. Adam 1987:ix.

159. In West Germany, the Social Democrats reformed the law when they came to power in 1969, quite without American influence. The university gay groups that later emerged drew on internationally diffused models, including Rosa van Praunheim's film of American gay life, *Not the homosexual is perverse, but the situation in which he lives.* Scandinavian and Dutch homophile organizations and publications emerged shortly after the end of World War II (Adam 1987: 60–61) and gradually won homosexual rights without inspiration of post-Stonewall New York theatrics. In Paris, many of the founders of GLF there had been involved in the general insurrection of May 1968. On gay mobilizations elsewhere (often with censorship of any "promotion" of homosexuality), see Adam 1987:86–89, 124, 138–43.

160. Opp 1988.

into gay liberation than the Stonewall raid had. GLF grew out of the demonstrations following the Snake Pit raid (and GAA grew out of GLF). In San Francisco, police harassment in 1965 mobilized straight supporters as well as homophiles and led directly to changes never achieved in New York by GLF or GAA.

Two

The Growth and Diversification of Lesbian and Gay Institutions

Political mobilization was slow. Gay institutions (with some lesbians in them) attained visibility more quickly. Early social science discussions of the "homosexual community" treated it as static, rather than recently emerged.[1] Since at least the mid 1970s, sociologists writing about North American gay culture and gay communities have noted changes, particularly growth and diversification.[2] This advance to diachronic analysis was more nominal than real, however, marred by a recurrent American penchant for taking differences across space as surrogates for historical data.[3] For instance, after a synchronic tour of urban gay ghettoes, Levine (1979c:201) suggested that other places represented earlier stages in a single *process* of ghettoization:[4]

> Societal antipathy toward homosexuality sets the stage for their formation. Conditions of total suppression and zealous persecution inhibit ghetto development, but with a modicum of tolerance, the process begins. At first gay institutions and cruising places spring up in urban districts known to accept variant behavior, resulting in a concentration of such places in specific sections of the city, . . . turning the districts into homosexual culture areas. Tolerance coupled with institutional concentration make the areas desirable residential districts for gays. Many homosexuals, especially those publicly labeled as gay or open about their orientation, settle in these areas. . . . Recent modification

1. E.g., Leznoff 1954; Leznoff and Westley 1956; Hooker 1961; Simon and Gagnon 1967c; Hoffman 1968; Soneschein 1968; Warren 1972, 1974. Cf. Wescott's journal's contrast (1990: 248–49) of the 1949 present to 25 years earlier, when there was not "so unabashed and homogeneous and self-conscious a homosexual society as such."

2. E.g., Humphreys 1971, 1972, 1979; Humphreys and Miller 1980; Harry and Devall 1978b; Lee 1979b; Levine 1979b; Murray 1979b.

3. Redfield 1941 is an excellent example.

4. Already in 1970 in his gay manifesto, Wittman (1970:330, 339) used the term "ghetto" in discussing San Francisco as a refugee camp.

of social attitudes towards homosexuals explain the transformation of the West Village, Castro Village, and Boy's Town into fully developed gay ghettos.[5]

Not all the gay "recreational centers" have been in residential areas.[6] I would suggest the location of many in warehouse areas has been partly a result of the absence of nocturnal competition for the ecological niche: the best way to avoid neighborhood challenge (and other gawkers) is to locate where there is no neighborhood (where rents also tend to be low).

Clearly, lesbigays were leaders in gentrification of old housing stock in North American cities. Although I think that Manuel Castells (1983; also Castells and Murphy 1982) uncritically perpetuated some folklore about the history of the San Francisco gay community, he rightly challenged the widespread view that the renovation of deteriorating urban housing was middle-class gay speculation.

> Although some of this action took place within the broader context of middle-class, childless professionals desiring to live in the city, a very significant proportion of housing renovation and neighborhood improvement seems to have been the result of moderate-income gays making special efforts to invest their own work and time to share a limited dwelling space in exchange for the feelings of freedom, protection and self-expression provided by a gay territory. . . . Many gays were able to live in their neighborhoods because they organized collective households and they were willing to make enormous sacrifices to be able to live autonomously and safely as gays. (Castells 1983 : 166, 160)

> A majority of the gay community could not afford to buy a house in San Francisco. So they formed collectives to either rent or buy inexpensive buildings, and fixed them up themselves. This practice was not only an expression of an economic need but a tradition initiated by the counter-cultural collectives of the 1960s in an attempt to supersede the role of the family in the traditional household structure. (P. 159)

These are micro bases for the "macro" process of gentrification. The process led to redirection of the lives of some participants as well. Some of those who learned the skills necessary to renovate dilapidated housing outside their (often lower-level service sector) jobs during the 1970s began a cycle of "trading up," deferring the profits of improvements in one dwelling while acquiring and redoing more expensive housing for themselves and, in some cases, forg-

5. In contrast, Herrell and Herdt (1993:53) recognize the continued contest for less than officially recognized "gay turf." In more than a decade of participant observation in San Francisco government, I have only seen maps with "Eureka Valley" and "Upper Market" as a name for the area including "the Castro district," just as in Chicago "New Town" is the gay designation for the eastern half of what is officially labeled "Lake View" (p. 39).

6. And those that have been tend to have a lot of non-family housing stock, whether furnished rooms or flats shared by people not related by kin. See Chauncey (1994:152–58, 302–4, 445–466) on prewar New York City.

ing careers in urban gentrification. In San Francisco, and other large North American cities,[7]

> gay realtors and interior decorators discovered the possibilities of a new housing market and decided to use it as a way to earn a living. Using their commercial and artistic skills, they bought property in low-cost areas, and repaired and renovated them for a high profit. It would be simplistic to label this activist as "real estate speculation." What in fact happened was that gays, discriminated against in the labour market, discovered the hard way how to survive the tough San Francisco housing market, and then decided to use their newly learned skills as a means of earning a living. (Castells 1983:158; see also Knopp 1990a)

Cultural changes in scale and in content came about in urban North American gay neighborhoods from some of the same structural bases that made gay political organization possible. The coalescence of a critical mass, the conception that change was possible, the "mobilization of symbolic resources" (including embryonic gay press, distorted mass media coverage, and public examples), and other factors adduced in the discussion in chapter 1 of the emergence of gay political organizations apply to the "evolution" of gay culture at the same time in the same places.

GAY BARS

In folk conceptions of the past, "everyone knows" that "in the beginning was the bar." Like most of what "everyone knows," this isn't quite right. Before bars, an aggregation of a critical mass of homosexual people in relatively delimited segments of space was necessary, and the first public places, as opposed to friendship networks, were temporal and spatial *segments* of bars, along with outdoor cruising locales for men, rather than gay bars. Bars seem to have been more important for white working-class men and women than for white middle- and upper-class or for black men and women, for whom private parties were and still are important.[8] In many places, no subsequent institutional development beyond bars has occurred.[9] That is, in many cities, segments of bars are still the extent of public gay life and the main site of lesbigay sociation and solidarity.

Contrary to what readers of novels set in Los Angeles or New York City

7. See, for instance, Noel 1978; Winters 1979; McNee 1983, 1984; Lauria and Knopp 1985; Godfrey 1988; Murray 1989b; Knopp 1990a,b.

8. For earlier times see Leznoff 1954; C. Warren 1974; Ponse 1978:82–85; Grube 1986, 1987; Faderman 1991b:161–67; Kennedy and Davis 1993; Newton 1993; Chauncey 1994. On "still" see F. Lynch 1992.

9. Including bar-sponsored softball teams (in contrast to urban softball leagues).

might infer, most gay men have jobs which at least intermittently distract them from cruising.[10] Especially before the development of gay ghettoes, gay life did not begin until after 5 p.m. or on weekends. Also, before there was the present range of gay institutions, what most lesbigays seeking fellow lesbigays did between work[11] and sex or sleep was to drink. The gay bar was the first gay institution, and for most members of the "pre-liberation generation," the only one. Before gay people demanded acceptance and forged our own institutions, profitable gay bars provided a modicum of anonymity and protection from official and unofficial interference with lesbigay sociation.[12]

Obviously, bars provide a marketplace for arranging sexual liaisons, and a locus of hope for finding love,[13] but their historical importance for the development of self-identified lesbian and gay peoples has more to do with revealing to many individuals that they were not unique: i.e., not only were there similarly homosexually inclined others, but these others were not (all) monsters, and were numerous enough to have meeting places, of varying degrees of furtiveness and friendliness. In that "open spaces like parks and beaches, commonly used by gay men, were too exposed for women to express interest in other women without constant male surveillance and harassment,"[14] bars

10. "Having renounced the world of work, duty, caution and practicality" (Holleran 1978: 88) is a good formula, but as even the frame of *Dancer from the Dance* makes clear, the "doomed queen" was not representative of most gay New Yorkers then.

11. Those unable or unwilling to conform with the culture's gender costumes and mannerisms consistent with their biological sex often could not obtain or hold "straight jobs." (Faderman 1991b:171; Kennedy and Davis 1993:82–83, 291). Working in jobs with gender-crossing or gender-mixing expectations or jobs for which there was no competition, some masculine lesbians and effeminate gay men acted out homosexual stereotypes at work, including, to some extent, same-sex cruising.

12. Hooker 1961, 1965, 1993; Achilles 1967; Cavan 1963, 1966; Lee 1978a; Noel 1978; Weightman 1980; Castells 1983; Adam 1987; the film *Last Night at Maud's*. Only a modicum, because police and state liquor control boards often interfered, as Wolf (1979), D'Emilio (1983), Faderman (1991b), Kennedy and Davis (1993), and Chauncey (1994) recalled. Like the temperance movement, their focus was at least as much on the public space and who was in it as on the flow of liquor. Chauncey (1994:348) shows (yet another unanticipated consequence of reform) that post-Prohibition liquor board surveillance fostered exclusively gay bars in place of speakeasies where straight tourists had gawked and smirked at fags and dykes while engaging in illicit behavior (buying drinks) with them. A similar concentration indoors occurred in South Africa (Gevisser and Cameron 1995:37).

13. "The modest, unstated proposition the bar rests on is: Everything can still be solved with a lover," Holleran (1988:181) wrote. "Although securing public space was indeed important, it was strongly motivated by the need to find a setting for the formation of intimate relationships," Kennedy and Davis (1993:5) wrote—with less skepticism for the extent to which such hopes were attained than Lorde (1982:187, 220, 224) and Gittings (in Tobin and Wicker 1972:209) recalled.

14. Kennedy and Davis 1993:30.

were even more important for overcoming the invisibility of gay women.[15] The location of bars in rough or nocturnally deserted neighborhoods made going to or from them alone imprudent, especially for women.

"In the beginning was the bar" will strike some as sociology again discovering the obvious. However, what is striking about bars being the first gay institutions to develop is that this also is the case in other cultures (including Latin America, southern Africa, and Polynesia) in which men have made only embryonic challenges to the equation of homosexuality with female gender appearance and behavior. Indeed, bars have been or are central locales for the flamboyant deviance from gender norms that sometimes is part of "coming out" (see chapter 6). In cultures where homosexuality is age-defined, neither gay bars nor gay identity has developed.[16] This is not because alcohol is a necessary catalyst for the crystallization of gay identity. Rather, drinking together represents a degree of solidarity lacking where one expects to "graduate" from the receptor role with age. Solidarity with peers (partners and potential partners) is what is important in sociable drinking, not alcohol dissolving inhibitions and/or generating addiction.

What Bronski (1993:83) recalled discovering two decades earlier remains true in many places for people unable or unwilling to have lesbigay newspapers, magazines, books, or videos:

> I remember, in the summer of 1972, going to Sporters almost every night for three months and realizing for the first time that gay bars were not simply for cruising, but that they were community centers, public meeting places, town squares, clotheslines people could hang over to gossip, and bulletin boards. There were no bar rags then or local gay papers. The bar was where you found your information: everything from who had been queer-bashed in the street the night before to whether or not Ken Russell's *The Music Lovers* really dealt with Tchaikovsky's homosexuality.

Bars were an early site of lesbigay male solidarity and visibility. In their generally higher drink prices, undesirability of locales, and poorer service, the gay bars of the 1950s and 1960s were the historical prototype of businesses selling us to each other. Manifestly, the business of a bar is to sell drinks, and the central importance of the bar, followed by the institution of the cocktail party, likely explains the high rates of lesbian and gay alcoholism—vitiating

15. Lorde (1982:150) recalled that in the early 1950s, even on Manhattan, "Just finding out another woman was gay was enough of a reason to attempt a relationship, to attempt some connection in the name of love without first regard to how ill-matched the two of you might really be" (see also p. 196).

16. Ironically, despite the euphemism "cupbearer" for Ganymede and the employment of handsome "serving-boys," especially in Arab and Persian societies (Murray and Roscoe 1996).

the need to appeal to orality, masochism, dependency, etc., as explanations. As Nardi (1982:18) put it, "Drinking is not used to escape from something; rather it is used to join something. Initial socialization into a gay community often occurs by attending gay bars and enacting the drinking roles perceived as essential to gay identity."[17]

If institutional elaboration (discussed in the following section) provides alternatives, and if predispositions for alcoholism and for homosexuality are not genetically confounded, we would expect gay alcoholism rates to be lower in larger cities than outside them, and lower for younger cohorts than for earlier cohorts when they were the age of the younger cohorts (i.e., differences of generation as well as of age). I realize there are formidable obstacles to testing these hypotheses. The prediction also presumes that Gans (1962) and Fischer (1975) are right to challenge the inherent pathology of urban life that Wirth 1938 and much other Chicago School work assumed.

Besides problems of sampling,[18] there are no agreed-upon indicators for *alcoholism*.[19] Rather than a set of symptoms evidencing lack of control over oneself or a volume of alcohol regularly consumed, what is "defined as alcoholism by the community is that drinking behavior which cannot be accounted for. . . . Getting drunk . . . is normal trouble in the gay community, rather than deviance."[20] It is deviance within the community, by community norms, which is of interest for the proposed interurban, intergenerational contrasts.[21]

17. See also C. Warren 1972:148–49, 1974:58–59; Ziebold 1979:40; Swallow 1983; Kennedy and Davis 1993:137, 91. McKirnan and Peterson (1989) on the basis of a survey of 3,400 gay and lesbian Chicagoans found a higher proportion of homosexuals who were moderate drinkers than in the general population (71% vs. 57%), with similar rates of heavy drinkers across the sample (21% of straight men, 17% of gay men, 7% of straight women, 9% of lesbians. In a random sample of 19 census tracts centering on the Castro in San Francisco, Stall and Wiley (1988) found that among never-married men who reported some homosexual behavior (not necessarily any gay identity), 20% consumed five or more drinks on at least one occasion every week. Although this figure is lower than other estimates of the extent of gay alcoholism, it is still quite high. Longitudinal data are not available, so that it is impossible to know whether the rate declined or whether earlier estimates were exaggerated.

18. I advise anyone setting out to test these hypotheses *not* to draw a sample in gay bars!

19. D. Robinson 1976:9; Nardi 1982.

20. C. Warren 1974:59, 58.

21. Readers reasonably could have expected Read's book (1978) about a Seattle Tenderloin bar to provide evidence of changes to contrast with Achilles's study (1967) of gay bars, but he avoided any consideration of alcoholism. Although purportedly providing a symbolic analysis, Read's study failed to address the symbolic (or any other) importance of alcohol in the culture, either synchronically or diachronically (see Chen and Murray 1984). More recently, contrary to moralistic expectations, connections between alcohol intake and increased involvement in risky sex have not been established (Bolton et al. 1992; Weatherburn et al. 1993; M. J. Perry et al. 1994—with Belgian, English, and American data, respectively).

OTHER INSTITUTIONS

I have argued above that the aggregation of a critical mass of homosexual people in fairly delimited segments of space was, and is, a necessary precondition for the establishment of any sort of homosexual institutions, including gay bars and gay (or lesbian or homophile or queer) organizations. Whatever the order of appearance of other institutions, organs for communicating a positive view of a group are essential to positive self-identification, as well as to political organization and social coordination.[22] In the United States, early homophile organizations produced periodicals. In particular, One, Inc. fought a protracted legal battle (1954–58) all the way to the Supreme Court (335 U.S. 371) to secure the right to send its magazine through the U.S. mail. As Harry and Devall (1978b:153) wrote:

> Gaining access to the use of the federal mails for gay organizations . . . was crucial to the development of a gay culture. It provided a means whereby gay organizations could communicate with their members, an essential requirement for all voluntary organizations. It thus provided the basis upon which the level of social organization within gay communities could rise above that of cliques and friendship networks and begin the "take-off."

They also noted that the gay press keeps readers informed about current political events affecting the group that are ignored by the straight press (p. 167).

In Latin America, police continue to seize gay periodicals as subversive, even when there is no conceivable prurience to interpret as obscene, e.g., in Mexico *la ley de imprenta* allows a judge at his discretion to declare printed, written, or duplicated materials *apologias de un vicio* (C. Taylor 1978). In Canada and England, charges of "obscenity" and even "blasphemy" are used to interfere with gay and lesbian publications. Outside metropolises with gay ghettoes, many people learn that homosexuality is a possible way of life from print media. The existence of printed material that describes homosexuality without condemning it as inherently wrong is now taken for granted by those living in gay worlds (not least gay/lesbian/queer scholarship), but is far from established in much of the world.[23] Representations (verbal as well as pictorial) published elsewhere are often seized by British, Canadian, and U.S. customs agents vested with some of the license Latin American policemen use to harass single women and gay men, while the boundaries of what is classified in the U.S. as "kiddie porn" continue to expand.

In introducing the conception "institutional completeness" to distinguish

22. More generally, see Brym 1980:26–31 and Oberschall 1973:246–48.

23. See Preston 1993a:30, 117. Hardcore videos and magazines corrode the equation of effeminacy and sexual receptivity among males and make an alternative to gender-stratified homosexuality more conceivable in many places.

the degree of community development, Breton (1964) stated that it "would be at its extreme whenever the ethnic community *could* perform all the services required by its members. Members would never *have to* make use of native institutions for the satisfaction of any of their needs" (emphasis added). He added, "In contemporary North American cities very few, if any, ethnic communities showing full institutional completeness can be found" (p. 194). By the late 1970s, gay communities included all three types of institutions Breton used to construct an index of institutional completeness—religious organizations, periodicals, and welfare organizations. Therefore, gay communities were (and are) "high" by his criteria.

The importance of institutional completeness is that the existence of a full range of institutions makes it *possible* to concentrate social relations within the group. Breton suggested that the degree of in-group sociation could be predicted from the extent of formal organizations, and Levine (1979a) found that in the cities with many gay institutions there were numbers of gay men whose meaningful social relations were more or less exclusively with other gay men,[24] although membership in organization of "one's own kind" may be even more important for sustaining identity for those not living in or near an aggregation of them, as Fugita and O'Brien (1991) showed for Japanese Americans.

Murray (1979b; see also chapter 8) found the institutional completeness of gay communities remarkable in that none of the factors that Breton saw as stimulating the elaboration of distinct institutions are relevant. These were (1) group distinctiveness, separate language in particular; (2) low level of resources commanded by group members; and (3) systematic (chain) migration. Immigrants often need services rendered in their native language, but all lesbigays speak languages served by existing institutions. Furthermore, most gay persons can "pass" and need not be confined to interacting with their "own kind." Second, affluent strata of the population engaged in homosexual activity patronize distinctively gay facilities. Third, although I think that I exaggerated the atomism of gay migration to urban centers (see chapter 10), it is often the result of discrete decisions by individuals, rather than the organized familial or village response that Breton (1964:171) saw as facilitating institutional completeness of ethnic communities.

It is certainly true that the institutions have not developed from the bottom social strata up. Clerical workers and middle managers are strata upon which much institutional elaboration rests. The neither lower- nor upper-class "bar crowd" paid for development of other gay institutions. The most

24. C. Warren (1974), Chauncey (1994), and Nardi, Sanders, and Marmor (1994) attest this was already the case earlier.

obvious case is the San Francisco Tavern Guild, which paid the expenses of the Society for Individual Rights. There is also a tradition of charitable fund-raisers, particularly from leather bars, which has expanded to raise money for AIDS service organizations.

A continuing influx to an increasingly gay neighborhood provides demand for more distinctly gay services—even as it may transform longtime non-gay residents into something analogous to Palestinians in the New Zion. The magnetic quality of a gay center draws more people, who make it a bigger magnet, but the same magnet may repel others. Conflict over space and political influence evidence such repulsion.

With greater mass, a minority population may resist assimilation.[25] Since the mid 1960s, the notion of inevitable assimilation has lost its hold on social scientists' imagination, and it is the reverse process—de-assimilation—of gay communities which makes them of particular interest to sociological theory.[26]

In the first serious attempt to explain gay de-assimilation, Humphreys (1971) presciently stressed the virilization of gay men—in individual histories, in the challenge to the traditional effeminate stereotype of homosexuals, and in thereby becoming desirable to each other as sex partners. Humphreys suggested tricking as the archetype of capitalist relations—short-term, contractual, and depersonalized—although not necessarily unique to capitalism, nor exclusively a product of capitalism (nor unique to homosexual relations).

In marked contrast to the then dominant view that a leisure society was imminent, Humphreys argued that technocratic executives lacked the leisure that earlier generations of capitalists had for romantic interludes ("love in the afternoon"),[27] i.e., increasing premiums on time promote impersonal encounters and vitiate lengthier affairs. The conventional wisdom that we have more time than our ancestors had may be wrong. Workdays have shortened simultaneously with increases in commuting time; labor-saving devices in

25. Breton (1964) introduced "institutional completeness" as a synchronic indicator of the assimilation of a minority group to the majority culture.

26. Even so articulate an opponent of the conventional wisdom of assimilationist urban sociology as Claude Fischer finds it probable that "extent of intensification [of urban ethnic subcultures] is . . . often transient" (1975:1333). It remains to be seen if the gay and lesbian communities will re-assimilate. History is not over, and gay/queer men and women coming out in the age of AIDS may participate less in gay-identified institutions than their elders did. Whether this is a general trend will depend on stigmatization of homosexuality within majority culture institutions and on any changes in attempting to enforce surface conformity.

27. Humphreys was contrasting 20th-century managers with 19th-century capitalists. Lacking evidence on the typical workdays of the latter, I suspect that those building financial empires also worked long hours, so that Humphreys was engaging in some wishful thinking about a "golden age" of adultery. More generally, see Schor 1991.

the home may have changed standards of cleanliness, but do not appear to have reduced the hours of housework.[28]

Rather than contrast conjectures about relative amounts of leisure, let us dally with the alleged consequences of less leisure time, specifically, a "decline of cruising." At least for the rest of the decade after Humphreys wrote (i.e., the 1970s), this was hardly a trend in gay circles. The locales may have changed from free parks and public toilets to commercial establishments, and the participants may have stopped defining the insertor as "straight," but a decline in cruising? Hardly. Although, again, there is a lack of quantitative data, I tend to believe informants who say the "Stonewall" and "clone" generations spent "more time cruising, a lot more time posing, and less time with any one trick than we used to." If the institutions of the clone generation existed to facilitate sexual contact, as Lee (1978a, 1979b) argued, they were not particularly time-effective, nor are the successors in the AIDS era any more so.[29] Just as standards of housecleaning rose with the spread of labor-saving devices, so criteria for partners rose with the increases of potential choices. Umans (1982) offered two explanations for the failure of the "sexual revolution" to deliver more connections. One is that if there are no obstacles, there can be no excitement.[30] The other is that revealing desires which were once forbidden and are still widely stigmatized carries an extra charge to the devastation of rejection.[31] Murray (1979c)[32] appealed to the Simmel/Wirth thesis that mental hygiene in the metropolis requires one not to attend to most of what is going on around one and to Granovetter's (1974) discussion of strategies for handling information gluts to explain the necessity of efficiently reducing the number of potential partners for serious scrutiny.

More time cruising, or at least standing around gay bars and clubs, does not corroborate time becoming scarce(r)—especially for the large numbers of un- and underemployed men in gay ghettoes—but it still fits well the model of capitalist relations central to Humphreys (1971) and also to the neo-Marxist theorizing of Greenberg (1988) and Adam (1979, 1982, 1987) even though the latter wheels out the shibboleth of the transformation from production to consumption, which is usually tied to a trend to increasing leisure.

---

28. Oakley 1974.

29. On the wait even for jackoff parties to get going, see Wagenhauser 1992:276. Back in 1949, Glenway Wescott quoted a friend's remark on how "all these people who come here [to a bar] every night and hang around for hours, and all they really want is to be at home in bed with someone" (1990:261).

30. Borrowed from Tripp 1975.

31. Adumbrated by Cavan 1966:192; Hoffman 1968:55–56.

32. A revised version of Murray 1979c appears as the appendix to chapter 7 below.

The homophile movement tried to protect spaces in which commercial institutions could flourish, but support of even those profiting from these institutions who were gay was not automatic. In Weimar Germany,

> The almost legendary flowering of the homosexual subculture during the heyday of the "Golden Twenties" worked to the detriment of the emancipation movement. . . . A contradiction between personal and collective liberation emerged, for it was far easier to luxuriate in the concrete utopia of the urban subculture than to struggle for an emancipation which was apparently only formalistic and legalistic. (Steakley 1975:78, 81)

Self-styled "radical" critics leveled similar charges at the law reform orientation of San Francisco's Tavern Guild from the late 1960s onward.[33] Elsewhere, the profits of gay bars and clubs have gone to non-gay owners who have not supported even "formalistic and legalistic" gay causes.

Moving back from their functioning to their origins, Adam (1987) and Greenberg (1988) related the emergence of gay institutions (and, indeed, of a gay people) to reduction of the functions of the family.[34] State provision of insurance against disaster (Medicaid, workers' compensation, disability and unemployment insurance) and old age (Social Security) is perhaps the most important replacement of family function.[35] Just as parents no longer needed to rely on offspring for support in old age, children could not depend on parents to find them non-agricultural jobs.[36] The inability to guarantee a livelihood for the next generation, and increased geographical mobility, eroded parental control. Job opportunities beyond the reach and often beyond even the view of parents increased in industrializing and industrialized states. "Choosing a mate could become a more personal decision . . . among industrial workers"[37] than among feudal landholding families.

Welfare-state protection of individuals clearly reduced the necessity of reliance on the family and may well be a prerequisite to gay society.[38] In the first chapter I questioned whether geographical mobility was necessary to populate gay proto-ghettoes. The correlation between capitalism and romantic love seems to me weak, since "the romantic heresy" flourished long before the rise of capitalism (and also away from the emerging Italian centers of mercantilism), and even longer before the rise of gay ghettoes.[39] Similarly,

---

33. D'Emilio (1983:182–89) well chronicled the naiveté of some members.

34. This was a prominent "Chicago School" theme (Ogburn 1928, 1933, 1935; Burgess and Locke 1945), also discussed by Parsons and Bales (1955) and picked up by D'Emilio (1983:11).

35. Gramsci 1971:295; Fabrega 1971.

36. See Granovetter 1974.

37. Adam 1982:51.

38. Contrast the situation in Latin America: Murray 1987b:118–28, 1992b, 1995a:33–48.

39. Adam 1987:8–10; Lee 1977; see Rougemont 1955.

while "newly created public places such as railway stations and parks provided anonymous meeting places in the 19th century,"[40] there had been recognized trysting places in pre-capitalist mercantile centers, such as Venice, Florence, Paris, and Seville.[41] And, while "women's economic independence declined in the Victorian period,"[42] increased after United States entry into World War II, precipitously fell, and then rose again after the war; in a longer time perspective, women's participation in the market economy is unremarkable—even for societies dependent on subsistence agriculture.[43]

While I am not satisfied that the explanations advanced are adequate, prerequisites have been isolated: critical mass, welfare protection, geographical mobility, voluntary relationships, all releasing individuals from dependence on and control by the family. That monasteries and the militaries in Western history at least adumbrated these[44] provides reasons to believe that genuine social processes are involved, rather than unique/unpatterned events. That is, social theory, not just particularistic histories, is necessary and possible, although to date insufficiently developed.

THE CONTINUED SALIENCE OF DIFFERENCES

Emphasis on similarities and differences also seems to oscillate. During the early 1980s, the "Where am I? That's not me!" responses to a masculinist clone "gay community" and to an egalitarian, feminist "lesbian community" undercut the pretensions of gay and lesbian ideologists to have reached (markedly different) Promised Lands. Not only those who did not fit the dominant 1970s gender images,[45] but some of those who considered themselves working-class or impoverished, expressed an alienation from representations of urban middle-class, white lesbian and gay life.[46] In examining

40. Adam 1979:3.

41. Murray and Gerard 1981; Ruggiero 1985; Rocke 1988; Goodich 1979; M. E. Perry 1980; Murray 1988a. Adam (1987:7) passes too quickly over mercantilism in Italy.

42. Adam 1982:51; see also 1987:9–10.

43. Whitehead 1981.

44. As Adam (1982:51), Boswell (1980, 1982), and Greenberg (1988) suggested.

45. Although *clone* was used to represent only male uniformity, the rigidly egalitarian, politically correct lesbian-feminists were as much clones in appearance and more so in attitude than their male counterparts. The dress of each kind prescribed(/fetishized) previously working-class models (such as jeans and flannel shirts). I think that the look did not just signal that a particular wearer was gay or lesbian but demonstrated our numerousness. They were "the first widespread, visible [to everyone] signals that gay men exist in great numbers. They are not attempts to idolize straight men, they are announcements of gayness—perfectly obvious to both the wearer and the onlooker" (Preston 1993a [1982]:179).

46. Soon enough there were new fashions: a resurgence of butch/femme dichotomization among women (Faderman 1991b:260–70), increasing prominence of "lipstick lesbians" reject-

shifting representations of collectivities in lesbian fiction, Zimmerman (1990:222) wrote of "some nostalgia at the close-knit communities that once existed in the shadows." She also captured the disillusion from the utopian aspirations of 1970s lesbian-feminism as the dissatisfaction with politically correct behavior (in particular, having to eschew butch and femme roles), and showed that the insistence on the central importance of class and ethnic disparities undercut the view that heaven (or even a *Bund*) had been achieved:

> At first, we new residents of Lesbian Nation felt ourselves to be united in the warm glow of "sisterhood," sexuality, and community—what June Arnold, in *Sister Gin* (1975), was to romantically label the "safe sea of women." But as sisters often discover, even the closest relationship can be undermined or destroyed by fear, misunderstanding, and differences. . . . The lesbian community, like the lesbian self, was envisioned by white women in the 1970s as monochromatic and uniform. As that uniformity broke down, however, smaller and smaller units containing more and more narrowly defined categories of self became the rule. Eventually, it seemed, in place of Lesbian Nation, we had microscopic rooms containing one or two women apiece. . . . Though vestiges of Lesbian Nation can still be found, it is a far less powerful and cohesive idea than it was a decade ago. The influence of feminism is weaker, or more diffuse, as in society at large. Consequently, lesbian fiction is less visionary and mythic, its voice less communal and more individual, even idiosyncratic. (Zimmerman 1990:xiii, 200, 208; also see S. Krieger 1983; Wolf 1979)

Not just lesbian fiction, but also lesbian and gay organizations and their constituents. Less articulately expressed dissatisfactions with the insistence on ultramasculinity, and unequal access to gay male institutions arose; even before the first cases of AIDS were diagnosed, gay male burnout from both political and fast-lane sexual gay life was reported.[47]

During the new American dawn of Reagan-Bush America in which persons with AIDS were written off, lesbians and gay men mobilized to care for those living with and dying from AIDS. Although taking care of one's own would seem proof of communal feeling, the 1980s were also a time of a sort of ethnic retribalization within lesbigay communities. Feeling insufficiently welcome or valued, lesbigays "of color" formed groups for narrower "own kinds." The impetus for ethnic lesbigay organizations included negative re-

---

ing lesbian feminist anti-fashion (Stein 1989), and among gay men the "boy look" (Gorman 1992:100) consciously differentiating a new generation from clones (especially sick and dying ones). It would be hard to argue that these fashions were more egalitarian, and I am not convinced that they were any more ethnically inclusive (contra Leger 1989:44 and the fantasies or pretensions of many others).

47. See Adam 1978c; Harry and Devall 1978a; Murray 1980a; Preston 1983:74, 87.

actions from lesbigay institutions perceived as "white," along with positive pride in members' cultural background and wishes to provide mutual support as well as more socializing with "our own kind." The number of "kinds" available in San Francisco is very numerous. Those that have been bases for lesbigay organizations include Vietnamese, South Asians, Pacific Islanders, Native Americans, Latinos, Latinas, and African Americans.

For a younger (post-liberation, post-clone, post-feminist) generation coming out in the 1980s and 1990s, building some kind of "family" seemed a more feasible goal than attaining the overarching communion of the liberated "new man" and "new woman" envisioned by the gay liberation generation.[48] My generation saw itself as creating new social arrangements that would be models for backward straight people.[49] As I discuss more in chapter 5, many of us who came out within a gay liberation milieu find the early 1990s movement goals of being able to be a soldier and to marry someone of the same sex as rather unexciting, if not positively suspect as salvaging oppressive structures by making gay/lesbian copies. However, our "do your own thing" ethic is strong enough that we tend to shrug and say, "Well, if that's what you want to do, you should be able to do it," even while thinking "But why would you want to do that?" We didn't just want to "find ourselves" in a mass ("ghetto") of duplicates in looks and thoughts and sexual deeds. We wanted to be the "new man" and the "new woman," to overthrow the gender order, and to live a new communal life of interethnic comity. Even recognizing that we failed to remake the world, it's hard for us to accept lowered expectations, even when we admire those working out humane, viable ways to live and to create and maintain ties longer than a trick and wider than a couple.

48. See chapter 8; Weston 1991; Carrington 1995. Cf. Adam 1978a; Altman 1982.
49. See the frame of Lee 1978a.

Three

After Gay Liberation

S&M AND GENDER UNIFORMITY?

Gay men do not simply like other men, they are like other men.
John Stoltenberg in Jay and Young (1979:109)

Masculinity was desired in [gay male] erotic partners to the extent
that it was valued in the self.
Joseph Harry (1984:142)

The paradox of the 1970s was that gay and lesbian liberation did
not produce the gender-free communitarian world it envisioned, but an
unprecedented growth of gay capitalism and a new masculinity.
Barry Adam (1987:97)

This chapter veers back to socio-sexual types of the 1970s. Feminine appearance was regarded with suspicion and increasingly stigmatized both in lesbian and in gay male circles during the late 1970s, though the male and female circles hardly overlapped during that time of pronounced separatism. The approved and readily identifiable lesbian-feminist look was not called *clone*, though lesbians had as uniform a look as gay men, and though flannel shirts and jeans were also part of both uniforms.[1] Within systems of gender endogamy, relations ideally were between men aspiring to masculinity and between women aspiring to be neither masculine nor feminine ("post-gendered" seems apter than "androgynous" for this). Rather than undertake a history of fashion, I will focus in this chapter on the prototype of 1970s sexual dissidence, S&M, as playing with gender stereotypes (shifting rather than eliminating the theatricalization of gender).[2]

1. Footwear differed: Birkenstock sandals for women, various kinds of boots for men.
2. Chapter 6 discusses reasons for display of gender deviance. As discussed in chapter 1, various reformers have claimed that for homosexuality to be accepted (to deserve "a place at the table" of society), gender conformity must be imposed. These would-be leaders condemn either exaggerating or dissenting from conventional gender appearances, while others regard challeng-

Especially in New York GLF, there was a strong streak of effeminism with dreams of future universal androgyny. The defiance and assertion of pride of other gay liberationists inspired many men whose distaste for effeminacy persisted. As Vollmer (1989:9) wrote, "What they found appealing in the Stonewall radicals was not their politics but the new gay role they presented, a role that was direct, active, and aggressive—in short, one that seemed masculine. Ironically, out of the revolt of the queens emerged not the androgynous individual of the future but the butch gay man of the ghetto." The sex they had, frequently, though I am not convinced more frequently than that which the World War II generation had during its youth, had little to do with heterosexual models. That is, gay sex often was neither a prelude to nor a part of forming a relationship (*nesting*); was not role stratified, so that it was no longer more blessed to give than to receive, and neither role was associated with gender expectations; and was recreational rather than procreative. Men tried to be, or at least to look, like what they sought to have: masculine men. Sexual practices, especially those involving demonstrations of endurance, produced for many "an intense sense of communion and identification with the new vision of tough, masculine gay role[s]. For all practical purposes, they were the rites and rituals of a quasi-religion, the glorification of the male" (p. 9). S&M provides the clearest example.

WHAT IS S&M?

As gay and lesbian participants in the S&M subculture(s) use the acronym "S&M," it does not refer to the clinical psychopathological concepts of sadism and/or masochism. Pain and humiliation may be parts of the more global roles of slaves and masters, but only parts of these roles, and means rather than ends. The center is dominance and responses to it of resistance and submission.[3] It seems to me that one would abbreviate sadomasochism "s-m," whereas (by general abbreviation principles) "S&M" follows from "slaves and masters." It could stand for "sadism and masochism," but no one

---

ing the conventional gender order (among others) as central to the (cosmic and/or political) mission of lesbigay people.

3. Obviously, submission to and resistance to domination, and eroticization of the slave–master dialectic, are not new, after a by no means completed liberation. The work of Petronius and Suetonius show that acting out such fantasies long predated Sade and Masoch. As Wescott (1990:313) wrote, "It seems to be a disgrace to have named so mighty and universal and multifarious a characteristic aspect of humanity after a French lunatic and a pornographer." (He suggested coercion and submission instead, and rejected mapping the poles onto gender. "Coercion" misses the consent, desire even, of the "coerced.")

uses that label. Califia (1982:246), who writes "S/M," reported a speaker who preferred "Sexual Magic" (SM).

No researcher seems to have bothered to ask gay men or women "into S&M" whether they think "S&M" stands for sadomasochism, slaves and masters, or sexual magic, or has escaped its etymology to become an arbitrary sign. According to Ian Young, "S&M has come to be a generic term for any inventive sexuality in which ritual is often important."[4] Mains (1984:11, 30, 29) added that "leatherfolk" was preferable as a label, since

> gay sexual role play with emphasis on limits and couched in fundamental equality bears little resemblance to what the world and psychiatrists term "S/M." . . . The leather community is fundamentally egalitarian. . . . If there is one constraint that is almost universally applicable throughout the leather community it is that the acceptability of an action must be certified by both its partners. A man's limits must be recognized and any transgression must be a willing one. There are strong social sanctions reserved for individuals who break this trust.

What little social science research has been done on S&M/leather scenes has followed the sociological tradition of normalizing stigmatized behavior, thus challenging cultural presuppositions (including, in this case, those widespread among lesbigays not involved in S&M). In their study of 52 victims of homicides relatable to homosexual encounters, Miller and Humphreys (1980:175) found none that had stemmed from S&M play.

Of the 35 adepts interviewed by John Lee (1979c:75–76), nine reported having been involved in a total of eleven incidents that resulted in physical harm requiring some form of medical treatment. He argued that this was a low rate in contrast to incidents of violence among straight married couples, and also a "very low rate per sexual encounter, since most men in my sample are quite promiscuous and may meet one new partner per month or more."[5] In *The Body Politic* soon thereafter, the late Michael Lynch countered that the rate of almost one person in three shows that, sooner or later, most of those involved in S&M scenes are seriously injured.[6] "Most of the injuries were not serious, certainly not life-threatening and 9 of 35 is closer to a quarter than to a third," John Lee responded (personal communication, 5 August 1993). Gayle Rubin (1982:202–3) suggested that those outside

---

4. In Jay and Young 1979:85–86.

5. If that was "quite promiscuous" ca. 1980, it says something about differences between Toronto and San Francisco, or between the leather community and gay society generally.

6. A sensationalistic 1980 CBS pseudo-documentary "Gay power/gay politics" twisted San Francisco coroner Boyd Stephens's statement that 10% of homicides in the city were gay to the claim that 10% of homicides in the city derived from S&M (see Rubin 1982:201–2; Califia 1982:269).

"S/M communities" are the ones who get injured, so that stigmatization of S&M rather than S&M scenes between trained/socialized adepts is responsible for injuries:

> Among the people I know, there are more health problems caused by softball or long-distance running than by whipping, bondage, or fist-fucking. The S/M community is obsessed with safety and has an elaborate folk technology of methods to maximize the sensation and minimize danger. These techniques are transmitted largely by older or more experienced members to neophytes. S/M oppression renders this transmission difficult. Scaring people away from the community puts people in some real danger of trying things they do not know how to do.

Like other S&M apologists, Rubin and Lee seem to me on the one hand to describe accurately the ability of adepts to maintain role distance (within S&M scenes) and to take precautions in selecting partners in ways that minimize the likelihood of real risks, but systematically to ignore those (marginal to the scene) who are not committed to the ethos of sexual play, for whom the scenarios are real life—the only real life they have. Generally, Simon (1994: 16) is right that "the social segregation of the sexual ensures its limited claims upon larger identities," but this is not true for everyone. Not everyone shares the apologists' own ability to fantasize, and I strongly suspect some people with fantasies of being violated require significant real (unstylized) risks in order to be excited. However, no more than the existence of pathological heterosexuals establishes that heterosexuality is a sickness, do the clinically sadistic and masochistic fringes of S&M prove that S&M is psychopathology.[7] What the leather fraternity has in common, Rinella (1993: 3) wrote, "is our individuality, our radical sexuality, and our desires for safe and sane good times. . . . What leather is all about [is] empowerment, ecstasy, and bonding."

Against those who link enjoyment of S&M with proto- or neo-fascism, Scott Tucker (1987: 46) noted that "people who play with power are likely to question it as well." Ian Young asserted the existence of

> a close connection between our opposition to political power and injustice . . . may be one of the most effective ways to fight political power and even render it unnecessary is to understand the impulses to power and submission in oneself and integrate them, rather than trying to extend them in political systems. Involvement in S&M tends to take away a person's "need" to oppress and be oppressed, manipulate and be manipulated socially and politically—another

---

7. The eroticization of danger was hardly a novelty introduced by those in the S&M subculture during the late 1970s. It was common in "traditional" queens' fantasies of "rough trade" and avoidance of "incest" with "sisters" for the risky excitement of finding out "What will he do afterwards?"

reason why political power-trippers tend to oppose it strongly. S&M can be part of an outright rebellion against social, structuralized oppression, which again is part of the reason anarchists and libertarians are over-represented among S&M people. (In Jay and Young 1979:104)

Simon (1994:24) asserts that S&M "can represent an escape from both the practice and legacies of hierarchies by playing past its realistic imperative." "May be," "can be," but for how many does it? For some, acting out fantasies of dominance and submission may expiate feelings of guilt, reduce anxiety, provide relief from the usual ambiguities of hierarchy, and/or provide insight into the charged relationship between sex, gender, and power—as Lee (1979c), Kamel (1983), Mains (1984), Simon (1994), Brodsky (1993a), and others have claimed—but, so far, no one has suggested even qualitative indicators for these outcome variables. It is also fair to wonder, if acting out fantasies of dominance and submission expiate long-stored guilt and provide new insight, why do those involved in S&M scenarios repeat or elaborate the same few scenarios rather than leave the "classroom" of S&M behind to apply the lessons in everyday "real life?" Of course, this is not the only proposed therapy that turns out to be interminable, nor the only proposed defusing of oppression or repression which becomes an end in itself rather than a step toward other social or individual goals.

Obviously, sexual scripts of all sorts, not just S&M ones, are repeated; both transcendence and sexual release are routinely sought again along familiar roads. Mystics develop reliable techniques for achieving ecstasy and getting out of the self. "Sexual passion often promises—and threatens—a loss of self. . . . We deliberately concentrate sensation in order to diffuse personality," Tucker (1990:30) wrote. Indeed, increasing pain and mortification are among the most tried-and-true techniques in the history of religion,[8] although "pain largely remains a mystery, even to insiders. Among sane and experienced leatherfolk, pain is a path and not a destination."[9]

The "status-loss humiliation" of being feminized in private, and, even more, of being displayed (exposed) in public is an important part of heterosexual male masochism (see Kronhausen and Kronhausen 1970:184), and in the accounts of many Christian saints eschewing the prerogatives of their class or gender status. Baumeister (1988:492) wrote that North American heterosexual masochism contains

8. The spirituality of trust and abnegation in S&M life bears more study. On the relationship between "filthy, disgusting rites" and oppositional identities, see Greenblatt 1982. Mains (1984) appealed to many religious traditions' paths through pain to transcendence, although he was more interested in the physiology than in the social structuring of rituals and identities (cf. Brodsky 1993a).

9. Tucker 1987:44.

some resemblances to certain cultural stereotypes of femininity. . . . These elements appear to reflect socially and culturally determined ideals about femininity rather than any natural or innate aspect of women. The most important evidence in this regard concerned the feminization of [heterosexual] male masochists, as contrasted with the lack of any masculinization of female masochists. Changing one's gender seems an important and viable means of escaping one's normal, everyday identity, and so it might well appeal to masochists. Yet only male masochists used it. . . . When female masochists do use gender symbolism, this tends to involve further feminization rather than masculinization. . . . Both male and female masochists assimilate the submissive role to the stereotypically female role.

The feminization of bottoms and masculinization of tops seems to be less salient when both roles are enacted by those of the same sex. Schrim (in Samois 1981:8) pointed out that in lesbian S&M "roles do not correspond to male dominant/female submissive social patterns. I've seen many feminine lesbian tops and many butch lesbian bottoms." Faderman (1991b:261) also asserted that S&M is opposed to gender hierarchy.[10] Age is a more salient symbolization of hierarchy in gay male S&M than is gender. For reducing one actor to a status less than that of an adult male, gay male S&M scenarios cast boys, or naked men (sometimes shaved of body hair), rather than forcing bottoms to don women's clothes. "Daddy's boys" on leashes are more common than "bad girls."

As in often painful initiation rites in African, Melanesian, or Native South and North American tribes, demonstrating the ability to persevere and to withstand pain evidences masculinity. To become men, boys have to show that they can "take it," where the antecedent for "it" may be adult penises, or tattooing, being strung up, etc. The male role in North American culture, among others, is often defined by activity and manipulation of the environment. One important part of the male role is seeking intense sensation, including risking danger and being toughened by pain.[11] Enduring pain without screaming or swooning is an important part of masculinity. Proving to oneself and demonstrating to others an ability "to take it" was central to self-conception as masculine—not just to bottoms in S&M scenarios, but to

10. See also Samois's collection *Coming to Power* and Alexandre 1983. As for straight male bottoms, public display heightens humiliation for lesbian and gay male bottoms, whereas display *is* the primary humiliation for straight women within S&M: "Male masochists submitted to display as a means of accentuating some other humiliation; for example, the man might be embarrassed to be put on a leash or dressed in lingerie, and being displayed in front of others might intensify this. Female [heterosexual] masochism, in contrast, often seemed to involve display for its own sake, that is, simply being displayed naked. . . . Display may be an end in itself for females, but only an auxiliary means for male masochists" (Baumeister 1988:487). For a dyke wanting to be *made* to dress up in femme costume, see Barker 1982:103.

11. Baumeister 1988:493–94.

clone masculinity more generally in the late 1970s and early 1980s. For instance, "Jerry," who brought up an analogy to Mandan warriors' initiation, told Mains (1984:68), "I've always been proud of my capacity to withstand. I'm physically strong and I've been through shit. Sure, I like myself. But I also like to see what a man can do to me. I like to see how much more I can take." [12]

There is also a nurturing aspect to being a top and a necessary sensitiveness to what the bottom is feeling and wants.[13] Devotees reiterate an ethic of care and responsibility. It is not true that adherents have been "unable to provide any moral judgments beyond merely formal ones (i.e. consent)," as Seidman (1992:134) mistakenly claimed. Young (in Jay and Young 1979), Lee (1978a, 1979c), Mains (1984), Thompson (1991), and others contend that gay/lesbian S&M is a more evolved form of sexuality in the general direction of human sexuality away from reproduction (both of babies and of gender models) toward greater mutuality, communication, and community.

WHY THE VISIBILITY, THEN?

Along with those who supplied the epigrams to this chapter, Edmund White (1980:55) raised the interesting historical puzzle, "Why [has] S&M emerged after the advent of gay liberation, which was supposed to have banished all role-playing?" He rejected the psychological theory that hypermasculinity is overcompensation to deny the disvalued characteristic of "essential" male homosexual femininity, or an escape of repressed desire to be like women (masochistic) within an increasingly masculinized gay world during the 1970s. Rather than answer his own temporal question, White contrasted across space, specifically, between northern European Protestant cultures and circum-Mediterranean Catholic ones (including Latin America) which dramatize punishment and family structures. An adequate culture area explanation, however, must at least account for the elaboration of S&M in Japanese gay culture, a phenomenon of which White appears to have been unaware in making his north/south contrast. The popularity of S&M in Japan also poses a challenge to those such as Simon (1994) who relate increasing or increasingly visible S&M to the breakdown of meaning-providing hierar-

12. Mains (1984) and Brodsky (1993a) discuss adrenaline and endorphin releases in a cross-mammalian perspective.
13. See Ehrlich 1985:50–51 on the maternalism, patience, and resilience of real cowboys (in contrast to the Marlboro man): "Their job is 'just to take it,' one old-timer told me." AIDS made gay nurturance more visible to non-gays (see Adam 1992).

chies, or those such as Baumeister (1988) who relate S&M to radical individualism, for Japan remains a society with clear and legitimated hierarchies and with expectations of less individual initiative than is expected of Latin American machos.

Another approach to explanation suggests that growth leads to specialization.[14] In *The Division of Labor* (1893), Durkheim long ago observed that increase in scale almost always leads to diversification, hardly ever to competition. This is a well-established regularity for all sorts of institutions. The particular specialization of bars and clubs focused on S&M can, then, be seen as having led to greater explicitness of desires within these settings and thereby reduced the likelihood of mistaken identities of would-be participants. Lee (1979c) listed a number of techniques used to avoid going off with someone interested in criminal mayhem rather than in mutually satisfying sexual theater. Most of these depend on being part of a "regular crowd" wherever partners are found. This protection was not as available before the clubs and bars began, so more cautious persons may have eschewed acting out such desires, or have been unaware of them. Implicit in this explanation of the flowering of S&M subculture is the assumption that there were large reservoirs of repressed S&M inclinations that could be released when the risks lessened.[15] In an anti-repression tradition,[16] S&M apologists prefer such an assumption to any consideration of desires being created (rather than merely released). Unfortunately, the existing store of knowledge is inadequate to answer so important a question as the innateness of specific desires.

Contrary to this native essentializing of constant and timeless S&M desire, it seems to me that during the 1970s gay male S&M came to involve less total and enduring commitment to particular roles than during the 1960s: contrast the prescriptive role fixation in the first *Leatherman's Handbook* (Townsend 1972) with the normative role fluidity in the second (1983) edition. To refine their own and their partners' pleasures, effective tops must be able to imagine how the bottoms feel about what the top is doing (i.e., mentally taking the role of the other). Doing this plays with divisions within the self.[17] Bottoms also may, but I do not think must, be turned on by trying to view their objectification, humiliation, etc., as their tops views it.[18] Versa-

14. Schiller (1982) applied this to S&M. Harry and Devall (1978b) and D'Emilio (1983:11–12) provide more general examplars.

15. E.g., Califia 1982:275.

16. See Robinson 1969.

17. Simon 1994:16. Dillard (1993) provides a vivid illustration.

18. An especially vivid representation of this is Steven Saylor's 1980 story "The blue light."

tility came to be more highly valued in lesbian and gay circles, including S&M ones, as the inversion in the top/bottom order in the acronym "S&M" (i.e., from "sadomasochism" to "slaves and masters") exemplifies.[19]

Adam (1987:98) noted that there is a sense in which "the new masculinity" realized "one of the deepest aspirations of the movement, that is, to develop egalitarian relationships free from role-playing"—or at least to involve *alternations* in the roles played rather than permanent type-casting of "the queer" as the bottom worshipping a "straight, real man" top.[20] An adept master "understands limits and responsibilities. . . . He has learned his limits like a true leatherman through reversal of position, and through the insight and humility that comes from such a reversal."[21]

Lee (1979c), with his emphasis on "role distance" (not being taken in by one's own act), suggests, at least to me, another explanation: that the S&M subculture is a transformation of the camp subculture, i.e., that leather is just another kind of drag. In an earlier version, Lee (1978d:14) wrote

> Gay men, who are best at theatrical performance in other areas of life, are the best (and least risky) S/M partners. Thus, gay men who are skilled in "grossing out" and "camping" behavior may well make the best partners. Such men are able to distance themselves from their homosexual orientation and laugh at it and are therefore less liable, I suspect, to dangerous role engulfment in the dungeon.

Kamel (1983:77) also emphasized the development of acting skills over the course of an S&M career.[22] Camp was always about artifice, and especially typified by a relish for the exaggeration of gender characteristics—Steve Reeves and Victor Mature, as well as Jayne Mansfield and Tallulah Bankhead, were camp icons in the 1950s.[23] During the late 1970s, especially the Cowboy and the Indian of the Village People were masculinist camp icons (along with more credible urban types like the Policeman, the GI, the Leatherman, and the Construction Worker). The exaggerated masculinity of the "clone" as well as of the "leather daddy" and his "boys in need of discipline" differs in

19. It bears noting that not everyone wanted to be "liberated" from enacting a polarized gender role (see Faderman 1992; Kennedy and Davis 1993; Nestle 1987).

20. For a celebration of the un- or pre-modern exogamy between "queers" and "real men" willing to penetrate them, see Arenas (1993:108), although in his memoirs he also recalled a number of apparently masculine men who wanted him to fuck them (e.g., pp. 103, 113, 152) and noted that gay–gay endogamy was not unknown in Cuba (p. 78).

21. Mains (1984:72; see also 48, 67, 73–76, 89, 128, 133, 154, 169, 175) somewhat confuses imaging the role of an other with experiencing it.

22. Mains (1984) was ambivalent about theatrical metaphors: using them (e.g., pp. 72, 74, 84) while at other junctures rejecting them (e.g., pp. 46, 67).

23. Sontag 1964:281. "Anything but reality!" (Monette 1992:88).

direction from drag queen performances, but both exaggerated female impersonation and exaggerated male impersonation act out stereotypical gender roles, very consciously aimed at commanding attention from potential sexual partners by being, or at least seeming, what one wanted to have.[24] "Your muscles are as gay as my drag," as a drag queen told bodybuilder/hustler John Rechy.[25]

The taste for artifice may not have changed, only its predominant direction within a relatively fixed firmament of gender stereotypes and often very specific fantasies. Renaud Camus (1981:108) wrote, "I like fake butch types better than real ones." Some of the same men have moved from female drag to male drag (again, quantitative data have yet to be collected about earlier cross-dressing of men who in the early 1980s dressed hypermasculinely), as the fashion in exaggerated conformity to a gender stereotype shifted during the 1970s from Mother Camp to Father Camp.[26] Gay men did not have to simulate femininity in order for their sexual availability to be noticed or the masculine gender identity of their partners to be sustained. We could look like what we wanted our sexual partners to look like with some confidence that they sought the same look (while preferred sexual behavior—or at least the image of what one wanted—could be signaled wordlessly by keyring placement or by what color handkerchief we wore on which side).

I think that this had less to do with ideologies of egalitarianism than for lesbians. In the pre-liberation era, when gathering places were few and/or dangerous, gender nonconformity signified homosexual interest for women, just as for men. During the 1970s, North American homosexuality became

24. The risk of advertising homosexual desire—in the readily identifiable hypermasculine clone or leather garb as much as in gender-mixing, gender-crossing drag—is that it is visible to those hunting targets for purposes other than sex (fag-bashing in particular).

25. Quoted in Leyland 1978:267. He also reported that "I've always had a good body but I prefer to have a constructed body" (p. 257).

26. Humphreys 1971; Murray 1983b. Joel Brodsky suggested that Newton (1972) and I overestimate the "pre-liberation" importance of female drag: "Pre-transition era gay life was hardly dominated by the drag clubs described by Newton. At least by the mid-1960s the audiences in these were already straight. By then, one could find men without dressing up as Marilyn Monroe. . . . Gay (and lesbian) fashion trends have lots to do with who you want to go to bed with and who you imagine would want to go to bed with you if you project a certain image" (personal communication, 30 Sept. 1993).

If less hegemonic than it appears in schematic accounts of radical discontinuities, drag did not die in 1969, but continues to coexist with other gay scenes (especially in "Imperial Courts" and "vogue balls"). Something of a revival of traditional camp during the late 1980s (see Vollmer 1990 and the diffusion to Hollywood of the mid 1990s) did not supplant masculinist leather. Though both continue, neither kind of "drag" has hegemony in North American (or European) gay communities in the 1990s.

less hetero-gender for both men and women,[27] though theatricalization of gender seems to me to have shifted rather than disappeared.

Evidence supporting the transformation of terms within the camp structure (of theatricalized, exaggerated gender performances) is supplied by such terms as "vanilla sex" and "bambi sex." These were generated by traditional camp processes of manufacturing pejorative two-word labels to refer to what seems to some as simple-minded, old-fashioned pleasures. Susan Sontag, the original explicator of camp to straight intellectuals, claimed that "fucking and sucking come to seem merely nice, and therefore unexciting."[28] Sontag (1964) noted that the proselytizers of the camp sensibility considered themselves to be "aristocrats of taste." An aristocracy, especially one without an economic basis, must flee emulators.[29] Sontag (1980:103) suggested this as a basis for those committed to being exceptional to delve into "sexual theater, a staging of sexuality. Regulars of sadomasochistic sex are expert costumers and choreographers as well as performers, in a drama that is all the more exciting because it is forbidden to ordinary people." I see, in the common focus on costuming and in choreographing near caricatures of gender, a continuity between female and male drag rather than the crypto-fascism that Sontag (p. 94) and others feared.[30]

OTHER DEFAMATIONS

In his analysis of the partial success of gay political organizing in San Francisco, Castells (1983) merely parroted the negative view of the South of Market (SOMA) subculture held by the politicos of the Harvey Milk Gay Democratic Club of the late 1970s and early 1980s, sharing "the considerable embarrassment" of those who saw SOMA dress and events as "cultural expressions of the need to destroy whatever moral values straight society had left them with" (p. 168). Other than a certain sympathy for the less affluent

27. The increased availability of sex change operations during the 1970s removed many of those who wanted to be another sex (transsexuals). Also, the "free love" ideals at least somewhat reduced the market for prostitutes (transvestite and other), as did reduction of police harassment of "public sex."

28. Sontag 1980:103–4. Surely this was true for some, but is easily over-generalized—and wholly unspecified by Sontag. Those writing out their suspicions of S&M are even less inclined to seek empirical data than are S&M advocates!

29. Weber 1947:188–93.

30. I also think she overestimated the popularity of Nazi regalia. As Califia (1982:250) illustrated, the equation is made even in the absence of any examples, let alone systematic evidence. In an analogous way, anti-porn crusaders read "violence of men against women" into consensual sex and into any representations of sex, even if those engaging in it are of the same sex.

and less educated, Castells imagined only individualistic nihilism, no positive culture south of Market:

> While sharing the aspirations to a self-controlled 'private territory,' many gays could not afford the high rents landlords were forcing them to pay if they were to have that kind of freedom [in the Castro]. So they started another colonization in the much harsher area South of Market, where transient hotels, warehouses, and slums were awaiting redevelopment. Their marginality to the [clone] gay community was not only spatial, but also social: they tended to reject the politicalization and positive counter-culture of the new liberation movement. Instead, they emphasized the sexual aspects of gay life, and the more the gay community strove for legitimacy the more an individualistic minority, who were also poorer and less-educated, evolved new sexual codes, many of them joining the sado-masochistic networks. The South of Market area became the headquarters of the leather culture. (P. 156)

This picture badly distorted many things. First, Castells neglected to mention that many of the landlords hiking rents in the Castro were gay men, not a few of whom belonged to the progressive organizations from which Castells recruited his informants.[31] Second, the participants in the nocturnal SOMA culture were mostly not residents of the area. The area is much less residential than the Castro Valley or Polk Gulch, and the section between 4th and 6th Streets remains wino territory. Many old warehouses southwest of this "Bowery" within census tracts 176 and 178 were converted into artists' studios, so that there were some gay artists living in the area with no involvement in S&M.[32] Third, the leather segments of gay San Francisco predated the clone florescence in identifiable masculine homosexuality. Fourth, it is difficult to imagine how gay men who gravitated to South of Market bars "emphasized the sexual aspects of gay life" any more than those who went to Castro ones. Other than dancing, they mostly did the same things with comparable frequency. The bathhouses to which clones flocked were south of Market (Rich Street, 8th and Howard), while the largest and most dramatic S&M bathhouse was in the Tenderloin.[33] The sexual activity in one SOMA

31. The only person he interviewed who was expert on the neighborhood was Gayle Rubin, whose name he mangled (p. 356). For a more empirical though still resolutely Marxist analysis of gay gentrification, see Knopp 1986, 1990a, 1992.

32. Hudson (1987) discussed a similar phenomenon in the Chelsea neighborhood of Manhattan.

33. John Lee (personal communication, 5 Aug. 1993) opined that leather bars in Detroit, Washington, and Toronto deliberately located themselves away from gay ghetto bars so that they would be harder to get to ("you need wheels," preferably [fetishized] motorcycles). More important than the residual glamour of daytime working-class men in the area, in such locales there is less chance of gawkers and tourists. Leather bars that are accessible, especially if located in the main gay ghetto, soon cease to be leather bars (e.g., the Barn in Toronto and Kox in Montreal).

alley did not differ from that in a Castro schoolyard after the bars closed. Fifth, it is difficult to imagine what Castells meant by "more individualistic." If anything—the culture, especially the etiquette—of the leather world has a longer and more elaborate history than the clone world's. Tucker (1988: 126) asserts that "leatherfolk are some of the few people I know who understand the communal and sacramental value of sex" and noted that "precisely because sexual communalism is a strong element in the leather scene, leatherfolks have also taken great initiative in organizing community events to promote AIDS education and safer sexual practices," suggesting that these are a "natural extension of negotiating sexual roles and limits."

Castells's own map 14.3 shows a concentration of gay gathering places south of Market predating the rise of the Castro. Collective celebrations and benefits for charity occur south of Market at least as often as in the Castro—while many participants in both gay worlds are self-absorbed hedonists. Allegiance to traditional values except in sexuality was not and is not confined to the gay urban professionals of Pacific Heights' south slope. Gay Republicans also party in the Castro or at the Eagle. Castells provided no data on differential political attitudes or involvements of clones and leathermen, whereas I agree with Rubin (1982:213) that "the idea that there is an automatic correspondence between sexual preference and political belief is long overdue to be jettisoned."

Probably a majority of gay men gravitating to either area scoffed at, rejected, or ignored the messianic message of urban salvation proposed by the gay liberationists Castells finds most congenial. Castells (1983:325) concluded that gay San Franciscans "won their right to existence but at the expense of their capacity to transform the city and society in unison with other oppressed minorities. Thus, coalition politics led to a series of victories by different oppressed groups, but ended in a collective stalemate."

The brand of radicalism of the leather culture playing with power and humiliation is incomprehensible to Castells's urban project, even though "the personal is the political" could be a SOMA slogan as easily as a feminist one,[34] and even though Castells approved of the connection made by the women's movement (p. 170) and extolled lesbians for "creat[ing] their own rich, inner world . . . 'placeless' and [thereby?] much more radical in their struggle. . . . Lesbians are more concerned with the revolution of values than with the control of institutional power" (p. 140). At least to me, this suggests

---

34. There was a sense among "sex radicals" of being pioneers in "the pursuit of happiness" beyond all hitherto-existing limits for the future liberation of all, not just that of gay men (Holleran 1988:24; Lee 1978a). This had little to do with leftist political theory, even for a former labor organizer like Lee.

a double standard and is of little help in understanding the goals or accomplishments of the South of Market leather community.

The lack of comment on the resemblance between the distaste assimilated/straight-identified gay men express for those in leather and the obvious analog in late 19th century Western Europe is strange. Those convinced that they are accepted by the dominant society despite their (in their view, minor) difference nervously deny that "we" (the respectable stratum) are like "them" (those misguided people who enact the stereotypes "we" evade and despise), perhaps more than do those who can take their respectable place for granted. In the early years of this century it was assimilated English-, French-, or German-speaking Jews denying any kinship with "funny-looking" and -dressing Yiddish-speaking Jews from Eastern Europe; in the 1950s and 1960s in gay circles, it was drag queens; recently in the same circles it is has been "responsible" feminist gay men and lesbians deriding leatherclad sexual outlaws and other gender deviants. Rather than challenge the stigmatization of the Other, assimilationists merely try to redraw the boundaries to include themselves and to increase the exclusion of those they scorn as genuinely deviant (other).[35] Those stigmatized as fitting majority stereotypes of the whole category by those most committed to the majority values are denounced as too obvious, too loud, too oversexed, and in general keeping alive the bad image we combat as typifying us.[36] Before accepting the views of the assimilationists fleeing from stigma while imposing it on those less enlightened denizens gravitating to south of Market Street, as Castells does, it would be good to remember that the carefully maintained Occidental/Oriental boundaries of the assimilated European Jews were ignored when the Nazi regime set out on its attempted purging of the body politic of Jewish "contamination."

I think that the confused discourse about S&M yields some rudiments of an explanation of the trajectory fairly straightforwardly from female impersonation to male impersonation, even as the nightmare of respectable gaydom shifted from "those awful drag queens" to "those sleazy sadomasochists." The question remains: Why a transformation? Even if both gender extremes were always there, why did the balance shift? Humphreys (1971) noticed the change in style and its roots in the "Muscle Beach and motorcycle set," or, as Esther Newton (1978:xii) snarled, "The S&M crowd, once a small and marginal subgroup, are now trend setters; their style and, to a lesser degree their sexuality have captured the gay imagination." Even if both

---

35. See Gilman 1986; Nestle 1987:100–9, 144–52; Preston 1983.
36. See Adam 1978c.

Mother Camp and Father Camp are products of "self-hatred" (as she suggests), the conceptual puzzle remains of explaining the opposite manifestations at different times.

Brodsky (1993a) took up this question—in apparent contention with my 1984 discussion. I certainly agree with him that there was, and is, "an interior, deadly serious side" to traditional female-impersonating camp.[37] "The serious side of 'Father Camp' might be the lack of anticipatory socialization for male erotic relationships in American society," as Brodsky (1993a:237) suggested.[38] Anticipatory socialization is a central problematic for explaining how a culture not based on biological descent maintains and reproduces itself and has been too little discussed in work on gay identity formation.

Specifically about S&M, apologists claim that novices learn about S&M as bottoms and later apply what they learned (especially about what gave them pleasure) as tops.[39] However, there is a lack of empirical evidence that

37. Newton (1978) perhaps overromantically described drag performers as gay cultural heroes (see n. 26 above). Murray (1979a, 1983c) dealt with stigma-challenging aspects of intragroup camping.

38. Brodsky (1993a:250 n. 3) also suggested the opposite, i.e., nostalgia for the bad old days rather than anticipation of a totally liberated future: "The Mineshaft's decor, for example, was in some ways suggestive of a late evening at some of those outdoor sites in its vicinity [empty meat trucks and abandoned wharves] at which many patrons would have erotic experiences under conditions of considerably greater personal danger of, among other things, being mugged. . . . The Mineshaft's location was as out-of-the-way and its admission policies as elaborate as anything necessitated by police surveillance during the early 1960s."

The concurrent presence and popularity of glory holes and cell blocks in gay sex clubs of the late 1970s and early 1980s made even some observers who did not see self-hatred in S&M scenes wonder about the desire to recreate the venues in which homosexuality had been confined by a society hostile to open affirmation of gay male sexuality. An enthusiast told me that no one wanted to recreate "the real thing," that these were "symbols of safe, gay places." Brodsky (personal communication, 30 Sept. 1993) offered the following explanations: "The 70s commercial fantasy 'nostalgia' for jail-cells, tearooms, army barracks, and dark corners was possibly intended to turn people on by reminding them of milieux in which they had previously experienced sexual (and, doubtless, adrenal) excitement. These themes were always treated by customers as camp come-ons rather than turn-ons. I don't know if they really turned anyone on, but they may have reassured some patrons that the given establishment was a 'safe' place. More likely, they reassured patrons that anything was permissible, even though this was never the case, by celebrating socially devalued settings. This in turn may have suggested to potential customers that if they patronized a given establishment, something exciting would happen to them."

Peter T. Daniels (Sept. 1995 comments) suggested, "The explanation for glory holes and general gloom is much simpler: so ugly men could get sex too. Also, some people don't like to be seen having sex."

39. E. g., Kamel 1983:77; Mains 1984:33. The temporal and psychic primacy of masochism is also the orthodox Freudian interpretation: "Where once the suffering of pain has been experienced as a masochistic aim, it can be carried back into the sadistic aim of inflicting pain, which will then be masochistically enjoyed by the subject while inflicting pain upon others,

most tops began as bottoms, let alone that while "some individuals have strong and consistent preferences for one role or the other, most S/M people have done both, and many change with different partners, at different times, or according to situation or whim," as Rubin (1982:222) claimed. John Lee (personal communication, 5 Aug. 1993) faulted my discussion for insufficiently attending to fantasy in S&M in general, and particularly in regard to solo anticipatory socialization:

> Many (not all) tops began as bottoms. This is not an argument in terms of top–bottom interaction per se, but an argument based on masturbation fantasies. In my observation, most tops began not with experience as a bottom, but with masturbation fantasies carried out alone. It is obviously a lot easier, alone, to tie oneself up in some way, spank oneself, insert toys in oneself, etc., while having in mind a master–slave fantasy (or watching master–slave scenes on video)—in short, to play the slave role in masturbation—than it is to find some inert object that will serve as a slave, and spank and bind it, while acting the master. Thus masturbation fantasies usually begin in the slave role, and merge readily into at least a few interpersonal enactments in which the novice plays slave, before moving on to what he may all along have preferred to do: be master. There is no suggestion in my observation that everyone starts by preferring to be a bottom, and then some or all move on to preference for top fantasies. Some tops most certainly knew that they wanted to be a top from the beginning, even while apprenticing as a bottom to "learn the ropes" (literally).

Lest it be thought that hardcore videotapes and magazines are necessary to provide models in channeling desires, Lee related (ibid.) the instance of a recent immigrant who had heard there was open homosexuality in North American cities, but not that there were S&M venues:

> He had definite ideas of what he wanted to do, had had fantasies of homosexual slave roles since puberty (down to specifics about the way he wants to be tied up) in spite of the fact that he had no exposure whatever to any media representations of such acts. He had tried some of these fantasies on himself while masturbating, long before he had any knowledge that there existed an S&M gay subculture where he could find men to play the role of master for him.

---

through his identification of himself with the suffering object" (Freud 1915, quoted by Bonaparte 1973:176).

"Sadism could never be primary, for how could pleasure be felt in inflicting pain if one had not already experienced both antagonistic and mysteriously linked sensations? Passivity generally precedes activity" (Bonaparte 1973:167).

In Euro-American S&M I do not see a prescriptive shift from initiate service to a master to becoming a master initiating later generations of novices (as, for instance, for boys inseminated during their initiations in traditional Melanesian culture and for Azande warriors' boy wives when they grew up). Most "bottoms" do not "graduate" to becoming "tops," though they may try out the dominator role, while some regularly switch roles.

Perhaps the best known case is Yukio Mishima's (1958) recounting of his childhood erotic reaction to a painting of a bound St. Sebastian. Several men have told me that they were turned on as young children by bondage in such Hollywood epics about the ancient Mediterranean as *The Robe, The Ten Commandments, Spartacus,* and various Steve Reeves movies, or in Westerns in which Indians capture and tie up or stake out one of the invading white men. Some tried out bondage and whipping in childhood playgroups, while others stored the images for later masturbation and still later reenactments.

I am not sure what capitalism has to do with explaining the reversal of gender poles (in Brodsky 1993a), although greater openness about being gay made it more feasible for openly gay capitalism to replace the (also much discussed but little documented) Mafia control of gay bars in New York City and elsewhere. Recognition of new markets clearly affected the options available to gay immigrants to North American cities and, therefore, socialization patterns. Although the gay bars of the 1950s were commercial enterprises no less than those of the 1970s, the increase in number and differentiation of public gay institutions contributed to the waning influence of private coteries in which a respected elder would advise and bring out young protégés. Grube (1986, 1987, 1990) discussed the networks in which neophytes submitted sexually to the desires of older men in exchange for entrée to the underground gay world, and the disappointed expectations of some who did not succeed to their turn at being in charge of the bodies and destinies of the next generation when the system was supplanted by commercial meeting sites. This pattern was especially strong among those interested in S&M. One recalled:

> When I first entered the scene, the S-M community was a small, private subculture with a rigidly defined hierarchy and inviolable rules of behavior. A man was expected to "earn his leathers" by serving an older, experienced top until he was deemed adequately prepared, and if he wanted to become a top in his turn (as did I), the training was much longer and more strict. (Dykstra 1989:7)

He bemoaned the admission of masses of tourists by "bar owners [who] eventually realized that there was more profit in allowing everyone into the bars and selling drinks to anyone with ready cash." The openness of a more public world annoyed those who felt they had paid their dues and should be having their turn at dominance. Training by elders remained more common in the leather subculture than elsewhere in gay and lesbian communities.[40]

40. E.g., Dillard 1993.

Nonetheless, gay male S&M initiations during the 1970s were more likely to be self-directed and to occur in the more anonymous commercial gay world(s).[41] With the closing of many commercial leather spaces during the mid 1980s, private parties and quasi-private clubs again became the main venue in United States, but not Canadian, cities, as they had been all along for S&M lesbians.[42] John Preston (1993c:41) remarked, "Lately, more and more, it's the bottom who does the training," and joined Dykstra in bemoaning "declining standards since when I paid my dues": "It seems to me that the top should be the mentor and the initiator. That was my experience. To have an S/M scene run by a bunch of pushy bottoms is very bizarre to me."

Devotees claim that the leather subculture is less "ageist" and "lookist" than other lesbigay locales. Specifically, novices, who still generally learn about S&M in the bottom role, defer more to the experience of elders. The initiate might later do to others what an experienced master did to him/her. However, not everyone wants to graduate this way, so a skillful top who might be rejected as too old in other gay settings may continue to dominate eager bottoms appearing in the leather bars and clubs. Youth and beauty are such little valued attributes of bottoms that Lee (personal communication, 5 Aug. 1993) reported "cute younger visitors often tell me they don't come to the [Toronto S&M bar/hotel] Toolbox because 'everyone ignores me,' and there is, indeed, little competition for them."

For the breathless young, or for anyone lacking experience in reading the signs of potential risk, it was much safer to have sex in the semipublic arenas of backroom bars, clubs, and bathhouses than to go home with a stranger. The maternal mentors of the old gay world would warn new boys of potentially dangerous partners. In larger, relatively anonymous settings like the Mineshaft, initiation into gay sex was/is largely self-directed, though it seems to me that the roles enacted were relatively few.[43] Gay employees patrolled the premises to provide some protection, and other nearby men could respond to any calls for help. A range of public for-profit institutions catered to private needs—not least, safety. As Brodsky (1993a:246) put it,

> While each participant performed his own ritual with his own meanings, the Mineshaft [et al.] hooked up all these performances with a common set of

41. Califia (1982) and Rubin (1982, 1991) portray a more communitarian, less profit-motivated milieu constructed during the 1970s by gay men and accepting women. Given the deemphasis of insertion of penises into orifices in S&M, lesbians and gay men could play scenes with each other while maintaining gay/lesbian sexual identities (see, especially, Rubin 1991).

42. Tucker 1987:48–49; Califia 1982:248.

43. Brodsky 1993a:245. I would not presume to claim knowledge of the range of meanings denizens attached to the small array of stereotyped/ritualized behavior.

facilities, rules, symbols, and emotions. . . . [Such an institution with a finely-tuned etiquette provided the possibility of] a non-violent community in a fragmented, specialized, and culturally atomized society.

In common with Weinberg, Kamel, Lee, Mains, and others, Brodsky stressed that over the course of time, and even in a single night, one could change costumes and enact a variety of roles—tops, bottoms, polymorphous parts of orgies, along with specializations within each of these roles. The question unasked by S&M apologists is, How many did? and, in contrast, How many repeatedly enacted the same role in similar scenarios? In other words, How improvisational are the adaptations (performances) of most of those making "the leather scene?"

We know rather little about what the meaning people attach to their sexual behavior or to representations of bodies and acts in mass media, so it is not surprising that there is a lack of knowledge about what behaviors and attitudes stigmatized by more respectable and politically correct lesbians and gay men mean to any but a few articulate writers committed to S&M. Even the ecstasy of self-transcendence on the dance floors of discos pulsating with other sweating gay men has been little discussed.[44]

The considerable body of research on sexual behavior that has been a byproduct of AIDS has asked people to count or estimate frequencies, not to limn the meanings of sexual conduct. Rather than focusing on what transmits HIV, lesbigay conventional moralists took the opportunity to include what they disapproved of (particularly S&M and multiple partners) as *unsafe sex*. The next chapter details attempts by some gay men in concert with public health authorities to impose traditional moralism under the guise of AIDS prevention.

44. Roscoe (1995a [1978]) stressed an important component: knowing that gay men had made this alternate world. In the most popular 1970s continuation of the doomed queen novel from the 1950s and 1960s, Holleran (1978) showed the central role of dancing. Any sense of tribal affirmation is missing in his novel (as also in Kramer 1978).

Four

The Promiscuity
Paradigm, AIDS, and
Gay Complicity with
the Remedicalization
of Homosexuality

We didn't grow up with all these shifting facts and attitudes. One day they
just started appearing. So people need to be reassured by someone in a
position of authority that a certain way to do something is the right way or
the wrong way, at least for the time being.
Don DeLillio, *White Noise* (1985, pp. 181–82)

AIDS was first identified in the U.S. among urban gay men. Demonized
by some and devalued by many (particularly in the Reagan administration), sick gay men and drug users were written off. Heterosexism, although
certainly important in understanding the American response to AIDS, is not
a sufficient explanation. While AIDS reactivated the paradigm of homosexuality as intrinsically diseased[1] and fit a well-established American tradition
of blaming the victim, it also revealed the inadequacies of much-vaunted
medical knowledge and the inequities of health care delivery.

From the era of Koch and Pasteur to that of antibiotics, the great successes in finding cures or means to eradicate infectious diseases in industrialized societies enormously increased the prestige of medicine within industrialized societies, and also raised expectations of technological "fixes." The

---

1. Bayer (1981) describes the removal of "homosexuality" from the list of psychiatric disorders. The picture of Nebraska gay men and their physicians painted by Brodksy 1989 and
Weitz 1991 suggests that many physicians continue to try to avoid touching homosexual patients
(i.e., treat them as literally "untouchable").

high status and concomitant rewards of medical professions rest—especially in the United States, where they are highest—upon expectations of cures. This produces a strain between recognizing the limitations of scientific medical competence[2] and wanting to maintain or, preferably, enhance prestige and rewards. Such strain—which is probably a universal attribute of the healer role—leads physicians to pretend to more understanding of illnesses and of what to do about them than their scientific knowledge and therapeutic art can support.

Credibility crises are generally avoided only because the hopes of clients parallel practitioners' pretensions.[3] When the miracle workers can do nothing at all, anxiety—profession-wide and individual—mounts. Clients' perception of their inability to work more miracles exacerbates physicians' frustrations. Temptations to blame the patient or some other scapegoat increase when failure becomes common knowledge. "We don't know" is a difficult answer for healers (of any sort) to give to the question "What should we do?"[4]

There is a push from within medical organizations and professions to increase the domain of medicine to achieve still higher status for medicine. There is also a pull from policy-makers, as well as from patients, to apply medical knowledge. Neither push nor pull waits for a knowledge base to develop. Individuals terrified about what is going wrong with their bodies want immediate reassurance that someone knows what to do, and is undertaking to do it. Public health bureaucrats also want to be able to say that everything possible is being done to protect the public and to cure the sick.

Visible efficacy in dealing with dramatic physiological crises best supports the legitimacy of the high status and ever-increasing share of resources accorded scientific medicine. Failure to demonstrate efficacy endangers the reputation and influence of scientific medicine.[5] Any occasion of such failure triggers attacks on those who manifest inconveniently incurable or chronic diseases not amenable to displays of capital-intensive medical virtuosity for bringing their problems on themselves. If no high-tech cure or management of the disease is available, explanations increasingly involve patient "non-

---

2. See Stelling and Bucher 1973; Fox and Swazey 1978; Bosk 1979.

3. The "client" for American medicine includes the state as well as patients and families of patients.

4. See Kleinman 1980.

5. An instance of possibly direct importance for federal government epidemiologists was the congressional inquiries about the failure to establish the cause of "legionnaire's fever" (Culliton 1976). Despite a seeming "lifestyle choice" label in the name, "Legionnaire" was not considered a risk group, and the deaths of legionnaires were not seen as divine punishment for conventioneering in Philadelphia or for belonging to the American Legion. Perhaps the briefness of the outbreak spared those who died from being blamed.

compliance," lifestyle, personality, or genetic predisposition.[6] Individualizing responsibility for illness has been a major priority for medical research during the 1980s and 1990s. Blaming the victim is more likely than reconsideration of the basic conceptual and clinical organizations of illness or of medicine.

Moreover, as social control increasingly operates under a medical guise in industrialized societies,[7] categories from the discourse of scientific medicine become bases for public policy. Expert opinion on how to safeguard public health is sometimes pressed, sometimes sought, but rarely is it presented as heuristic and hypothetical rather than as established fact[8]—not even when it interferes considerably with the lifeways and life chances of various populations. In their own view, as well as in that of many others, doctors know best. Saving lives is what medical professionals try to do—without asking questions about the quality of life after (technical) salvation. Despite some challenges from persons with AIDS (PWAs) and mounting rejection of artificially keeping people alive, doctors remain accustomed to violating the bodily integrity of their patients without question or challenge to the legitimacy, rationality, or effectiveness of their orders and invasions.

Physicians tend to generalize from their routine experience of overriding personal autonomy in doctoring individuals to doctoring communities (i.e., taking "public health" actions). At both levels of practice, many doctors do not distinguish between trying their clinical guesses and applying a widely accepted scientific consensus. In their view, no one should question them: therapeutic intentions should be good enough.[9] At both the level of treating individuals and that of intervening in the name of "the public," medical professionals take any second-guessing of their prescriptions as "noncompliance," irrational "resistance," or outright "mental illness." It is genuinely difficult for those dedicated to medicine to conceive that preserving life may not be everyone's highest value. Most medical professionals remain insensitive to quality of life and individual liberty issues.[10]

In analyzing the challenge to the psychiatric medicalization of traditional Western condemnation of male homosexuality, Conrad and Schneider (1980:

6. Duster 1990.
7. Zola 1972; Kitsuse and Spector 1973; Conrad and Schneider 1980; Foucault 1980.
8. Murray 1980c; Goodfield 1982; Duster 1990.
9. Early AIDS activism pushed a parallel view. Believing that a cure was out there, the problem was conceived as bureaucratic obstacles to testing and evaluating drugs before the Food and Drug Administration licensed them. "This might help" or "this kills HIV in test tubes" were reason enough in the view of desperately ill PWAs and their friends not to wait for information about long-term side effects or more than anecdotal evidence of efficacy.
10. The extent to which this is trained incapacity deserves investigation.

211) predicted, "If a behavior is demedicalized but not vindicated (absolved of immorality), it becomes more vulnerable to moral attack." Besides showing the competition among would-be agents of social control, Conrad and Schneider suggested the possibility of remedicalization following demedicalization. Soon after their book was published, a new cycle began with the discovery of a new medical basis for proscribing male homosexual behavior. Just as with the psychiatric proscription, medical claims far outstripped the scientific evidence plastered onto traditional Judeo-Christian intolerance of male homosexuality. Also repeating the history of the psychiatric colonial expeditions into male homosexuality are struggles over territory between different medical specialties and organizations.[11] Most like the old one, the new medical model of why male homosexuality is unhealthy does not include any cure.

In this chapter I show how the original identification of a syndrome of opportunistic infections in gay men living in the most institutionally elaborated gay communities made it a "gay plague" and therefore sexually transmitted, and how such identification constrained thought and research subsequent to the initial "explanation" of "gay promiscuity."[12] Attempts to fit cases into the promiscuous male homosexuality etiology not merely delayed, but continue to mute the "discovery" of cases in populations with less access to medical facilities (viz., heterosexual Haitians, central Africans, and American intravenous drug users).[13] The symbolic politics of sustaining conventional "morality" has constrained—and, at times, has driven—"application" of AIDS science to public health. Blaming victims is a leitmotif of public discussion of AIDS, derived directly from the view that "promiscuity" is an invariant, defining characteristic of gay men. Public health interventions were and continue to be inhibited by moralistic pressures, so that tactics of high cost to individual liberties and little likely benefit in preventing cases of AIDS have been adopted, while those which would be challenged

11. Most visibly between the National Cancer Institute and the Centers for Disease Control within the U.S. Department of Health and Human Services but also between immunology and virology in the scramble for research funds.

12. For compelling analysis of sensationalism of the promiscuity paradigm to fit conventional prejudices within mass media coverage of AIDS, see Albert 1984; Crimp 1988; and Gilman 1988:245–72. The focus of the present chapter is on the conceptions, selective attention, and actions of public health professionals and organizations, but I want to stress that "elite" scientific discourse is not just a source selectively drawn upon by vulgarizers, but is directly affected by such popularization.

13. In 1987, the New York City Department of Health reexamined drug-related deaths during 1982–86 and classified many as AIDS-related, but did not extend the analysis to "junkie pneumonia" during the late 1970s (Crimp 1988:249 n. 11). At the other extreme, white heterosexuals sometimes press successfully not to have AIDS recorded on death certificates and/or physicians don't test such "respectable" folks, especially women (see McCombie 1986; Wermuth 1995).

by moralistic Christians as "condoning immorality" have been avoided despite their greater likely benefit and lower cost.[14]

PARADIGMS

> As new medical terms become known in a society, they find their way into existing semantic networks. While new explanatory models may be introduced, changes in medical rationality seldom follow quickly.
>
> Good (1977:54)

Not just medical practitioners, but medical researchers apparently accept "scientific" claims without any empirical evidence, if it fits with prejudices, whether these are theoretical and/or religious.[15] Indeed, in borrowing the term *paradigm* from grammatical analysis, Kuhn (1962, 1977) argued that not just the "folk," but also scientists think along lines constrained by the terms of particular theories, sometimes failing to see what does not fit into the terms or within the theory, sometimes seeing what doesn't exist (archetypally, phlogiston). *Conceptions shape perceptions, even if they do not entirely determine them.* In particular, paradigms channel inquiries along established routes. Before scientists undertake the laborious and expensive task of drawing a new map, they are likely to proceed along well-mapped and well-traveled roads which have led to payoffs in the past.

Within the dominant paradigm of Western "scientific" medicine, chronic illness is barely recognized, let alone understood.[16] Chronic illness leading to the death of men in their twenties and thirties is hard to accept, for clinicians as well as for theorists and researchers.[17] The clinical entity conceived in the early 1980s within Western scientific medicine as Acquired Immune Deficiency Syndrome was forced into the theoretical procrustean bed of an acute, discrete, sexually transmitted disease rather than being conceived as a chronic illness triggered by introduction of a virus into the bloodstream.

Labeling a Syndrome

The first reports in 1981 contained a variety of labels for a mysterious outbreak of Kaposi's sarcoma and pneumocystis pneumonia among previously

14. See Crimp 1988:259–65; Bolton 1992a:167–88; E. King 1994. More explicit educational material has been shown to be effective in continental Europe and even in Thailand, where censorship of genital representations was nearly total before the AIDS epidemic there.

15. See Roth 1957; Lipton and Hershaft 1985.

16. See Strauss et al. 1985. From the title, one would expect chronicity to be the focus of Fee and Fox 1992, but, alas, it is only asserted, not demonstrated, nor the basis of any of the analyses contained therein.

17. Lessor and Jurich 1985.

healthy gay men.[18] By the end of 1981, "gay compromise syndrome" (GCS) seemed to be emerging as a consensus in medical reporting, "gay cancer" and GRID (gay-related immunodeficiency) in the gay press.[19] As Albert (1984:12) observed, "The major source for early information on AIDS was the CDC [Centers for Disease Control] in Atlanta. CDC reports tended to emphasize who got sick rather than the nature of the disease itself." The first mass media attention in the summer of 1982 presaged the media onslaught of the first months of 1983 by focusing on "hotbeds of homosexual promiscuity," "living playgrounds for infectious agents."[20]

The leader of the CDC task force, James Curran, recognized a predisposition that I would extend to CDC epidemiologists: "You get heterosexual doctors examining gays, and they jump on the first possible hypothesis, that it must be due to the sexual behavior of gays."[21]

It was almost a year into CDC reports in the *Morbidity and Mortality Weekly Reports (MMWR)*, in June 1982, before mention that almost 20 percent of the first 355 U.S. cases were heterosexual male and female intravenous drug users, and another three years before official notice of homosexual IV drug users was taken (discussed below). By the end of the year, CDC trackers noted AIDS in heterosexual hemophiliacs, and the 4 March 1983 *MMWR* acknowledged transfusion of blood as a vector for infection.

During this same period, a label crystallized. In the 24 September 1982 *MMWR*, "AIDS" replaced the previous "Kaposi Sarcoma and Opportunistic Infections in Previously Healthy Persons." The new label was already current in *Science*, though not in medical journals, a month earlier. Although no longer containing "gay" as a preface, as in GCS and GRID, AIDS was already indelibly stamped as a "gay disease," a "gay plague" as some gay writers called it. Because early cases were urban gay men, from the beginning epidemiologists presumed the syndrome was a "sexually transmitted disease," an already trendy classification in the zeitgeist of "sexual counterrevolution":

18. Centers for Disease Control 1981a,b.

19. *Newsweek* 6 Sept. 1982. Murray and Payne (1989) list labels used before the consensus on "AIDS" as a label. It bears noting that GRID was not a locution used (at least in print) by epidemiologists. It was used in a clinical abstract by the discoverer of AIDS (Gottlieb et al. 1982), but mostly in the gay press (and more in outraged retrospect than at the time).

20. The subtext of much scientific and most popular AIDS discourse is that gay men went shopping outside conventional morality and acquired a syndrome, like acquiring a leather jacket. Presumably a celibate nun or a monogamous, heterosexual man injected with blood containing HIV in the 1970s was no more choosing to acquire a syndrome of infections than was a man who was exposed to HIV while engaging in homosexual activity during the 1970s; yet transfusion cases, along with children born with congenital syndromes of immunodeficiency, are often presented as "innocent victims."

21. In Astor 1983:56.

Once a disease is classified as being transmitted sexually, the disease and its spread arouse strong negative emotional reactions of a kind not aroused by waterborne or airborne diseases or those carried by insects. The emotional reactions are often as marked in doctors and scientists as they are in other people, and like any powerful emotion, they are liable to impair clear thought. The recent classification of many diseases as venereal has been accepted very uncritically. . . . Because of the emotional overtones, once doctors are convinced that a disease is transmitted through sexual contact, many assume that any patient with the disease must have acquired it by promiscuous sexual activity. Those afflicted are assumed to be guilty till they can prove their innocence. This medical attitude is not only arrogant, but potentially dangerous, because other means of transmission will inevitably be overlooked. (Seale 1985:38)[22]

The initial epidemiological discourse focused on sexual promiscuity. Although CDC publications did not use the word "promiscuity" itself, the number of (self-reported) sexual partners over varying durations of time was the datum most frequently gathered and analyzed in epidemiological work. Others, including writers in the gay press, did not emulate CDC employees' semantic asceticism in eschewing the heavily loaded and imprecise term "promiscuity."[23]

Urban public health officials and CDC epidemiologists were familiar with endemic gonorrhea, hepatitis B, and epidemic ameboasis among sexually active urban gay men. Etiological agents for those diseases had been identified. Their ultimate causes were not sexual practices, although sexual practices could transmit those agents. Similarly, the occurrence during the 1980s of relatively high rates of diverse ailments, many of them induced by parasites, had given rise to a clinical concept, "gay bowel syndrome" (GBS), in the late 1970s. Parasites thought to be the province of tropical medicine became a new focus of health care for urban practices including many gay men. Young American men were not supposed to turn up with such parasites, just as they were not expected to present Kaposi's sarcoma (KS) or Pneumocystis carinii pneumonia (PCP). This model of a syndrome of exotic (for young middle-class Americans) diseases was already waiting. Work during the 1970s developing a vaccine for hepatitis B also familiarized some medical scientists with the anal sexual practices and high number of sexual partners of the gay men

22. On the original construction of a sexual transmission paradigm to replace astrological and metallurgical explanations of syphilis, see Fleck 1979.

23. For heterosexual behavior, "x-marital" (x may be "non-" or "extra-" or "pre-") tends to be used rather than "promiscuous" (Bolton 1992a:148). It also bears noting that "partner" and "sex" are not transparent terms to those engaging in or to those studying homosexual behavior (see Murray and Payne 1985; Coxon 1988:132–33; Bolton 1992a:166).

whose bodies were culturing antibodies to be used in the vaccine—the *in vivo* factories as well as the test site.

A predisposition existed to equate an outbreak of unexpected diseases among gay men with anal transmission;[24] and, despite considerable differences in contagiousness between the two, even now hepatitis remains the favorite analog of the epidemiology of AIDS.[25] So satisfied with anal intercourse as an explanation for AIDS were American health officials that a 1984 AIDS information pamphlet from the New York State Department of Health attributed heterosexual African cases to it—even without any evidence of actual sexual practices in central Africa.[26] Similarly, CDC researchers attempted to persuade those with AIDS in Belle Glade, Florida, where the per capita rate of cases is the highest in the United States, that they must be homosexual or intravenous drug users.[27]

"Risk Groups"

The CDC's classification system continuously reinforced identification in the U.S. of AIDS as a "gay disease." During the first five years of reporting, rather than listing all cases with each characteristic, the tables in *MMWR* suppressed interaction effects: e.g., a gay IV drug user was categorized as a gay case, a Haitian IV drug user as an IV drug user, etc. Such tidy classification precluded independent judgment of the relative weight of risk factors and of their prevalence in the population at risk. Although eventually the CDC added a "gay/bisexual IV drug user" category to the hierarchy, most behavioral data gathered by epidemiologists dealing with anything other than sexual behavior and needle use have gone unpublished.[28]

24. I do not question that viruses, including the putative AIDS-causing virus, HIV, can be transmitted during anal intercourse. Direct transmission to the bloodstream, however, not sexual orientation(/identity) nor even the number of sexual partners in itself (i.e., independent of the sexual behavior) is salient. Exposure to HIV or something else co-occurring with HIV— if HIV infection is an indicator rather than the cause of AIDS—appears to be a necessary but insufficient condition for damage to immune functioning.

25. The general public conflates cause with transmission. Some of the difficulty health and school officials have had in convincing parents that pupils with AIDS going to school with their children do not constitute a threat to their children can be attributed to the dissemination of the hepatitis analogy. This "folk" equation did not originate among the masses!

26. Lieberson 1986:44. Various hypotheses about anal sex and genital ulcers in Africa have been advanced without being evidence of prevalence of these explanatory variables. For instance, female "circumcision," which occurs in areas to the north of the central African societies beset with AIDS, was supposed to lead to substituting anal for vaginal sex, though if this were so one would expect a higher ratio of female to male cases.

27. Fettner 1986; Norman 1986.

28. Peter Duesberg's attacks on the HIV etiology model (S. Epstein 1993: 70–319) posit very high drug use rates for gay PWAs but lack any empirical base (and spectacularly fail to meet the high demands of proof he demands to establish HIV as the cause).

Published analyses were strikingly univariate in an age when sophisticated multivariate analysis is the norm in social, biological, and medical science, and when multifactorial disease models were supposedly paradigmatic within epidemiology.[29] As Lauritsen (1985:7) concluded, CDC hierarchical presentation of risk factors along with confining "drug use" to intravenous injection "de-emphasizes and under-represents every patient characteristic *except* homosexuality. One cannot help but suspect a theological mindset behind this statistical misrepresentation of reality: that which is most 'sinful' is presumed to be most dangerous." As elsewhere, the scientistic veneer over traditional Judeo-Christian condemnation of homosexuality is very thin.

That risk factor classification is subject to extra-scientific consideration is perhaps even better demonstrated by the 1983 removal of "Haitian immigrant" from the CDC's hierarchical list of risk groups.[30] Assertions that Haiti had been a favorite vacation spot for gay Americans were unaccompanied by case-control evidence. Examination of official U.S.–Caribbean air travel statistics for the years preceding the recognition of AIDS shows that, while travel to Haiti increased slightly, both the absolute magnitude and the rate of increase in travel were greater for other Caribbean countries than for Haiti. Insofar as gay travel can be estimated from gay guidebooks, Haiti was one of the least favored destinations in the Caribbean for gay travelers during the 1970s, and the less favored half of the island of Hispaniola. Epidemiological data published through 1995 do not include data on Haitian travel of American AIDS cases ("gay" or other).[31]

Although the director of the Centers for Infectious Diseases, Walter Dowdle, justified dropping the Haitian risk group because it was "the only risk group identified because of who they were rather than what they did,"[32] it is in fact the risk group *most* difficult to understand in terms of behaviors thought to transmit HIV. The non-Haitian risk factors are also *all* kinds of people: drug users/abusers/addicts, homosexuals, bisexuals, hemophiliacs, even recipients of blood transfusions—although all these classifications can be resolved into behavior proposed to be means of transmission: sharing

29. Oppenheimer 1988:269.
30. The case is elaborated in Murray and Payne 1989.
31. The 1986 and 1987 CDC's Multi-Area Cohort Study (MACS) interviews (except for Los Angeles) included questions about travel to Haiti and Zaire and about sex with persons native to them—but only within the previous two years. Responses remain unpublished. Such data could not be expected to bear on behavior prior to 1981, or indeed on HIV infection, given the ever-lengthening estimates of incubation periods. (The current estimate of the median is nearly 12 years.) I am grateful to Steven Nachman for supplying me a copy of the interview protocol.
32. Quoted in *American Medical News*, 19 April 1985, p. 11.

needles, unprotected receptive anal intercourse, injecting clotting factor or blood containing the virus. As early as the 4 March 1983 *MMWR*, CDC personnel recognized that "each group contains many persons who probably have little risk of acquiring AIDS."

The logic of Dowdle's doing/being dichotomy of AIDS risk groups could easily have been extended to the "homosexual/bisexual" (identity) risk category, making clear that the risk was male–male anal intercourse (behavior). Instead, the facile CDC equation of homosexual behavior and "homosexuals" ignores the large literature about the problematic link between homosexual behavior and identity.[33] It continues to lull those who do not identify themselves as being in a risk group into thinking that they are safe regardless of what they actually do.[34]

The role of symbolic politics in the identification of an etiologic agent of AIDS and the assignment of risk factors was considerable. AIDS slid easily into the paradigm of consequences of "promiscuity," with drug use as well as stigmatized sexual behavior included within "promiscuity." This mindset led directly to paternalistic and punitive policy initiatives. The symbolic politics of conventional "morality" drove American "application" of AIDS science to public health even more obviously than it channeled "scientific" investigation into its etiology. Blaming victims is a leitmotif of public discussion of AIDS, derived directly from the view that "promiscuity" is an invariant, defining characteristic of gay men.

DOING SOMETHING

> Experience should teach us to be most on our guard to protect liberty when
> the Government's purposes are beneficent. Men born to freedom are
> naturally alert to repel invasion of their liberty by evil-minded rulers. The
> greatest dangers to liberty lurk in insidious encroachment by men of zeal,
> well-meaning but without understanding.
> Justice Louis Brandeis in *Olmstead v. U.S.*

> If an intervention does not produce results, and yet is supported by officials
> and the public, one must look to secondary reasons to explain that support.
> The issue thus becomes not the desire to protect the public from

33. Reiss 1961; Humphreys 1975; A. P. Bell and Weinberg 1978; T. Weinberg 1978a; Ross 1984; Carrier 1995; Murray 1987b, 1995a, 1997. On the similar lack of self-identification and sense of belonging to a group defined by "risk factor" of "intravenous drug use and their sexual partners," see Kane and Mason 1992.

34. This sometimes literally fatal effect is elaborated by Bolton 1992a.

hazard. . . . Rather, these activities indicate a transformation from
protection to punishment.
Brandt 1988:165

Relatively quickly, HIV testing protected the nation's blood supply, removing exclusively heterosexual, non–injection-drug–using white males other than those who received blood products between the mid 1970s and March 1985 from all but the remotest risk of AIDS. In March 1985, the Food and Drug Administration licensed the ELISA test to detect HIV antibodies (with an explicit statement that the test was to screen blood and was not a diagnostic test). Simultaneously, legislators more concerned about avoiding any appearance of state "condoning of immorality" than with saving the lives (or the liberties) of those they regard as "immoral" have blocked funding for tactics to increase the safety of such behaviors. Trying to make sex safer (rather than simply condemning it) is also too controversial for most U.S. public health departments. Politicized religious pressure insists that the only legitimate goal is enforcing pre- and extramarital chastity.[35] Throughout the 1980s and into the 1990s, the U.S. Senate annually banned funding for any educational material that shows—and thereby "condones" the existence of—homosexual sex. In American public health, empiricism, realism, common sense, and rational weighing of costs and either benefits or dangers must oppose a flood of moralistic doublespeak, transparently specious rationalizations, and feverish anxiety about sex and disease.

In the following section I outline the lack of scientific/statistical basis for an early public health "application"[36] of "knowledge"/misinformation about AIDS in what is generally conceived to be the most enlightened and liberal American city health department.[37] If the ideology of the sexual counterrevolution can force the kind of symbolic politics that upholds "traditional morality," however slight the likelihood that they affect AIDS transmission, in San Francisco, it can drive health policy anywhere in the United States. Personal privacy is more cherished in California than in many other states, as evidenced both in initiative balloting and in state constitutional decisions. Yet, freedom of assembly was overridden without any demonstration of countervailing medical necessity in a city with a cherished history of tolerance for diversity. The case is further deserving of special attention because

35. In 1994, Roman Catholic prelates condemned condom use even within marriages in which one partner is HIV-positive. This has not led to public health intervention in marriages—or to closing Catholic churches as health hazards because they promote HIV transmission.
36. Others were discussed in Murray and Payne 1988.
37. E.g., by Altman (1986).

of the dangers of the well-meaning interference with liberty warned against by Justice Brandeis in the first epigraph to this section and because a best-selling and then filmed historical novel by one participant is taken, even by some sociologists, as factual reportage.[38]

Closing Gay Baths

Until 1984, resisting pressure from San Francisco's Mayor, Dianne Feinstein (whose distaste for gay male "promiscuity" was a matter of public record prior to the identification of AIDS,[39] and who is viewed by local civil libertarians as extraordinarily insensitive to civil liberties issues in general), and from others, Dr. Mervyn Silverman, Director of Public Health for San Francisco, had refused to close down bathhouses and private sex clubs in the county, maintaining that it was behavior rather than its locale which mattered in risking AIDS. Bayer (1989:32–33) quotes 1983 letters from Silverman asserting, "Because the facilities of most bathhouses do not present a public health hazard, I feel it would be inappropriate and in fact illegal for me to close down all bathhouses and other such places that are used for anonymous and multiple sex contacts" (10 May 1983) and "I do not share your impression that the subculture who use bathhouses would not immediately switch to other locations where we would have less access to post warnings and provide some education" (12 Sept. 1983). Public health warnings and guidelines were distributed in the baths, whereas no education campaign was feasible in locales of "public sex." The formula for the alternative was "Out of the tubs, into the shrubs." Silverman also stressed that those engaging in homosexual sex in the baths, tearooms, and parks were not necessarily gay-identified and therefore could not be reached with information via the gay press.

Silverman could have rationalized continuing not to interfere with the

---

38. See Crimp's (1988:238–49) critique of Shilts's (1987) sensationalism and fictionalizations. In particular, Crimp shows how the unsubstantiated portrait of Patient Zero is made of the genre conventions of a villain seeking to destroy the innocent and the stereotype of uncontrolled homosexual male promiscuity. It was this story based on conventional American demonology that was serialized in newspapers across America and on *60 Minutes*. With this focus, purporting to be "the facts" about how AIDS came to California (or to North America in some versions), the portrait of federal government unconcern and inaction in the book was ignored. Patient Zero, not Ronald Reagan or the Department of Health and Human Services in his administration, could be blamed for the spread of AIDS. Leaving aside questions about the basis for Shilts's knowledge of what Patient Zero thought about whether Kaposi's sarcoma was contagious, the time between his sexual contacts and the appearance of opportunistic infections regarded as AIDS was too short to be consistent with the current model of HIV incubation into AIDS.

39. Bowman (1990) reviewed the history.

(federally recognized) right of assembly and the (state-recognized) right of privacy for adult consensual sex by citing the indicators of behavioral change, viz., the drop in rectal gonorrhea from 1400 cases in the first quarter of 1980 to 400 cases in the second quarter of 1984,[40] and a still-unreleased CDC study of bathgoing which failed to establish bathgoing as an AIDS risk factor.[41]

However, two gay San Franciscans took it upon themselves to force closure of the baths. Randy Shilts, a *San Francisco Chronicle* writer, who viewed the constitutional rights of privacy and freedom of assembly as "let[ting] gay businessmen murder gay people,"[42] was the more peripatetic. His first tactic was to supply a *California Magazine* attack on the San Francisco Department of Public Health for minimizing the threat of AIDS to the wider community.[43] At the height of general paranoia about blood banks and the safety of living in the same city as gay men, this was in itself a signal contribution to enhancing homophobia. At the same time, it was a means of waging a new offensive in the interminable internecine struggle between San Francisco's two largest gay Democratic clubs—politics far too complex to explicate here.[44]

Shilts's second offensive, in the 2 February 1984 *Chronicle*, was to seize on a minuscule fluctuation in the trend of decreasing incidence of rectal gonorrhea (figure 4.1) as evidence that San Francisco gay men were resuming unsafe sexual practices. The rates of rectal gonorrhea were taken to be indicators of the amount of unprotected receptive anal intercourse. Since the latter is the major means of transmitting HIV among gay men, the rates were

40. Schultz et al. (1984:296) reported a 59% drop in rates of rectal gonorrhea in Manhattan—from 485 per hundred thousand in 1980 to 201 in 1983. For an overview of behavioral changes made during the mid-1980s, see J. Martin (1987), and Becker and Joseph (1988).

41. Bayer (1989:43) had access to the communication of the findings of no distinct risk factor from the principal CDC epidemiologist working on AIDS, William Darrow. The existence of this finding was reported in the April 1984 *Coming Up!* Bayer also reports that Silverman and his deputy for communicable diseases, Dean Echenberg, complained about the finding to Darrow's superiors at CDC. It is extremely difficult to imagine that data showing sex clubs to be a risk factor for AIDS would have been suppressed in an administration signally insensitive to the gay community and to civil liberties. Not issuing a report exonerating gay institutions is far more in character.

42. Quoted by Hippler (1989:130).

43. Shilts (1987) omitted mention of this venture.

44. Of particular perceived relevance at the time was that the Department of Public Health's gay and lesbian liaison, Pat Norman, a leader of the Alice B. Toklas Gay Democratic Club, was preparing to run for the Board of Supervisors, where Harry Britt, a former president of the Harvey Milk Gay Democratic Club, was running for reelection to one of six at-large seats filled in that election. (The conventional wisdom then was that no more than one lesbigay supervisor could be elected. Since 1994 there have been three.)

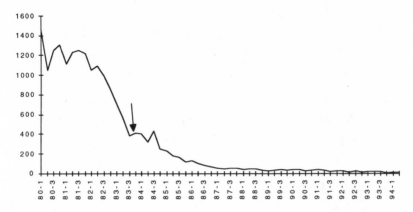

Fig. 4.1 San Francisco Cases of Rectal Gonorrhea by Quarter. Arrow indicates rise Shilts reported as trend reversal. (Source: San Francisco County Department of Health, Sexually Transmitted Disease Office)

taken as indicators of future AIDS rates—the time lag being due to the hypothesized incubation period of the posited virus, which is a median of 11.8 years in the estimate of Lemp et al. (1990: 1499). If this indicator is accepted, obviously its trend is important in predicting future AIDS cases.[45] However, Shilts sensationalized a small *fluctuation* in the fourth quarter of 1983, ignored the trend, and, when the rate resumed dropping, he did not bother to report that; nor did he report the larger increase following the bath closure (i.e., the third quarter of 1984). Indeed, years later, in his book, Shilts (1987:415–16) again reported the fluctuation as if it were a change in the trend line.[46]

The other offensive by a San Francisco gay man in 1984, the real "triggering event,"[47] was undertaken by Larry Littlejohn, a gay deputy sheriff later shown to be engaged in competition with bathhouses—he was dismissed from his job in 1987 after being charged with pandering for young male prostitutes.[48] Littlejohn did not attempt to organize a gay community response, such as demonstrating in front of the establishments or talking to patrons inside or outside them. After meeting with Shilts and Leonard Mat-

45. Behavioral change was so considerable that gonorrhea became less endemic, making inferences from rectal gonorrhea frequencies less plausible an indicator of the extent of anal sex.

46. The slope (the speed of decrease) does seem to have changed then, and from 1987 on. There appears to have been a downward trend in 1981–82. The precipitous decline (1982–83), as is obvious in figure 4.1, preceded demands for governmental action. I would like to thank William Kohn for providing me data for 1985 to (provisional) 1994. 1980–84 data were taken from 1985 charts from the Sexually Transmitted Disease Clinic that were published quarterly in the *Bay Area Reporter.*

47. In the sense of Galliher and Cross 1983.

48. As they had left the state, the case did not go to trial.

lovich,[49] Littlejohn's *first* resort was to seek governmental intervention. He began seeking signatures for a city initiative closing the baths in the spring of 1984, arguing, "We must not fool ourselves. There are no educational programs that will effectively change high risk for AIDS sex habits of bathhouse patrons to safe sex."[50] Matlovich explained:

> Some people argued that they were a place to educate. But I thought it was a far better strategy to close the places down first and then to educate, because people wouldn't have paid attention otherwise. Furthermore, I thought it was very foolish for our community to start drawing battle lines at the bathhouses.[51]

Under pressure from Mayor Feinstein,[52] and supported by some leaders of the Harvey Milk Gay Democratic Club eager both to close the baths and to avert a plebiscite, Silverman assembled a group of gay medical and political leaders to discuss closing the menaces. The orchestrated gay demand to close the baths to protect gay bathgoers from themselves was more dissonant than expected. The Bay Area Physicians for Human Rights, a group of doctors concerned with gay health issues and recognized for special expertise about diseases affecting gay men, refused to endorse any governmental action to close bathhouses. The National Gay Task Force stated its opposition in traditional civil liberties terms:

> NGTF feels most strongly that personal behavior should not be regulated by the state, which historically has been an instrument of our oppression. Furthermore, state closure of such establishments would be largely symbolic, a largely symbolic gesture that would provide a false sense of security that the AIDS epidemic had somehow been contained. (*NGTF Update*, 28 March 1984)

Shilts (1987:436–41) detailed his own "squeeze play" of telling gay leaders that Silverman would close the baths while telling Silverman there was community support. The consensus of gay community leaders for bath closure, which Shilts and Milk Club leaders assured Silverman existed, was far from evident at a 29 March meeting with gay physicians. The next day, at the news conference scheduled for announcing closure of the baths, Silverman merely announced that no decision had been reached pending determination of the legality of various courses under consideration. Mayor Feinstein continued to press for bath closure, but it bears stressing that gay doctors and their organizations did not support governmental intervention.

49. Hippler 1989:122.

50. *California Voice*, 5 April 1984, p. 2.

51. Quoted by Hippler (1989:123). Littlejohn, Matlovich, and Shilts chose the battle line without attempting to see if anyone would "pay attention" to educational programs. I have heard allegations of another sense of no one paying attention to these men in the bathhouses that undergirded their "revenge."

52. *Chronicle*, 28 March 1984, p. 20.

For instance, the president of the American Association of Physicians for Human Rights wrote Silverman,

> The closing of businesses to protect people from themselves cannot be accepted. . . . AAPHR strongly discourages sexual contact with multiple anonymous partners. But we cannot and will not support any effort to enforce that viewpoint. (2 April 1984 letter, quoted in Bayer 1989:37)

Bayer (1989:38) asserts that "action against the baths was inevitable" in San Francisco. In his retrospective accounts of his pacing of bathhouse closure,[53] Silverman has contended that in addition to waiting for opinions about the legality of various actions he could take (including quarantine), he was waiting for gay leaders, or at least gay physicians with experience of the ravages of AIDS, to orchestrate closure of private clubs in which anonymous sexual interaction with multiple partners continued, or at least to mobilize support for action by the Department of Public Health. The scientific literature available to him was the same as that available to directors of public health in other jurisdictions. If evidence existed that the locale of multiple sexual encounters could be differentiated as a risk factor for AIDS, he would have had it. If scientific evidence, new or not so new, suggested a course of action, let alone demonstrated the need for this particular one, it would be very remarkable that public officials elsewhere, particularly in places without vociferous and organized gay rights organizations, did not draw the conclusions Silverman did.

From New York City, where the preponderance of AIDS cases were, both the Commissioner of Health and the director of New York City's Office of Gay and Lesbian Health stated that they would not act to close private clubs, the latter stressing that "there is no science to support the closing of the bathhouses."[54]

Bayer (1989:38–39) reports a long meeting of health officials on 3 April at which the tactic of regulating rather than closing private sex clubs was agreed upon. Such a meeting was not reported at the time, and so would almost certainly violate California laws requiring meetings at which public policy is determined to be open to the public. On 9 April, Silverman held another press conference and announced a ban on sex between individuals in "public facilities."[55] Behind him were twenty-four of those with whom he

53. To Fitzgerald, to Bayer, and in Silverman 1986.

54. Quoted in the April 1984 *Coming Up!*, p. 9.

55. Traditionally, clubs requiring membership have been called "private member clubs" rather than "public places." Bayer (1989), though ostensibly concerned with the boundaries of private and public, did not question the semantic sleight when Feinstein, Silverman, et al. redefined private assembly as "public" because such establishments are licensed by the county. It should be obvious that the county also issues marriage licenses without claiming that this pro-

had discussed what to do. Within a few days, eleven of this group publicly rejected the policy.[56]

Banning sex rather than closing the baths outright was a compromise sufficient for Littlejohn to halt collecting signatures for his initiative petitions. However, Mayor Feinstein was not satisfied that this was sufficient. Although the Department of Public Health was supposed to enforce the edict, and also to monitor its implementation, some weeks after the promulgation of the bath sex ban the mayor sent policemen (presumably in towels) to observe and report to her. She refused to release the report even to the Board of Supervisors. Certainly, it indicated that sex continued to occur in the baths and clubs. No arrests for violating the sex ban were made, nor were any licenses to operate clubs or baths revoked, so there was no court test of whether Dr. Silverman had the legal authority to override the state's law protecting consensual sex in private. Toronto police got around the problem of how to accuse men in locked cubicles in Toronto baths of having sexual relations in public by breaking down the doors.[57] San Francisco public health regulation aimed to accomplish the same end without such clumsy force: Silverman's draft revision of Section 263 of the San Francisco Police Code (under which the baths are licensed) banned doors on cubicles.

Surveillance by private investigators reported continued (primarily oral or manual) sex in various places. On the morning of 9 October 1984, Dr. Silverman decreed that the operation of three bookstores, two theaters, and nine private clubs

> contributed to the spread of the virus that causes AIDS; accordingly, the Director of Public Health has determined that the continued operation of the above designated businesses constitutes a hazard and menace to the public health; then by virtue of the power yielded to him by the law of the State of California, the Charter of the City and County of San Francisco, the Director of Public Health for the City and County of San Francisco hereby orders the above designated businesses to close no later than 12:00 noon (notice posted on doors of closed businesses).

---

vides a basis for regulating conduct within that institution. Building codes, public recording of deeds, etc. involve the state in homes, so that "public concern" has precedent there (as well as in hotels, a locale which the New York City Health Commissioner included within the bounds of his AIDS policy jurisdiction). The analogies of seat belt laws and motorcycle helmet requirements are less apt in that governments build and maintain roads in addition to licensing drivers; moreover, the clear medical evidence about motorcycle helmets has only intermittently led to the state protecting persons from conduct dangerous to their health and costly to the public. I can also report from personal experience that smoking was still permitted in meetings within the Department of Public Health at the time.

56. *Bay Area Reporter*, 19 April 1984, p. 8.
57. Fleming 1983.

His press statement elaborated:

> The places I have ordered closed today have continued in the face of this epidemic to provide an environment that encourages and facilitates multiple unsafe sexual contacts, which are an important contributory factor in the spread of this deadly disease. When activities are proven to be dangerous to the public and continue to take place in commercial settings, the Health Department has the duty to intercede and halt the operation of such establishment.[58]

Because the order was delivered by armed policemen and alluded to power vested by state law, the order was initially perceived to be a quarantine. However, the power invoked was that of "abating a public nuisance" (i.e., a local rather than state grant of authority to the county Director of Public Health). Once they understood this, six of the businesses reopened to challenge the authority of public nuisance regulation.[59] Within a week, San Francisco Superior Court Judge William Mullins signed a temporary restraining order that reclosed the clubs (but left theaters and bookstores open, out of First Amendment considerations), pending a 30 October hearing on the City's petition to close them indefinitely. In his request for a temporary restraining order, Silverman again equated "commercial" with "public," contending that "altering sexual activity is a matter of individual privacy; when that sexual activity takes place in a commercial setting, this government has the prerogative and duty to intercede," and emphasizing that his professional judgment as a public health officer was that it was necessary to "bring to an end commercial enterprises that involve exploitation for profit of an individual's willingness to engage in potentially lethal forms of recreation."[60] As Bayer (1989:48) notes, "Perhaps most remarkable in the city's [actually county's] well-prepared case was the failure to obtain a clear declaration of support for closure from any nationally known epidemiologist involved in the study of AIDS and the patterns of sexual behavior among gay men."

The defendants' response cited the lack of scientific evidence that bathgoing was a risk factor for AIDS, challenged the unsafeness of the sex reported by private investigators, and rejected Silverman's equation of "commercial" and "public," arguing that

> there is simply no legal basis to distinguish the right to engage in consensual sexual activity in defendants' premises from the right to engage in consensual

58. The relevance of "commercial" in this is unclear (see n. 54). The overwhelming majority of acts observed in these places were not and have not been proven dangerous. The whole safe/unsafe distinction so carefully nurtured by the Department of Public Health in San Francisco prior to 9 April 1984 was abandoned in the blanket proscription of sex in gay clubs.

59. *Bay Area Reporter*, 11 Oct. 1984.

60. *People of the State of California v. Ima Jean Owen et al.* memorandum from Mervyn Silverman.

sexual activity in hotels or private homes, no difference between someone who rents a cubicle in a bathhouse and someone who makes a mortgage payment on his house.

They contended that the burden of proof that closure "will be sufficiently effective to justify the obviously serious intrusion on property rights, privacy rights, and associational rights" should rest on the county health department. They were also able to do what San Francisco officials had not been able to do: present briefs from experts outside the county government (specifically, public health officials from Los Angeles and New York) to argue that the proposed closures could not be expected to have any reasonable likelihood of affecting the rate of AIDS cases.

Judicial review in late November by Superior Court Judge Roy Wonder rejected the county's case for closure. On 28 November, Wonder ruled that the clubs could reopen, but ordered them to remove private rooms, to hire monitors (one for every twenty patrons), to survey the premises every ten minutes to ensure that no unsafe sex acts were occurring, and to expel patrons observed to be engaging in "unsafe sex practices." To the amazement of almost everyone, the delineation of "unsafe sex" was initially assigned to the San Francisco AIDS Foundation rather than to the County Department of Public Health. (The definitional power was later reassigned to the Department when Judge Wonder issued "technical" clarifications on 21 December 1984.)

The weekend after the bath closure in San Francisco, an Oakland bathhouse owner reported that his business increased 142 percent, repeating the pattern from 1950s crackdowns on San Francisco gay bars, when patrons also relocated their cruising across the bay.[61] The decision was not appealed, and, over the course of the intervening years, owners closed all the San Francisco bathhouses that Silverman left open. An attempt to open one in the Tenderloin in 1994 (after the expiration of Wonder's rulings) was blocked by Mayor Frank Jordan's personal intervention with his planning commission. Many commercial venues for safe sex (mutual masturbation) operate in the county, and facilities with private rooms for unregulated sex continue to operate in nearby counties.[62]

Other Jurisdictions

In late 1985 in New York City, where most of the diagnosed U.S. AIDS cases then were, parallel moves to close several gay bathhouses on the basis of

61. Bérubé 1984:18.
62. The number of gay baths in the country has declined from 169 in 1982 to 61 in 1994 (Tattelman 1995:29), mostly from lack of business rather than from governmental action.

117

private investigators' reports of unsafe sex (mostly fellatio) occurred. As in San Francisco, the reversal of policy about bathhouse closure can be directly related to pressure from above: there, from New York Governor Mario Cuomo, who like Mayor Feinstein had a track record of insensitivity to gay civil rights and a penchant for statist regulating of conduct. Also as in San Francisco, the New York City health department was bypassed, and surveillance of activity in clubs was conducted by investigators from another department. Also as in San Francisco, they observed and reported practically no anal sex. In New York City, the most visible and gay-owned establishments, the Mineshaft and New St. Mark's, were targeted. Less visible, allegedly Mafia-owned, establishments remain open.

The major difference, other than a lag in timing, between the New York and San Francisco actions is that the New York judge, Richard Wallach, did not devise a policy of his own for regulating sex clubs. In *City of New York v. St. Marks Baths* he deferred to the health department and did not evaluate the evidence about sex clubs as a risk factor. In May 1986, in upstate New York, in *Commissioner of Health of the County of Erie v. Morgan Inc., et al.*, closure was rejected because the county did not sustain the burden of proof of dangerous behavior occurring. Los Angeles County Department of Public Health sex club orders were overturned in the summer of 1986, again because the county failed to establish any likelihood that its regulations would reduce the spread of AIDS. Also during the summer of 1986, the San José Water Garden, the largest and plushest gay bathhouse in northern California, was given special recognition for its contribution to AIDS education by the Santa Clara County Department of Public Health.

Just as public officials elsewhere did not rally to Silverman's side in 1984, Dianne Feinstein, who was chair of the U.S. Conference of Mayors, unsuccessfully tried to enlist support from her peers for a resolution urging closure of sex clubs.[63] In August 1988, the California Assembly and Senate passed the Bradley Act to assist San Diego County efforts to shut down bathhouses under the guise of nuisance abatement. Gay bathhouses continue to operate in California, with some unknown number of gay San Franciscans visiting them. California County Public Health Directors' quarantine power has yet to be used in any AIDS matter.

The "Scientific Evidence"

No one had (or has) published any evidence showing bathgoing to constitute a risk factor for AIDS. As mentioned in the chronology above, 1984 CDC

63. Bayer 1989:69.

data still unpublished in 1995 found bathgoing to have no statistically significant effects. A more or less simultaneous report of an ongoing, Department of Public Health–funded survey of changing sexual behavior among San Francisco gay men appears to have been influenced by the policy of closing bathhouses more than it could have contributed to the policy. At least, its authors showed more interest in contrasting bathgoers with other gay men in the report than in their data collection: McKusick, Horstman, and Carfagni (1984) compared only two self-reported behaviors for bathgoers and bargoers. To the surprise of many (and no doubt the consternation of some moral entrepreneurs), they found that those in their bathgoer sample were no more likely to have received anal intercourse with new or secondary partners five or more times during the previous month than their bargoing sample. Furthermore, 56 percent of the bath sample in contrast to 50 percent of the bar sample reported none.[64]

Considering that only two of the reports of behavior contrasted the bath subsample with the other subsamples, both the abstract and the conclusions of McKusick et al.'s 1984 report (abridged and published in 1985) gave inordinate attention to bathgoers, whom they characterized as more rigid and more compulsive than other gay men, although the evidence for these psychological characterizations is nowhere in the report. Similarly, the following indictment seems to have been pulled from the air or from officials' prejudices rather than from any data reported in the study:[65]

> It is apparent that the identities of men in the bathhouses are more attached to sexual behavior than men in other groups and that these men as a group are the most rigid and inflexible in their sexual response patterns. There may also exist in certain members of the bathhouse group a type of fatalism that is not subject to the influence of information, since they may already believe that they have come in contact with the hypothetical transmission agents. (McKusick et al. 1984:29)

If this was "apparent," it is on the basis of evidence other than that presented in their reports. In neither study did McKusick et al. (1983, 1984) attempt

64. It cannot be assumed that the sex reported by the bath sample occurred exclusively in the baths. Perhaps owing to the professional bias of psychologists for constructing personality patterns, McKusick et al. made no attempt to distinguish the number of sex partners bathgoers had sex with in the baths from the number outside. The cherished notion of the promiscuous personality, of course, undercuts the rationale for government interference with the operations of the specific institution of the baths. Since, at the time the questionnaire was prepared and distributed, the official public health view was that if the baths were closed, gay men would go elsewhere, the explanation for this failure might be historical rather than occupational, i.e., the authors did not anticipate that their results would be used to justify a policy shift.

65. Or in then available literature on the baths, such as Lee 1978a, 1979b; Styles 1979; M. Weinberg and Williams 1975.

to determine whether bathgoers have more sex or are more "addicted" to sex than any other human group,[66] nor did they use any psychological scales for rigidity.

Moreover, their assertion that "the efforts of the Public Health Department have been ineffective in influencing sexual activity at the bathhouses"[67] was misleading. According to their own data, more of those in the bath sample than in the bar or (an added) couple sample listed "public information brochures or posters" as a source of information about AIDS (p. 13). They also showed that "knowledge of the disease process and the risk reduction guidelines closely parallels opinion of experts and is well disseminated across subgroups" (p. 13). That is, for transmitting information, the public education efforts of the gay press (the main source of information for most sampled gay men), public health authorities, and others were successful before Silverman's attempts to regulate or close gay clubs.

Sixty-five percent of the bar and bath samples, 88 percent of the coupled sample, and 85 percent of the volunteer sample indicated they had already made the changes in their lives needed to adapt to AIDS. Whether the behavioral changes were sufficient was, of course, open to question. Hessol et al. (1987), analyzing blood stored from gay volunteers attending San Francisco's STD Clinic in the mid 1970s and participating in a hepatitis B study, found most of the seroconversion occurred between 1979 (when 5% were already infected) and the beginning of 1984 (by which time more than 50% had seroconverted).[68] Gay men's changes in risk behavior were mostly made before bath closures and the "professionalization" of AIDS prevention education.[69]

In Los Angeles County, where bathhouses have remained open, Richwald et al. (1988) interviewed 807 men who could speak English leaving bathhouses in 1986. Fifty percent reported that information about AIDS received in bathhouses played a major role in their understanding of AIDS prevention; another 37 percent reported it played a minor role. Ninety-seven

66. See Levine and Troiden 1988; Coxon 1988; Murray 1984:62–63.

67. McKusick et al. 1984:2.

68. In the 13 July 1984 *MMWR* (p. 377), slightly different preliminary figures from the San Francisco City Clinic Study were available: 25% (of 48) in 1980 to 65% (of 215) in 1984. This latter figure was used as the best estimate of HIV infection among sexually active gay men in deliberations by Silverman and other San Francisco physicians concerned with AIDS (personal communication from a BAPHR member who wishes to remain unnamed), although it is now regarded as an overestimate due to the biased basis for recruitment into the study from an STD clinic (cf. Winkelstein et al. 1987a,b).

69. Bolton 1992a:179–88, 1994; E. King 1994. The failure of "professional" education to stop new cohorts from seroconverting is increasingly obvious, especially among Latino and African American gay men (Harper 1993:133).

percent were familiar with bathhouse information on AIDS prevention. Despite this information, 5 percent reported receptive anal intercourse without a condom. The 10 percent involved in anal intercourse without a condom[70] were significantly more likely than those who did not practice this highest risk sexual activity to be aged less than 30, to be Hispanic, never to have attended college, to be earning less than $20,000 per year, and to have had five or more male sexual partners in the past month. If one can extrapolate from Los Angeles in 1986 to San Francisco in 1984,[71] it would seem that those who were not heeding the message of condom use were the segments of the population most difficult to reach *outside* the bathhouses. It would also seem that the small minority of bathgoers who continued to receive unprotected anal intercourse with multiple partners from a population of whom half were HIV-positive were already infected, so that closing the baths would not afford them any protection.[72] Whether it would protect their sexual partners, including (for 7% of those reporting anal intercourse without a condom) women, or would distribute unsafe sex more widely, is not easy to predict or to measure.

Two years after closing the bathhouses and sex clubs, Silverman (1986: 34; see also his similar secondary elaborations to Bayer and Fitzgerald) still could not point to any evidence establishing bathgoing as a risk factor. Like any good politician, he could, however, provide folksy non sequiturs to make his policy sound plausible: (1) allowing bathhouses to continue to operate was like providing crop subsidies to tobacco growers at the same time public health education funds are spent to stop smoking; (2) "some people would feel that their civil liberties would be violated if we told them they could not have sex in a restaurant or a church"; and (3) what gay leader would want to create the institution of the bathhouse if it didn't exist? Obviously, the first is not unthinkable, since it describes policies of the federal government. The second is a peculiar comparison, since banning sex in restaurants and

70. This figure includes insertive as well as receptive; 30 of 84 reported both roles in the same night. Unfortunately, no data were obtained from monolingual Spanish-speaking men, who constituted 5% of the population from which the sample was drawn.

71. At least some justification for such an extrapolation is the earlier heightened visibility of AIDS and AIDS prevention efforts in San Francisco, including the bathhouse closure controversy. Also, the Winkelstein et al. 1987a data from San Francisco census tracts show a similar (to the Los Angeles bathgoer sample) proportion of the gay population continuing to engage in anal intercourse without a condom.

72. Bayer (1989:61) quotes a 9 Oct. 1985 memorandum from Director of the New York City Office of Epidemiological Surveillance and Statistics, Alan Kristal, to the Health Commissioner, David Sencer, which says, "The prevalence of infection in the sexually active gay population is already so high that the environment from which one selects sexual partners has little relevance."

churches would not interfere with the purposes for which people assemble in those settings. The third non sequitur, the hypothetical question Silverman posed to gay opponents, is counterfactual, so the answer is irrelevant to public policy. One could as easily ask, "If there wasn't a Bill of Rights in the Constitution of the United States, would there be an impetus to amend the Constitution to add it in the 1980s or 1990s?" Whatever the original purpose of social institutions, with the passage of time additional meanings attach to them. Gay bathhouses symbolized uncontrolled male promiscuity to some, a haven from violence and homophobia to others,[73] and the rights to privacy and freedom of assembly to others.[74]

The symbolic politics of Silverman's shifting or evolving policy (and Judge Wonder's modifications of it) attempted to balance competing demands of persons with markedly differing definitions of the situation. Verifiable medical facts were not necessarily of interest to those pressing any of these actions. If compelling medical evidence existed, the director of public health had and has sweeping quarantine powers.[75] American courts have shown great reluctance to question official claims of "medical necessity" or "military necessary"[76]—this is perfectly exemplified by the judge's refusal to question the cogency of the health department's case in *City of New York v. St. Marks Baths*.

As was mentioned above, the failure of neighboring counties to follow Silverman's precedent is prima facie evidence that the decision stemmed from local political considerations rather than from compelling scientific evidence. Yet another indication of the essentially political motivation of the decision is the frequency with which Dr. Silverman referred to a public opinion poll published in the 8 April 1984 *San Francisco Chronicle*, in which most respondents favored forcing the baths to close. As Brian Jones (1984: 6) commented, "When a doctor makes a decision because the voters favor it, that doctor is a politician."[77]

It is impossible to believe that the bath closure was motivated by new

73. On the history of bathhouses as havens see Dynes 1990a; Chauncey 1984:207–25, especially p. 223 on collective memory; Bérubé 1984; Tattelman 1995.

74. Silverman (1986:33) also asserted that six months after the bath closure, "mail from the gay community was over 60% in favor of closing the bathhouses." He did not mention how many letters he was receiving at that point. I would guess few. The civil rights precedent was already set, although Silverman has continued to fail to understand a distinction between admiration for the bathhouses and opposition to governmental interference with rights of privacy guaranteed in the constitution of California.

75. Novick 1985.

76. See Murray 1987a.

77. See Perlstadt and Holmes 1987.

scientific evidence rather than by political pressure.[78] As Bolton, Vincke, and Mak (1994:270–71) noted, closing bathhouses

> provided health authorities with a means of taking popular action with a minimum investment of resources. . . . It is more expedient politically to denounce "promiscuity" than it was [or is!] to advocate sex-positive approaches to prevention. While the bathhouse issue may have had symbolic value in alerting gay men to the seriousness of the epidemic, it also sent a symbolically inappropriate message, i.e., that partner reduction was a valid strategy for HIV prevention.

"Reduce the number of your partners" and "Know your partners" provided a false sense of security. Insofar as such prevention efforts encouraged men to believe that they had "cleaned up their act" and were safe, instead of pressing for safer sex with all partners, strangers and lovers, "prevention" and "education" increased infection.[79]

No new clinical or epidemiological evidence about bathgoing justified a change of policy, especially since doing so undercut the credibility of the thrust of the safe-sex education campaign and its most visible proponent until then, Dr. Silverman himself. Even a decade later, no link between bathgoing and AIDS has been established, and the CDC has not listed bathgoing as a risk factor. Indeed, in a study in Belgium in the late 1980s, Bolton, Vincke, and Mak (1994) found bathgoers more likely to use condoms in anal sex than non-bathgoers—they contend (in n. 7) that Belgium was at a stage of the AIDS epidemic comparable to that in San Francisco five to six years earlier.

On several occasions I have asked San Francisco County epidemiologists where the effect of bath closure appears on AIDS infection rate charts. They have not claimed any effect. As for the slight increase of rectal gonorrhea in one quarter sensationalized by Shilts, no serious epidemiologist, statistician, or experienced public health figure would have staked his or her credibility on the assertion that so slight an increase indicated a trend back to earlier levels. Subsequent data (in figure 4.1) show that this was a fluctuation, not a trend. The Public Health Department's own reports included information about both medical opinion and changed behavior, including a 90 percent reduction in the number of gay San Francisco men "practicing receptive anal

---

78. The same is true for the actions of the Health Commissioner of the State of New York in October 1985. David Axelrod claimed to change the state's policy on the basis of "new evidence" rather than political pressure (*New York Times*, 25 October 1985, p. B3). One can hardly expect public health officials to state explicitly that they are subordinating their professional judgment to political demands!

79. Louganis (1995:169–73) provides a chilling example.

intercourse with non-steady partners" between 1978 and 1985.[80] The results could be interpreted as suggesting that more education was not going to lead to more change, although no one publicly interpreted them that way.

CONCLUSION

Public health thought (or, at least, discourse) immediately added AIDS to the class of exotic diseases transmitted by promiscuous sex, especially promiscuous homosexual sex. Although needle use and heterosexual "promiscuity" now supplement homosexuality within the paradigm of immoral excess, the explanatory model persists among medical researchers at least in accounting for transmission of a virus believed to be the cause of AIDS, and for many non-scientists as the underlying "real cause."[81] Because a syndrome was initially identified among gay men with medical access lacking to most intravenous drug users, it was obvious to medical researchers that whatever it was must be sexually transmitted. The preference for a sexual explanation persisted, obstructing consideration of drug use by those already "explained" as "homosexuals." Between mid 1983 and late 1986, epidemiologists avoided the anomaly to this explanation posed by the existence of heterosexual Haitian and African cases by assuming that the Haitians were lying and that the Africans were engaging in heterosexual anal intercourse (and were also probably lying). There was never any evidence that African, Haitian, or Haitian American men are more likely than men of other origins to conceal homosexual behavior when suffering from fatal diseases, or that central Africans are more likely to engage in heterosexual anal intercourse than are North Americans.

Beginning in 1984, another kind of sexual being, the prostitute, was medicalized and added to explanations of AIDS transmission—with no attention to prostitutes' drug habits, or even to their usual sexual behavior. Again, "being a prostitute" rather than behavior was the focus of attention. Given the apparent difficulty of female-to-male sexual transmission, this broader conception of "promiscuity" does not explain etiology. Instead, it reinforces attempts to condemn and eliminate extramarital sex. A focus on prostitutes is certainly consistent with the CDC taste (paradigm) for multiple-partner sexual transmission as an explanation of whatever they can't explain without the help of emotional reactions to "immorality." In American epidemiologi-

80. McKusick, Horstman, and Carfagni 1983, 1984; Werdeger et al. 1987.
81. S. Epstein (1993) documents how homosexual "promiscuity," and some exceedingly implausible accounts of "typical" gay behavior, periodically creep into Peter Duesberg's explanation of the etiology of AIDS as drug use rather than HIV.

cal work in central Africa, the number of sexual partners is also a source of seemingly endless fascination.

The commitment to the inadequate promiscuity paradigm derives from more fundamental features of American medicine than the homophobia and erotophobia of some clinicians and researchers, however. Doctors need to explain AIDS away as "their own fault," quite apart from preexisting hostility to homosexuality, prostitution, and recreational drug use, or of contempt for drug users and prostitutes. A disease that kills previously healthy men in their 20s and 30s is both personally and professionally distressing. It is even a threat to the reputation (and, therefore, the rewards) of medicine in American society. American doctors prefer to deal with acute diseases amenable to capital-intensive, high-tech remedies involving considerable control over patients. No such remedies are available for AIDS.

Opportunistic politicians, inside and outside public health, have used sexual transmission of AIDS to legitimate reinstituting prohibitions of homosexual acts. In this, some gay men (such as Randy Shilts, Larry Kramer, Leonard Matlovich, or Larry Littlejohn), loathing what some gay men do and/or what they themselves do or did, have been eager allies in popular condemnation and official suppression of gay institutions. Under the guise of public health, homosexuality *in toto* has been remedicalized, while new extensions of social control of sexually active adults have been proposed regularly to protect a "public health" in which the "public" is only a righteous, monogamous, heterosexual elect.

Five

The Initial Surrender and Eventual Tentative Reassertion of Autonomy under the Shadow of AIDS

In the account of bathhouse closure, I stressed that several gay-identified men seeking governmental intervention to close gay institutions rather than attempting to persuade and organize other gay men to their view of health risks (e.g., by demonstrating or leafleting outside bathhouses) triggered state repression. Paralleling this demonization of promiscuous degenerates who were killing each other and (worse?) giving respectable homosexuals a bad name and who (therefore) probably deserved to be condemned by right-thinking leaders like Mayor, subsequently U.S. Senator, Dianne Feinstein and who needed to be controlled, in many ways AIDS organizing during the 1980s revived the 1950s' homophile movement's reliance on "sympathetic" outside "experts," such as Mathilde Krim in New York and Donald Francis and Marcus Conant in San Francisco. "Stop them" and "Lecture us" were the messages delivered to allegedly "gay-sensitive" politicians and physicians by Randy Shilts and other would-be "gay leaders" contemplating coercing gay masses unwilling to be obey/follow them[1]—even while major behavioral changes were under way that maintained hard-won control over sexual self-determination while avoiding infecting or being infected.[2]

Enforcing celibacy or monogamy on wayward brothers was the first pri-

1. Unsurprisingly given his own activities, Shilts's (1987) tendentious novelization of early (non-)responses to AIDS ignored grassroots gay organizing (unless his own small conspiracy to misrepresent the views of Silverman and leaders of the Bay Area Physicians for Human Rights to each other counts) to celebrate Conant, Francis, Krim, Selma Dritz, et al.

2. King 1994:276, 49; Siegel et al. 1988. It bears stressing that these changes were made *before* HIV antibody testing became available.

ority. Research was the second. The alliance between gay AIDS activists and biomedical researchers produced immediate benefits for the latter, little more than a slight and ever-dwindling basis for sustaining hope for the former.[3] From the fringes of one of the major American biomedical research institutions (the University of California, San Francisco), I observed researchers reformulating previously rejected grant applications, adding claims of some relevance to AIDS, then being funded as "AIDS research." Such grants then counted as part of the federal effort to "do something." Laboratories and research programs, especially in retrovirology and immunology, that had been moribund in the early 1980s were suddenly reinvigorated with infusions of money, and its concomitant: researchers starting their careers where the money is.

The activists who pressed for more research money had no say in how it was spent. For many nominally involved in doing "AIDS research" it was business as usual, only better business. Those who really did focus on AIDS, on the other hand, tended to quit too soon. Epidemiological research was largely abandoned after the discovery of HIV, despite the inadequacy of explanatory models involving HIV slaughtering T-cells. Similarly, AZT (azidothymidine, now officially Retrovir) swept the field too quickly, without any demonstrated survival benefits.[4] Instead of assessing AZT's efficacy, most research focused on dosage levels. Through the 1980s, drugs other than nucleoside antivirals were not tested.[5] Gay AIDS activists must bear some of the responsibility for both these premature foreclosures of inquiry. A virus— indeed, any etiological agent—somewhat delegitimated attempts to blame gay men for AIDS.[6] Untangling new drugs from red tape to get them immediately into the bodies of gay men was the aim of the third wave (exemplified by ACT UP, AIDS Coalition To Unleash Power) of gay AIDS activism. This goal dovetailed with the pharmaceutical industry's interest in

3. The main funding has been thrown at blocking HIV replication, and has so far failed: anti-retroviral drugs made huge profits for drug companies, but do not prolong life. Some treatments and prophylaxis for opportunistic infections do.

4. With increased realization of the costs of ineffective but toxic drugs to our bodies as well as to our resources, placebo trials seem less immoral to 1990s AIDS treatment activists than to earlier ones. Temporary increases in surrogate markers, CD4 count in particular, no longer seem to be a sufficient basis for getting drugs out of testing into the bodies of the masses, even to activists hoping to save their own lives. See S. Epstein 1993.

5. The late Joel Brodsky said that this sounded like I'd joined the "AZT kills" legion. The Concorde (1994) study showed no effect of three years' high dosage (1.2 grams daily) on survival: AZT neither increased nor decreased life expectancy. Its toxicity and cost have detrimental effects on quality of life, but I don't think that "AZT kills" any more than "AZT will save us."

6. The initial equation of AIDS and homosexuality, discussed in the previous chapter, is very hard to expunge from the collective consciousness (Crimp 1988; Murray and Payne 1988; Plummer 1988; Gamson 1989; Edwards 1992; Murray 1994a).

faster and looser FDA approval of their products, whatever their efficacy, thereby realizing sales and profits sooner after product development (before something better might come along). This was a part of the Republican Party's policy of deregulating businesses, the most famous and expensive example of which was loosening government oversight of savings and loan institutions.

Sick gay men's desperate hope for a quick fix, a "magic bullet," made them willing to try almost anything that seemed to help as few as one other person.[7] Our eagerness to try drugs far exceeded anyone's knowledge of probable efficacy or side effects of the drugs singly, let alone in the baroque variety of combinations that proliferated. Pressure to get drugs into and through clinical trials led to approval of AZT partway through its clinical trial. With demonstrated severe side effects and without any demonstrated prolongation of life, AZT became standard therapy not only for persons with AIDS, but for "early intervention" into the bodies of asymptomatic persons whose blood contained HIV antibodies.

Other toxic and even less effective antivirals followed AZT into a profitable northern European and North American market, expanded to include asymptomatic HIV-positive persons. We and our insurers, including governments paying for prescription drugs, have paid vast sums to drug companies in hopes of buying time.[8] Besides their high costs in both money and toxicity, antivirals cannot be counted on to do more than slightly slow illness progression. Physicians, therefore, prescribe diverse drugs for symptoms and prophylaxis. HIV-infected persons, particularly gay men, have turned our bodies into drug cocktail shakers. Adding drugs that seem to make one feel better and subtracting those that don't feels rational, but, to put it mildly, no one knows what the effects are of the combinations of these arrays of

7. Rothman and Edgar (1992) show that the government does not require double-blind placebo studies for studying the effects and toxicity of treatment for terminal cancer, so there is a precedent for relaxed requirements—and for very ill persons trying highly toxic substances of very uncertain efficacy. While I feel that people with a terminal illness should be able to try whatever we want to try, I think that we are particularly unlikely to make rational judgments about efficacy and risk, and are very vulnerable to slick purveyors of false hopes.

8. "Be here for the cure," a long-running advertising slogan for early intervention sponsored by the San Francisco AIDS Foundation, implied that not being here for the cure was an irresponsible, individual choice. In this instance, the message is that if one does not get tested and then take antivirals he (or occasionally she) is committing suicide. Just do what your doctor tells you (no matter how often the directions change!) and you'll be around for the cure (which must certainly be on its way . . . It just *has* to be . . .). This is a good example of the increasingly powerful American tendency to blame the victim. A predominantly lesbigay organization thus foisted more blame on those dying, while enriching laboratories performing blood tests and the manufacturers of toxic and expensive drugs of no particular efficacy.

drugs.[9] Moreover, other drugs study participants are taking at the same time—often, but not always, unknown to those running the clinical trials—contaminate clinical trials. "Do something, anything, whether it is effective or not" describes the conduct of HIV-positive persons, as well as that of public health authorities. Rather than possession of that amorphous entity "cultural capital" (S. Epstein 1993), I would relate AIDS treatment activists' belief that they could read medical literature for themselves and challenge the credentialed "experts" to earlier engagement in solo searches of books and libraries to find out about same-sex desire, reading between the lines of much, and skeptically processing negative materials about homosexuality.

While initial gay AIDS activism involved lobbying for established biomedical research and then for drug companies eager to get products of dubious efficacy to the market, by the late 1980s gay AIDS activists were frustrated enough by the slowness of progress to take matters into their own hands. Community-based organizations began distributing drugs, evaluating "promising" therapies and combinations of drugs, and even collecting data in advance (or in lieu) of official clinical trials—most famously (albeit inconclusively) in the case of the Chinese melon root extract, compound Q.

While community involvement in the evaluation of drugs increased and community-based activists attained considerable expertise, forced wider access to experimental trials, increased provision of "compassionate use" prescription of drugs while they were being tested, and even began to have some impact on decisions by the FDA on what to test,[10] provision of services to PWAs went the other way: from community-based to professionalized. Once funds for AIDS research, education, and care started to become available, credentialed, generally heterosexual professionals supplanted the gay male volunteers who had resolutely stepped in to meet the needs of PWAs that were not provided for by the partially developed, mostly crumbling welfare state in the United States.[11] Governments and umbrella charity organiza-

9. It is not unusual to find 30–50 prescription drugs in the possessions of PWAs, who may be taking more than a dozen different drugs concurrently.

10. See Harrington 1990; Arno and Feiden 1992. S. Epstein (1993) focused on two facets: how attempts to "democratize" decision-making about drug trials led to the inclusion of some experts whose initial credentials were that they spoke from the population of PWAs from which participants in clinical trials must be drawn; and how such new "experts" were increasingly isolated from their roots in community activism. Against those who blame gay AIDS activists for pressing too hard to get drugs approved, he reminds that "activists such as John James had been complaining all along that clinical trials were asking the wrong questions—that they should be oriented around the real-life issues confronting patients and doctors, rather than the thumbs-up/thumbs-down logic of FDA approval" (p. 504).

11. And also in the United Kingdom. See Plummer 1988; E. King 1994:169–224. Schneider's assertion (1992:168) that half the volunteers in American AIDS organizations are women

tions such as United Way require bureaucratic rationality for the PWA-serving organizations they fund. They demand bureaucratic accountability not only in financial record-keeping, but also in providing at least the semblance of "rational, bureaucratic delivery of services to a series of usually mutually isolated, passive clients" rather than to mobilized groups.[12] Although funders are little interested in evaluations of services by those supposedly being served, the bureaucrats in funding agencies are quick to suspect that recipients of service will try to circumvent eligibility and other requirements to get more than managers have decided they need or are entitled to receive. Therefore, they welcome surveillance of attempts to "work the system."[13] Moreover, PWAs have had many occasions to bristle at organizations, such as Gay Men's Health Crisis in New York and the Shanti Project in San Francisco, and staff eager to help "victims" die rather than to help autonomous adults to live and possibly to make decisions with which those who "know best"—i.e., medical and welfare professionals—disagree. The dying often have to comfort those they are leaving behind. Ensuring the spiritual self-satisfaction of gay and non-gay caregivers too often has been an additional burden on PWAs.[14]

Altman (1988:302) claimed that "AIDS has forced governments to recognize organizations they had previously ignored, and this has resulted in strengthening gay organizations." Although gay men's relationships, institutions, and lifeways unquestionably are more visible to more people now than they were in 1981, it seems to me that the organizations governments in the U.S. and U.K. have dealt with are AIDS-centered organizations that did not exist before (e.g., Gay Men's Health Crisis, the Treatment Activists Group, the Terrence Higgins Trust, the San Francisco AIDS Foundation)

---

differs from my impression, which is that lesbians occupy paid and/or leadership positions disproportionately to their numbers in the population (whether the population is AIDS cases or the whole society) or as volunteers in the AIDS organizations. To resolve our differing impressions requires quantitative data on frequencies of paid and unpaid personnel by sex and sexual identity. Meanwhile, a national survey found that homo-/bisexual men were nearly twice as likely to have cared for someone with AIDS than were lesbians (H. Turner, Catania, and Gagnon 1994:1547, table 2). Though proportionately much less likely to have provided AIDS care, heterosexual total numbers exceeded homo-/bisexual caregiver ones.

12. Adam 1992:179. For an example of successful community organizing and empowerment in building peer support for safe sex, see Mutchler 1995. Renewal funding was not available for that project, while more funds for testing are readily authorized despite the lack of demonstration that test results enhance safe(r) behavior.

13. The major focus of the American welfare system is surveillance, i.e., finding reasons to deny help rather than trying to deliver resources to those in need. See Piven and Cloward 1971.

14. Brodsky 1993b.

or that were radically redirected toward AIDS (e.g., the Shanti Project). Before AIDS, they were mostly not there to be ignored, while older gay organizations (the National Gay Task Force, the Human Rights Campaign Fund, etc.) remain as marginal and impotent as ever. If anything, through the 1980s and into the 1990s, AIDS agendas largely eclipsed/superseded other gay agendas,[15] and organizations founded by gay men increasingly focused on outreach to everyone except gay men. Even protest organizations populated mostly by gay men downplayed the fact that most PWAs in the U.S. and "the West" generally are gay men. In 1991, Robin Hardy complained,

> ACT UP's failure to ground its politics in the identity of 98 per cent of its members has diverted it from goals which are critical to gay men. As ACT UP embraces the politics of inclusion, it cuts itself off from the community which has provided the core of its tactics, theory, membership and funding. Implicit in ACT UP's brand of coalition politics is an assumption that homosexuals must subordinate their gay/lesbian identity to attract other communities to the ranks of AIDS activism. No one has stopped to ask what attention to the political agendas of other minorities might be costing the gay community. Or if it's even working.[16]

Any "partnership" between government and [gay] community-based organizations was very unequal, with government agencies calling the shots, the organizations whoring after trickles of money, and "accentuating the trend toward leaders who can claim professional expertise instead of activist credentials."[17] Watching new "AIDS professionals" who had shown no interest in AIDS until there were funds to grab alienates (the surviving!) gay volunteers, both the political ones and the previously apolitical ones. As in the instance of bath closure, gay men have been centrally involved in diverting prevention funding away from those most at risk, i.e., gay men.[18]

NEW SOCIAL MOVEMENTS THEORIZING

In the first chapter I stressed the increased prominence since the Second World War of social movements that are not working-class and do not legiti-

15. As Rist (1989) complained, and Altman (1988:309) somewhat acknowledged.

16. Quoted by E. King (1994:192).

17. Altman 1988:303, 309.

18. E. King (1994:254–77) makes a sustained argument for returning control to community empowerment rather than professional(ist) bureaucratic administration, i.e., for "re-gaying AIDS." We currently have the worst of both worlds—a disease blamed on gay men while governmental AIDS funding goes to everyone but gay men, though we remain those at the highest risk.

mate their actions in the name of that allegedly universal class. What is seen[19] as "new" in the "new social movements" (NSMs) attended to by sociologists is primarily their middle-class membership. More restricted aims than the total transformation of society (to make room for the New Man and the New Woman) also characterize them. That is, their goals are more concrete and limited than saving or redeeming the world. "We're going to get aerosol pentamidine a lot quicker than we're going to get social justice," as one ACT UP member explained to Gamson (1989:39).

Despite much rhetoric about coalitions and inclusivity, the members of "queer" and AIDS street theater groups have been mostly white and from middle-class family backgrounds.[20] As with "old" class-based movements, the easiest enemy to locate and to denigrate is not the distant "ruling class," or even managers of key institutions, but those most like the "radicals" except in not being "radical" enough and/or belonging to rival organizations (i.e., following false prophets). Just as communists often seemed more interested in attacking democratic socialists, young "queer" and AIDS activists have focused on their allegedly too accommodationist (whether closeted or merely "lesbian" or "gay" instead of "in-your-face-queer") elders. Locating the enemy and taking effective action against it have been even more difficult than were locating and challenging "the establishment" for my own generation, one that also was eager to shock the bourgeoisie (along with the working class) and was similarly confident that changing coiffures and hurling four-letter words would change the world.

ACT UP, Queer Nation, et al. seem to me to have revived the tactics of earlier gay liberation zaps (kiss-ins, die-ins, etc.) that followed upon the symbolic rejection of mainstream cultural values by the more flamboyant parts of the 1960s' youth "movement."[21] Blocking entry to an FDA building has a connection to goals—changing FDA drug approval processes—that almost everyone can grasp, whereas disrupting traffic on the Golden Gate Bridge

19. Possibly erroneously.

20. Generation after generation of Japanese and Korean student radicals has set aside opposition to take their place as salarymen. Some of those involved in 1960s North American counterculture substitute for political action stayed dropped out, but many more only temporarily renounced class privilege. It remains to be seen how enduring will be the diffuse opposition simultaneously to "heteronormativity" and "gay/lesbian conformity." "Not very" is the likely answer.

21. I.e., those who supposed that donning androgynous clothes, growing their hair long, using drugs, and listening to acid rock constituted a "revolution" that would lead to the collapse of capitalism, universal brotherhood, and peace on earth. The male focus of this characterization is quite deliberate. Obviously, the state, capitalism, and warmaking all survived that "revolution."

puzzled and irritated commuters, including those disgusted by lack of concern about AIDS. Both actions exhilarated the self-styled "activists" involved—especially if they later saw themselves on television news—but it is very dubious that unfocused assaults on the sensibilities of the general society accomplished anything, thus recapitulating that aspect of the New York media-focused gay liberation movement of the early 1970s. So far as I know, the social scientists involved in ACT UP, Queer Nation, et al. did not undertake research measuring the impacts of public actions on those they hoped to move. The inability to decide what audience they were seeking precluded serious investigation of how any target audience viewed their antics.[22] Indeed, those staging ACT UP or Queer Nation actions were indifferent to whether the prejudices of heteronormative bourgeoisie present were lessened or were reinforced.[23]

But, hey! Until the impossibility of achieving consensus in seemingly endless meetings wore them down, young "queers" felt good and solidary about challenging taboos; that is something! Changing consciousnesses and rejecting the status quo are not enough, but may be valuable. They even may be prerequisite to more effective action, as long as the survivors don't burn out. Demonstrating that "We are everywhere" is as central to "queer nationalism" as it was to "gay liberation." Impatience with closetry has mounted. Public display (literally, embodiment) directly challenges the assumption that we must be ashamed of our "affliction" and will try to hide our shameful secrets to the extent we can.[24]

22. See Gamson 1989:47; Gamson 1994; A. Williams 1994. Simultaneously with confrontational AIDS activism, the "queer" activists recapitulated the behavior of an earlier generation: in the 1970s, de-assimilating gay liberationists had similarly dismissed our elders for being too concerned with respectability and straight approval. Also like us, "queers" trumpet difference both from their homosexual/gay elders and from (even "liberal" and "sympathetic") straight people. For all the confusion of audiences found by Gamson (1989) in the symbolic politics of ACT UP, the two Bay Area ACT UP chapters were focused and instrumental in contrast to the diffuse rage and flamboyant public performances of Queer Nation and TANTRUM. Older generations recurrently question the effectiveness of upstart generations' actions aimed more at attracting media attention than at producing concrete changes. Like Cleve Jones earlier (in his involvement with the infamous 1980 CBS report, "Gay power/gay politics," on the alleged dominance of San Francisco government officials by kinky gay men), ACT UP members overestimated their ability to manipulate mass media.

23. Similarly, assertions about reclaiming and transforming *queer* have been unaccompanied by any even anecdotal evidence that fag-bashers or school children hear or use the epithet differently since it has been "reclaimed."

24. Visible evidence that we are not ashamed is valuable, though "shameless" is not a highly valued category in American (or any?) culture. Insofar as we are concerned about societal conceptions, it is important to include representations of men and women oriented toward their

Distaste for "identity politics" has led NSM writers mostly to ignore what seems most genuinely new in recent years, namely the mobilization for rights and scarce resources of "disabled" persons (both generally, and the more particularistic mobilizations by the Deaf, those with breast cancer or infected by HIV, etc.).

Increasing the acceptance and protection of those not confined to heterosexuality involves more than feeling good about ourselves, excavating coded representations in mass or elite texts,[25] and increasing the range of representations of sexualities. "New Social Movement Theory" tells us some things about the mobilization of somewhat focused middle-class people around fairly specific disaffections with some aspect of their society—or of middle-class people who have been moved to take action by the plight of people or animals further afield. Few attempts to apply or to extend new social movements theory to gay/lesbian/queer or AIDS activisms have been published.[26] The leading NSM theorist, Alberto Melucci, is as heteronormative as, say, Talcott Parsons. Rather than explicitly denigrating homosexuality(/ies) as Melucci does,[27] other NSM theorists ignore gay/lesbian/queer movements. Similarly, Pierre Bourdieu's own intellectual habitus seems to be entirely heteronormative.

In an interesting unpublished confrontation of San Francisco Queer Nation activities to NSM theory, A. Williams (1994) reveals what I see as residually Leninist assumptions within NSM theory. While the Mattachine Society and ONE operated as vanguard parties with tight organization, Queer Nation (even more than GLF and ACT UP) tried to avoid institutionalization:

own sex who are not extreme instances of gender stereotypes (hypermasculine or hyperfeminine). This is not a demand that everyone be colorless or that the flamboyant remain hidden, only that what the mass media show not be *only* the flamboyant gender extremes.

25. The "challenge to heteronormativity" that Michael Warner (1991:17 n. 8) finds in textual criticism might as well be out of this world. It certainly does not impinge on those making decisions in the society that has indulged its development. I am less delighted than he that gay/lesbian/queer studies are confined to English and French departments of (mostly elite) U.S. universities. I am tempted to think that some measure of acceptance has been possible there because they matter so little. I would be more impressed by acceptance of those challenging heteronormativity in economics departments—or in the Department of Defense. And I would be more impressed if the interpretations churned out were less idiosyncratic, more intersubjective, had some plausible theory about society, and were less overwhelmed by gender as an explain-all. In particular, I would like to see some evidence that critics' interpretation of cultural products have any correspondence to how audiences that are larger than one person consume/receive such products.

26. S. Epstein 1988; Gamson 1989; and V. Taylor and Whittier 1992 are exceptions.

27. See Melucci 1989:152 and 159 and Warner's (1991:4–5) apposite response.

Few opponents are named. Few targets are defined. Concrete goals per se are avoided. Many queers understand their potential influences upon the mainstream to be cumulative rather than direct. . . . Actions are often small and the messages diffuse. . . . The actual actions themselves have the unique characteristics of little or no emphasis on organization and the capacity to exploit the fragmentation that generally pervades social life. . . . Actions are intent on opening a space rather than filling it. (Pp. 27–29)

Queer Nationists do not aim to seize power, though I doubt that their disaffection from seeking power owes much to having thought about what Leninist vanguard parties did with the state power (and ownership of the means of production) they seized. Queer Nationists are more interested in being in a cultural vanguard than in affecting—let alone taking control of—the state. In trying to shock "straights," they are more akin to surrealists and yippies than to earnest Bolsheviks or Vietnam-era draft resisters. Transforming society was not a game, in Lenin's view, nor is it in that of NSM theorists.

The easy answer is that in avoiding either strategic goals or "identity consolidation,"[28] Queer Nation is not a movement. It is easy to conclude that its members (and nonmembers who consider it "radical" to call themselves "queer") are deluded in believing that they have avoided "identity politics" ("queer" being an identity whether the contrast is with "normal" or with "gay," and even diffuse actions form/consolidate identities), that their consciousnesses are false, and that their actions are as alienating of others as they are based on their own alienation. Obviously, their slogans were quickly co-opted and marketed.[29] I expect that, despite their self-exalted advanced consciousnesses, many will drift into competition for fame, fortune, and (even modicums of) power. Modern states and economies have survived and absorbed many waves of acting out of adolescent rebelliousness and expression of opposition to the status quo.

If power is everywhere, as Foucault maintained, resistance can be anywhere. For Queer Nationists, as for Foucault, this rationalized the focus on (privileging) cultural representations (texts). The result for both was a sense of hopelessness, as no discernible effects followed upon diffusely targeted actions and analyses of cultural representations. New social movements may expand the domains of mobilization and action, but opposition to the whole of society tends to lead to withdrawal rather than to confrontation.

28. This is the NSM alternative, in the formulation of A. P. Cohen 1985.
29. The T-shirt industry, both production and distribution, would be an interesting phenomenon to study. I am amazed by the rapidity with which new slogans are inscribed and marketed. The role of wearing slogans in consolidating identities, not least that of the allegedly post-identity "queer," also merits investigation.

... AND IN THE MOST CONVENTIONAL
INSTITUTIONS OF AMERICAN SOCIETY

Young "queers" are far from being the only ones alienated and outraged by the range from hostility to indifference displayed by society toward those outside gender and sexuality norms. AIDS has taught many middle-class gay men how irrational and inequitable the American health care financing (non-) system is. Expressions of our fear and outrage are part of the stimulus for Bill and Hillary Clinton's failed 1994 attempt to overhaul how health care is delivered and paid for in the U.S. Across the U.S., those pushing for recording and penalizing hate crimes have included sexual orientation as one of the categories. In contrast to the early homophile movement's focus on combating police harassment, lesbigay antiviolence organizations now work with police in many cities to hasten and improve police response to fag-bashings, to document the extent of such attacks, and to train people to avoid or escape increasingly numerous and violent assaults.[30]

A gay rights issue that appears to me to have come from the bottom up, rather than from the top down, is military service. The right of openly lesbigay people to serve in the military was not a priority for established gay rights organizations during the 1980s. The General Accounting Office estimated the cost of investigating and separating from the services suspected "homosexuals" during that decade as $27 million. Massachusetts gay congressman Gerry Studds managed to get the report released. Defended generally by ACLU lawyers with little contact from gay rights organizations,[31] various military personnel with exemplary and long service records fought discharges in courts with increasing success. George Bush's Secretary of Defense, Richard Cheney, abandoned the traditional arguments about blackmail potential and unfitness to serve, leaving the fears of young straight military personnel and unwillingness to "condone sinfulness" as rationales for the expenses of ferreting out "homosexuals." As a presidential candidate, Bill Clinton said that he would sign an executive order similar to the one Harry Truman had signed to desegregate the armed forces. Immediately following his inauguration, President Clinton ordered military recruiters not to ask applicants or inductees about homosexuality. Opposition to lifting the ban on "homosexuals" in the military, especially from Sam Nunn (senator from Georgia, chair of the Senate Armed Services Committee), and from the

30. Jennes 1995. See also Herek and Berrill 1992.

31. M. Friedman (1993:35) contests this, pointing to the Human Rights Campaign Fund as a major culprit in usurping AIDS at the top of the gay agenda with "an issue which involves a few thousand people at most."

Chairman of the Joint Chiefs of Staff, General Colin Powell, led to a media circus in which the right to privacy—a right denied to civilian gay men by the Supreme Court's *Bowers v. Hardwick* decision—was extended to include a right to not be in the presence of lesbigay people for those in the all-volunteer American military, a locale heretofore notable for a lack of privacy and for a complete absence of concern for the privacy of its personnel.[32] Clinton's interim policy of "don't ask, don't tell, don't pursue" was reduced to what had been the de facto policy before, i.e., "Don't tell."[33] Challenges to both old and new policies (which on the ground appear to be the same: continued hot pursuit)[34] are moving through the courts. At this writing, courts have ordered branches of the military to reinstate challengers of both old and new regulations, but only one successful case (that of Perry Watkins, who had stated his homosexuality at the time of his first enlistment), has passed final (i.e., Supreme Court) review.

Although being known to be homosexual, not committing homosexual acts, has been the major target of the military all along, it was precisely young men and women who came to see themselves as gay and lesbian while in military service who pressed for acceptance as openly lesbigay, not those content to remain closeted. The Senate codified a view of gay or lesbian identity as evidencing "a propensity or intent to engage in homosexual acts" and as constituting "an unacceptable risk" to morale, discipline, and unit cohesion.[35]

The issue—especially the hysteria about sharing showers—was almost entirely about gay men, although women in the military have been more than twice as likely as men to be dismissed from service for homosexuality.[36] The Senate hearings in particular, and public discussion in general, excluded those knowledgeable about military homosexuality in history, American or foreign. The originally espoused goal of easing the implementation of lifting the ban was quickly abandoned. Gay and lesbian witnesses were excluded, and justifying continuation of a ban became the focus of the Senate hearings. Claims that straight men would stop enlisting or reenlisting were made by witnesses without any empirical data, while empirical data were ignored. With perhaps typical ignorance about (and contempt for?) the rest of the world, the "debate" covered by American news media and permitted by Sam

32. Dalton 1995.

33. Montini (1995) illustrates in a nonmilitary setting the variety of help offered by those who do not want to know in "repairing" and ignoring statements of lesbian identity before shunning those who recalcitrantly insist on it making it known. Not just in Islamic and Latino societies is there what I call a will not to know!

34. Miles 1995.

35. 1993 S. 1337, 546(a)15.

36. Enloe 1993:92.

Nunn before his committee was almost completely devoid of scrutiny of allied countries' experiences with accepting homosexual military personnel.[37]

For my present purposes, the eventual outcome is less important than noticing that a lesbigay issue unrelated to the continuing devastation of AIDS was raised to intense national discussion by lesbigays with no history of activism. Michelangelo Signorile's quip that people who were interested in military inclusion mostly had never protested before, while those who protested had little particular interest in the issue, has considerable truth. Those seeking to challenge the bases of society found their slogan "We're here, we're queer, get used to it" modified to demands for acceptance in straight institutions: "We're here, we're queer, we want to serve our country"[38] and "We're here, we're queer, we want to marry each other."

The other major lesbigay cause meeting with some success in courts (at least in Hawaii) is also one of inclusion in what an earlier gay liberationist considered another of the most oppressive of patriarchal institutions, marriage.[39] By legislative means, various jurisdictions have recognized "domestic partners" and some have extended benefits to "domestic partners" of government employees, as have some companies, while some northwestern European lawmakers and the Hungarian Constitutional Court have extended legal benefits of marriage to same-sex couples.

The gay liberationists of the early 1970s, and the queer nationists of the late 1980s, would have been hard pressed to name institutions they were less interested in joining and reforming from within than the military and matrimony,[40] but these have become the lesbigay priorities of the 1990s. Some see this as a wave of assimilationism, a hyperconformity going beyond dress (such as the recurrent insistence on "gender-appropriate" garb in marches). But others see renunciation of the privileges depending on "passing as what I'm not" on the part of those who not only could, but *did* "pass" and whose demand for acceptance challenges symbolic bastions of heterosexuality to acknowledge gay and lesbian personnel and relationships.

Based particularly on the research done by Laner and Laner (1979, 1980), in which lesbians and gay men who were not visibly gender-deviant were

37. Canada in 1991 and Australia in 1992 joined Israel, Japan, Austria, France, the Netherlands, Denmark, Sweden, and Spain in accepting *homosexuals* in their militaries (Enloe 1993: 280 n. 45).

38. Herrell 1993:1.

39. See, e.g., Wittman (1970:333) on mimicry of straight marriage as evidence of self-hatred. Cf. Sherman 1992, esp. pp. 13–26.

40. Adam (1987:162) presciently provided a less assimilationist framing for the latter: "An enduring issue will certainly be the battle for the right to love and live with the person of one's choice and to disestablish the state-supported patriarchal family."

more threatening to those most intolerant of homosexuality than were obvious "queens" and "bull-daggers," I suspect that conventional-appearing men and women demanding places in the military without disguising their sexual orientation are more threatening than lesbigay enclaves are. I would also infer from Laner and Laner that such persons are more likely to be the targets of violence even than obvious "sissies." When the place to be gay is Camp Pendleton rather than Greenwich Village or the Castro, challenges to the valuation of heterosexuality and to the equation of homosexuality with gender variance directly confront straight authorities and rank and file personnel. Not accepting the traditional assigned place (the closet and inferiority), those who reject the stereotypes and the status quo make themselves very visible targets. As Edmund White (1980:51) wrote, "Straights are amused by drag performers, but they are alarmed by more 'normal'-seeming gays"—and lesbians.

We will have to wait and see whether they will change the institutions, and whether the changes are more backlash than increased acceptance. While "we're the same as you" threatens some, the ardent embrace and eagerness to be a part of the military and marriage seem to many longtime activists to sustain two of the most patriarchal institutions of this society. Advocates counter that once lesbigays are included and accepted in the strongholds of heterosexual privilege, we cannot be excluded or rejected anywhere in the society. My own guess (which is based on European outcomes)[41] is that if the initiatives are successful, not much visibly will happen, i.e., relatively few military personnel will come out; relatively few same-sex marriages will occur. But I have no idea whether chances to test these surmises will arise. Mobilization against same-sex marriage and open lesbigays serving in the military are considerable and may well prevail in a politics in which rational analysis or comparative/historical evidence very rarely matter.

41. In that hysteria about homosexuality and mobilization for maintaining discrimination have been uniquely Anglo (American and British), one cannot generalize from Europe with much confidence, especially since a price of demanding acceptance for espousal of lesbigay identity has been that those who have chosen to put themselves on the line as test cases have had to refrain from homosexual sex. I have not seen challenges to military prohibitions of sodomy. Prohibiting both sodomy and discrimination based on sexual orientation, Massachusetts and the Roman Catholic Church provide (schizoid!) civilian "models" of "You can be gay/lesbian as long as you don't do anything."

2

Different Units
of Analysis

Six

"The Homosexual Role" and Lesbigay Roles

As originally conceived by social scientists, *role* contrasts with *self, identity, personnage*. In dramaturgical sociology, as on theater stages, an actor plays many roles over the course of a career, or even on a single night. Similarly, persons with varying degrees of commitment in appropriate settings and who play other roles at other times and places enact *homosexual roles*.

In the basic social science introduction to the concept, Ralph Linton (1936:113–14) defined *status* as "a collection of rights and duties," and a *role* as "the dynamic aspect of status, what the individual has to *do* in order to validate his occupation of the status" (emphasis added).[1]

Linton noted that each person in a society occupies more than one status and therefore plays multiple roles. Even on a stage with a predetermined script, there are complex characters, not just the stereotypical figures of allegories. Shylock and Othello, for example, balance multiple statuses. Everyday life does not come with playbills that list who is going to play what part(s), and it is also far less clear what status is relevant to the players. The salience of roles and status categories for ongoing, embodied social interaction or for self-conception is even less clear.[2] Moreover, even within functionalist role theory, Merton (1968:423) showed that a single status "involves, not a single role, but an array of associated roles": e.g., the "teacher" role in relation to students is not the same as the "teacher" role to administrators, to the PTA, etc. Thus, even in the relatively mechanistic functionalist conception of role, there are crosscutting simultaneous roles, not a one-to-one correspondence of a single overriding ("master") status to

---

1. Even before Cottrell (1942)—back in Linton's original formulation—role was envisioned as being enacted in behavior.

2. Rosenberg 1979:21.

a predetermined, wholly predictable, perfectly internalized role or sequence of roles.

In the Harvard wing of abstract microsociological theorizing (Parsons 1951:208–9), behavior flows from the internalization of norms appropriate to one's parents' social status. Secondary socialization outside the family refines role expectations and solidifies the child's personality structure— already formed, for Parsons, as for Freud and to a considerable extent for George Herbert Mead—by primary socialization in the family. Other sociologists have found this childhood determinism implausible or unpalatable. These include especially those who examine adults in new milieus.[3] Early on, the Columbia wing of American structural-functionalism recognized not just crosscutting roles, but overtly contradictory role expectations.[4]

Analysis of the enactment of shifting, overlapping, and multiple simultaneous statuses easily becomes very complex.[5] Sometimes, it seems that an abstract "situation" or organizational structure determines rather than constrains status presentation; at other times it seems that role theorists believe that any sort of role can be presented, i.e., that there are no constraints on what can be feigned in any interaction.[6] Phenomenological analysis can make the "local accomplishment" of even the simplest communication seem miraculous with or without invoking roles, or formal and informal codes of behavior demanded or expected of persons occupying particular statuses in a society. Perhaps even more confusingly, as Goodenough (1965) noted, use of the term "role" often drifts from this definition of enacted rights and obligations of a status to any and all kinds of statements about social categories, selves, and "personality structures." As Goffman (1961:143) complained,

> Much role analysis seems to assume that once one has selected a category of
> person and the context or sphere of life in which one wants to consider him,

3. E.g., Thomas and Znaniecki 1927; H. Becker et al. 1961; Zurcher 1970, 1977; R. Turner 1988. For direct critiques of oversocialized conceptions, see Wrong 1961 and Wentworth 1980.

4. E.g., Komarovsky 1946; W. Goode 1960.

5. The heuristic value of the concept "role" is vitiated by recognition that complete specification of appropriate behavior even for one role is probably impossible (Hilbert 1981). The difficulty of sorting out the various possibly relevant statuses even in a dyadic interaction is immense. Determining whether these statuses have enough salience for the interactants to justify a claim that they are enacting the rights or obligations of any particular role is very difficult.

6. Although Goffman (1961:101, 103, 143) stressed that commitment to and definition of roles vary from person to person, such criticism has frequently been leveled at his writing. Ralph Turner (1962 et seq.) circumscribed what can be constructed in formal organizations, especially military and bureaucratic settings, to such an extent that Hilbert (1981:209) argues his interactionist conception of "role" is not essentially different from the functionalist conception of Linton, with both "presuppos[ing] a standard of literal role conformity with which empirical behavior can be compared" and with both overeager to fill "self" with role expectations and performances.

there will then be some main role that will fully dominate his activity. Perhaps there are times when an individual does march up and down like a wooden soldier, tightly rolled up in a particular role. It is true that here and there we can pounce on a moment when an individual sits fully astride a single role, head erect, eyes front, but the next moment the picture is shattered into many pieces and the individual divides into different persons holding the ties of different spheres of life by his hands, by his teeth, and by his grimaces.[7]

"THE HOMOSEXUAL ROLE"

In the case of "homosexual role," discussion has gone as far as positing psychological entities apart from any interaction or audience. Some social scientists forget that "'role' makes sense only in the context of persons enacting reciprocal roles. . . . The actions of one participant in a social act are not organically separable from the actions of other participants" (Sarbin 1982: 24). As Turner (1962:28) said in the basic symbolic interactionist statement of role, it is by imputing motives to someone that her/his behaviors can be interpreted as reasonably plausible and consistent enactments of the rights and obligations of a status. An actor preparing a part for the stage may go over his or her lines alone, and only imagine how the audience will react or how the other players will deliver lines—with much greater certainty about what will follow than is available in everyday life. As is discussed further below, someone "rehearsing the homosexual role offstage" at least imagines what interaction might be like, how others playing heterosexual or homosexual roles might react to the behavior being fantasized or considered. It is at least conceivable that one can act alone, but role does not make any sense outside *inter*action—although the interaction may be imagined by the native of a culture, or abstracted as an "ideal type" by a social scientist, instead of being actual interaction. "Role" may not be either a necessary or a sufficient conception to explain behavior or the interpretation of behavior by interactants or by non-participant observers, but it has no chance of being a heuristic concept unless it is related to the behavior or expectations of persons other than the one said to be enacting a "role."

At least to those in the interactionist tradition that does not assume that

7. Yet he also wrote, "Personal qualities, effectively imputed and effectively claimed, combine with a position's title, when there is one, to provide a *self-image* for the incumbent and a basis for the image that his role others will have of him. A self, then, virtually awaits the individual entering a position; he need only conform to the pressure on him and he will find a *me* ready-made" (Goffman 1961:87–88). Cf. Rosenberg's more reflexive conception of "self" and interpretation of social labels (1979:xiv, 24): "The individual is indeed influenced by social forces, but not in the sense of being molded by them, but in the sense of responding, of dealing, of coping with them. . . . The individual is both subject and object."

norms and meanings are shared, enacting a role plausibly does not require role commitment. "Some roles are put on and taken off like clothing . . . [and even] identity can be strictly situational."[8] Roles are not just played. Some are "played at."[9] For some persons, homosexual intercourse may involve only an ephemeral role. As Zurcher (1970) showed, someone may play ephemeral roles recurrently over the course of many years. Despite the pressure to role commitment and to simplistic (essentialized) conceptions of roles,[10] as the grandfather of Symbolic Interactionism put it,

> We can carry on a whole series of different relationships to different people. We are one thing to one man and another thing to another. . . . We divide ourselves up in all sorts of different selves with reference to our acquaintances. . . . There are all sorts of different selves answering to all sorts of different social reactions. (Mead 1934:142)

Notwithstanding Mead's tendency (not least in this quotation) to organize all experience into a self, he also noted that "the body can be there and operate in a very intelligent fashion without there being a self involved in the experience" (pp. 135–36). In examining whether "role" is a useful conception of such interactional experience, I will bracket the question of a gay or homosexual self here. What such a self might be or mean is another vexed conceptualization.[11]

Mary McIntosh

Although McIntosh (1968:184) wrote that "sociologists should examine this process [labeling of "homosexuals"] objectively and not lend themselves to participation in it," in her oft-cited paper which consolidates Anglo-American societal stereotypes into a "theoretical construct," she reproduced a dichotomous homosexual/heterosexual categorization apart from any interaction. Neither for those who allegedly conceived this "homosexual role" in everyday life (heterosexual "natives" of Anglo cultures), nor for the sociolo-

8. Turner 1978:1–2.

9. Goffman 1961:99.

10. See Turner 1978. John Cheever (1991:344–47) provided an interesting example of seemingly internal pressure to define himself by homosexuality and the unthinkability of publicly declaring it, even after having given up an earlier resolve to "cure" himself of it rather than trying to change the world (p. 215; see also 171–72, 245–47). As one fictional alter ego says, "If I should have to declare myself a homosexual it would be the end of my life" (1982:53; see 1991: 144, 181, 216, 257, 289, 364, 374–77).

11. I find heuristic Ewing's formulation (1990:69) that "our various self-representations constitute a repertoire of possibilities organized into response structures," just as even a monolingual can shift styles and others can shift languages (often feeling like a different person in each language).

gist analyst (McIntosh herself), were the contents (behaviors or expectations) of this role based on empirical contact of any sort with those purportedly playing the role, although McIntosh's stated aim in "propos[ing] that the homosexual should be seen as playing a social role" was "to handle behavior [that] does not match popular beliefs" (p. 184). McIntosh's "homosexual role" is devoid of all the subtle multiplicities of situated meanings of "role" as used by Linton, Merton, Turner, or Goodenough (none of whose readily available writings she cited).

McIntosh's "homosexual role" is a functionalist, not an interactionist construct,[12] a bogeyman used to scare boys away from homosexuality and thus to reinforce the superiority of a heterosexual social order.[13] In common with most functionalist sociologists, McIntosh—citing Talcott Parsons on acceptance of societal norms by "deviants"—presumes a single moral community. For functionalists, rather than being negotiated in actual interaction, roles are "part of the categorical system of a society, the socially recognized and meaningful categories of persons, the kinds of people it is possible to be in that society" (Cohen 1965:12). Functionalists treat the set of roles in a society as relatively static and conceive the individual as searching for his or her appropriate role, which eventually will be integrated into self-conception, the individual-level equilibrium to which functionalist theorizing tends. For symbolic interactionists, in contrast to functionalists,

> (1) The role is regarded not as a cultural given, but as a product of a social interactional process and as a matter for subjective interpretation and definition. (2) The emphasis is placed upon the function of role in facilitating interaction between persons, or of offering lines of action in situations where the cultural requirements of behavior are not fully specified. (Miyamoto 1963:119; also see Sarbin 1982)

The kind of role McIntosh (1968) described, Harry (1987) calls a *gender anti-schema*. I would call it a "bogeyman-woman." Why anyone would enact such a role is unclear, for "one needs to see oneself as approvable in the eyes of some significant others."[14] McIntosh did not suggest who the significant

---

12. Although McIntosh's paper had no discernible influence on the study of lesbigay lifeways and emerging communities during the 1970s, it has been represented as foundational by those seeking an earlier Anglophone and/or female alternative to Foucault as a charter for constructionism (badly as her discussion of the mollies fits with there being no conception of homosexual types separate from particular acts prior to medical discourse created *the homosexual*). The functionalism has been ignored, and it has been assumed that she, like her Essex colleague Ken Plummer, was applying labeling theory (e.g., by Epstein 1994:191).

13. See the discussion of functionalism in chapter 1.

14. Miyamoto 1973:281.

others might be for those playing "the homosexual role," or who is expected to approve the behavior of enacting the expectations of this role. What those enacting a (the?) heterosexual role expect from those playing "the homosexual role," according to McIntosh (1968:184–85), are exhibition of (1) effeminacy, (2) more or less exclusive homosexual feelings and behavior, (3) attraction to and (4) attempted seduction of all young men, or, perhaps of all men ("sexuality will play a part of some kind in all his relations with other men"). She did not mention where, when, or whether someone playing her version of "the homosexual role" has a *right* to act effeminately and to seduce men and/or boys. Implicitly, this un-male "role" was enacted to/for a heterosexual male other.

As noted in chapter 1, in some other cultures with a gender-crossing societal conception of homosexuality, blatantly effeminate homosexual men could be tolerated, because such persons provided vivid warnings of what boys must avoid becoming. According to Levy (1973), there was only one *mahu* per Tahitian village. They did not meet other *mahus* and therefore could not learn the gender-mixing role from other occupants of the role. In traditional Tahiti, the *mahu* did have a right to act effeminately and to seduce men and/or boys, without risking the violence that is often a consequence of attempting to enact "the homosexual role" with males enacting "the heterosexual role" in Anglo-American societies. There is a sense in which these roles were complementary and even approved in Tahiti that is little evident in Anglo-American societies.[15]

Although, as Whitam (1977) noted, McIntosh's treatment of roles "violates the prevailing definition and conventional usage of this concept in sociology," there are homosexual roles to analyze apart from the monster of the heterosexual imagination conjured by McIntosh. Within homosexual interactions and relationships, complementary roles exist. For instance, mentor/initiate or sodomite/catamite occur where age differences structure homosexual relations; hustler/trick or patron/protégé in class societies, especially where there are "homosexual occupations" such as dancing boys; trade/queer, *hombre/maricón*, or brave/berdache where gender distinctiveness organizes homosexual relations.[16] I have listed each of these pairs in insertor/insertee order, although sexual behavior is only one aspect of these roles. A person may play one or more of these roles while conceiving of the self as heterosexual, without any strong commitment to or preference for homosexuality.

15. Recall the lack of payoff for the "queers" in Reiss 1961 from chapter 1.
16. On the recurrent types of organizing homosexuality see Murray 1984:45–54, and the introduction to 1992a.

ROLE DISTANCE

"Role distancing involves an active and self-conscious attempt to foster the impression of a lack of commitment or attachment to a particular role in order to deny the virtual self implied" for various stigmatized categories,[17] especially when imputations based on appearance, behavior, or location are incongruent with self-identity and/or are socially disvalued.

An individual's "role distance" (intrapsychic non-reification of a social role into a self or a component of a self) actually may facilitate plausible performance, whereas totally embracing a role lands a person in the realm of psychopathology.[18] Moreover, strain between the demands of one's roles is "normal: in general the individual's total role obligations are over-demanding" as well as incompatible, as William Goode (1960:485) wrote. People routinely manage complex repertoires of distinct roles without inordinate stress, especially if they compartmentalize roles and/or are rewarded in the settings in which they play different ones.[19] Indeed, some homosexual roles may not require even feigned homosexual desire. Affectation of indifference may be an eroticized part of the hustler role, quite apart from any ambivalence or attempts to maintain role distance to preserve a non-homosexual self-conception. The role obligation for a hustler at work to appear indifferent should be separated from denial of a homosexual self-identity.[20] For estimating the latter, patterns of association provide better indicators than verbalizations on this particular stage.

Routine accounts disavow responsibility for any choice of a same-sex partner, and/or devalue the behavior as unimportant, atypical, not the person's preference, not the basis for one's identity, and so on—not just for hustlers, but for many persons who engage in homosexual behavior. Hencken (1984:55) listed some of these accounts offered both by persons who later identified themselves and their earlier discounted behavior as "really gay" as well as by those who dropped homosexual behavior from their repertoire (for whom "there is rarely any external pressure to think about it, and there is usually internal pressure not to"), or who continue to have homosexual encounters that "don't really count":

1. Boy was I drunk (and I don't remember what happened very well or at all . . .).

17. Snow and Anderson 1987:1350.
18. Goffman 1961.
19. Sieber 1974; Marks 1987.
20. The ideal norm for the ancient Greek boy beloved similarly proscribed any registering of desire or pleasure. Complaints of boys' infidelity (e.g., by Theognis) suggest that boys were not so uninterested as they were supposed to be. See Murray 1991b.

2. It's just physical release/getting off with what was available when I was horny. It was the only game in town . . .
3. I was just curious/experimenting. It was just a phase.
4. Variety is the spice of life.
5. I was seduced.
6. I didn't really like it. I just let him/her . . .
7. We were just friends (and I didn't know it "counted" as "sex.").

Especially those who used one or more of these discounting accounts before identifying as gay or lesbian view them very skeptically. However, the accounts have sufficient plausibility, necessity, or legitimacy to persist from generation to generation.[21] Unchallenged—as they are likely to be if they are offered to spouses or friends who do not want to believe the person "could be gay" rather than to skeptical lesbigay-identified audiences—these accounts have a social reality in explaining away even overt, public, insertee sexual behavior.

UNLEARNING "THE HOMOSEXUAL ROLE"; LEARNING ABOUT LESBIGAY ROLES

Novices learn how to perform the sexual and other rights and obligations of homosexual roles in a variety of different situations. Boys and girls learn how to be "homosexuals" directly in primary socialization with one's natal family even less than they learn how to be a husband or a wife. One may learn *about* such roles, i.e., learn the cultural script for each. Boys may learn about "the male role" without male role models, just as they may learn about "queers" without seeing any. Similarly, girls may hear about "dykes." Learning about a "homosexual role" of the sort McIntosh portrayed may motivate the suppression of homosexual desires. It may also motivate acting out exaggerated cross-gender behavior before realizing that such behavior is not a necessary adjunct to homosexuality within gay or lesbian worlds.[22] Gagnon and Simon (1973: 147–49) and Erich Goode (1981) alluded to a transient stage of enacting effeminacy in the process of coming out, before novices to gay male scenes distinguish societal expectations of effeminacy from actual gay cul-

21. It is difficult to believe that these recurring accounts are transmitted within the very subculture with which the individuals are seeking to avoid contact and identification.

22. Betty in Faderman 1991b:128 provided a corrective to Faderman's view that discourse about psychopathology inspired emulation: "I didn't think that what I'd read in an abnormal psych text applied to us in any way." Also see Vicinus 1992, and, on emerging political consciousness, Esterberg 1994 and Weitz 1984.

tural expectations.[23] Chauncey (1994:102) documented a decline in this necessity in New York City in the early years of the twentieth century, reminds readers that many could turn the mannerisms off and on as easily as they could change clothes (p. 56), and that the feminine figure such men cut was modeled after prostitutes whose appearance also advertises sexual availability (pp. 61, 83). Wanting to attract a man is not the same as wanting to be a woman.[24]

Similarly, a butch phase may have made a woman's sexual interest in other women visible, rather than indicating any deep-seated need to be manlike. As Marisa recalls in Moraga 1984:13–14), "I never wanted to be a man, I only wanted a woman to want me that bad."[25] In Thailand and Mesoamerica, getting the attention of male sexual partners remains a motivation for some men to appear and act flamboyantly feminine,[26] and Thongthiraj (1994) described a somewhat analogous contemporary Thai situation in which the appearance of the butch *tam* (from tomboy) woman cues femme *dees* (from ladies) who make the approaches.

Nevertheless, many persons who were committed to same-sex relations and relationships before the challenge to cross-gender role-playing either did *not* pass through a cross-gender stage or have repressed any memory of it. None of the men born between 1895 and 1930 interviewed by Vacha (1985) reported a "femme phase" within homosexual subcultures. Instead, those who became involved in the pre–gay liberation subculture categorized their initial roles as *trade, gay trade, butch,* and one *boy dyke.* Only one of 23 self-identified gay men born between 1910 and 1930 whom I interviewed in 1980

23. Philip Gefter provides a good example in both his own recollection and Neil Alan Marks's generalization (in Denneny 1979:34, 110). Some men never make this distinction (see Sullivan 1990). Also, insofar as there is a phase or stage of flamboyant gender deviance (in either the masculine or feminine direction), there are no clear graduation rites and far less certain graduation from "bottom" to "top" than in cultures in which the sexual receptive role is age-graded (Brodsky 1993a). On gay hypermasculine self-presentation, also see Levine 1986, Humphries 1985, and Connell 1992.

24. McIntosh (1993:43) continues to miss this and to confuse displays intended to obtain access to a male sexual partner with deep-seated (essential) desire, claiming that homosexual men "wanted to be desired and courted as a woman is—by a man."

25. See Gagnon and Simon 1973:198; Kennedy and Davis 1993:203; and Newton 1984 on an ultra-butch phase for lesbians coming out.

26. Murray 1992b, 1995a; Morris 1994; Carrier 1995. The need to be visible to prospective partners (by which I do not mean only sexual liaisons), more than any sense of being "a woman trapped in a man's body," may account for the flamboyantly unmasculine dress of homosexual prostitute roles such as the Omani *khanith* and the South Asian *hijra*, for both of whom homosexual desire seems more compelling than gender (Wikan 1977, 1982:172–73; Nanda 1990; see Roscoe 1991b:121; Murray 1996).

reported coming into the gay world as a "femme."[27] Four had longstanding homosexual relationships without any subcultural contact predating the Second World War. Those who had regular sexual partners before knowing about a gay world continue to be unlikely to go through an extreme gender-nonconformity phase when coming out.

Another way of acting out the fervor of recent conversion to affirming a gay or lesbian identity is a phase of sexual hyperactivity.[28] A phase of intensive sexual acting out seems to me more common than a phase of heightened cross-gender acting out. I suspect that the increasing visibility of lesbians and gay men who do not differ from conventional gender expectations has decreased the frequency of gender acting out, and that the "promiscuity" framing of AIDS may have reduced sexual experimentation phases.[29] Clearly some coming-out youths continue to go through such phases, and the evidence for shifts is very tenuous impressions. I do not know of anyone who has collected longitudinal data on frequency of sex or the number of partners of those coming out, let alone related these to rejection by significant others, to preconceptions of what being gay or lesbian means, or to later conceptions.[30]

Grube (1987, 1990) described an age-graded system of homosexual relations dominant in the 1950s and 1960s in which the young initiate, usually living at home, would "let down his hair"/"camp it up" in private gay networks, and often "submitted sexually to older men to gain entrance to the underground gay world" with the expectation of later graduating to molding and sexually using subsequent generations of young men seeking entrée into a secret gay world. As one of Grube's informants recalled, his mentor "had a nice manner of explaining things to me, and once when I said to him, 'You know, I don't know how to thank you for what you do for me!,' he said, 'You pass it on, that's your obligation.'" Leznoff (1954:97–106) described a not particularly affluent "queen," resented by some for "sell[ing] people to each other" (p. 103), but whose sponsorship of safe parties and liaisons was ap-

27. Some did mention taking greater care with grooming than was normative for men at the time. These data may suffer from retrospective distortion, and from changes in societal markers of gender since then. Documents generated at the time may become available, though routine destruction of them continues.

28. See, for instance, Hippler 1989:87; Harry and Devall (1978b:150) suggested that a phase of ghetto involvement lasts less than five years. See also Sable 1979:17.

29. That it only increases fatalism is a distinct possibility.

30. Vincke et al. (1993) found that disapproval by significant others of being gay was associated (to a statistically significant degree) with more frequent receptive anal intercourse without condoms. They drew the practical conclusion that to increase condom use among gay men who are in the process of coming out requires acceptance and support from those with whom they feel close.

preciated by others. Mary McIntosh (personal communication, 1989) and many older gay men have told me that in days of old, novices were sponsored and "brought into" gay circles, rather than finding public spaces and "coming out" on their own.

The opening of the gay world in the 1970s and the ease of coupling with agemates who could be met in public places disrupted this role succession, depriving men who had "paid their dues" of their anticipated opportunities—for sex and for deference. Of course, many older men lamented this. The common attitude is that "everyone should go through what we went through"—to earn the right to be gay, or to attain other relatively privileged adult statuses.

Generally, anticipatory socialization is incomplete and either ambiguous or stereotyped. Even what is recognizably training for a role may also be quite discontinuous.[31] Moreover, as Thornton and Nardi (1975:875) noted, anticipatory socialization "helps only to the extent it is accurate. . . . If it is not accurate, it may actually impede adjustment, for performing the acquired role will necessitate unlearning as well as further learning." When it fails as a deterrent, anticipatory socialization into the societal gender-deviant stereotype may be an impediment within gay or lesbian communities.[32]

An unstudied empirical question is whether neophytes directly learn stigmatized roles about which they are likely to be ambivalent.[33] The extent of copying specific known others or of acting out societal expectations in early encounters in homosexual careers (both of those who become committed to homosexual roles and of those who, despite recurrent homosexual sexual encounters, do not) deserves study, especially for the generation(s) coming out since the era of public gay affirmation. Before it, there were couples in enduring relationships who did not have contact with gay worlds and did not need to find a succession of short-term sexual partners by hyperstereotypical gender displays. I doubt that such isolated pairs have ceased to exist.

Children in many societies (including Thailand, the U.S., Mexico, and

31. R. Turner 1978:12.

32. As advertising for same-sex sexual partners it may be effective, especially at the high school level.

33. Heiss (1981:105) asserts that in Anglo-American culture, "Non-interactive forms of anticipatory socialization are not conducive to adequate role acquisition. . . . Attention, coding and rehearsal are likely to be quite low." Many lesbians and gay men recollect being very attentive—indeed, searching out information in the absence of role models. In other cultures, notably Native American ones (Darnell 1981; Basso 1981; Scollon and Scollon 1982)—in which noninteractive socialization is the major means of socialization—attention, coding, and rehearsal are quite high.

Canada) learn about the equation of homosexuality with gender deviance in early socialization—often in warnings and scoldings. "Learning about" may heavily condition initial attempts to do what (one thinks) is expected of a sexual partner (husband, wife, or homosexual), but there is also secondary socialization on-stage in the role, as well as intrapsychic rehearsal for playing it. Divergent individual meaning generated within interaction (sexual or otherwise) is always possible:

> Individuals sexually acting in virtually identical ways may, in fact be doing so for different reasons, in pursuit of different configurations of desire, and, as a consequence, find themselves experiencing that event in different ways. . . . Even to oneself, behavior is often not a fact but a sign, often an enigmatic sign. (Simon 1994:2; see the discounting accounts—the seven "excuses"—listed above)

Gender roles (how to act masculine or feminine) are central to primary socialization in North America, among other places. The roles enacted in heterosexual marriage, as well as those enacted in gay subcultures, are part of later learning/socialization, however. For decades, a key part of secondary socialization within gay and lesbian communities has been breaking the popularly supposed link between homosexuality and gender deviance.[34] Neophytes tend to rigidly (ritualistically) play their preconceptions of a role.[35] As already discussed, persons who decide they are gay or lesbian without having directly observed gay or lesbian people are more likely be guided by societal stereotypes, akin to McIntosh's "homosexual role," than those who have been exposed to openly gay or lesbian role models. Those without such role models are less likely than those with them to recognize that role expectations vary with situations, or that different persons have different definitions of "the same" situation.

Hyperconformity to perceived distinctiveness is a common part of a conversion experience when living the new role is taken seriously as a defining attribute (master identity).[36] Converts to anything are notorious for their zeal. Both adolescents coming to terms with gay feelings and married adults who decide to come out tend to act "gayer" or "dykier"—along whatever dimensions they consider distinctive—than gay people who have settled in and take being gay for granted. As Brian Miller (1987:184), who studied the essentializing of homosexual roles previously played with considerable role distance remarked, "The process of gaining a new identity seems to necessi-

---

34. Fein and Nuehring 1981.
35. Goffman 1961:130, 152.
36. See E. Hughes 1945.

tate 'going overboard.'" Although I think "necessitate" is too strong, at least a period of intense commitment or of considerable acting out is common.

Without experience within a lesbigay world, one is unlikely to know how to relate to other lesbigay people, except sexually.

> Gay husbands and fathers often report awkwardness in approaching and conversing with other gays, because they feel deficient in gay social skills. . . . [Having] perceived other gays as merely sex objects, . . . finding new friends in the gay world may require new social approaches and techniques . . . [and many] report a dissonance between the newly encountered realities of the gay world and the fantasies that enticed and sustained them during the marital conflict and divorce. (Miller 1987:185)

Within gay or lesbian communities or networks, one unlearns the requirements of the "queer" or "dyke" role, at least as conceived in the dominant society, and learns what others involved in homosexual scenarios really expect. This generally differs substantially from what individuals with little or no experience of openly lesbigay people or of lesbigay media imagine will be expected of them.[37] In North America, many of those who find their way to urban gay communities find out that gender variance is not requisite and indeed is stigmatized by many within the communities.[38] This was already so in the 1920s and 1930s in New York City.[39] In recent years, exaggeration of the socially appropriate gender has also occurred, with "lipstick lesbians" and gay male "clones," and a phase of testing hypermasculinity has been central to socialization into some gay male worlds (as discussed in chapter 3).

The traditional phase of cross-gender role exaggeration may be attenuated for those growing up with homosexual desires who can see positive representations of lesbians or gay men who do not act or appear crossgendered. Still, the trend in the U.S. toward greater tolerance for homosexuality should not be overemphasized. Even the young who find their way to the combination therapy group and lesbigay finishing school of Horizons (in Chicago, described by Herdt and Boxer 1993), begin with some of the dev-

---

37. I do not mean to imply that societal stereotypes are never eroticized, or otherwise unconsciously maintained (see chapter 3; Brodsky 1993a; B. Miller 1978, 1983, 1987:185; Klein 1989; Nestle 1987; Kennedy and Davis 1993). For an example of the realization that lesbians and gay women were not all "obvious," see Lorde 1982:160–62. I am not convinced that what Paul Monette (1992:1) called "imprisonment [in] the self-delusion of uniqueness" has ended. More representations are available, but "I can't be like that" remains a reaction to some of the most pervasive ones. In particular, the equations of homosexuality with effeminacy or with isolation remain robust.

38. Gagnon and Simon 1973:147–49, 152.

39. Chauncey 1994:102.

astating old patterns of believing "I'm the only one who feels like this."[40] Sears (1991) and Zeeland (1993) attest that some members of the same generation still act out "if I'm gay/lesbian I have to be gender-deviant," and "'faggot' remains the most humiliating insult a male teenager can give another."[41] Rap performer Milk "says that on the street 'faggot' is a major 'dis'—a term of disrespect—but it's generic, not always a reference to sexual preference."[42] Escalating levels of violence involved in fag-bashing also indicate something less than sexual or gender pluralism among the young of the post-feminist, post–gay liberation 1980s.[43]

Thornton and Nardi (1975) distinguish formal, informal, and personal stages of role-taking after anticipatory socialization. For homosexual roles, a "formal stage" with the presupposition of "incumbency" does not seem heuristic. For "the homosexual role," a neophyte stage such as that suggested by Troiden and Goode (1980) precedes the "informal" stage in which the person discovers that one does not have to act and appear effeminate in order to engage in homosexuality, i.e., that there are homosexual roles, not just the "queer" or "butch" role he or she has been acting.

In Thornton and Nardi's "informal" stage, one learns what those playing a role may do. This may supplement or supplant expectations about what playing the role requires. If testing the limits reveals a role with which the person is comfortable, self–role congruence may occur.[44] If the obligations seem too great for too few rights and gains,[45] the individual may enact the role perfunctorily, or not at all. Also, disengagement from a role can occur at any of the stages.

"Fixation" also may occur. Thus, despite the disparity of "the homosexual role" and lesbian and gay roles, some persons never test the limits of "the homosexual role" and continue (regularly or intermittently) ritualistically acting out societal or group expectations without discovering possible variability. For instance, like the traditional Tahitian *mahu*, the classical

40. See also discussions by Monteagudo (1986), Bergman (1991:7), Preston (1993b:30, 117, 192–93), Plummer (1995:7, 85), and Del Martin and Barbara Gittings (in Tobin and Wicker 1972:49, 207–8) of the quest in books for evidence that others "like me" exist, given the lack of personal contact or publicly acknowledged role models. "A. Nolder Gay" (1978:20) recalled that his "homophile consciousness was formed primarily in the [library] stacks, not in the streets, much less in the sheets" (see pp. 9, 18 on the discouragement from psychiatric texts, paralleled by Delaney and Beam 1986:196).

41. Alonzo 1983:20; see also Louganis 1995:75; Fine 1987.

42. Block 1990:6.

43. Harry 1982a; Comstock 1989, 1991; Nardi and Bolton 1991; Herek and Berrill 1992.

44. Sarbin and Allen 1968:524.

45. In the view of Sarbin and Allen (1968), perceived incongruity of role and self is a particularly major hurdle.

"town queer," who lacks any contact with others enacting "queer" or gay roles either within the same town or elsewhere, provides sexual "service" to males who do not consider receiving blow jobs as implicating them in homosexuality. Such socially isolated homosexuality occurs, although mass media make it increasingly difficult to maintain ignorance either of the existence of gay men or of the societal view that any homosexual behavior (insertor as well as insertee) implies a homosexual self—and therefore compromises/ threatens other self-images, even if no one else knows about it.

Conclusion

Homosexuality is more polyvalent than either realists or nominalists (particularly special creationists) suppose. There is a variety of homosexual roles in a single society, and only a limited number of roles have been attested in the societies about which there are records. There is homosexuality outside the subcultures, outside and/or against the cultural scripts for who should play homosexual roles how. As the architects of "sexual script theory" recognized, "Even in the seemingly most traditional social settings, cultural scenarios are rarely entirely predictive of actual behavior."[46] Actors who merely read lines without interpreting their roles are not very interesting or convincing under prosceniums or on "the stage of life." Those who write stage plays find their lines changed, rearranged, and performed in unexpected ways, so it should not be surprising that unwritten sexual scripts are not mindlessly performed the same way by everyone who enacts them. There is neither total consensus nor invariant intensity of commitment to any role in any society.[47] Especially those who play a role badly and/or disvalue it are unlikely to merge role and self.[48]

Not just in "postmodern" states does "the necessity for creating interpersonal scripts transform the social actor from being exclusively an actor trained in his or her role(s) and add[s] to his/her burden the task of being a partial scriptwriter or adaptor . . . of relevant cultural scenarios into scripts for context-specific behavior" and for the achievement of intrapsychic meanings.[49] This does not lead to the inchoate flux of sexual possibility yearned for by creationists and other "queer theorists," because "deviations from prevailing cultural scenarios tend to be limited to a universe largely created

46. Simon and Gagnon 1986:98.
47. Miyamoto 1963:121.
48. R. Turner 1978.
49. Simon and Gagnon 1986:99. Cf. Shibutani 1961:116–17. Sarbin (1982:32) contrasts dramaturgical roles, which the actors improvise, from dramatistic roles, in which "the identity of the playwright is lost in antiquity." However, his model of role transition seems to me still to assume eventual role–self merger.

by such cultural scenarios,"[50] and because there are norms and attempts to regulate sexuality in all societies. Even with their Durkheimian stress that society pre-exists any particular interaction, Simon and Gagnon's "script theory" leaves considerable latitude for generating, as well as replicating, meaning in and from sexual behaviors that are diverse but very limited in number. There is not a monolithic, homogeneous, static, closed gay world. There is intracultural variance,[51] and even those for whom being lesbian or gay or queer is the most salient part of their self-identity may differ in their understanding of "lesbianness" or "gayness"/"queerness," in their expectations of other participants in lesbigay worlds, and in their overlapping but not identical social networks.

Role–self merger is not inevitable. There is certainly pressure to crystallize roles into predictable, more or less permanent consistency. Since lesbian identity and community are more tenuously established than gay male identity and community, pressure for commitment appears greater from lesbians.[52] The pressure on others to "choose" (fit into a role) seems stronger among women than among men, even though (or because?) lesbian (and "queer") women tend to be less certain than gay men that their identity is "natural."[53] Vera Whisman (personal communication, 16 Dec. 1994) suggested that "perhaps lesbians are more inclined to believe bisexuality exists although one should not act upon it, while gay men doubt that one's deepest desires can truly be bisexual but tolerate those who wish to behave as though they are."

Whether or not one achieves the "final stage" of self–role merger,[54] indi-

50. Simon and Gagnon 1986:106.

51. Having demonstrated marked intracultural personality variation (Wallace 1952a,b), Wallace (1956, 1961) explained that complementary understandings rather than shared meanings make interaction possible. Interactant A may assume that interactant B interprets A's conduct in the same way A does, but, unless the two understandings are expressed, neither interactant may realize they do not share the other's interpretation. Even when one interpretation leads to expectations which are not met, the clash of perspectives may still not be recognized by the interactants. Apparently independently of this very famous work in psychological anthropology, Turner (1988:4) concluded, "Conformity is merely a special way of achieving the more fundamental interactive condition of predictability."

52. Ponse 1978:107–8, 132; Wolf 1979; S. Krieger 1983; Fuss 1989; Silber 1990; Rust 1992, 1993a,b; Ault 1994; etc.

53. Murray and Montini 1994; Whisman 1993.

54. See R. Turner (1978) on identity essentialization reinforced by a reference group. Turner is careful to consider variable role commitment/identity merger—indeed, predicting variance is the problematic of his paper. Nonetheless, there is a strong functionalist strain in social psychology to presume common definition of a situation and of the identity of interactants (e.g. Blumstein 1973:347), integration of roles into "personality structure" (e.g. Spiro 1973: 282), a quest to reduce role strain (W. Goode 1960:483; Sarbin 1982:30), and general underestimation of the possibilities of individual meaning underlying role enactment. Among the theor-

vidual conception of any role is possible: the process of role acquisition is not mere training in enacting pre-existing expectations of fixed roles. Conceptions of what homosexual roles require vary—historically, situationally, and from person to person.

"HOMOSEXUAL OCCUPATIONS"

In particular, the occupational requirements Whitam and Mathy (1986) posited are only the destiny of those who define themselves by homosexual desire and have not glimpsed other ways of being homosexual than societal expectations of effeminacy in some societies. Concentrations of men involved in homosexual activities in some occupations is indisputable. However, if there is a biologically based drive to become a waiter or a hairdresser linked to or part of the posited gene for homosexuality, one wonders how the proponents of the theory managed to become sociology professors![55]

Recourse to genetics or even to "gay sensibility" is not needed to explain homosexual concentrations in occupational slots. This is especially so for occupations in which few succeed in securing an income with which to support a family, especially the performing arts.[56] In most places the prototypically masculine occupation of construction worker requires knowing someone to get him into the union or hired by a patron (foreman or employer) at a non-unionized site. Obtaining a position in what hairdressers consider a good salon similarly depends upon personal sponsorship from inside. In any field, there is routine insider trading of information about job vacancies and even secrecy about them.[57] Therefore, any concentration (of any category of employees) is likely to be replicated or reinforced over time. That is, getting jobs for those one knows best, are most like one, and with whom one most wants to work is a common motivation. Those who possess job information transmit it first to their intimates. Moreover, they are likely to "put in a good word" for them as well.[58]

---

ists drawn from in this chapter, Shibutani (1961:116–17), Miyamoto (1963), Thornton and Nardi (1975), R. Turner (1978:12–13), Heiss (1981), Simon and Gagnon (1986), and Snow and Anderson (1987:1347, 1366–67) all attempt to reserve some conceptual space for varying intrapsychic meaning.

55. See Murray (1991c), a challenge to Whitam's claims and explanations with data from Mesoamerica, one of his research sites. The following two paragraphs derive from that article. An early (1930s) study of a network of Salt Lake City lesbians discussed by Bullough and Bullough (1977:899) reported only 16% doing what was conceived as "men's work."

56. Ashworth and Walker 1972.

57. Spector 1973.

58. Granovetter 1974; Murray, Rankin, and Magill 1981; Wegener 1989, 1991.

There is also discrimination against persons viewed as homosexual and/or gender-deviant.[59] Havens or niches developing over time need not reflect genetically intrinsic occupational correlates of homosexuality, as Whitam and Mathy (1986) suppose.[60] They are aware that not everyone secures the kind of job s/he wants, noting "Some ambitions, given the nature of the economic, educational, and stratification structures of these countries, are unlikely to be fulfilled" (p. 88). Some ambitions, childhood or adult, are more impossible than others. There is certainly no reason to suppose that discrimination against those known as homosexuals is invariant from occupation to occupation, firm to firm, or workplace to workplace within a company. Similarly, there is no reason to suppose that information about job openings spreads randomly. Specific concentration in service sectors may also stem from more meritocratic (i. e., less paternalistic) evaluation of candidates than in other occupational sectors.

THE ULTIMATE REDUCTION

There are certainly occasions in which one person ignores the complexity and individuality of others, reducing the other to a social category with no interest in whether the other person conceives of him/herself as an instance of that category. The prototypical example is a violent reaction to "the enemy" recognized at a distance by their uniform or skin color. Presumptive identification of "fags" by "fag bashers" also fits this pattern, and the danger of violent attack constrains public display of homosexual affection as well as avoidance of locales "fags" frequent. "Fag bashers" don't stop to make inquiries about the sexual orientation of those they find, and stereotypical conceptions of "fags" have very real social consequences for men in public unaccompanied by women, especially at night, especially in certain locales. This not unimportant kind of categorization has little or nothing to do with learning to perform the role of a stigmatized social category competently, and does not require so complex a conception as "role."

59. See A. P. Bell and Weinberg 1978; Levine 1979a; Adam 1981; Levine and Leonard 1984; Schneider 1987.

60. Even were one to take Whitam and Mathy's childhood recollection data (1986:101; see also Whitam and Dizon 1979:141–47) as free of retrospective bias and knowledge of social stereotypes (especially by those reporting themselves to be heterosexual) and as a valid indicator of something important to adult occupation, a "universal" drive to be a hairdresser seems to vary substantially among their transvestitic homosexuals—from 22% in Phoenix to 80% in Cebu.

APPENDIX: A NOTE ON A PURPORTED "THIRD-GENDER" ABORIGINAL ROLE

An indigenous liminal/sacralized "third gender" role that used to be called *berdache* (derived from the Persian *bardag*) is now called 'two spirit' in an ongoing attempt (already manifest in W. Williams 1986 and Roscoe 1988b) to shift the emphasis from homosexuality to spirituality.[61] From the seventeenth century into the late twentieth century, observers of European derivation applied the label *berdache* not only to Native North and South Americans but to Polynesians, generally conflating—or at least not distinguishing—sex, gender, and sexuality.[62] In recent decades, many North American and other social scientists have been careful to distinguish these aspects.[63] Those identifying themselves as lesbian or gay in a range of cultures have challenged any necessary connection between sexuality and gender, so that a woman whose primary emotional and sexual relationships with women may be both female and female-identified, and a man who loves men may be both masculine and male-identified. A vast literature has grown on the cultural achievement of masculinity in a range of cultures,[64] along with a smaller one on femininity.[65] Those working with records of cultures that have been destroyed or significantly disrupted by colonial and neocolonial penetration and domination have had to try to interpret whether earlier writers were describing variances from the observers' dichotomous conception of gender, sex, or sexuality; or native, possibly multiple, categories of gender, sex, or sexuality.[66] Seemingly, very little thought has been given to what should be the prior question of whether such division into distinct domains (of sex, sexuality, gender, economics, medicine, religion, and more) is universal—or generally salient to those in even one culture.

61. For the most nuanced contemporary attempts to sort out the components of the historical roles in societies in what is now the southwestern United States, see Roscoe 1991a, 1994, 1995b. The currently faddish "two spirits" fits the phenomenon back into an at least implicit dichotomy of "one-spirited" in contrast to "two-spirited."

62. See Murray 1987b:145–47, 159–64; 1992a:185–89, 249–56.

63. Rubin (1975) proposed a "sex/gender system" to overcome structuralist and Freudian dualisms. She later (Rubin 1982, 1984) faulted her earlier, widely influential model for failing to account for homosexuality. Herdt (1994:47) asserted that "sexual orientation and identity are not the keys to conceptualizing a third sex and gender across time and space," but neglected to mention whether there are keys, and if so, what they are; or to identify the "clear examples" of third gender that he claims (on p. 51) "are found."

64. E.g., Fine 1987; Gilmore 1990; Herdt 1982.

65. E.g., Bernard 1981; Dalby 1983; Breines 1992; Murray 1992a:120–2, 133–35; Thorne 1993.

66. The most heroic attempt is that of Greenberg 1988.

Fulton and Anderson (1992:607) are among those who have interpreted the old records as confused attempts to describe "a distinct gender—one separate from 'male' and 'female.'" On the way to this conclusion, they made the very peculiar claim that *man* and *woman* are "the only words earlier writers had at their disposal for describing gender," as if *male* and *female* (the usual terms for sex in English), or *masculine, feminine,* and *effeminate* (the usual terms for gender in English), or *butch* and *femme* (common terms for gender among lesbians and gay men) were coined only recently. Murray 1992a:151–63 includes a number of application of these terms (except for the last pair) to Polynesians from the first British visitors to Tahiti onward. I think that the confusion we experience reading earlier accounts of travelers and ethnographers derives from a *profusion* rather than from any lack of English words. For instance, what could Cora DuBois (1944:101–2) have meant by *male hermaphrodite* and *female hermaphrodite?* A third and fourth sex? Or Alorese (rather than American) sexual-part metaphors for gender or sexuality?

It is not the case that "Westerners' terms always ascribe to the 'man-woman' a sexualized term" (Fulton and Anderson 1992:608). Of the labels Fulton and Anderson repeated from Roscoe (1987:138–53), *effeminate, gender-crosser, transvestite,* and *amazon* are terms for gender, not sexuality; *hermaphrodite* and *transsexual* are terms for sex, not sexuality; *berdache* is exceptionally polysemous and ambiguous, with occupational specialization being the most common meaning in my reading of the recent literature; and the natives who so self-identify themselves contend that *gay* and *lesbian* are terms for identity with neither a necessary nor a sufficient connection to (homo)sexuality.[67] Even *catamite* and *prostitute,* particularly as applied by many Christians, may refer to economic dependence more than to sexual preference or conduct.[68]

Even if we interpret absence of attestation in the historical records and outright proclamation of absence of "berdaches" (etc.) in this or that Native American culture as due to failed observation rather than to absence of the phenomenon, and believe that there was a single sacred role across all of aboriginal North America, we are still imposing an alien "Western" (Northern) label, 'third gender.' *Gender* is a "Western label" (specifically Latin-

67. See chapter 8. Moreover, not everyone considered by himself and by others to be a 'gay man' "performs same-sex sexual relations exclusively." While I agree with Fulton and Anderson that to relexify 'berdache' with 'gay role' is confusing, their reduction of 'gay' to 'exclusive homosexual' increases confusion.

68. See Standing 1992:478–79; Callender and Kochems 1985:172.

ate)—more so than is *berdache*, which derived from Persian via Arabic (the original antithesis of "Western").

Unfortunately, we cannot ask, for example, pre-contact Hidatsa whether those called *miati* were third-gender, transvestite, homosexual, or merely tended to do work considered women's, although we can speculate endlessly about what Dorsey (1890:516) meant by "woman-inclined" and what he and other observers missed or distorted. I consider it more fruitful to think about what it would take to establish firmly that some human group has a conception of three genders. Before proposing a standard, I would like to proceed through two negative examples.

The first is a classification of *sex* I encountered in the collection of information about clients of San Francisco County Community Mental Health clinics. The intake forms (completed by an employee, not by the client) had "Sex: M F T (Circle one)." When I saw this, I thought I had found an official definition of reality in which transsexuals are a 'third sex'. But when I looked at the instructions, I learned that the categories were 'male', 'female', and 'in transition'. Note that these are gender categories for "sex," because I am going to contend that the "sex"/"gender" distinction is not made consistently outside social science elite discourse (if even there!). Despite the existence of three categories, sex is still dichotomous in this conception. There are men (called *male*). There are women (called *female*). There are men in the process of becoming women and women in the process of becoming men. These are officially labeled *in transition*. Once they have finished medical "correction" of their sex, they are not a "third sex" (*transsexual*), but are legally classified as one of the two sexes.

My second negative example of a "third gender role" in the U.S. is *basketball superstar* in American English texts about Earvin "Magic" Johnson. I have never seen him (or other National Basketball Association players) referred to as *a male basketball superstar* (nor as *a female basketball superstar* nor as *an effeminate basketball superstar*), although *Magic* is not a conventional sex-specific male or female name in American English. Also, I have never heard a statement to the effect "There are men, there are women, and there are basketball players." After being identified as a *basketball player*, Johnson and others are subsequently referred to with *he*, but so are many players of allegedly third-gender roles (as in Wikan 1977, Roscoe 1991a). Basketball players have distinctive dress, baring their legs as other men at work do not (although when they go to press conferences or to meetings of presidential commissions they do not wear this distinctive dress). Basketball players have highly specialized skills, and an exceptional occupation, being few in number and very highly rewarded. One would expect someone called "Magic" to have special spiritual powers.[69] A case could be made that he follows visions. Allegations of homosexuality have been made and denied . . . There are many similarities to reports of berdaches!

Clearly, there is a role "basketball superstar." It combines certain attributes considered masculine in the culture (such as physical strength and ruthless competitiveness) and others considered feminine (display/commodification of a skimpily dressed and widely fetishized body, frequent public embracing of each other). To ascertain whether "basketball superstar" is conceived as an 'intermediate gender' or a 'third gender' or not a 'gender role' at all, we need native contrast sets (as in traditional structural linguistics or its application in classical ethnoscience) or answers to direct questions from natives of the culture. As argued above in chapter 6, not all terms for roles are terms for gender roles, even if there are cultural expectations about the distribution by sex and/or sexuality of incumbents of those roles.

I do not think that natives of my culture think of "basketball superstar" as a gender role. Insofar as it is associated with gender, it is a masculine role. I have used this case, because it seems to me that for Native American and other cultures, the existence of terms for roles does not suffice to establish how many genders (or sexes or sexualities) are (or were) conceived. There are many terms for roles. Knowing that one is a "gender role" or a "sex role" requires contrast with categories that are established sex or gender roles. Still less does a role term indicate that dress, work, sexual behavior, and sacredness matched, or that one of them is criterial.

To me, the best evidence of a native conception is a direct statement such as "There are three genders. Some people are male, some are female, and some are professional basketball players. One of the greatest of these magicmakers is named 'Magic,'" or—more plausibly, especially since the distinction between sex and gender is not widely diffused—"There are three sexes: men, women, and hermaphrodites."[70] Use of a pronoun other than those

69. In common with shamans in many cultures, other basketball superstars (notably Michael "Air" Jordan) can fly, as anyone watching U.S. television commercials regularly can see. On Johnson's shifting image, see S. King 1993.

70. Though I think it is more common for sex to change (by fetal or newborn decision in West African and Canadian Inuit cultures, as part of a shaman's eventual recognition of vocation in Siberia and Borneo) than for there to be three categories of "sex," "third sex" is plausible for eunuchs (including South Asian *hijras*) and "hermaphrodites." Will Roscoe (personal communication, 1994) maintains that Sanskrit and Pali categorization includes multiple genders. My preliminary examination suggests that the Sanskrit one is a typology of conditions precluding heterosexual intercourse, not a typology of "genders," and I have not had a chance to review the Pali.

Jacobs and Cromwell (1992:55) report one Tewa's definitions of four sexualities involving

used for men or for women would also constitute strong evidence, especially in languages such as English with more than two genders of pronouns.

Anthropologists project contemporary North American and northern European conceptions of distinctions between sex, gender, and sexuality on peoples in other times and places on the basis of evidence less compelling than in the case above for "basketball player" as a third gender. They do not—and I believe could not—demonstrate that at the time of Western contact (if ever!), Native Americans made the contemporary "scientific" distinctions among sex, gender, and sexuality.

I do not think this trichotomization is a well-established folk systematic in Anglo, African, Asian, or Latino America. To take an example from the last, when pressed to assign primacy to one of these three in explaining the pejorative Spanish term *maricón,* one Mexican American told me, "It doesn't mean that he is homosexual. It's someone who can't take care of himself and therefore gets fucked over." So, I thought, here is a label for gender, not for sexuality. To confirm this, I asked, "Gets fucked over or gets fucked?" A second Mexican American replied, "Both: he can't take care of himself, so he gets taken care of." His friend concurred, "Yeah, he gets fucked over and he also gets fucked, just like a woman." In this instance, there was some conception of gender as primary, but the cultural expectation is for symmetry in gender (effeminate) and sexuality (receptive)—and, at least functional sex: the cultural expectation is that the penis of the *maricón* is useless (or useful only as a handle). In the much discussed case of the Omani *khanith,* although Wikan (1977, 1978) moved from third sex to third gender, it seems to me that in the Omani view, as she described it, there are two sexes, two genders, and the expectation of a one-to-one correspondence between sex and gender. Attributes of the *khanith* are intermediate between those of men and women, but jurally the *khanith* is a man and is referred to with the masculine pronoun. Rather than being a third gender, the *khanith* seems to me to be a kind of man. The dichotomous categorization of "fallen"/"virtuous" applies to both sexes.[71]

From the available data, I do not think that we can ever sort out which of these or which combinations of these were conceived in aboriginal American

exclusive or inclusive sex with three sexes (men, women, and *kwidó*). This falls short of a native statement that there are three Tewa genders. It is the contemporary Northern valorization of "gender" as the most important aspect, not a Tewa one, that leads to reading a set of terms for sexualities into the currently privileged domain of "gender." Moreover, if "traditionally, when *kwidós* engaged in sexual liaisons it was with married men, which is considered part of married men's 'normal' heterosexual behavior" (p. 56), then this attestation of the fourth sexuality was probably an innovation that would be unfamiliar to most Tewas.

71. For a more detailed review of this case, see Murray 1996.

cultures. It would be useful to find a contemporary culture that conceives of three genders that are distinct from sexes and sexualities. Lacking that, I feel that data are being forced into a contemporary specialist Northern schema in which religion, sexual division of labor, sex, gender, and sexuality are distinct, with the contents of each believed to vary without limit between cultures (even while being completely determined by the schema *within* any one).[72] I think that these analytically separable constructs are highly correlated in many (most?) cultures. Those who do not fit cultural expectations may be intermediate.[73] (If masculinity is achieved and the default, unmarked category is lacking masculinity, then an effeminate man or a butch woman may be "a half man.") Or they may be conceived as lacking gender (a zero on a scale with integers for a first and second sex, and thus not capable of being initiated into either sex's adult status; as among the Pokot, as described by Edgerton 1964). Or they may be conceived as less than prototypical cases of a fuzzy gender category ("a kind of a man, but not a good example").[74] That they are conceived as a third, or *n*th, gender in cultures with multiple gender categories is only one possibility.

Questions about what some earlier observer really meant, or might have seen if s/he had seen the way those in some no longer observable culture saw, cannot achieve resolution and are unlikely to lead even to consensus among specialists. Before trying to decide whether there was a transcontinental "third gender" (or "two-spirit") role in the past, it would be better to firmly attest such a categorization somewhere, whether among contemporary Native Americans or in some other human group outside academia. The reductive essentializing of a unitary role across aboriginal America provides an opportunity for overdue questioning of the conception of "third gender" that has been increasingly popular among anthropologists, and of the premature universalization of the distinction between biological "sex" and sociocultural "gender" from contemporary elite discourse(s) into the world's cultures.

72. Breaking with the view that categories determine conduct, in another recent advocacy of the preeminence of gender, Jacobs and Cromwell (1992:48) asserted that even hegemonic category schemata don't matter: "The dominant cultural gender ideology does not prevent a suppressed gender ideology from existing, nor does it constrain flexibility in sex, sexuality, and gender variance." Surely, categories at least *somewhat* constrain thought and channel socialization!

73. Given the ongoing fascination among anthropologists (including Fulton and Anderson) with liminality, one might have expected them to focus on intermediateness rather than to proclaim a third kind, especially because those glossed as 'berdache' often seem to be intermediaries between Native communities and intruding officials from the nation-states, as Chiñas (1995) and Roscoe (1994) noted.

74. See Schlegel 1990:39; Dickemann 1993:59; Murray 1983a.

Seven

Couples

Intensely devoted same-sex couples considered to be inspirational models include Gilgamesh and Enkidu, Damon and Pythias, Achilles and Patroklos, Jonathan and David, Jesus and the Beloved Disciple, Han Aiti and Dong Xian, Hadrian and Antinous, Gertrude Stein and Alice B. Toklas, Christopher Isherwood and Donald Bachardy.[1] The sexuality in several of these relationships continues to be controversial, although those who take these couples as models assume they included genital relations.

Even in the extreme situation of Nazi Germany, homosexual relationships at least sometimes occurred. Relationships also develop in some societies prescribing universal (though transient) homosexual intercourse.[2] Devoted relationships occurred in societies, including Classical Greece and within the Ottoman Empire, where some claim that homosexual relationships between peers did not occur, as well as in cultures inclined to organization of homosexuality by age, where "love between comrades" cannot be disputed, notably China and Japan.

In the legendary cases and those from the ancient world, the stresses of a long life together rarely challenged the intensity of passion. The modern role-model couples from the list above exemplify durability as well as intensity of same-sex love. Such models reassure lesbigays that long-term relationships are possible, despite the obstacles posed by social arrangements and by social conceptions of homosexual relationships as necessarily transitory due to a supposed essential promiscuity. Heterosexist bigots (especially

1. My focus in this chapter is on dyads. On the larger quasi-family entities, see Weston 1991; Carrington 1995. On gay fathers see B. Miller 1979, 1983. On lesbian mothers, contrast the "brave new world" ideology elicited by Wolf (1979:136–65) with the "same old [material and emotional] realities" recounted to Lewin (1993) by mothers in the same place (San Francisco) a few years later.

2. See Herdt 1984.

Freudian psychoanalysts and Roman Catholic Church hierarchs) regard homosexual relationships as more serious (sinful, neurotic) than fleeting anonymous sexual encounters, because a relationship entails greater acceptance of homosexuality—"flaunting living in sin" rather than committing distinct "sinful acts." As De Cecco (1988:3) observed, "That two men who have sex together can also love each other symbolizes the ultimate detoxification of homosexuality."

Both institutions such as church and state, and social groupings such as natal families and employers, provide positive sanctions for heterosexual relationships while denying legitimation and rewards to same-sex couples. Thus, traditionally religious and socially conservative parents may mourn and punish divorces among their heterosexually married children, but celebrate and reward the dissolution of their lesbian or gay children's relationship as marking a return to normalcy, or as at least opening the possibility of "growing out of a homosexual phase."[3] Although there are similarities among all kinds of relationship, lesbigay couples routinely encounter obstacles not generally encountered by those in heterosexual relationships.

ROLE-PLAYING

Given the importance of gender as an organizing principle, many people in many cultures routinely assume that for a relationship to exist, distinct gender roles must be enacted: one partner must play the part of the wife (femme) and the other the husband (butch). Although there are instances of such replication among lesbigay couples,

> Most contemporary gay relationships do not conform to traditional "masculine" and "feminine" roles; instead, role flexibility and turn-taking are more common patterns. Only a small minority of homosexual couples engage in clearcut butch-femme role-playing. In this sense, traditional heterosexual marriage is not the predominant model or script for current homosexual couples. (Peplau, in De Cecco 1988:34–35)

Indeed, with a historical change in the functions of the family from economic production to companionship, and with feminist challenges to traditional female roles, heterosexual relationships increasingly came to resemble the companionate dyad of gay relationships.[4] One might question the extent to which "traditional heterosexual marriage" can be the predominant model in

3. See Vaughan 1987:48, 193.
4. As DeVault (1991) and Carrington (1995) show, the domestic work to sustain households continues to be considered women's work. Gay men often fail to notice domestic labor, as do many males in heterosexual relationships. Sometimes discounting seems to be an attempt to maintain the image of one's partner's masculinity.

heterosexual couples in which both the man and the woman pursue careers and/or do not raise children.

Harry (1984) found that the increased visibility of gay enclaves provided a larger pool of potential partners than were available in earlier eras when, as argued in chapter 6, only cross-gender appearance or behavior publicly signaled homosexual availability. Chances of finding an approximation to one's conception of a desirable partner increase in a larger pool.[5] Specifically, a preference for butch–butch relationships increasingly typified North American urban gay men. Harry found that men who value masculinity in themselves also seek masculine-appearing partners. He also found that those living in cities with gay communities were more likely to cohabit with their partners and were more interested in emotional intimacy than those living in suburbs and small towns, where the chances of meeting a partner and of being able to live together with the approval of neighbors were less.[6]

DECISION-MAKING

Although reports of enduring same-sex pairs come from many locales, there is a dearth of systematic data on same-sex couples even in North American cities, so that it is not possible to estimate whether the age and status disparities of some of the examples listed at the beginning of this chapter typify same-sex relationships. Many gay writers assert that gay male relationships cross racial, class, and age discrepancies more often than do heterosexual or lesbian relationships. "Opposites attract" is the predominant folk wisdom— except, of course when "birds of a feather flock together." What "everyone knows," thus, provides little resolution. The number of long-term lesbian and gay relationships that cross social discrepancies remains a question for systematic research. The extent to which the ideology of egalitarian relations is realized in gay and lesbian couples also remains unclear.[7]

In what little empirical evidence exists, choice of long-term partners in same-sex relationships is based on similarity of social characteristics *(homophily)* and on opportunities for contact *(propinquity)*, just as in the usual choice of heterosexual marriage partners and of lesbian and gay "best friends"—many of whom are former sexual partners.[8] Undoubtedly, racial

5. Increases in specificity of requirements easily and often offset this (Murray 1979c, revised as the appendix to this chapter).

6. See F. Lynch 1992.

7. J. Lindenbaum (1985) and Carrington (1995) begin to clarify this.

8. Nardi 1992b, 1994. See also Soneschein 1968; Warrren 1974:75; S. Krieger 1983; Harry 1984; Laner in De Cecco 1988. Cotton (1975) found homogamy more typical of lesbians than of gay men (in Cotton 1972), as have later observers.

and cultural differences often enhance sexual attraction. The same differences that initially intrigue and attract may become problematic for transforming a sexual affair into an enduring relationship, however. Long-term gay and lesbian relationships in which there is not the friction between male expectations and female expectations may thrive relatively better than heterosexual relationships with conflicting cultural expectations,[9] but there remains the tendency to marry one's "own kind" despite being attracted to and even sexually involved with persons of other classes, races, and/or ethnicities. The attributes of those with whom one wants to have sex and those with whom one would consider settling down (marrying) are often quite distinct. Moreover, the kinds of relationships someone wants and seeks are not necessarily the kinds he or she has.

Most self-identified lesbians and gay men have some experience of living in a relationship. In a study conducted in San Francisco during the late 1960s, A. P. Bell and Weinberg (1978) found 51 percent of white homosexual men, 58 percent of black homosexual men, 72 percent of white homosexual women, and 70 percent of black homosexual women were in a relationship. As in most surveys of lesbigay populations, most of the rest reported having been in a relationship at some time in their lives. In a national survey of 530 black lesbians, Mays and Cochran (1988a:59) reported 66 percent currently in committed relationships. Of these, 53 percent lived together. The median length of the longest (lifetime-to-date) relationship was 42 months, and the median number of serious/committed lesbian relationships was three. In my own 1988 nonrandom sample of gay male San Franciscans, 40 percent were coupled.

In the Bell and Weinberg study, there were not age discrepancies in 5 percent of the couples including a white male respondent, in 10 percent of the couples including a black male or white female respondent, and in 3 percent of the couples involving a black female. There were differences of more than five years in 51, 40, 35, and 47 percent of the couples, respectively. Sixty-four percent of white gay male respondents judged their social position to be similar to their partner's, compared to 39 percent of black males, 56 percent of black lesbians, and 72 percent of white lesbians. Three percent of black homosexual couples reported equal income, in contrast to 17 and 18 percent of white female and male couples, although negative effects of income disparity were reported by only 2 percent of the gay white men, 4 percent of black gay men and women, and 6 percent of white lesbians.

9. Bernard (1981), Maltz and Borker (1982), and Tannen (1990) contend that gender differences between white North Americans are of the magnitude of ethnic differences and attribute the basis of these differences to early socialization.

Blacks in the sample were substantially younger than whites when they began their relationship (just as black gay men tend to have initiated homosexual sex at earlier ages than white or Asian American gay men).[10]

In a large-scale survey of contemporary American couples, Blumstein and Schwartz (1983) found that couples in which both people felt they were genuine partners with equal control over economic assets were more tranquil. Harry (1984:141) found age to predict power in decision-making within gay male relationships, especially among those couples living together, but also suggested that "in gay relationships it is more likely that partners will be more similar to each other in the possession of bases of power than in heterosexual relationships."

Other studies with smaller samples of lesbians and gay men also found perceived equality in making important decisions to be central to their successful relationships. Perceived equality in decision-making is not necessarily lacking in couples who differ substantially in age, status, or income; but the older and/or more affluent partner tends to dominate decision-making in such relationships. Greater sexual marketability may also be a factor. That is, the partner who is more desirable by conventional standards of beauty may use this ("You can't do as well as me, so you'd better do what I want!"). Yet another complication, related to the immediately previous one, in predicting power within relationships is "the power of the least interest": the partner who seems to the other to be least concerned about preserving the relationship can deter opposition to his or her choices by threatening, implicitly or explicitly, to leave the relationship.

These same factors operate in heterosexual relationships. The person who brings more resources to a relationship tends to make decisions when the two disagree. In heterosexual relationships, the man typically(/historically) has higher status and more economic resources and also often claims to have less interest in the relationship. Moreover, in many cultures, including North America, women are raised to support relationships and to be defined by their relationship, while men are socialized to and defined by what they do outside the domestic sphere. Despite recent social changes, North American women often continue to defer to male partners' career contingencies while men pursue their careers, either ignoring a partner's preferences or jettisoning partners unwilling to go along with their choices.

Blumstein and Schwartz's discussion of the negative consequences of perceived "failure" in the work world for couples of all kinds, and the relatively great instability of the lesbian relationships (fewer of which endured than

10. Documented in chapter 9.

any of the other kinds of relationships they tracked over time), suggest that success in the work world is important to the duration of a relationship. Moreover, they found that "lesbians in established relationships who have unequal income or unequal influence over spending are more likely to break up" (pp. 310, 588 n. 14).[11] Rather than supporting the contention by Parsons and Bales (1955:24) of role complementarity, these data seem to indicate that durable relationships require roughly equivalent success in the outside world on the part of partners who are not work-centered. Neither lesbian rhetoric about not letting income differences affect their relationship, nor gay men's greater tendency to pool incomes, necessarily preserves same-sex couples. Moreover, the problems of two-career relationships which same-sex couples have long faced (e.g., competition, allocation of housework, resolving the pulls of uncoordinated careers) are increasingly problematic for heterosexual couples as well (p. 188). This historical drift should enhance the theoretical interest of studying same-sex couples even beyond the opportunity to sort out what can be attributed to gender, what to the legal institution of marriage, and what to heterosexuality in the marriage and family literature.[12]

McWhirter and Mattison (in De Cecco 1988) outlined a natural history of predictable stages within committed relationships: blending, nesting, maintaining, collaborating, trusting, and renewal. The stages are labels for recurrent patterns, not causal models of what every relationship must pass through in what order. Moreover, their model does not take any account of different kinds of love.[13] Despite its limitations, a model of stages does draw attention to the changes that affect relationships over time. In particular, a

11. Kennedy and Davis (1993:82–83, 291) noted that gender-conforming fems often made more money than their gender-nonconforming butch partners (and often supported them), but did not explore the consequences. (On p. 103 they injected a defensive judgment that the majority of butches didn't exploit other women, though some butches acted as pimps.) On sexual satisfaction, particularly of fems, see Rosenzweig and Lebow 1992, Tanner 1978, and Weston 1993a.

12. Although the similarities between gay and straight relationships are as interesting as the differences, Vaughan (1987) in her very sensitive and insightful book on uncoupling unnecessarily obscured the sex and the sexual relationships of the 103 people she interviewed. The extensive quotations identify occupation, age, duration of relationship, and whether the couple was married or living together, but she did not provide even any summary descriptive statistics. She quoted fewer lesbians than gay men, and, especially in the discussion of reuniting, both seem to disappear. The person who leaves a relationship (whom Vaughan calls the "initiator") may have been the relationship-focused partner or have focused on work and other identities outside coupledom, so her dichotomy of the "initiator" or the "partner" (the one who was left or at least recognized trouble in the relationship later than did the "initiator") does not correspond to the instrumental/affective dichotomy of the Parsons-Bales tradition.

13. Lee 1976b.

period of initial romance and mutual discovery tends to give way to everyday coexistence and reduced frequency of sex in relationships that endure.

The gay, white, Southern California males they studied did not merge money and possessions until the trusting stage—which McWhirter and Mattison estimate as ten or more years into the relationship—after some questions about individual autonomy have been resolved to both partners' satisfaction. Whether or not it usually takes so long, if the relationship endures, lesbian couples, and even more so gay male couples, tend to pool assets. Such pooling reinforces decision-making equality among those making differing economic contributions to the relationship and maintains the stability of the relationship. Very few same-sex couples (5%) believe that one partner should support a non-working partner. Fewer still do so: Harry (1984) and Weston (1991) each reported 1 percent. Yet, even in same-sex couples in which both members work, income inequality often remains an underlying stress. Male socialization to competitiveness, a tendency to assess success in monetary terms, and a devaluation of domestic labor make economic inequality particularly problematic in male–male couples. Blumstein and Schwartz (1983) suggest that the egalitarian ideology of two strong women fighting together may also become an unconscious solvent of relationships between women of unequal income, propelling the more economically successful partner out of the relationship thinking, "If you were really strong, really my match, you'd do as well as I do!"

Blumstein and Schwartz reaffirmed that being poor and happy in a consumer society is difficult. Whether or not one can buy happiness, relative wealth generally establishes power within relationships for gay and lesbian couples, as for heterosexual couples. Monetary comparisons are less predictive of relative power in lesbian couples (in part because large income differences between women are less common). The more affluent partner has more control over the couple's recreational activities for lesbian and gay male couples.[14] Sharing more activities outside work than heterosexual couples do may account for greater satisfaction within the couple for lesbian and gay men in relationships. Much of the social life of heterosexual men and women is homosocial in most cultures. To the extent that primary and secondary socialization shapes interests differentially depending on the sex of the child,[15]

14. This differs from the pattern Blumstein and Schwartz found in married heterosexual couples, where this is often the domain where the wife makes choices.

15. See M. Goodwin 1990; Thorne 1993. Socialization is an active process, not something done to a passive tabula rasa. Recent fascination with "performing" gender (much of it misreading Butler 1990) tends to obscure how children cultivate stereotypical gender self-identification

same-sex couples are likely to have more compatible interests than mixed-sex couples.

Various studies have found lesbian couples more likely to live together than gay male couples. The extent to which this is a result of temperament or a difference of economic resources is not clear from the available data. Partners who have lesbigay friends are also more likely to cohabit. Probably integration into gay/lesbian circles cannot be separated from self-acceptance as lesbigay, and both individual and social acceptance of homosexuality make living together more conceivable.

SEX

Blumstein and Schwartz (1983) found that relationships with at least one partner more concerned with the relationship than with his/her career are more likely to endure. They also found that the relationship-centered partner usually initiated sex, whereas the more powerful one, who was more likely to be career-oriented and to have higher income, was more likely to refuse sex. The frequency of sex decreased with the duration of all types of relationships, but especially in homosexual ones. Forty-five percent of married heterosexual couples had sex three times a week or more often, compared to 67 percent of gay male couples, and 33 percent of lesbian couples. For couples who had been together ten or more years, the percentages fell to 18 for married couples, 11 for gay may couples, and 1 percent for lesbian couples.

At least prior to the devastation of AIDS, many men in gay couples were relatively casual about extramarital sex. For some, outside sex often replaced sex between partners—without being conceived as a threat to the relationship.[16] In contrast, lesbian lovers associated non-monogamous sex with dissatisfaction and lack of commitment to their relationship. Given cultural prohibitions against females engaging in casual sex,[17] women, including lesbians, have tended to have protracted affairs more than the one-time "tricks" with little emotional investment sought by men (gay or not).[18] Affairs represent a greater threat to a relationship than casual encounters, so that lesbian

---

and routinely also underestimates the massiveness and obdurateness of cultural expectations of a simple concordance (conceived as "natural") of gender and sex.

16. See also Kurdeck and Smith in De Cecco 1988. Cf. Leznoff 1954:190–9 on an earlier era.

17. Based on sex-specific dangers, notably pregnancy.

18. The extent to which this remains true for women who identify themselves as "queer" would be an interesting research topic.

non-monogamy is more serious for primary relationships than gay male sexual encounters outside relationships. That is, the character of the non-monogamy, not its frequency, matters. Of course, gay men sometimes have affairs as well as or instead of tricks, and possessiveness is not a monopoly of women. (Moreover, all these differences are statistical, not absolute.)

Blumstein and Schwartz also found that lesbians (along with gay men and straight men) are happier both with their sex lives and with their relationships the more they engage in oral sex. Roles in both oral and anal sex raise sensitive issues of dominance and reciprocity in gay male couples. Traditionally, anxieties were settled and sexual incompatibilities compensated for outside the relationship. Reciprocity also mutes anxieties about seeming to "submit." Blumstein and Schwartz (1983) found that "the partner who performs anal sex is no more 'masculine' or powerful than the partner who receives it," and that "for both partners, anal intercourse is associated with being masculine: in couples where both partners are forceful, outgoing, and aggressive, there is more anal sex" (p. 244). The gay ideology that it's not who does what to whom (in particular, who penetrates whom), but getting what one wants, that matters also undercuts the dominant culture's equation of sexual receptivity with "womanliness" and powerlessness.

DID GAY MEN FORM COUPLES MORE DURING THE 1980s?

Indisputably, the late 1970s was an epoch of exploration of many varieties of sex with many seemingly interchangeable partners. "Smashing" monogamy (as ownership of a person by another) was even a tenet of lesbian feminist political correctness of that era (Faderman 1991b:232). One of the anthems of the late 1970s gay discos was Gloria Gaynor's song "I will survive." It spoke directly to and for men who felt they had shaken loose from self-immolating relationships (gay and straight, natal families and dysfunctional adult relationships). "Go on! Walk out that door: / You're not welcome anymore" seemed to speak not just for one person who felt trampled in an earlier relationship, but of relationships in general. Many of us had decided that we'd rather dance than cry over exes, and rather trick than try again to build and sustain a new relationship.[19]

Explaining what this conduct that now seems unimaginable to our juniors

19. Dancing "is all that's left when love is gone," Holleran (1978:97) wrote in an early elegy for mid 1970s disco communitas. The long-running battle to be able to dance together without state harassment had only recently been won, but quickly was taken for granted.

meant to us then, without the retrospective bias of knowing about AIDS, needs to be done, but is not what I want to do here. Instead, I want to consider factors in addition to the appearance of AIDS that shape recent gay male conduct.[20] In regard to the shift in cultural emphasis from "too many men, too little time" to "one man or no man and little or no time" and/or to withdrawal,[21] we need to remember that sexual license and suppression alternate in a cyclical history of revolutions and counterrevolutions. The most famous instance is English Restoration comedy following the Puritan Revolution. In the U.S., the 1920s stand out as a similar era of loosening restrictions following the First World War. To a limited extent, the Second World War was another phase of release in contrast both to the Depression era and to the witch hunts of the late 1940s and early 1950s, as Bérubé (1990), Faderman (1991b), and Kennedy and Davis (1993) show. Alongside changes—whether these are linear trends or cycles of repression and expression—at any particular point in time, there is diversity within a community, especially in ethnically diverse urban communities.

Throughout the cycles of emphasis on nesting or tricking, there are large numbers of individuals who do not conform to the prevailing sexual zeitgeist (to the dominant societal representation of homosexuality), whichever focus is in the ascendant.[22] Clearly, during the clone era, there were gay men frustrated by the prototypically American male flight from commitment. There were gay men hunting for "husbands"; 86 percent of the gay men in a survey published by Harry and Lovely (1977:179) had or wanted a long-term lover. Some even found them. J.B., the narrator in the 1980 section of David Feinberg's 1990 novel *Eighty-sixed*, searched for a lover; his friend Dennis found one; and Feinberg represents at least one other monolithic, long-term gay couple. Although written from a different gay world, devastated by AIDS, the focus in the book on finding a lover does not seem to me retrospective

20. Despite the low incidence rate of AIDS among lesbians, AIDS frightened some lesbians (back) to serial monogamy, too (Faderman 1991b:281). The rate of coupling within the generation that has grown up and come out knowing about AIDS also deserves investigation. My impression is that it is not appreciably higher than among baby-boomers on the eve of AIDS (when "promiscuity" was positively evaluated in the visible gay may culture). Fear may prolong relationships for some time, but not indefinitely. See Bolton (1992a) on the dangers of this and similar fear-based HIV infection prevention strategies.

21. I include celibacy, chastity, phone sex, as well as "self-conscious self-removal from the active gay world" (Bronski 1988:140).

22. I have similar doubts about drug use. "Clean and sober" contingents are more visible now, and asceticism in regard to alcohol and drugs is more fashionable, but I am not convinced that young gay men now are less likely to use whatever recreational drugs are currently fashionable than were clones during the late 1970s. Clone mix-and-match drug-taking also continues with drugs (prescription and other) for opportunistic infections and immune system boosting.

falsification. *When the Parrot Boy Sings* (Champagne 1990) provides another example. I remember hearing the term "husband-hunting," and—along with the more common propositions—I received a number of proposals of marriage during the clone era of San Francisco. Indeed, I accepted one! Not everyone sang along with Donna Summer, "There's nothing for us here. Enough is enough is enough." Just as there were gay couples in the late 1970s, "sexual outlaws" still prowl and trick.

I am not certain that even the percentage distribution of gay men in couple relationships has shifted. As noted above, during the late 1960s in San Francisco, 51 percent of white gay men and 58 percent of black gay men were coupled. During the late 1980s, various studies have reported between 43 percent of gay men in New York City and 58 percent in San Francisco to be coupled (see Table 8.1). Although the specter of AIDS encouraged some to nest, the success and durability of relationships motivated by fear are questionable. I know of no evidence of any direct effects of AIDS on the frequency of durable gay relationships.

In addition to the threat of AIDS and governmental action to close private sex clubs discussed in chapter 4, three other factors facilitated a shift in emphasis from sexual promiscuity to coupling. I have already mentioned a cyclical shift in public emphasis between sexual expression and restriction. Another factor is the burnout with "life in the fast lane" which was being discussed before the recognition of the first AIDS cases.[23]

Coupling certainly became symbolically more central. This publicized trend to coupling, settling down, and raising kids was partly a function of age as well as a reaction to AIDS.[24] The baby-boom generation is so large, and so used to being taken as coterminous with the world in general, that as its members have visibly settled down, we have paid less attention to our juniors or to our elders. The baby boomlet in straight people of the same age and the transformation in the stereotype of my own generation from yuppies to couch potatoes evidences the more general aging and "settling" of the baby-boom generation. As the country has become more conservative—both politically and in regard to lifestyle experimentation—gay men have also become more cautious and less willing to experiment with unconventional

---

23. Adam 1978a; Harry and Devall 1978a,b; Altman 1982. I suppose that the major fictionalizations of clone self-hatred, Andrew Holleran's *Dancer From the Dance* (1978), and of clone-hatred, Larry Kramer's *Faggots* (1978), might also be advanced as evidence, though it seems to me that both were smoldering with disgust before having had any experience of the gay clone world of the 1970s. Cf. Brodsky 1993a:233–51 or Lee 1978a for more sympathetic analyses.

24. Gorman (1992:100, 104) also stressed this in his account of Los Angeles gay communities.

forms of sex and relationships than we were in the heyday of sexual liberation. Hardly anyone even remembers communes.[25]

We need to overcome our particular generational myopia and facile journalistic analyses[26] and realize that, just as we didn't invent promiscuity in the 1970s,[27] we didn't invent coupling in the 1980s. In the 1970s, those expanding gay traditions celebrated the models listed at the start of this chapter. We should learn or remember that there were many gay men in committed relationships even during the clone era, just as we should recognize that there have been same-sex couples, as well as homosexual "sexual outlaws," through a number of supposed sexual "revolutions" and "counterrevolutions." Fashions of/in discourse are continually in motion—although the motion seems to me cyclical or Brownian rather than linear. What isn't in "the news," even when "news" is "lifestyle/soft news," does not change as much, or change directions as often!

APPENDIX: SCREENING INFORMATION;
THE FUNCTIONS AND FETISHISM OF "MY TYPE"

Someone cruising in a setting where there are many unknown others potentially available as sexual partners must have some criteria to narrow the field of possibilities. In a short amount of time, it is impossible to gather very much information about very many people. One tactic is to wait to be selected for approach. This considerably narrows the field and shifts screening problems primarily to others willing to take the risk of a rejected approach. For those taking the initiative, as for the "buyer" in the job market, "The problem is not to get in touch with the largest number of potential applicants; rather it is to find a few applicants promising enough to be worth the invest-

25. See Weston 1991. On the shift in focus in lesbian discourse from utopian vision of commonality to dystopic preoccupation with differences, see Zimmerman 1990.

26. Confusing of prominence in discourse with social change plagues historical writing on gay history. Research on the manufacture of news, such as E. Epstein 1973, Fishman 1978, and Gitlin 1980 should enhance skepticism about relying on discourse to infer social change, or, indeed, even fluctuations in supposed empirical occurrences.

27. I think that some members of my generation think that we invented extramarital sex. In reality, having sex with multiple partners was not an innovation of our generation. Gay men from the generations which fought World War II and the Korean War recall availing themselves of many sexual opportunities, as memoirs in many gay oral history collections attest: see Bérubé 1990; Vacha 1985; Chauncey 1994. The age of AIDS did not eliminate "promiscuity," nor need it: not how many but what and how are important for avoiding AIDS transmission within homosexual sex, as much as moralists inside and outside the gay community would like to eliminate non-monogamous sex, using AIDS and the promiscuity paradigm for rationalizing it (see chapter 4).

ment of thorough investigation . . . reducing the number of applicants to manageable proportions."[28] That is, screening out prospects (risking eliminating one who would be a good choice) is the first order of business, wherever there are many prospects.

More time and effort are then available to expend in the second stage, selecting from those who seem plausible prospects. On the job market, prospective "buyers" seek evaluations from trusted colleagues. "Personal contacts are used simultaneously to gather information and to screen out noise, and are, for many types of information, the most efficient devices for doing so."[29] In the cruising environments of smaller cities or within an ongoing group, such techniques are feasible.[30] They are not feasible in the more anonymous cruising environments of large cities. Choice of territories somewhat offsets this:

> Just as hunting animals prefer the territories of their favoured prey, so a gay man hunting a partner can assess the various territories and spend longer where it is most likely to pay off. Where there is a high proportion of "my type," there are less people to filter through to get what I want. This sounds predatory, but it is not when you consider that the targets have offered themselves with the same consideration.[31]

Regardless of territory, there is considerable reliance on reading appearances. "Is X (the potential quarry) already with someone?" is frequently of interest to the cruiser—whether or not a positive answer will eliminate X from further consideration.

In the gay ghettoes, and even more so in S&M locales, an elaborate set of signals developed during the late 1970s. Attire and stance had always been read both to gauge availability and role. The side on which keys hung was a clearer signal of intent—insertive or receptive. The code of handkerchief colors quickly elaborated beyond most men's ability to remember what code was signaling what desired practice.[32] The depersonalization of

28. Reese 1966:561. According to Simmel (1950) and Wirth (1938), staying sane amidst the plethora of stimuli in cities requires not attending to most of them.

29. Granovetter 1974:98. Revealing that one is looking and specifying what one is looking for may be a cost for seeking evaluations—of sexual partners or of employees—and "an individual seeking information that is potentially discrediting may avoid asking intimates" (Murray, Rankin, and Magill 1981:134 n. 3).

30. They are especially important for scenes involving bondage (Lee 1979c).

31. Lee 1979a:9. See also Lee 1978c.

32. Besides the confusion from excessive complexity, both the efficiency and the substantive rationality of this system were undercut by some signaling what they wanted to be thought to seek, which was not always what they really sought (i.e., they were unwilling to advertise what they really wanted—in some cases because it seemed too "tame," in others because it seemed too "outrageous").

this system appalled many, both because of the exclusive emphasis on sexual behavior and because it reduced the need for verbal interaction. Such systems, however, are formally rational within any setting in which people gather seeking sex. They produce a very cheap way to screen information, first because there is no emotional risk of rejection in gaining the information, and second because practically no time needs to be expended to read the data.

Scrutinizing appearances for clues, then, is rational behavior in selecting a short-term sexual partner from a wide range of seeming possibilities. As often happens, however, means may become ends in themselves. Specifically, some feel that conformity to some set of visible characteristics is necessary for any relationships, not just for "tricks." In his book *Lovestyles*, John Lee (1976b) identified crucial valuation of physical appearance as one of several basic types of love.[33] For anyone so motivated, seeking a particular type is rational, though others may regard such patterns as fetishism, false consciousness, or an escape from humane interrelations.

In most times and places, the pool of suitable prospective partners has been socially restricted. A "right" to live with anyone with whom one thinks oneself to be in love is a relatively recent idea. Even in contemporary North America, accidents of birth account for most marriages—propinquity, class, parents' religion, and even education being among the corollaries of birth. Being born Mormon is no more an achieved characteristic than being born with black hair.[34] The point is that there are criteria used to narrow the range of possible partners always and everywhere. Criteria are necessary to discriminate within what would be an unmanageable flux without some way of efficiently eliminating consideration of most prospective partners—especially if the selection is going to be repeated the next night or more times in one night! In many societies (though fewer than in the past), marriages are arranged, or most matches are defined as unsuitable.

A "good" criterion depends on what the one using it wants. The content is culturally variable (and to some extent socially constructed). A man taught to want many children might consider a woman's hip structure. Someone wanting companionship might consider class. Someone seeking good sex might consider physical characteristics that turn her/him on and advertisement of role complementarity to what s/he wants to do. Of course, such formally rational behavior perpetuates whatever structure fostered the values

33. He expropriated *eros* as a label for this type of love. Lee (1976a) applies his typology to gay male relationships.

34. Remaining either is the default, though one may decide to change either.

(large families, companionship, sexual fantasy fulfillment in the examples). In a similar way, formally rational behaviors of individuals on the labor market cumulate in perpetuating inequities in the society and hence are not substantively rational.[35]

35. See Granovetter 1974.

Eight

Gay Community

N o community composed of ethnically diverse persons[1] dispersed, albeit nonrandomly, through an urban, post-industrial metropolitan area is going to be monolithic. Assertions about complex societies must necessarily be statistical distributions, not categorical, exceptionless pronouncements. However, given the history of derogation of gay men, it seems necessary to stress that evaluative norms as well as statistical ones exist in urban gay communities. Despite the acceptability of factors extenuating the extent of aid, gay men can and do reasonably expect other gay men to attempt to help them to find jobs and places to live, and to care for those stricken with AIDS. Similarly, despite a longstanding, albeit fraying, tolerance for not announcing that someone is gay in many circumstances, and lack of agreement about what *gay* means, a moral imperative not to deny gayness exists *within* the gay community.[2]

In this chapter I endeavor to show some patterning of diversity within the San Francisco gay community. I begin by reviewing *community* as a technical term in social science, showing that insofar as the term is applicable in urban settings, it is appropriate to identify *gay community* as one. Turning from the usage of social scientists, I discuss what San Francisco gay men mean by *gay community*. This ethnosemantic analysis of a folk category shows that gay self-identification is the most important criterion of membership, in the native view, and that this centrality has been stable over time. The chapter

1. The number of "kinds" available in San Francisco is very numerous. Those that have been bases for *gay* organizations include Filipino, Vietnamese, Malaysian, South Asian, Asian/Pacific Islander, Latina, Latino, Native American, and African American.

2. Chauncey (1994:276) quotes a recollection that, in the 1930s, "What was criminal was denying it to your sisters. Nobody cared about coming out to straights." Chapter 9 takes up ethnic variations and changes over time in coming out and moving to a metropolitan gay community.

concludes with scrutiny of newer locutions, *queer community* and *families we choose*.

Although one can identify oneself as part of a gay tradition with no particular location in space, those men who consider themselves part specifically of the San Francisco gay community live in the San Francisco Bay Area. Most of us originated elsewhere. Many of us also came out elsewhere. Numbers in what follows derive from responses of respondents in 1980, 1988, and 1993 snowball sample of San Francisco Bay Area self-identified gay men.[3] This sample overrepresents Asian men if contrasted with the Multicenter AIDS Cohort Study (MACS) random sample of gay men from the 19 San Francisco census tracts with the highest 1983 AIDS rates, centered on the Castro district; or with the random telephone sample of the San Francisco Bay Area conducted for the *San Francisco Examiner* in the spring of 1989.[4] Other ethnic representations, age, percentage in a relationship, age of initial homosexual experience, and educational attainment of the two samples are roughly equivalent, as can be seen in Table 8.1's contrasts of four San Francisco gay community samples with samples from five other U.S. cities.

COMMUNITY AS A SOCIAL SCIENCE TECHNICAL TERM

Debate over the existence of *gay community* stems partly from the dissensus about what a *community* is,[5] and partly from a separate standard for *gay community* in contrast to other kinds of urban communities.[6] North American

3. A snowball sample involves one informant directing the researcher to others. See Sudman and Kalton 1986:401–29; J. Martin and Dean 1990 for details.

4. Samuel and Winkelstein 1988; Hatfield 1989; Winkelstein et al. 1987a,b, 1988; Ekstrand and Coates 1990. Whether my sample overrepresents gay Asian Americans, or whether they are less concentrated in the environs of the Castro district, cannot be settled definitively, but I believe the latter is the case, and that gay Asians (also Latinos and African Americans) live in areas of ethnic residential concentration more than in areas of quasi-ethnic (lesbigay) concentration.

5. Along with Toennies's contrast of *Gemeinschaft* (community) to *Gesellschaft* (society), it is necessary to deploy Schmalenbach's contrast of *Gemeinschaft* to *Bund* (communion). There may be bunds within the gay community, but the whole gay community is only a bund on Gay Freedom Day (see Herrell 1992), and not always even then. At least, asserting solidarity outweighs providing a spectacle for straight amusement then, unlike Halloween, called by some a "gay holiday."

6. This is typical of other concepts preceded by the adjective *gay*. I have suggested that the invocation of such special standards for gay phenomena is a function of societal prejudice, including individual self-hatred. See Murray 1983a, 1984:21; Dynes 1990b:229; Roscoe 1988a:9. Affixing simple labels on complex realities is the norm for social categories, and certainly for aggregations of persons with multiplex ties inside and outside "boundaries" of "differences" that are labeled *communities* (A. P. Cohen 1985:101). People generally share symbols without

TABLE 8.1 Gay Community Characteristics

CHARACTERISTIC	SAMPLE										
	SF this study	Random SF MACS sample[a]	Random Telephone SF sample[b]	Non-random SF[c]	Random LA[d]	LA MACS[e]	Chicago MACS[f]	New York City[g]	Pittsburgh MACS[h]	SF white c. 1969[i]	SF black[i]
Mean education	16.7						16.3	16.5		15.6	15.1
Percent with some college	86.5	90	88	70	84	89	88	94	81	75	77
Mean age in 1988	40	40.5	37	40	36	35	35	39	35	37	27
Percent white	70	89	77[j]	91	78	95	93	87	96		
Percent in a relationship	56[k]		58[k]	58	36		53	43		51	58
Mean age at which began homosexual activity	17.0					17	19		17		
Mean age at coming out	23.8	21.3[m]								23[l]	21[l]

a. Winkelstein et al. 1987b.
b. Hatfield 1989.
c. McCusick, Horstman, and Carfagni 1985; McCusick et al. 1990.
d. Kanouse et al. 1991.
e. Kaslow et al. 1987.
f. Kessler et al. 1988.
g. J. Martin and Dean 1990.
h. Valdiserri et al. 1988.
i. A. P. Bell and Weinberg 1978.
j. Figure includes lesbians as well as gay men.
k. Figure inferred from "living with someone." From Martin et al. (1989:274) one might extrapolate that 85% of those living with someone else are living with a lover.
l. Age of first affair, which is generally later than first sexual activity.
m. Mean age at which first socialized as gay. In contrast, mean age at which first thought of self as gay was 18.7.

gay male communities fit all the criteria suggested by sociologists to define *community* as well as or better than urban ethnic communities do.[7] Lesbian communities exhibit the same features, albeit to a lesser extent.

Territorial Concentrations

The first, commonsense component of *community* is territory. The imaginary "traditional" rural village is supposed to have been geographically distinct, internally homogeneous and harmonious, and untrammeled by external influences. Nowhere are rural villages entirely isolated from each other, however, and in some places the boundaries of rural villages are difficult to draw.[8] Levies of taxes, soldiers, and labor come from outside, and even in extremely mountainous regions, some persons look beyond the immediate locale to larger worlds.[9] Intravillage variability and conflict are more common than anthropologists once supposed.[10]

To make communities out of geographical aggregates, people must experience spatial boundaries as important ways of conceiving and distinguishing kinds of people within those boundaries. These differences may be quite minuscule. "The community boundary is *not* drawn at the point where differentiation occurs. . . . The conceptualization and symbolization of the boundary from within is much more complex" (A. P. Cohen 1985:74).

Endogamy, restriction of trade, local cults, and other such social creations supplement geographical distance and obstacles to make socially salient (meaningful) boundaries. Moreover, geographical distinctions may be unnecessary as well as insufficient.[11] Isolation and propinquity alone do not

---

necessarily attaching identical meanings to the symbol. See Wallace 1961; Kay 1978; Schwartz 1978.

7. I used the update by Sutton and Munson (1976) of Hillery's (1959) review of how sociologists defined "community" in a more extended formal analysis of the Toronto gay male community ca. 1975–78 in Murray 1979b.

8. See Geertz 1959; Skinner 1964; Lansing 1987.

9. Merton 1968:441–74.

10. Although Robert Redfield is considered the chief perpetuator of the myth that they are rare, in his ideal type "folk society," his description (1950) of Chan Kom, his main research site in the Yucatan, revealed quite virulent factionalism as well as considerable influence from outside the country, not just outside the village.

11. Shibutani (1961:130) pioneered the notion that social worlds need not be grounded territorially. Webber (1964:108–110) argued for abandoning "place" altogether in defining urban communities: "In a very important sense, the functional process of urban communities is not placelike. . . . The idea of community has been tied to the idea of place. . . . But it is now becoming apparent that it is the accessibility rather than the propinquity aspect of 'place' that is the necessary condition. . . . Spatial distribution is not the crucial determinant of membership. . . . Interaction is." See also Ward 1989; Knopp 1986.

Delph (1978) argued for an international community of cruising gay men who feel connected

produce solidarity.[12] Contrariwise, seemingly trivial similarities (such as living in a red housing project rather than a brown one, one side of a street rather than another) may come to symbolize distinctiveness important enough to lead to collective action, and even to violence.[13]

North American cities lack walled-in ghettoes. Nor do checkpoints prevent the flow of persons between perfectly segregated areas.[14] Thus, one may travel from a predominantly Italian territory to a predominantly Chinese one, or to a predominantly gay one in San Francisco (or Toronto or other North American cities). None of these areas is inhabited exclusively by Italian, Chinese, or gays; yet residents of a city are able to report where such communities are. At least, they can specify where the centers are. Boundaries often are not distinctly conceived. Categories of everyday cognition are generally fuzzy sets.[15]

Several neighborhoods with lesbian and/or gay residential concentrations exist in large North American cities.[16] In Toronto in the late 1970s, there were two, shown on Map 1: a downtown one on both sides of Yonge Street north of Dundas Street, and the Annex. More than half the members of gay organizations lived in less than 2 percent of the total area of Toronto. Table 8.2 includes residential data from a lesbigay organization from 1980 and the two gay ones reported in Murray 1979a.[17]

Map 2 shows San Francisco neighborhoods. In San Francisco, major areas of lesbigay residential concentration during the 1980s and 1990s in-

---

to those they have not met who are prowling similar locales and share a common sense of being stigmatized, common enemies, and a common commitment to shield their sexual activity from public view. Plummer (1995:45, 93) stressed technological bases for non–face-to-face contact.

12. See Foster 1965; Selby 1974; and many studies of witchcraft in villages from around the world.

13. Weber 1978:388–89; Suttles 1972:156–232; Moerman 1965; Barth 1969.

14. Even the Jewish ghetto within the Pale was not ethnically totally homogeneous (Wirth 1928:3). Nor were the "defended neighborhoods" in the city on which the ecological approach to urban communities was based: "Very few of the defended neighborhoods in Chicago which Park, Burgess, and their followers described seem to have been exclusively or almost exclusively occupied by a single ethnic group," according to Suttles (1972:27). On historical changes in San Francisco gay concentrations, see Godfrey 1988.

15. See Zadeh 1965; Brown 1976; above, pp. 34–36.

16. Chauncey (1994:151–63) discusses early 20th century concentrations in rooming houses and YMCAs in New York City. I have heard of similar concentrations in other cities. Gevisser and Cameron (1995:19) note a concentration of gay men in the Hillbrow area in Johannesburg, South Africa, during the Second World War.

17. John Firth mapped addresses for Community Homophile Association of Toronto and For Your Information members; I mapped the 1978 male membership of the Toronto Gay Academic Union (there were only a few lesbians in the organization; as I recall, all lived in the borough of Toronto). Both recreational and residential concentrations have spread eastward from Yonge Street since then.

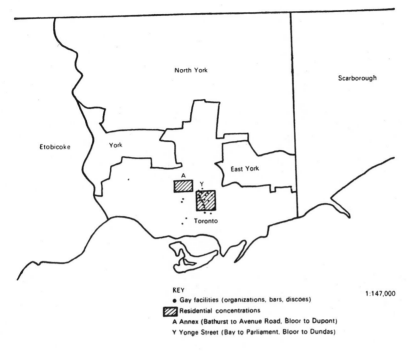

Map 8.1 Concentration of Toronto Homophile Organizations and Members

TABLE 8.2 Residential Concentration of Lesbian and Gay Members
of Three Late-1970s Toronto Gay/Lesbian Organizations

	FYI (1980)		CHAT (1976)	GAU (1978)
AREA	*Percent of lesbians resident within*	*Percent of gay males resident within*	*Percent of gay males resident within*	*Percent of gay males resident within*
Toronto: Yonge/Wellsley[a]	20	37	33	31
Toronto: Annex[b]	12	5	17	27
Toronto: Other	48	38	33	35
Other boroughs	20	22	16	7
N	*123*	*810*	*109*	*78*

a. Census tracts 34, 35, 36, 63, 64, 65, 66.
b. Census tracts 91, 92, 93.

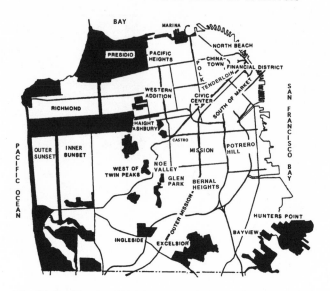

Map 8.2 San Francisco Neighborhoods. Shaded areas are the larger parks. Smaller parks are not shown. (Map by Keelung Hong)

clude the Castro, Bernal Heights, and Potrero Hill (for lesbians and gay men, mostly in multiple-person households), the Valencia Street corridor of the Mission district (for lesbians), Polk Gulch side of the Tenderloin, and South of Market (for gay men, mostly living alone).[18] Thirty-five percent of my San Francisco sample lived in these (including the hills above the Castro), with additional concentrations (totaling 27%) in Noe Valley and the Western Addition (respectively to the south and northwest of the Castro). Similarly, three other concentrations of Chinese business and residence in San Francisco exist (Clement, Irving, and Noriega) along with the original, expanding, and increasingly Chinese "Chinatown."

Data on what gay men in my San Francisco sample considered to be the

18. The first concentrations were in North Beach, spilling southwest into the Tenderloin/ Polk area in the early 1960s, overlapping with concentrations of hippies in the Haight later in the decade. Gay gentrification pioneers moved into the Castro area and "lower Pacific Heights" ("upper Fillmore" in the northern part of the Western Addition) in the early 1970s. Lesbigay residential areas without gay bars, especially Potrero Hill and Bernal Heights, began in the mid 1970s simultaneously with lesbian cultural institutions and residential concentration in the Valencia corridor. This expansion looked to some of the natives and some of those they considered "invaders" like a new form of "manifest destiny" to conquer a last frontier of the Far West without noticing that people were already there. Only North Beach seems to have lost lesbigay population in this expansion, so immigration must account for populating the other concentrations. My sense of the timing and direction derive especially from a realtor, Norm Dale; the late Nick Ardell (both of whom were 1950s immigrants to San Francisco); and Karen Murphy.

TABLE 8.3 Percentage of Neighbors Reported by Gay San Francisco Men
to be Gay/Lesbian, by Neighborhood

| NEIGHBORHOOD | REPORTED | | 1990 CENSUS DATA |
	gay/lesbian percentage	N	Percentage of male–male "partner" households
Buena Vista Heights	72.5	2	2.8 (Haight)
Castro	66.9	23	10.1 (Upper Market)
Eureka Valley	50.0	1	6.0 (Eureka/Noe)
Diamond Heights	43.3	3	4.5
Duboce Triangle	43.8	4	10.1 (Upper Market)
Hayes Valley	34.7	7	3.4 (Western Addition)
Richmond	33.3	3	1.0 (Inner Richmond)
Potrero Hill	32.8	9	4.3
Balboa Park	30.0	2	3.9 (Glen Park)
Mt. Olympus	30.0	2	—
Haight/Ashbury	29.2	8	2.8
Fillmore	28.3	3	3.4 (Western Addition)
Noe Valley	28.2	19	6.0 (Eureka/Noe)
Western Addition	28.2	17	3.4 (Western Addition)
Twin Peaks	25.9	9	6.9
Panhandle	24.3	3	2.8 (Haight)
Polk/Civic Center	20.0	3	1.2 (Tenderloin)
Pacific Heights	19.6	4	1.4
Mission	19.4	9	1.8
Dolores Heights	19.0	2	1.8 (Mission)
Nob Hill	17.0	5	1.4
Presidio	12.5	4	0.0 (army base)
Glen Park	11.2	4	3.9
Russian Hill	9.2	4	0.1
Sunset	8.5	2	0.6
North Beach	8.0	2	0.7
St. Francis Wood	8.0	1	0.1
Tenderloin	5.0	4	1.2
Telegraph Hill	5.0	1	0.1 (Russian Hill)
Marin County	17.8	17	0.3 (San Rafael)
Berkeley/Oakland	9.7	10	0.6/0.4
Daly City	3.0	5	0.3 (San Mateo)
Contra Costa County	0.0	4	0.4 (Concord)
West Oakland	0.0	2	0.4 (Oakland)

concentrations of lesbigay people in their neighborhoods should not be mistaken for objective measures. Conceptions of shared characteristics matter, and conceptions of residential concentrations to some degree can become self-fulfilling prophecies.[19] The rightmost column of Table 8.3 lists the percentage of households composed of unrelated males who checked off the relationship category "unmarried partnerships" in the 1990 U.S. census.[20] My

19. Merton 1968:475–90.
20. L. Krieger 1993.

guess is that at most half the couples would have checked this off on the census form. If somewhere between a third and a half of gay men are coupled, 10 gay men will be distributed into about 8 households.[21] I would, therefore, multiply the numbers in the rightmost column by a number between 4 and 6 to estimate the number of households containing gay males. There were 5,437 male same-sex partner households, in comparison to 1,379 female ones, approximating what I think is the true ratio of three or four self-identified gay men for every self-identified lesbian.[22] From a random sample of households in three multi-ethnic San Francisco neighborhoods, Binson (1994) reported 3.4 times as many exclusively homosexual men as exclusively homosexual women.[23]

That my respondents' estimates still exceed the results of even the high algorithm (of multiplying by 6) may stem, at least in part, from a much smaller sense of what one's neighborhood is: perhaps as small as the two sides of one street for one block. Beyond that, no doubt, is some exaggeration of how gay "gay neighborhoods" are and of how totally lacking in gay people places such as West Oakland and Contra Costa County are.

Institutional Completeness/ Elaboration

Clustering of recreational facilities, particularly nocturnal ones such as bars, fosters in-group perceptions of a gay or lesbian territory. The existence of distinctive institutions is more salient to the identification of a community— both for insiders and for outsiders—than is residential segregation or concentration. Although Hooker (1961:356) noted that gay social life was not randomly distributed through Los Angeles during the 1950s, she felt that there was "not a community in the traditional sense of the term, as it has been used by sociologists, in that it lacks a territorial base with primary institutions serving a residential population." Gagnon and Simon (1973 [1967]:153) used the term, but called attention to its "very limited content":

21. For simplicity's sake I will assume that the number of couples living separately is approximately equal to the number of uncoupled gay men living in the same household. I suspect more of the latter than of the former exist, so that perhaps there are only 6 or 7 gay households for every 10 urban gay men.

22. In West Hollywood, the male:female census same-sex partner household ratio was 20:1, in Oakland 1:1.2. Although there is a concentration of lesbian couples in Oakland, I believe that Oakland also has more gay men than lesbians. I also believe that lesbians are somewhat more likely to be in couples at any particular time than gay men, as in the 1980 Toronto data: 53% in contrast to 43% of FYI members, though only 53% vs. 50% in the 1970 San Francisco data of A. P. Bell and Weinberg 1978:278.

23. The prevalences of men who said that they had had sex with men during the preceding ten years that she reported were 37.2% for (the Castro side of) the Western Addition, 15.9% for the Mission, and 13.5% for Bayview/Hunter's Point. Of these, 72% self-identified as gay.

"the homosexual community, as it exists at the present time, is in itself an impoverished cultural unit" (p. 154).[24] Hoffman (1968:8) wrote that "the homosexual community is not so much defined by geographical factors (although homosexuals tend very often to live in certain sections of the city rather than in others) as by certain common values and behaviors, and by shared public places."

Over the course of the 1970s, gay men in Australian, Western European, English, and North American cities developed a fairly complete set of basic social services beyond the bars. These included bookstores, churches and organizations within churches, travel agencies and other specialized businesses, periodicals, sports leagues, historical societies, musical groups, mental health and substance abuse programs, charities, etc., as well as local, national, and international political organizations. Indeed, San Francisco and other cities have "Gay Yellow Pages" featuring myriad other gay businesses and services, just like the "Hispanic Yellow Pages" and "Chinese Yellow Pages." As I argued in Murray 1979b:170, urban North American gay communities were, even then, more institutionally complete than ethnic communities,[25] and, more importantly, were in the process of adding rather than abandoning distinctive institutions. That is, urban gay communities not only were more institutionally complete than ethnic communities, but were moving in the opposite directions: de-assimilation into specifically lesbigay institutions in contrast to assimilation away from ethnic institutions. *Institutional elaboration* is what I called the process.[26]

Solidarity and Collective Action

Contemporary gay male (and also lesbian) urban North American enclaves nevertheless differ from ethnic immigrants, past and present, in some important ways. In contrast to the relatively impoverished immigrants speaking an alien language whom sociologists expect to form distinct (ethnic) institu-

24. They contrasted *gay community* with other ones rather than with longed-for communion: "For both male and female homosexuals one can talk about the existence of a community, at least in most relatively large cities. As for many ethnic or occupational groups, which also can be said to have a *community*, the subcommunity does not require a formal character or even a specific geographical location. It is, rather, a continuing collectivity of individuals who share some significant activity, begin to generate a sense of a bounded group possessing special norms and a particular argot" (p. 194; p. 195 discusses functions the community serves for members).

25. In contrast to Breton 1964. See pp. 72–73.

26. The term has been picked up and used widely, generally without attribution. On the substantial growth in numbers of gay organizations between 1972 (when cities with populations of less than 300,000 other than college towns generally had no gay organizations), and 1985 (when almost every city with a population greater than 200,000, even in the South, had one or more), see Weiser 1986:288–89.

tions, gay men were relatively integrated into a the full range of occupations, and mostly had native command of English, before gay institutional elaboration began. Most gay persons could and did "pass" in everyday life.[27] We *choose* to interact with "our own kind," rather than being restricted to those who speak the same (alien) language. Given a previous homosexual exogamy (a preference for straight *trade* rather than for *sisters* as sexual partners), sexual endogamy (self-identified gay men coupling with other self-identified gay men) was crucial to the formation of gay pride, consciousness, and collective action.

As noted several times in this book, some men who engage in recurrent homosexual behavior do not recognize "sexual orientation" as defining any important component of their self. They do not see a "we" with whom they have anything important in common and therefore see no reason to associate with openly gay men in nonsexual interaction. Others feel that they have a distinct sensibility shared with other gay people. Some individuals fight the expectation to be part of any such "we," while others eagerly seek a sense of commonalty. Consciousness of kind is not innate or automatic, but emerges over time, depending on experiences (and the feelings about and cognition of those experiences) and sympathetic identification with others of a kind. This is true of ethnic consciousness or class consciousness as much as of gay consciousness.[28]

Social stigmas inhibit identification. Sometimes, however, as discussed in chapters 1–2, a critical mass develops to challenge a stigma—either by asserting "We are not like that" or by proclaiming "The ways we are different are fine, or even valuable." Stigmas then become badges of honor. They may also become stimuli to collective action challenging discrimination and affirming the value of the group's formerly stigmatized characteristics.[29] In a pluralistic society, group identification is an achieved status, not automatically and irrevocably established at birth, nor in primary socialization.[30]

Advocates and adversaries both foster collective identification, which is a necessary but not sufficient prerequisite to collective action. Some opportunistic politicians use definitions of a "kind of person" to advance a

27. On the invisibility of networks, see Leznoff 1954; Burnham 1973; Chauncey 1985; Bérubé 1990; Grube 1990.

28. See Shibutani and Kwan 1965. Gusfield (1975:35) defined community as "people who see themselves as having a common history and destiny different from others." Similarly, A. P. Cohen (1985:16) wrote, "The quintessential referent of community is that its members make, or believe they make, a similar sense of things . . . and, further, that they think that that sense differs from one made elsewhere."

29. See Kitsuse 1980; Gamson 1989.

30. See Glick 1942; Pitt-Rivers 1973.

minority's status, while others organize against any (sometimes only fanta-sized) gains—and, sometimes, against the very existence in a society of such a people. Public discourse about the value or threat of a kind of person crys-tallizes the identification of some persons with a group, while scaring off others from identification or even association with the stigmatized group. Partly through political conflict, some people who are defined categorically come to see themselves as having a common history and destiny distinct from other kinds of people, public supporters, and public enemies. Gay leaders have pressed economic boycotts, political coordination, and mass demon-strations.[31] Other moral entrepreneurs have promoted legal discrimination and harassment, as well as criminalization of homosexual behavior.[32] None-theless, it bears stressing that even those who have the feeling of being part of a group may still not join in collective action, which is rarely—if ever—characteristic of *any* population. Homosexual behavior does not necessarily lead either to a lesbigay identity or to associating with gay men and women. Even gay identity and gay sociation do not necessarily lead to gay collective action.[33] One could substitute "ethnic derivation" and "ethnic" for "homo-sexual behavior" and "gay" in these false inferences without loss of validity. Sporadic action by a self-selected vanguard is more common for class-based or ethnic-based groups, as well as for lesbians or gays. And with a decline in the closure and the geographical boundedness of communities in late twen-tieth century North America, insofar as "communities encompass only one aspect of their members' lives, except in that domain, they lack the coercive power on which the effectiveness of norms, status, and reputation depend."[34]

Site of Primary Group

For some gay persons, the primary group consists of other gay persons. For some lesbians, the primary group consists of other lesbians. Perhaps in urban lesbigay worlds—or at least in discourse about them—the term *families we choose* has become popular, as is discussed at the end of this chapter. Already in the early 1950s there were urban coteries characterized by

31. Violent resistance to the police (most spectacularly, the torching of a line of eleven police cars in the "White Night riot" of May 1979 in San Francisco and the October 1977 barricades in the middle of Montreal) has been collective, but not premeditated.

32. On moral entrepreneurs, see Becker 1963:147–63; Dynes 1979; Gusfield 1963; Zurcher and Kirkpatrick 1976; and chapter 4.

33. In interviews with white gay men who reveled in the strength of numbers in the visibly gay neighborhood around Dupont Circle in Washington, D.C., Myslik (1995:20) found that they did not believe that gay men were more likely to come to the rescue of someone being attacked there than straight men.

34. Coleman 1993:9.

(a) unselfconscious and unrestrained practice of homosexuality; (b) a high degree of social isolation [from straight circles]; (c) little or no concealment from any heterosexual primary group; (d) total involvement within homosexual society; (e) no conception of sexual deviation as a threat to one's social position; (f) little concern with informal sanctions applied by heterosexual society. (Leznoff 1954:74; see also 94–97)

In the clone era, gay men told me (as others did Levine 1979b, 1986) that they lived in a gay world, restricting interaction with straight people to jobs and occasional visits to families of origin. AIDS has decimated some of those networks, and those who have come out under the shadow of AIDS seem to socialize more with (more accepting) straight friends and also with more lesbian–gay male contacts than was the case for lesbian separatists and clones in the late 1970s.[35]

Shared Norms

Lesbians and gay men learn norms for appropriate speech and behavior, especially cruising etiquette.[36] With the catastrophe of AIDS, an ethic of responsibility not to infect partners and to care for the sick and dying has become central.[37] Not everyone is equally adept or equally committed to any (sub)culture's norms: intracultural variability is ubiquitous. Even nuclear families contain diversity without anyone denying that *families* exist.[38] There are shared meanings and recognized signs, but not shared and not recognized by everyone who identifies as gay, lesbian, etc. For instance, while "camp" is a gay perspective, it is far from being universally valued. While some consider it as "resistance," delightfully destablizing heterosexist hegemony, hypocrisy, and cant, others see it as perpetuating sexism, misogyny, and self-hatred—and many less theoretically inclined and lesbigays regard it as degrading (of them, of those who enact camp, of the collective image). There is diversity not only in evaluation, but even in comprehension.[39]

"Community" as a Process

Although the traditional sociological and—even more so—anthropological conception of *community* has been an entity with a catalog of attributes, I

35. Herdt and Boxer 1993; Carrington 1995. Cf. Gorman 1992:99–101.

36. Quick wit is highly valued. On language norms and play, see Murray 1979a, 1983c; Hayes 1976, 1981; J. Goodwin 1989; Leap 1995a,b. On cruising etiquette, see Lee 1978a,c,d; M. Weinberg and Williams 1975; Brodsky 1993a; Wagenhauser 1992; Murray 1995b.

37. See Adam 1992; Kayal 1992, 1993; King 1993; Plummer 1988.

38. Suttles 1972:35; see C. Hart 1954.

39. See Bergman 1991 on creating an alternative culture controlled by gay wit.

argued in 1979 that *community* is a process of creating and caring about a kind that is constantly being constructed and reproduced:

> Consciousness of kind is an emergent quality, not at all innate. . . . Gross categories may not be experienced as meaningful by some of those to whom they are applied, so that a Cantonese is Chinese (Glick 1942) or a Sicilian is Italian only in the eyes of others. But such perception by others can have real consequences for life chances. (Murray 1979b:173–74)

I quoted Suttles's observation (1972:13) that "it is in their 'foreign relations' that communities come into existence," and suggested that only since the mid 1960s had some gay men and smaller bands of "dykes" and gay women been willing to undertake foreign policy in a generally hostile public glare. Not just institutions, but collective consciousness and collective action increased over time, despite an ongoing stream of denigrations from within and without that "there is no gay community."

My view remains that the gay community is at least as much of one as any other urban community, so that if we are to jettison the notion *community*, then *gay community* should be the last, not the first to go.[40] Even more than the Toronto of the late 1970s that I took as an example, the San Francisco gay community (then or now) evidences the criterial features of *community* either as an entity or as a process.

A Community, *Not Just a "Lifestyle Enclave"*

Since that time, an influential interpretation of American culture, *Habits of the Heart* by Robert Bellah and four colleagues (1985:72), sought to preserve the sacred term *community* from application to what they term *lifestyle enclaves*. This superficial, second-rate kind of grouping is based on "the narcissism of similarity" in patterns of leisure and consumption. "When we hear such phrases as 'the gay community' or 'the Japanese American community,'" they write, "we need to know a great deal before we can decide

---

40. For a defense of applying *community* to cities, see Suttles 1972:4–81; Rosaldo 1987: 182, 194. Some writers continue to dismiss *gay community* without providing examples of what they might consider "real" communities. For example, Grover (in Crimp 1988:24) asserted that gay people "are too diverse politically, economically, and demographically to be described meaningfully by such a term," but doesn't mention a people in American cities who are not also too diverse. In rejecting the locution *gay community*, Mohr (1988:12–13) at least suggested an alternative term—a *people*—with Jewish Americans as an analog of "open-textured unity." At the other extreme, despite their interest in stress-buffering social relationships, J. Martin and Dean (1990:548) adopted a wholly intrapsychic criterion ("private recognition that one was a homosexual or bisexual man") of *gay community*. I also think that Kennedy and Davis (1993) are too ready to call networks (in Buffalo ca. 1930–60) *community*.

the degree to which they are genuine communities and the degree to which they are lifestyle enclaves."[41]

One criterion of *community* for Bellah et al. is "to reproduce the entire institutional complex of a functioning society in rural and even, as far as possible, in urban settings" (p. 73). If, as I think I demonstrated in Murray (1979b), gay Toronto met this test in the late 1970s, San Francisco, then or now, has more instances of every institution, including four gay political clubs,[42] its own health services (including Operation Concern and 18th Street Services and, earlier, the Pride Foundation), two rival weekly newspapers *(The Sentinel* and *The Bay Area Reporter),* two biweekly magazines *(Frontiers* and *Bay Times),* and approximately six choruses. Almost all of these predate the florescence of AIDS organizations—protest ones such as Mobilization Against AIDS, Stop AIDS Now, and two ACT UP groups; and service ones such as Project Open Hand, the AIDS Emergency Fund, the AIDS Foundation, the Shanti Project, and others.

The most important criterion for Bellah et al., deeply concerned as they are about the failure of civic involvement in ultra-individualist America, is the extent to which serious commitments among geographically concentrated people similar in lifestyle "carry them beyond private life into public endeavors" (p. 74). It seems to me that even before the trauma of AIDS launched major political and charitable initiatives, San Francisco was already notable for gay political involvement in neighborhood, environmental, educational, labor, arts, and civil rights issues. These concerns extended beyond protecting and advancing specifically gay self-interests. In a long-running political battle with "downtown" interests pitted against "neighborhoods," gay County Supervisors Harvey Milk, Harry Britt, Roberta Achtenberg, Carole Migden, Susan Leal, and Tom Ammiano have been leaders in battles for a wide range of "progressive" causes, including height limitations on buildings, rent control, preserving open space from encroachment, civilian oversight of police, municipalization of electricity, etc. Although some gay male San Franciscans oppose one or more of these policies, the heavily gay precincts consistently turn out the highest percentages of votes not just for the gay "progressive" candidates, but for the more "leftist/progressive"

41. Fugita and O'Brien (1991, especially pp. 101–15) show the inappropriateness of *lifestyle enclave* for Japanese Californians. It is striking that Bellah et al. took as examples two groups that have experienced and reacted to marked discrimination. Shared stigmatization is probably more important to the persistence of consciousness of kind and solidarity than are items of lifestyle, even though people may regard the latter as symbols (Barth 1969; Hechter 1975; B. Anderson 1983).

42. The Republican Log Cabin Club; Alice B. Toklas, Harvey Milk, and Stonewall Democratic clubs.

straight candidates, and for environmentalist state and local initiatives. In addition to elected officials, openly lesbian and gay members serve on the boards of most local political, charitable, and arts organizations.

At an occupational-choice level, too, long before AIDS, gay people were

society's servants, its comforters and nurturers. . . . We work as nurses, thera-pists and teachers beyond our proportion in the populace. There is more to the gay lifestyle than Sunday brunch. . . . [And those standing by PWAs] are not stereotypical, flighty, sex-addicted faggots. (Kantrowitz 1986)

By defining "gay" as purely a sexual activity, and a wrong and sinful one at that, the heterosexual world [43] has not allowed itself to see any social, familial or nurturing aspects of the gay community. (Bronski 1988:134)

Beyond an active involvement in the civic culture of the Bay Area and the personal involvement of many lesbians and gays in the "helping profes-sions," the extraordinary mobilization to lobby for and care for persons with AIDS surely transcends the hedonism and shared leisure of a "lifestyle en-clave." Contributions of resources—not least, time and energy—by many gay San Francisco men protecting and caring for mortally ill peers show that gay men share more than jargon, costumes, and transient sexual encounters. Although the larger society disvalues and seeks to undermine our relation-ships, gay men for the most part have stood by their ailing lovers and friends. Whether in fund-raising or in providing services to persons with AIDS (and not just gay ones), gay men over the past decade have demonstrated their willingness to take on onerous burdens of caring for others. To put it mildly, it is hard to conceive the gay male response to AIDS as that of a "lifestyle enclave" with superficially committed individuals concerned only with nar-cissistic self-gratifications or reveling in "the narcissism of similarity" in consumption patterns.

Bellah et al. (1985:153–54) further specify that "a real community" is

a "community of memory," one that does not forget its past. . . . Stories of collective history and exemplary individuals are an important part. . . . A genu-ine community of memory will also tell painful stories of shared suffering that sometimes creates deeper identities than success. . . . Where history and hope are forgotten and community means only the gathering of the similar, com-munity degenerates into lifestyle enclave.

This certainly describes the gay community. Already in the late 1970s, I could write that "in recent years efforts to learn about the history of subor-dinated groups has gained momentum. The quest for forerunner heroes

43. Along with special creationists who see acts without selves in history and anti-identity "queer theorists" today not wanting to be defined by sexual preference (i.e., "wrong" in another sense than "sinful") . . .

("Shakespeare, Michelangelo and me" or *From Jonathan to Gide*) has been supplemented by serious historical research on the everyday life of oppression" (Murray 1979b:172). As a survey of a gay bookstore or of history journals would show, this trend continued to gain momentum. If Bellah and his associates examined the activities of either the gay or the Japanese American community, they would see intense activity in preserving accounts of suffering in oral history projects and autobiographical publications, as well as celebration of exemplary and of "common" members of each community.[44] In addition to a florescence of professional historical scholarship on homosexual pasts, community-based groups collect oral history in many American metropolises, including the very active Gay and Lesbian Historical Society of Northern California.[45] The Names Project AIDS Memorial Quilt would seem to me to be a model of community-generated public remembrance. Krouse (1994:73–74) stressed that the quilt is a collective endeavor that commemorates relationships: of panel makers to dead lovers, friends, and relatives. "In a society in which the message is that those dying of AIDS are expendable, the quilt involves passionate expression that these people matter" and are remembered (p. 74).

NATIVES' VIEWS

Having shown that the gay community well fits the new criteria for *community*, as well as the older ones in social science discourse, I would like to turn from the ethnological outsider criteria of *community* to analyzing the native sense of what *gay community* means for those who consider themselves a part of it. In 1980, just before the first cases of AIDS appeared, I surveyed 61 gay-identified San Francisco men about their understanding of *gay community*. I framed questions that systematically varied the criterial features suggested in pre-test interviews. These were (1) having a gay identity, (2) living in a gay neighborhood, and (3) having (socializing with) mostly gay friends. I then confirmed that for most of its members, gay identity is the salient, defining characteristic, not homosexual activity. As Michael, a white self-identified clone, put it,

44. I can, however, think of no other group whose academic elite is so bent on challenging the masses' quest for roots as gay and lesbian historians are. Lip service to social history by those who prefer to deal with texts, mostly, but not invariably literary ones, seems to me far more common than attempts to use records about recent or long-past everyday life in gay/lesbian/queer history. (Alan Bérubé's work is a spectacular and canonized exception. He recurrently stresses that he is a college dropout with community rather than academic credentials.)

45. See Roscoe 1988a.

It doesn't matter what you do in bed—or in the backrooms. Anyone who considers himself gay *is* gay.

[How does someone come to consider himself gay?]

God knows—and she ain't telling! Um, there's supposed to be a "gay sensibility," but again, there are people who are obviously straight who have it, and some very tacky fags. I'd have to say it's who you identify with. Like some of these straight people who I'd say have a "gay sensibility"—whatever that is—they're sort of "honorary faggots." There *are* people who consider it to be an honor, you know. There are others who have a lot of homosexual, um, "release" shall we say? Like they make it every day in some sordid tearoom, for instance, but would never admit to being gay, even while they're sucking your cock, right? Well, to me they aren't gay.

[What are they? What would you call them?]

They're homosexual, but they aren't gay.

[And some people who have never had sex with another man are?]

Yeah, sure. *The gay community is a state of mind, not body.* Anyway, gay men aren't real concerned about excluding people from this elite we consider ourselves to be. I've never hear of anyone's credential being challenged, like "I'm not going to believe you're gay until I fuck you."[46] We give everyone the benefit of the doubt: You wanna party with us? That's fine; you don't have to make it with other men if you don't want to. Your loss if you don't, you know?

Craig, an African American gay man, in 1980 also stressed the taste leader self-conception of a gay vanguard, saying,

Not all homosexuals identify with being gay, and not all people who are gay identify with the community. Sex may be its starting point, but it's more whom you party with and have a good time with. It used to be political, but now, it's not. Now, it's mostly hanging around in gay places and being chic.

Tony, a Filipino disco queen of that era, told me,

People standing out on the corner of 18th and Castro or in Ringold Alley at two in the morning [when bars close in California] aren't my idea of a community.

[What is *your* idea?]

Well, the Castro *is* a gay community, not just the corner where they flock to exhibit their sexuality. Who you want to be with *out* of bed is probably more important than who you want to be with *in* bed with. I mean, who your friends are, where you go to socialize, not just who you fuck with.[47]

46. Something of an exception to this statement is the North American Gay Amateur Athletic Alliance, the governing body of the Gay Softball World Series, which requires that "individual city champions qualifying for the world series must verify all roster players are gay. According to NAGAAA's definition, gay describes a player whose majority of romantic encounters are with members of the same sex" (Tracy 1989:50). In that this requirement is one of self-identification, it still does not provide an example of having to demonstrate sexual behavior to be included in a gay group or activity. This requirement is quite unusual, in contrast to the Gay Games and other gay sports organizations.

47. See Nardi 1992a,b.

In an earlier and more closeted milieu, Carol Warren (1974:150) distinguished gay identity from acknowledged homosexuality on the basis of sociation:

> A gay identity implies affiliation with the gay community in a cultural and sociable sense. A homosexual, for the community, is one who both practices homosexuality and admits it, whereas a gay person is someone who does all that and also identifies and interacts with the gay world.[48]

Similarly, and more recently, young Chicagoans told Herdt and Boxer that being gay is "a way of life," not about having sex (1993:118). I also asked about effeminacy and cross-dressing, not because I thought that these were components of the native view, but because homosexuality and gender deviance are so often conflated in social science literature (and not just old literature!). In the initial ("pretest") interviews, I went through formal questions that I thought would lead to nonresponse on questionnaires:

1. Are all effeminate men part of the "gay community?"
2. Are members of the "gay community" generally effeminate?
3. Are all men who dress as women part of "the gay community?"
4. Do members of "the gay community" generally wear women's clothes?

The answers to all four questions were negative, generally *very* negative ("Don't you know better?" or "What a stupid question!"). Nick, the informant most attuned to why I would ask questions to which I knew the answer would be strongly negative, commented:

> Femme drag queen is the stereotype, and, of course, there *are* some, but most transvestites, and probably most men who seem effeminate, are straight and *very* hostile to being regarded as gay. The compliment is returned. Most gay men are uncomfortable with drag queens and with flaming queens who reinforce the stereotype, and the drag queens are contemptuous of those they consider "male impersonators" and call "muscle queens" or "leather queens." Drag queens and flaming queens who aren't cross-dress[ers] are tolerated, but [are] often objects of fear and loathing.
>
> I think gay men generally like men and masculinity. You could even say we worship masculinity, so the effeminate stereotype is ludicrously wrong. Male homosexuality is "about" masculinity, not a form of femininity. Men who need women—who are, if you'll pardon the expression "pussy-whipped"—seem lacking in masculinity to many of us, though I'm told that in the "bad old days" the supposedly straight man was a premium object of lust for fags. I don't know of anyone who seeks men who claim to be straight as a sex object, and I don't even understand how a [lover] relationship with one partner claiming to be

48. For earlier, see Leznoff 1954:80–85; Chauncey 1994:272–77.

straight would work. I deal with enough schizophrenia without seeking it out at home!

[Don't you think that boys who are regarded as effeminate are channeled into gay life?]

You mean everyone already thinks they're queer, so they become queer? [Yes.]

No. I think they flee from homosexuality more than the jocks, who can suck cock and get fucked *because* they are respected in the masculine world of the locker room. . . . I don't mean to say that this kind of high school homosexuality usually leads to gay identification and the gay life, or that the high school or college jocks who get off with each other generally recognize themselves as gay, either at the time or later, but I think the really effeminate ones tend to be scared away from men, and even from wanting men. The boys who are loving each others are the high-status jocks. Those who seem effeminate or [have] girl's interests aren't receiving any love from boys. How can they not see males as threatening: they're being attacked, not loved by men? . . .

[Do you think there is *any* relationship between what is understood by most American teenagers as femininity and masculinity and becoming members of the *gay community?*]

No. I think we include the whole femme-to-butch range in high school, perhaps with more of those boys who were completely caught up in the all-male world of athletics and had no interest in "mere girls," even though they may sometimes have rammed their cocks into some. And maybe with fewer of the boys who weren't interested in "male pursuits."

[By which you mean?]

Football, wrestling, cocksucking—things men do better.

Feminine appearance and dress were not just unimportant, but exotic and incomprehensible in the gay male world of the late 1970s and early 1980s. Whatever the gender norms of the past may have been, masculine appearance, demeanor, and stoicism (literally, "taking it" without flinching, so that sexual receptivity, too, was defined as masculine, not effeminizing) were the clone's norms.[49]

The style of the post-clone, post-AIDS generation of young gay men (i.e., those coming out in the late 1980s and early 1990s, who for the most part were born after 1965) deemphasizes some of the masculinist markers of the clone epoch, in particular facial hair and pumped-up muscles, without reviving effeminacy as "the way to be gay." The "younger generation"—an ironic category for the baby-boom generation that still sees itself as "the youth culture" in eternal opposition to establishment elders—is underrepresented in the survey reported here.[50] However, the increased impatience with clo-

49. See chapter 3.
50. Herdt and Boxer (1993) provide data on a more recent cohort.

setry represented by the tactic of publicizing the homosexuality of closeted officials and other public figures suggests that public identification as gay remains central to the conception of *gay community* for a new generation. Moreover, as is shown below, the "younger generation" seems to be coming out at earlier ages than their elders did. Future research may show increased importance for friendship groups in their conception of *gay community,* but I doubt that gender will increase in salience, even among those who regard clone masculinity as exaggerated or excessive.

Alongside the resolutely secular view expressed by informants involved in what some view as "hypermasculinity" or "the alienating hypersexuality" of the urban gay scene, a variety of gay spiritualities coexisted. "Radical fairy consciousness" draws on exemplars from many cultures (e.g., Dionysos from ancient Greek religion, "two-spirited" Native North Americans, and historically untenable interpretations of "witches" from the history of European Christendom) to justify rejecting the violent, destructive strivings of patriarchal self-assertion and objectification of self and others in the lethal rituals of masculinity-proving.[51] Within this syncretic or ecumenical worldview, (homo)sexuality is no longer the "determining gauge":

> *Gay* implies a social identity and consciousness actively chosen, while *homo-sexual* refers to a specific form of sexuality. It follows that the path of "gay spirit" is not automatically adopted by everyone who has homosexual feelings [or engages in homosexual activities], nor is it necessarily limited to such individuals. It is merely a mode of personal growth commonly found among those who are gay. (Roscoe 1988c:48, quoting Thompson 1987:xi)[52]

This distinction between homosexual doing and gay being is common to gay politicos, gay spiritualists, and to the average José in the street who is not involved in either of those activities with their special discourses,[53] and who are quite unready to renounce masculinity (or to cease making sexual objects of themselves or of other men).

Eighty-eight percent of my 1980 sample considered gay-identified men who had never had a same-sex sexual experience to be part of the gay community. In contrast, only 43 percent included men within it who had same-

51. The self-styled "Red Queen," Arthur Evans (1988:178), labels rape, murder, fag-bashing, etc., as "the patriarchal psychosis." On the construction of a continuity between Native American berdache and urban gay Indians, see Roscoe 1988b, 1994; W. Williams 1986.

52. The centrality of identifying with women (with or without homosexual behavior) is entrenched among lesbians: see, for instance, Lorde quoted from Wekker (1993:153–54), in n. 15 of chapter 11.

53. Christian metaphors of communion and ecstasy shape the sense of themselves and rhetoric of self-conceptions of some gay men involved in AIDS service organizations and also within the rituals of the bathhouses and other sex-suffused locales in the pre-AIDS era (see Adam 1992; Brodsky 1993a,b and chapter 3).

sex experience but recognized no gay self-identity. "Credentials don't often get challenged," as Nick said in part of the interview quoted above. Tsunayoshi, a Japanese American gay man, reflected, "Some people say *gay* is a practicing homosexual, but I think you are practicing just by being, even if you're only thinking about, fantasizing about men. Your mind is practicing!"

In replicating these questions with a sample of 159 gay-identified men in the San Francisco Bay Area in 1988, considerably fewer gay-identified men included non–gay-identified men who recurrently engaged in homosexual sex to be within the bounds of *gay community*. Twenty-five percent of Asian gay men and 21 percent of Anglo gay men included within the gay community non–gay-identified men who were involved in homosexual activity. Anglo gay men in 1988 approximated the 1980 sample in including gay-identified men with no homosexual experience: 76 percent included "gay virgins." Asian gay men, who tended to have their first homosexual experiences later than men of other ethnicities (see chapter 9), were far more reluctant to include anyone without sexual experience within their conception of *gay community:* only 38 percent of them did. Otherwise, gay men in 1988 emphasized identity as the *sine qua non* of gay community even more than in 1980, as can be seen by comparing the 1980 and 1988 columns in Table 8.4. For Anglo gay men, gay identity is close to being a sufficient basis for including a man within *gay community*.[54] For Asian American gay men, both gay identity and homosexual behavior are necessary. For half the Latino and African American gay men in the sample, either of these will suffice.[55] The other proposed criteria are necessary additional requirements for only a few (2 percent each if set 6 with only gay identity is compared to gay identity with one of the other two features in sets 2 and 3 and with all three in set 1).

In 1980, those gay men who had at some time been involved with a gay political organization were more than five times more likely to exclude from their conception of the gay community men involved in homosexual activity without a gay identity than were gay men with no gay political background. A gay political background had little effect on explaining variance in the inclusion of other bundles of features. In the 1980 data I also found a statisti-

54. The original investigation was done at a time of pronounced lesbian separatism; see Wolf 1979. Only after preliminary results of this study were presented and Sue-Ellen Jacobs posed what should have been an obvious question—whether, by the late 1980s, any women were considered by gay men to be part of *gay community*—did I add the last two combinations of features, and I have not attempted to try to model a distinction between *gay community* and *gay and lesbian community*.

55. Hawkeswood (1990) reported that his 57 gay black Harlem men "insist on the necessity of homosexual behavior as an integral part of their gay identity" in contrast to the possibility of "being gay" without "doing homosexual behavior" conceived by white gay men.

TABLE 8.4 Percent Including Sets of Attributes in Category "Gay Community" in 1980, 1988, 1993

Set	Gay Identity	Gay Friendship	Gay Neigh-borhood	Percent Including 1980	1988	1993
1	+	+	+	98	100	
2	+	+	−	90	98	
3	+	−	+	80	98	
4	−	+	+	48	24	
5	−	+	−	50	15	
6	+	−	−	−	96	
7	−	−	+	−	7	
	Gay identity	Homosexual activity				
8	+	−		88	72	79
9	−	+		43	22	29
Exclusively heterosexual women who socialize mostly with gay men				68		
Lesbians who work with gay men for lesbian and gay rights or in AIDS organizations				100		
N				66	180	70

cally significant linear increase in inclusiveness for all the combinations based upon the year the respondent came out.

In the 1988 sample, the proportion of those with some experience of gay political involvement was lower (35%) than in the 1980 sample. Moreover, the effects of such experience were attenuated. Those with some gay political involvement were 1.65 times more likely than those without any to include within the category *gay community* gay-identified men without sexual experience, and 2.5 times more likely to exclude straight-identified men engaging in homosexual sexual activity from it. Gay political involvement continued to explain significant variance in inclusion of "gay virgins" in the 1988 data. Using stepwise regression, it was the most important explanatory variable ($r = .36$, $p < .001$), followed by a dichotomous white/nonwhite variable (raising the multiple $r = .463$, $p < .001$), and a slight effect from coming out more recently (which raised the multiple r to .48, $p < .05$).[56] That is, white men who came out in more recent years were most likely to include gay virgins.[57] As Table 8.5 shows, white gay men were more likely to include gay virgins than were nonwhite gay men, and less likely to include everyone who engages in homosexuality.[58] The linear increase on inclusiveness by coming-

56. The beta values for the model with the three variables that explained significant variation are .34 (gay political involvement), .33 (white), and .15 (outyear).

57. This probably relates to the AIDS-phobic increase in celibacy.

58. Although the difference is not statistically significant, Asian men were also more likely to include non–gay-identified homosexually involved men than were Anglo men.

TABLE 8.5 Ethnic Rate of Acceptance of "Gay Virgins" and
of Non–Gay-Identified Homosexuals as Part of
"the Gay Community," Pooled 1988 and 1993 Data

Ethnicity	Percentage including gay-identified virgins	Percentage including non–gay-identified homosexuals	N
White/Anglo	74	20	168
Latino	63	32	19
Asian American	58	33	33
African American	68	40	15

out year found in 1980 continued, but leveled off.[59] As already noted, the direct effect of gay political involvement on acceptance of gay virgins was reduced (from 5:1 in 1980 to 1.65:1 in 1988 to 1.1:1 in 1993).

Stepwise regression of including gay-identified men without homosexual experience in *gay community* produced a model with gay political background, year of birth, and an interaction of education and a dummy variable white/nonwhite involvement having statistically significant contributions (multiple $r = .36$).[60] Neither education nor white/nonwhite had a statistically significant independent effect. Nor did reported ages of first homosexual experience, coming out, moving to the Bay Area, a black–nonblack dummy variable, or a white–gay political interaction effect.

For including non–gay-identified homosexually involved men in *gay community,* gay political involvement (past or present) also remains the best predictor. Including a white/nonwhite dummy variable and year of birth (with decreasing acceptance over time) improve the explanatory model (to a multiple r of .31), with education, year of migration, a black/nonblack dummy variable, and various interaction effects not adding significantly to these three independent variables.[61] There was basically no variance to explain in inclusion of lesbians in *gay community:* only one of the 27 men asked excluded them.[62]

59. There was a slight, statistically insignificant negative relationship between year of coming out and involvement with gay politics in the 1988 data, in contrast to a steady rise in the 1980 data.

60. With a constant of .086, the beta values in a regression equation are .217 for gay political involvement, .01 for year born, and .01 for the white–education interaction.

61. With a constant of .75, the beta values in a regression equation are −.19 for gay political involvement, −.21 for white, and −.005 for year born. The first two are dichotomous variables. The last means that the later the year of birth (i.e., the younger the respondent is), the less the likelihood of inclusion.

62. I asked early respondents if AIDS had changed their conception of what *gay community* means. All said no, although several volunteered that the response to AIDS showed them that a

"Queer Community"

Since 1988, *queer* has been increasingly used by those born after the baby boom (of 1946–56, or up to 1960 in the view of some). In San Francisco, the 1993 Gay and Lesbian Freedom Day Parade Committee chose to use *queer* in the theme, which set off something of a generational semantic war. The liberation generation, once vehemently the "youth generation," was confronted with some of the same contempt we showed during the 1970s for our *homosexual* elders who balked at *gay*. The claim that *queer* was applied equally to women and men is historically ludicrous, and it was lesbian feminists in the 1970s who opted out of being called *gay women*, although many nonpolitical women sexually involved with women preferred *dyke* or *gay woman* to *lesbian*. Nonetheless, usage often escapes etymology, and some men and women now think that *gay* connotes male and that *queer* does not.[63]

As historically deluded as I find this interpretation, I consider it my job to describe rather than prescribe terms. Therefore, in the 1993 panel of my study of San Francisco Bay Area gay men's conceptions of community, I added questions about label preference and about sex and identity as bases for inclusion in *queer community*.

Although the sample is small (66) and disproportionately white and coupled, I would hazard the surmise that *queer* is more popular among whites than among nonwhites. Two of 42 whites preferred *queer* to *gay*, two had no preference between the two, and 39 preferred *gay*. In contrast, one Latino and one Asian preferred *queer*, while all six African Americans, six Latinos, and eight Asians preferred *gay*. Those preferring *queer* were on the average four and a half years younger than those who preferred *gay*, had their first homosexual sexual experience at a slightly younger age (means of 16.7 vs. 18.1), and came out earlier (means of 23.1 vs. 24). Those preferring *queer*

---

larger gay community existed than they had previously supposed, and that it included a wider range of kinds of people than they had previously encountered and/or thought about.

63. It is difficult to imagine how a term in overt contrast to *normal* "rejects a minoritizing logic" (as Warner 1991:16 claims). That "as a partial replacement for 'lesbian and gay' it [*queer*] attempts partially to separate questions of sexuality from those of gender" (ibid.) is impossible: *queer* is far more a gender than a sexuality term, deployed in part to include those not entirely renouncing heterosexual privilege (i.e., *bisexuals* and everyone else not wanting to be 'defined' by anything so unimportant as their sexuality). Moreover, both historically and today, the main connotations are exactly of *gender*—not sexual—deviance. It seems to me that attempts to take over the epithet might challenge gender dichotomies, but that the word itself is largely devoid of any dissent from or challenge to heteronormativity. This does not mean that those, like Michael Warner, who embrace the term do not challenge heteronormativity, only that the *word* does not. "Lesbian Avengers" already have opted out of *queer*, and I predict that women will increasingly claim that *queer* refers to white men.

had equivalent education (median 17.5 years vs. 17), but had substantially lower incomes (median $19,000 vs. $43,000) than those who preferred to be called *gay*.

Regardless of preference in term for self-reference, the sample considered *queer community* to be more restrictive than *gay community*. Whereas 82 percent of those who identify as gay include anyone who identifies himself as gay (even with no homosexual experience) within *gay community*, only two thirds of those who prefer to be called *queer* include queer-identified virgins in the *queer community*. Lesser willingness to consider all men who have sex with men as part of the *queer community* indicates that the difference between *queer community* and *gay community* is not a greater emphasis on sex. Only 16.7 percent of the queer-identified and 19.6 percent of the gay-identified include non–queer-identified men engaged in recurrent homosexual behavior as part of the *queer community*. In contrast, 33 percent include such men within the *gay community*.

Provisionally, I would conclude that rather than being more inclusive, use of *queer* is a fashion in the seemingly recurrent need to adopt a provocative label that will annoy elders who are judged as insufficiently confrontational of entrenched heterosexual society. In the 1970s, my generation railed at closeted, assimilated *homosexuals* among our elders without giving much thought or sympathy to the hostile environment in which they came of age as, simultaneously, lesbian feminists derided "gay women"—and, in turn, have become what "new lesbians" define themselves against.[64] Although it is difficult to consider the generation that has been most devastated by AIDS as too comfortable, some impatience with those perceived as being too ensconced with the political status quo—similar to what was articulated in the 1970s by self-styled *dykes* and *fags* against those seen (by would-be revolutionaries) as mired in accommodation and reform—recurs. Sighing "Plus ça change, plus c'est la même chose" is a temptation of age.[65] What differs is that there seemed to be some possibility of radical social change in the early 1960s, whereas now there seems a real possibility that reaction will triumph. What seems most the same to me is preferring to put each other down rather than to mobilize against external enemies. Each generation seems to have to define itself against the previous one, with a possible oscillation between

64. Whisman 1997.

65. Perhaps, so too is reflection on history. Although, as I have said, usage often escapes etymology, it is interesting that the earlier users of *queer* (ca. the 1910s and 1920s) sought to distinguish themselves from flamboyantly effeminate *fairies*. Not only was this earlier incarnation exclusionary, but gender was the basis for the distinction—and avoiding self-disclosure was one of the aims (see Chauncey 1994:16, 101–6,).

marking and not marking differences of sex. Whisman (1997) quoted a 1992 column from the *Philadelphia Gay News* by Al Patrick explaining that

> gays and lesbians try really hard to relate to their god-given genitals. Queers try really hard to keep everybody guessing all the time about what it is they do with [and what are] their god-given genitals. . . . Homosexuals and queers use one word for both men and women. Gays and lesbians like the separate identities.

Whisman (1993, 1997) showed how class and race complicate apparent generational succession and cautions against concluding that one "master narrative" replaces another. Increased popularity of one organization of homosexuality does not mean others have disappeared.

The "Family" Idiom

Joining attempts to revitalize *queer* in the lexicon of difference in North America during the late 1980s was promotion of *families we choose*. Weston (1991) interviewed 40 gay men and 40 lesbians of diverse class and ethnicity from the San Francisco Bay Area. She did not indicate how many of them used the idiom she exalted into serving as her book's title (or how many considered themselves *queer*), or whether there were any class or ethnic differences in use of this particular phrase. Indisputably, some lesbians and gay men consider their lovers and friends are their most real and important *family*.[66] Others believe that their life partners have been accepted into and are therefore a part of their families of origin. Others would like to construct a gay/lesbian/queer *family* but are unsatisfied with both their natal family and what they have been able to construct as an alternative family. Still others want to have nothing to do with *family* of any kind.

Lewin (1993) showed that 135 late 1970s Bay Area women who identify themselves as *lesbians* and had proved their reproductive capacity (i.e., borne children) feel that they cannot depend on their lovers or other lesbians for help in child rearing and must rely on their families of origin. Like Weston, Lewin did not report any bivariate analysis of her sample, claiming that there were no statistically significant differences, so that the reader must take on faith that the snippets from interviews are representative.[67] In their exchange

66. For some attestations (of the concept, not the exact term), see Preston 1992b:188, 222. For an earlier lesbian era see Barnhart 1975.

67. By chance one would expect every 20th relationship of random numbers to achieve the .05 level of significance, so it is difficult to credit Lewin's (1993:197) cavalier statement that household composition, sexual orientation, mother's age, and children's age(s) didn't matter for any dependent variable. It is also astonishing not to find any sustained narratives in what purports to be a study of lesbian mothers' narrativity. What is to me a paradoxical result of the sustained attacks on the ethnographer's authority (authoritativeness, authorial conjuring) over

of blurbs for each other's books, neither Weston nor Lewin has addressed how the lesbian world can consist of *families we choose,*[68] while these ties are viewed by lesbian mothers as unreliable and evanescent.[69] Perhaps lesbian mothers of the late 1970s were what we used to call *straight-identified,*[70] differing from the young dykes and queers of the mid 1980s for whom motherhood was not the highest or a defining status. Perhaps beliefs in the importance of natal vs. *chosen* families vary by statuses other than age, parenthood, and ethnicity, but these would be useful variables to attempt to relate.

To know, we need systematic analysis of differences in usage of the terms. Although giving lip service to "diversity" (especially when condescending to the naiveté of those who have written about and defended *community*), Lewin and Weston continue in urban postmodern San Francisco the authorial counterfeit of omniscience and unconcern about data selectivity that was traditional to anthropologists, and has been discredited even for mythic "simple societies." I have argued elsewhere (1988b) that when anthropologists started making pronouncements about places with which empirical social scientists were familiar, the latter began to wonder whether any credence should be put in an anthropological record also built more on vigorous omniscience than on systematic collection and analysis of data. Nonetheless, many anthropologists blithely continue to generalize their impressions of atypical acquaintances.

APPENDIX: A NOTE ON GAY GHETTO WAGES

For many of the gay men not struck down by AIDS, economic success continued during the 1980s and 1990s. Careerism often seems to substitute for

---

the course of the 1980s is that anthropologists' publications seem to me more than ever to consist of authors' interpretation with snippets of "native voices" and/or exemplary vignettes. Actual native voices were less celebrated but more audible in ancient, Boasian times than in allegedly "dialogic" anthropology—see Murray 1994c: 469, 476.

68. Both Weston (1991:123) and Lewin (1993:181, 200 n. 7) denigrate community in general and Wolf (1979) in particular on the way to at least as singular (and considerably more ahistoric) models. Astonishingly, in her book about San Francisco lesbian mothers, Lewin (1993) failed to mention Wolf's (1982, 1984b) publications about San Francisco lesbian mothers.

69. Lacking the numbers, the resources, and/or the interest to support lesbian institutions, lesbians tend to be more isolated from each other and less committed to lesbian identities than gay men are committed to gay identity (Murray and Montini 1994; Whisman 1993; Carrington 1995).

70. They were certainly very concerned about including fathers in their children's lives (Lewin 1993:143–62). The whole book shows a very conventional conception of *family* and its basis in *blood* among women fulfilling the traditional feminine vocation of motherhood as conventionally as they can manage.

sex (as among our straight agemates). Along with trends toward coupling and settling down to domesticity, effects of aging supplement the effects of AIDS in promoting investment of energy elsewhere than in sexual marketplaces for baby boomers now aged forty or more. Business and property are (along with love and AIDS) major topics of conversation among baby-boom-generation gay survivors in the late 1980s and early 1990s.[71]

In surveys of gay San Franciscans conducted in 1988 and 1993, I expected to find patterns of "paying for the privilege" of working for quasi-ethnic fellows similar to what Sanders and Nee (1987) found in ethnic economies (specifically, San Francisco's Chinatown and Miami's Cuban businesses): preferential hiring, some cultural sheltering, observable examples of entrepreneurship, and lower wages than outside the ethnic enclave economy. For New York's Chinatown, Zhou and Logan (1989:820) also found that ethnic "enclave workers have worse jobs at lower pay" than minority workers outside the enclave. Gay San Franciscans are not very encapsulated in "gay ghetto" firms. Most gay San Franciscans do not live in a "gay ghetto," and even fewer work there. Only 5.4 percent of my informants worked in the Castro, and another 8.2 percent worked in the South of Market or Polk Gulch areas where gay institutions are also somewhat concentrated, so my data are sparse, though suggestive of another similarity between gay and ethnic urban communities.

The mean annual income of those who worked in the Castro for gay employers was trivially lower than that of those working in the Castro for straight employers ($28,250 vs. $28,500), and $36,920 for those working elsewhere in the Bay Area.[72] The mean annual income for those working for gay-owned businesses outside the Castro was $29,100 in contrast to $38,653 for those working for straight-owned businesses outside the Castro ($F = 4.57$, $p = .017$). The mean annual individual income of the self-employed 10 percent was $48,538. (Medians were $30,000, $22,000, and $40,000, respectively.)[73] These data indicate that gay-owned businesses in the Castro form

71. Some gay men still talk about dance clubs and anonymous sex, but the cultural focus has changed—and not just for the aging "clone generation."

72. The medians were $16,000 for those working for gay-owned businesses in the Castro, $25,000 for those working for straight-owned Castro businesses.

73. The best predictor of earnings was year of birth (with an increase of $745.21 per year of age; $r = .24$, $p = .001$). Education also appeared to have a positive effect (with an increase of $1019.10 per year; $r = .15$, $p = .024$). However, with mutlivariate stepwise regression, there was not a direct effect of education. The variables with statistically significant effects were year born, a white/nonwhite dummy variable, and an interaction between education and white (betas of $-$600, $-$380, and $2,640 with a multiple $r = .345$; among variables not improving this

something of a labor ghetto. The possible thrill of working in the Castro area has a high cost in wages (on the average, $9,081, roughly one quarter of the average salary of gay men working outside gay ghettoes).[74] As in the ethnic enclaves studied by others, many self-employed men do not merely better, but well.

Including all three "gay ghettoes" (i.e., combining Polk and South of Market workers with Castro ones) does not change the picture of lower income from ghetto employment. The mean income of those working for gay-owned businesses in the three ghettoes was $31,500, in contrast to $41,470 for those working for businesses that are not gay-owned in those areas.[75] Those who work for gay-owned businesses outside the ghettoes do substantially better. On the average one year older with .08 more years of education than gay men in the sample working for non-gay employers outside the gay ghettoes, those working for gay employers make significantly more money: $43,636 in contrast to $36,222 ($F = 2.17$, $p = .01$).

Table 8.6 shows that the difference is not between "neighborhood" and "downtown" (financial district) employment. Some professionals work in neighborhoods, and many of the gay men working in the financial district are not professionals.

These data warrant further investigation of gay exploitation of gay labor in a quasi-ethnic enclave economy. In my small and nonrandom samples, those working in gay ghettoes pay for the "privilege" of working for and with one's "own kind" with lower wages in the ghettoes, while working for gay

---

model's fit were coming-out age, gay political involvement, having had a job before migrating, and other interaction effects), i.e., education increased income for whites (and for employed blacks), but not for Latinos or for Asian/Pacific Islander Americans in this sample. The mean annual earnings (and standard deviation) by ethnicity of respondents with any income were white $39,767 (32,957), black $41,375 (22,411), Latino $23,833 (13,210), Asian $30,194 (17.617). The very large standard deviations suggest that medians are better indicators of central tendencies. These were $30,000 white, $9,000 black, $17,500 Latino, and $25,000 Asian. (Half the black respondents had no income, and one very highly paid M.D. raised the mean.)

74. Typical conceptions of "human capital" investment cannot explain the difference. Those working in the Castro had more years of education than those not working there: 20.7 in contrast to 17.0. Insofar as age of first homosexual experience is an indicator of adolescent sexual repression, the Castroites were more repressed, with a mean of 18.10 in contrast to 16.68. They came out faster, at a mean age of 22.75 in contrast to 22.20. Only the education difference was statistically significant ($F = 33$, $p < .001$).

75. As was true of those working in the Castro, those working in the other two major San Francisco gay ghettoes had more years of formal education (18.3 vs. 17.1 years), began homosexual sex older (17.9 vs. 16.8), and came out younger (20.9 vs. 23.1) than gay men not working in the gay ghettoes. Only the education difference was statistically significant ($F = 13.85$, $p < .001$).

TABLE 8.6 Mean Income by Jobsite

Workplace	Mean Income	N
Castro/Upper Market	$29,100	10
Polk corridor	49,167	6
SOMA	41,222	9
financial district	35,147	34
at home	39,875	8
other SF	43,550	40
Outside SF	32,844	45
ghetto	38,280	25
SF exclusive of financial district	41,342	73

employers outside the ghettoes is more lucrative. The self-employed do substantially better, as in ethnic enclave economies.[76]

Eighty-four percent of the men with jobs in the 1988 sample worked for straight employers, so what gay employers pay gay employees affects relatively few respondents. In the perception of the sample, 96 percent thought that gay employers paid gay employees the same amount of money as they paid straight employees for doing the same job, and 4 percent thought that gay employers paid gay employees more than they paid straight employees for doing the same job.[77] Of the seventeen who had gay supervisors at work, 24 percent thought gay supervisors made greater demands on gay employees than on straight employees, while the remaining 76 percent thought there was no difference. Dan, one of the former, complained,

> Perhaps it's because the company is so small, rather than because it's gay. I know that it's generally the case that there is no ladder of advancement to higher-level positions in small companies, but working for a small gay company there is also this draining demand to work harder and make fewer demands, because I'm supposed to have this great desire for a gay company to succeed. This is supposed to substitute for the gratification of higher earnings.
>
> [And you're more concerned about succeeding yourself?]
>
> I like to see gay companies succeed, sure, but *I* would like to succeed, too. I'd like to share in the success more than I do. Instead, I'm supposed to be grateful to be able to work for the greater glory of gay enterprise and the greater profit of one gay enterpriser. And maybe, someday, more money will trickle down. Sounds Reagan Republican, doesn't it? But he [the gay owner] considers himself very progressive, still the radical he claims he was in college.

76. I did not collect data on firm size. If there is a relationship, I would hypothesize it is bimodal (a U-curve).

77. Unfortunately, I did not ask respondents if they thought working for gay employers was more or less lucrative than working for straight employers, and cannot contrast the earning patterns with whatever those expectations are. I did not repeat these questions in the 1993 version.

[And you're not grateful?]

Not grateful enough for him! I think I'm grateful, but also resentful about, shall we say, *excessive* exploitation. I think I should share more in the profits, not that I deserve all of them.[78]

Tsunayoshi similarly noted,

Everything is so fucking personal! I'm ungrateful or disloyal if I ask for anything, especially [for] more money. I think working for "your own kind" sets you up for extra guilt trips.

[Don't you think small companies where everyone knows everyone else expect more gratitude than larger companies, straight or gay?]

Sure, there has to be more personal expectations of employees from the top of a small company, because you all know each other and see each other all the time, but I still think there's an *extra* load of guilt trips and [those in] management saying they are *personally* disappointed, as if you [the employee] aren't being a good "gay brother" if you want money they want to put back into the business. On the other hand, they don't consider that *we* might be disappointed in them as good "gaybrothers" for what they put in their pockets instead of sharing with their "brothers." If we're brothers, we're "younger brothers" who don't deserve much; everything—in their view—is supposed to go to the eldest [i.e., primogeniture]. In this country, we expect that, without breaking up the family farm or family business, we should get a fairly equal inheritance. But we find we are not a real family, that we're being manipulated to be good little boys by an image of family, of being brothers working for the good of the gay family. Exactly the same thing happens for Japanese and Chinese: subordinate yourself to the good of the company, especially the family business: like, supposedly, "We're all in this together, and I [the owner] happen to get more money, but be happy that 'our kind' is doing well, and take what I give you." We Asians have this Confucian "please step on me, that's what I'm on earth for; of course, I'm happy to drink the dregs of bitterness" (as the Chinese say) background, but lots of white gay men seem to share it without Asian family pressure and indoctrination [primary socialization] when it comes to working for gay-owned businesses. It must be pretty easy to manipulate people this way. I used to think it was only Asians, but I was wrong. Maybe it doesn't even take being [part of a] minority.

Even these two skeptical, class-conscious employees preferred working for and with gay men, and there are others who are so relieved at the comfort

---

78. Dan was laid off in 1993 and is pursuing a wrongful termination (HIV discrimination) lawsuit against the company. When I asked him if he wanted to add anything to his quoted statement, he replied: "What I said seems right. [The employer] thought I was insufficiently grateful of his stingy largesse, and laid off all his HIV-positive employees when there was a dip in cash flow to use as a pretext, throwing us to fend for ourselves with 'preexisting conditions' in the insurance market. That's as close to a death sentence as employers have. I shouldn't have stuck around to keep my insurance. From what I said, I obviously knew not to trust his fake 'progressiveness.' Unfortunately, I didn't make it to disability as I planned, and the future looks very grim."

of being out of the closet on the job that they don't notice or report the kinds of underlying tensions about exploitation suggested by them. For instance, Alan reported, "I work harder than I would at a corporate, straight, higher-paying job, but it's worth it to me not to have to play the closet games, to have my sexual orientation taken for granted." Dave told me,

> I want San Francisco to succeed. I want the company to succeed. In a way it's just a job, and not that exciting a job, but I think the world will be a better place if there are successful gay companies, and if the City by the Bay can continue to be a beacon of gay acceptance and gay success.

There is nothing intrinsic to homosexuality or to lesbigay identity that keeps one from exploiting others, including the "own kind" with which one identifies, "chosen families," and natal families.

3

Diversity

Nine

Ethnic and Temporal Patterns of Gay Male Coming Out and Migration to San Francisco

A s are the "communities" of other "peoples" in urban interethnic settings, the San Francisco gay community is a loosely structured culture.[1] The real complexity of gay experience and the coordination of the people with these experiences is much greater than the simplifications herein. Categories such as "Latino" and "Anglo," and, especially, "Asian/Pacific Islander," include considerable internal differences, but such crude categories provide at least a start to the mapping of diversity.

Breaking from their tradition of treating cultures as integrated wholes, in recent years anthropologists have shown that behavior, knowledge, and cosmologies are heterogeneous even in small-scale social groups. There is certainly considerable intracultural variance within the San Francisco gay community, including warring political factions.[2] No one should expect the gay

---

1. Embree (1950) suggested that Thai culture is loosely structured, permitting considerable latitude in role performance in contrast to the extensive and ongoing demands made on individuals in tightly structured Japanese culture. Some interactions within Thailand, and some within gay San Francisco, have elaborate predetermined etiquette, even though there is considerable choice in taking on particular roles and engaging in particular types of interaction and voluntary association (Evers 1969; Murray 1992a:387–96, 1992b). Thus, "even though Thai society may have an appearance of relative fluidity when viewed in terms of the behaviour and movement of individuals, it is nevertheless a stable, ongoing social order with clearly defined and recurrent structural patterns. . . . The actors change, but the same types of action are performed regularly" (P. Jackson 1989:109).

2. Factionalism is far from unknown in villages (see Redfield 1950; Gallin 1968; Bosco 1992).

community, comprising ethnically diverse persons who are dispersed (albeit nonrandomly: see chapter 8) through an urban, post-industrial metropolis, to be monolithic in any regard. Thus, most generalizations must be matters of statistical distribution. In this chapter I endeavor to examine cohort and ethnic differences in two major rites of passage: coming out as gay, and moving to the San Francisco Bay Area. The sample is the same one as in chapter 8.

COMING OUT

Acceptance of being gay is not just the most important criterion for establishing membership in the category *gay community*, as is shown in chapter 8, but is the central moral imperative within it. Denying one's self, brothers, and sisters is the gravest sin. Denial of identity to a hostile assailant is forgivable, but—in retrospect—denial of one's self often looks corrosive. Therefore, accepting homosexual inclinations is prescribed with varying degrees of gentleness and pressure to others.[3]

Members of the community recognize and respect that gay men come to terms with identifying themselves as gay at different ages and to differing extents of publicness. Generally, no one challenges the pace of "coming out"; until very recently, there was also a general taboo against forcing a "brother" or "sister" out of the closet.[4] Based on his observations in Montreal during the early 1950s, Leznoff (1954:133) categorically stated a rule: "A homosexual should not expose others, even under conditions where he himself is identified." Men and women who identify themselves as gay (and, even more so, those who identify as lesbian-feminist) still are generally tolerant of others who do not tell their co-workers or their families that they are lesbian or gay. Although in some situations letting the assumption that one is straight

3. This may be a "cultural imperative" or the sum of individual conclusions about the therapeutic effects of ending denial. There are certainly plenty of folk maxims of the sort "You'll never be happy[/at peace, etc.] if you can't accept who you are." The term "denial," borrowed from the Freudian list of ego defenses, has been increasingly popular in American culture and is applied more appropriately to denying homosexuality than in many other of its applications. In my view, the earlier view of inauthenticity (more dominant in the 1960s and 1970s in American discourse, gay and other) has been medicalized, although the costs of denial (so far) are viewed as psychological rather than somatic. There are signs of attributing swifter mortality of some persons with AIDS to self-hatred, however, and I expect this medicalization to continue to expand its explanatory reach.

4. Faderman 1991b:109. "Outing," i.e., publicizing the homosexuality of politicians and other public figures viewed as contributing to gay oppression and/or AIDS underfunding, is directed precisely at those who do not behave as "gay brothers," and whose homosexuality is perceived as non-gay or anti-gay.

pass without challenge is readily accepted, denying that one is gay to men who identify themselves as gay and know about one's sexual habits (or who impute habits from captured glances or from noticing presence in particular locales) provokes denigration as a "closet queen" and, within gay settings, direct challenge. The prototypical response is a self-righteous "Don't pretend to me: I know better!"[5]

Coming out to natal family, co-workers, or other straight people is optional, but to accept being gay—at least simulating pride and rejecting shame—in the company of other gay men is as much a sign of adulthood as is paternity in other cultures. As Herdt argues, coming out is the most important rite of passage in lesbigay life.[6] Although coming out obviously is a process rather than an event—and a process with varying durations, differing ceremonies, ages of entry, and definitions—gay men almost invariably point to one particular time when they graduated from misguided rejection of homosexuality to affirming their own gayness;[7] that is, from the internalized normative societal stigma to the more sophisticated understanding of the properly initiated and subsequently "in the know."[8] What gay men mean by "coming out" is usually some public acknowledgment, such as the first

5. On this type of social control in gay settings see Leznoff 1954; Cavan 1963; Murray 1979a, 1983c; Grube 1990.

6. See Herrell 1992; Herdt 1992; Herdt and Boxer 1993. Even they understate the sacredness many men feel in this transformation. As with other social orders described in ethnographic literature, we cannot easily distinguish acquiescence with cultural views from acceptance of them. This is especially the case for bisexual behavior, which does not necessarily cease even with some public affirmation of a gay identity or following the symbolic extravaganza of a heterosexual wedding. Harry (1993:25) argued that "coming out is largely applicable to the transition to adulthood while having little applicability to adult homosexuals" and showed statistical relationships of income, occupation type, residence area, and individual nonconformity to being out to heterosexuals. Also see Lee (1978b) on public figures.

7. "Almost every gay man can pinpoint the time when he first came out to himself, when he finally accepted that he was gay," Hippler (1990:168) wrote. Only two of 275 men asked in this study proffered a range rather than a specific age at which they came out. Although what step was crucial varies from individual to individual, nearly every gay man remembers a specific breakthrough in his biography. The genre "coming-out story" is relatively easy to tap, although details in it would probably be less reliable (see Bradburn, Rips, and Shevell 1987 on differential retention of memory and the use of inference to supplement memory; and Abramson 1992 on the implications of research on memory for self-reports of sexual histories). Although the memory is generally very salient, several men said that in their view they were never in the closet, that everyone—including themselves—knew they were going to be fags from an early age.

8. In Spanish, a common non-pejorative term before the diffusion of the word *gay* was *entendido,* literally "in the know." The transformation from considering persons involved in homosexuality *queer* (or *maricones*) is a kind of conversion experience—but being converted to accepting gay people and accepting one's own gayness must be distinguished from sexual experience "turning" one homosexual. See pp. 153–55 on unlearning the dominant society's "homosexual role."

TABLE 9.1 Median Ages of First Homosexual Experience and of Coming Out by Birth Generation of Bay Area Gay Men

Ethnicity	Median age of first homosexual experience	Median age of coming out	Interim	N
born 1901–1935	14.5	26.0	11.5	44
1936–1945	17.0	25.5	8.5	46
1946–1952	18.0	22.0	4.0	74
1953–1960	17.5	21.0	3.5	72
1961–1965	17.0	19.0	2.9	31
1966+	18.0	18.0	0.0	8
Total	17.0	22.0	5.0	275
Examiner random telephone sample of Bay Area gay men reported duration between "when you knew you were gay and when you came out"			7.0	299

time they went to a gay bar or a gay meeting or told a friend. As Table 9.1 indicates, there is generally a lag between first homosexual experience and coming out.[9] Some of those without child or adolescent homosexual experience regard finding a man with whom to have sex as "coming out." Besides the 6 percent who reported coming out at an age less than the age at which they had their first homosexual experience, 17 percent reported coming out at the same age as the age of their first homosexual experience. Herdt and Boxer (1993:188) found 11 percent of boys coming out before reporting any homosexual experience. Unfortunately, my data do not permit distinguishing those coming outs and first homosexual experiences that are remembered as simultaneous from those which occurred over the space of the same year. In the "preliberation" era, "coming out" meant entering a public homosexual space such as a bar, so that it was really a "coming into" gay society, often being "brought out" by a (not necessarily older) sponsor already familiar with gay life.[10] More recently, "coming out" to family and friends has become more salient, but I think that venturing into the company of gay men with some presumption of commonalty remains the dominant meaning of "coming out."

9. See also Dank 1971; Harry and Devall 1978b:64; Troiden and Goode 1980; Hatfield 1989; Herdt 1992; Herdt and Boxer 1993:209. In the last of these, intrapsychic acceptance was the general meaning of "coming out," which may partially explain the lower mean age (16.75) Herdt and Boxer found.

10. Such a sponsor took the father's role in the established (debutante) sense of 'come into.' Mary McIntosh reminded me of this as a discussant of an earlier version of this chapter in 1989. See also Chauncey (1994:7–8). In his view the state built "the closet" in the crackdowns of the 1930s (p. 9).

"Initiation rites" are not strictly age-demarcated and the contents are fairly variable,[11] but the expected end result is acceptance of one's self as a member of a worthwhile people: "I'm OK, we're more than OK!"[12]

Despite the stigma of AIDS, openly gay men have not gone back into the closet in appreciable numbers. AIDS diagnoses and deaths forced out some closeted public figures (e.g., Roy Cohn, Malcolm Forbes, Rock Hudson).[13] Generally, I see no reason to think that the rate of coming out has changed. There is a longer term trend of coming out at younger ages, sooner after initial sexual experience (the age of which is rising slightly). Table 9.1 shows a decrease over time in the age at which gay men who ended up in San Francisco came out. The mean coming-out age for those born before the Second World War is 31.5, with some 50s, 60s, and even two 70s reported. The median is still markedly higher than for those born later with a less repressive climate in which to come out. The post–baby-boomers have been coming out shortly after high school, those not going to college one year earlier on the average than those with some college or more education in all age groups. The Chicago Horizons data extend the general trend of coming out at earlier ages to those born in the 1970s and coming out in the 1980s.[14]

It is tempting to interpret the earlier median age of first homosexual sexual experience for the earliest generation as indicating that there was less repression of homosexual behavior per se, along with a higher cost of being identified as "a homosexual." What makes me reluctant to proffer such an explanation is the sense that many men from those generations who "put off" homosexual sex until later never came out at all. For all age groups, there are men engaged in homosexual sex (as well as those thinking about and desiring it but not trying it) who will come out in the future. Samples

11. See the narratives in Saks and Curtis 1994.

12. A feeling that one's own people are superior to other peoples is well-nigh universal, and overcoming societal stigma probably requires some sense of a counter-elite. "Two, four, six, eight/ Gay is twice as good as straight" and the view of heightened gay sensibility are two examples of this affectation.

13. There has also been quite a boom of posthumous revelations by biographers of public figures such as John Maynard Keynes and Cary Grant.

14. By recruiting research subjects through a program only for those under the age of 21, Herdt (1992) and Herdt and Boxer (1993) necessarily underestimate what the age of coming out will be, insofar as those who come out at higher ages will not be sampled (as they explicitly noted on p. xiv). They have not reported ethnic differences in their data. A study of 90 gay-identified white South Africans found the same mean age as for white San Franciscans: 22 (Isaacs and McKendrick 1992:183). They did not ask about age of first homosexual contact. Instead, they asked respondents to recall the age at which they first became aware of same-sex attraction. Ninety percent gave ages less than 20, with a mean of 13 (p. 179), considerably higher than the mean 9.6 recalled by the "children of Horizons."

(including mine) of younger cohorts necessarily miss those who will come out later in life (and, in a longer perspective, will raise the medians for these cohorts). I think that the gap between sex and coming out is narrowing, but not quite so much as it appears to be in these data.

Complicating this historical trend are ethnic differences, displayed in Table 9.2. African American men who eventually identify themselves as gay [15] typically begin to have sex much earlier than Asian/Pacific Islander men.[16] Those whose first homosexual experience was at an age less than 10 tended to come out at higher ages than those whose first homosexual experience was at a higher age.[17] Specifically, the 10.1 percent of the sample who had engaged in homosexual activity before age 10 came out at an age 2.87 years later than those whose first homosexual experience was at a higher age (a mean age of 26.48 in comparison to 23.61, though the medians for both were 22).[18]

The correlation between age of first homosexual sex and education ($r = .07$) is not even close to being statistically significant, nor was that between coming-out age and education ($-.05$), suggesting that neither of the ages is a surrogate for repression (i.e., putting off expressions of sexual be-

15. The AIDS in Multi-Ethnic Neighborhoods (AMEN) study of 1770 households in San Francisco's Mission district, Bayview–Hunter's Point, and the Western Addition found that 10% of African American men in these neighborhoods had had sex with men during the past ten years. All those who had had sex only with men during that time identified as gay, as did 44% of those who had had sex with men and women. A matching 44% said that they were straight (the remaining 11% presented themselves as bisexual). Among Latinos in the same neighborhoods, 10% of the men had had sex with men during the preceding decade. All the exclusively homosexual ones identified as gay, along with 31% of those who had had sex with women and men. Another 31% represented themselves as bisexual and 39% as straight (Binson 1994; see also Peterson et al. 1992 on characteristics of a sample of 20–39-year-old Bay Area African American men who had sex with men—37% of whom had had sex with men for money at some time; 56% of the sample had some college education).

16. In the initial AIDS case-control study of urban gay men in 1981–82 (68 AIDS cases and 211 matched controls), more than half reported oral and/or anal sex with one or more males by age 16, approximately 20% by age 10, 80% by age 20 (Haverkos, Bukoski, and Amsel 1989:501).

17. Having been slow to see this pattern, I did not gather any data on early experiences and concealment practices. Seven of 17 African American gay men reported pre-teen homosexual experiences. These seemed to be sources of continued excitement for the two who provided some detail (I didn't interview the others myself). Harry (1985) found recollections of childhood effeminacy more frequent among gay men (ca. 1969) from working-class backgrounds, and noted that such "sissies" remembered earlier and more extensive homosexual experience than did more conventionally masculine boys.

18. Twelve percent of the boys in Herdt and Boxer 1993:185 recollected homosexual activity before the age of 10, but Herdt and Boxer do not discuss any subsequent differences in behavior or identification between them and other gay youth. In the study of young Bay Area men by Lemp et al. (1994:451), 19% of those born after 1970 had anal sex with men before age 15 (16% had never had anal sex with men).

TABLE 9.2 Median Ages of First Homosexual Experience and of Coming Out
by Ethnicity of Bay Area Gay Men

Ethnicity	Median age of first homosexual experience	Median age of coming out	Interim	N
Black	12.5	22.5	10.0	18
Latino	15.0	21.0	6.0	20
White	17.0	23.0	6.0	191
Asian/Pacific	18.0	21.0	3.0	33
Total	17.0	22.0	5.0	262

havior or identification while obtaining more education). There is also no statistically significant relation between either of those ages and later gay political involvement.[19]

I see no evidence of any return from gay endogamy to the old exogamy of seeking "real" men who viewed themselves as "straight" (à la Reiss 1961). Indeed, the popularity of "outing" shows less tolerance for a distinction between homosexual behavior and public gay identification.

MIGRATION

Coming out is the most important rite of passage on the way to becoming a part of a gay community. Getting to where there are other gay-identified men is a secondary but still important prerequisite of being part of the San Francisco gay community; only 4 percent of the sample were born in the Bay Area. At least since the end of the Second World War, some men have moved to San Francisco to "be gay." Some gay men continue to find it necessary to migrate to a metropolis before coming to terms with internally recognized but not publicly acknowledged homosexuality. For instance, Peter, a white gay man in his late 20s, said, "I was always a homo and knew it, but I didn't deal with it until I got to New York." Similarly Ning, an Asian American in his mid 40s, told me that he was attracted to men as early as primary school, but waited until his education was complete (at age 30), moved to San Francisco, and only then ventured for the first time into a gay bar to meet other gay men.

San Francisco long has been perceived as a place in which being gay is celebrated, accepted, or at least tolerated as "no big deal"—whichever was

19. There is a statistically significant correlation ($r = .18$, $p = .01$) between education and gay political involvement. Less expectedly, there are practically no relation between white and education ($r = -.02$) or white and gay political involvement ($r = .001$).

enough to be "better than where I am now." For some, San Francisco is a place in which it is possible to live in a relatively all gay world with few contacts except with gay people. For others, it is a place to be gay without being anomalous, i.e., where one will not be stigmatized for being gay. However, a perceived favorable social climate for gay sociation is only one factor among others determining individual and collective gay migration to San Francisco. Like all human behavior, migration is overdetermined: there is no single factor explaining the outcome.

Moreover, just as gay identity is achieved and then must be maintained, someone around to be sampled for a retrospective study of migration has to have moved *and stayed*. Such sampling necessarily misses the experiences of those who moved and then either moved on or retreated to the place of origin. Although moving on is also overdetermined, it doesn't seem unreasonable to suppose that those who moved to San Francisco and later left found it less than a Promised Land. In a letter in the 15 November 1990 *Bay Area Reporter* (p. 8), a bitter Scott Combs wrote from Lawrence, Kansas, "I'd rather live with upfront bigots than live in a place full of hypocritical, phony liberals," and asked,

> What's the use of laws protecting people in San Francisco in employment regardless of sexual orientation when it is virtually impossible to get a decent job in the city? . . . It is full of employers who know that people want to live there and are willing to work for almost nothing. Average wages for all occupations combined may be slightly above the national average, but they in no way compensate for the cost of living.

He is far from the only one to have given up the struggle to survive in the Bay Area, where homelessness is increasingly widespread. As he notes, "If you lose your job, you probably will not have a home for long." My friends who have moved from San Francisco to the suburbs extol having more house for a lower price (even including their cash expenditures on commuting; they prefer to spend more time getting to work by auto or by Bay Area Rapid Transit than they spent on San Francisco public transportation). Some feel that so many of their friends have died, that the ever-bustling Castro is haunted for them: Vollmer (1995:18) wrote that "nowadays whenever I go to San Francisco I feel like a ghost." Those interviewed by Fried (1989) paid in isolation, less developed AIDS service infrastructure, and lower wages for roomier dwelling space in a quieter, sunnier environment. Verghese (1994) provided some poignant instances of HIV-positive gay men returning to rural home towns they earlier fled. My sample, or any sample of gay San Franciscans, contains the residues not only of migration, but also of the process of gay identification.[20] Both men who moved on, and men who have sex with men but do not gay-identify, were not sampled.

Before trying to model some of the variance in migration experiences of gay-identified San Francisco men, I'd like to present some individual histories to show some of the variety of migration histories.

First, Larry: After release from the Army, he went to college in his Midwestern home state, funded by the GI bill. Upon completion of his studies in the early 1950s, he wanted to move to California, which seemed to him the land of the future. He did not know anyone in southern California, but had stayed in contact with a straight Army buddy in San Francisco. Larry stayed with this friend until he found a job (the first full-time job of his life) and could afford to rent a place of his own.

Michael moved from the South in the mid 1960s, because his lover was fed up with his job and wanted to move to a less oppressive climate. Michael was not especially enamored with his job or of the South, and was willing to relocate. Both did piecework while getting established, and they separated within a year of arriving in San Francisco.

Jay went back to school in the early 1970s. Upon completing his studies in the late 1970s, he applied for academic jobs all over the country and did not land one. When a long-term relationship ended, he decided to move to New York City. However, a woman friend who was getting divorced asked if he'd drive with her to San Francisco, where she was going to return to school. He agreed. They stayed with a friend of hers while apartment-hunting. He worked for a temporary office work agency for a year before starting his own business.

Also in the late 1970s, Lance's friend Joe called his friend Michael, whom we met earlier, and asked Michael to help Lance if he could when Lance arrived from his native country. Michael picked up Lance from the airport and arranged for him to stay with his friend Jay (for Lance, this was a friend

---

20. It took comments by Wayne Dynes, Harvey Molotch, and Bill Simon on my research for me fully to realize that the "casualties" (or "dropouts") of both processes were unavailable for sampling, even though I knew that differentiating those who migrated permanently from those who stayed home from those who moved back and forth, and distinguishing migration from adjustment to a new locale, are widespread conceptual problems in the literature on migration. For an exemplary study of migration as a continuing individual and communal process (rather than a discrete event), involving returning for various lengths of time to the natal community, see Massey et al. 1987. Ralph Bolton (personal communication, 1995) stressed that those who leave San Francisco do not necessarily return home. There is migration to other metropolises (notably New York and Los Angeles) and to more pastoral settings with lesbigay concentrations (such as the Russian River and Palm Springs areas).

of a friend of a friend) who had a vacant bedroom (the woman he moved with having decided she was a lesbian and couldn't continue to live with a man, even platonically). Jay not only provided free rent for six months, but arranged for Lance to work covertly (i.e., without a green card). Michael introduced Lance to his own extensive network, and also found work for him, as well as negotiating free consultation with a (gay) immigration lawyer.

In the early 1980s, Bill visited a friend who had moved to San Francisco. At a party he met Michael. Bill spent the rest of his vacation with Michael. Michael visited him and invited him to move into his house. Michael mobilized his friends and either found or made a job for Bill when he moved.

In the mid 1980s, the multinational corporation for which he worked transferred Peter to its South Bay office. He knew he wanted to lived in the city and used the company's generous moving allowance to stay in a downtown hotel while he shopped for a house in a sunny part of San Francisco. He did not know any gay people in the Bay Area.

Larry and Peter say they moved to get better jobs. Bill and Michael say that love was the primary reason for their moves. Jay first said that he never decided to move to San Francisco, and then said that if we had to assign a reason it was to get away from his ex. Lance also wanted a change of scenery. All knew of San Francisco's reputation as a good place for gay people to live; all had some notion of greater sexual freedom there. All felt more comfortable in being openly gay in San Francisco. Only Jay (and his woman friend) and possibly Lance were seeking more and/or different sex. All of them found jobs they judged better and more satisfying than any they had had before migrating to the Bay Area.[21]

The diversity of experiences of even these few individuals shows that migration is not a single normative rite of passage for San Francisco gay men.[22] Moving was a stage of coming out for some.[23] For others, it was more or less an accident.[24] Some moved seeking love, others seeking money. Some moved seeking a climate more tolerant of homosexuality, others a more temperate

21. Jay, Lance, and Larry were only entering the job market at the time they moved.

22. An argument could certainly be made for a liminal period immediately following migration for many, however.

23. Twelve percent moved to the Bay Area at the same age they reported coming out. The two events were within a year of each other for an additional 9%. Most gay men (69%) who moved to the Bay Area had come out before migrating. College towns and cities near military bases were generally where we came out (an intermediate step for those of us raised in small towns on the way to metropolises with gay communities, as well as for those raised in cities and suburbs).

24. The inclusion of the date of arrival in the Bay Area in many of the very condensed obituaries in the *Bay Area Reporter* shows that it was perceived and communicated as a significant event in the lives of many, as Hippler (1990:149) noted.

climate. Still others—those who acquiesced to moves initiated by family, lovers, or employers—weren't seeking anything in particular, not even change. It would be a mistake to imagine that gay men not native to the Bay Area thought about all the places in the country or the world they could live and picked San Francisco. Just as not everyone who changes jobs was looking for a new job before doing so,[25] not everyone who migrates did a cost–benefit analysis of possible places to live.[26] As Speare (1971:130) noted, "The biggest problem with the application of a cost–benefit model to human migration may not be the crudeness of the actual calculation, but the fact that *many people never make any calculation at all*" (emphasis added). There are patterns of mobility, but these patterns are somewhere between the strict order of initiation rites in some small-scale Melanesian societies, and the atomistic rationalist calculus of neoclassical *homo economicus.*

Over the course of the 1980s, migration to what was once the Gay Mecca seemed to slow, and both gay and straight print media publicized migration out to the suburbs (and beyond, to the countryside, fantasized as being AIDS-free). Dan White (a native San Franciscan who assassinated Mayor George Moscone and Supervisor Harvey Milk), and other murderers of gay men, along with nationally publicized attacks on lesbians and gay men, also tarnished the image of San Francisco as a haven of tolerance.

East Coasters—most influentially, Edmund White (1980)—overestimate the extent to which men abandoned careers to come to the sexual playground of San Francisco.[27] Of my informants, 34% of the black and white men had jobs in San Francisco before moving. They judged 89% of these jobs better than the one in the place they left. Moreover, it was the gay men who moved to San Francisco alone who considered the jobs they found in San Francisco better than the ones they had left: twice as many of those moving by themselves as those moving with someone reported that their first job after mi-

---

25. See Granovetter 1974; Murray, Rankin, and Magill 1981.

26. See Massey 1989.

27. Another unsubstantiated echo of the New York view is the "relative lack of achievement motivation" invoked by J. Martin and Dean (1990:558), who described San Francisco as a "magnate [presumably they meant magnet] for a more relaxed lifestyle in a physically attractive geographic area" in contrast to New York City. No more than in New York did most gay San Franciscans "renounce the world of work, duty, caution and practicality" exclusively to pursue "careers in love": the unrepresentativeness of the vivid representation of the "doomed queens" in Holleran's *The Dancer from the Dance* (1978) is clear in the framing exchange of letters in that best known of novels about the "clone" epoch; that novel also contains several typically New York condescensions toward California. Holleran (1988) asserted that "homosexuals who lived in that city [San Francisco] had gone there to be homosexual." (Note the "homosexual" rather than "gay.") Although Randy Shilts pursued a very successful career in San Francisco, he also disseminated this view (e.g., 1982:113).

grating was better than the job they had before moving. Some of these men subordinated their own careers to those of a lover advancing his career by moving, but this does not fit with giving up everything to move to San Francisco's sexual scenes during the 1970s.[28]

Further challenging the view of giving up careers and jobs for marginal existence close to the sexual playground is the finding that those who moved to San Francisco in the liberation era (1969–80) were twice as likely to be better satisfied with their first Bay Area job than with the job they left behind in migrating than were men moving in the AIDS era of sexual suppression and repression (i.e., from 1981 onward).[29] Those with higher education, those who moved during the 1970s, and those with jobs arranged before moving were more likely to report their initial San Francisco jobs were better than the jobs they had before moving. The first row of Table 9.3 lists the first-order correlations.

More than half the men who moved to San Francisco did not have a full-time job in the place from which they moved (78% of those who moved to San Francisco before 1969). Thirty-nine percent of those who did have a full-time job in the place from which they emigrated had a full-time job arranged in San Francisco before moving there. Of these, a third reported their first Bay Area job was not as good as the one they left (not always voluntarily) elsewhere, and a third reported moving to a better job. Of men who had a full-time job somewhere else and who moved to San Francisco before securing another, more found what they say were worse jobs than found what they say were better jobs (42% vs. 28% of 60).

Those who reported better jobs also reported a salary increase (of $1696 in unconstant and not readily comparable dollars). Substituting the seemingly more objective measure of difference in salary, the slight downward mobility for the sake of living in Gay Mecca in job quality disappears.[30] The

28. That primary socialization makes it especially difficult for either party in a male–male couple to subordinate his job/career to the other's is an important cultural stressor to which Gregory Baum first alerted me. With women's careers decreasingly subordinated to those of husbands, this stress on heterosexual relationships has increased in recent years.

29. For San Francisco, the liberation era could well be dated earlier (see the discussion in chapter 1). There is not a marked discontinuity in 1965 (the time of the California Hall incident in San Francisco) or 1969 (the celebrated Stonewall riots in New York), so I have opted to distinguish slightly more than a decade as the era of liberation. Demarcating the other end is at least as dubious, since changes resulting from consciousness of AIDS did not begin with the identification of the first case cluster (in Los Angeles). This tripartite division of eras facilitates comparison with other studies, but I consider them very fuzzily bounded categories for different men in different places.

30. The accuracy of recall of incomes is dubious. I am more confident about recall of the direction of change, and put more weight on a contrast of those who reported increased earnings

TABLE 9.3 Correlations and Means of Migration Variables

	Housing Satisfaction	Had Job Before Migrated	Migrated Before 1970	Gay Political Involvement	Years of Education	Mean
First job satisfaction	.24**	.04	−.24**	.03	.12	38%
Housing satisfaction		.16*	−.15*	.10	.22**	59%
Job arranged before migrating			−.17*	.11	.37**	28%
Migrated before 1970				.00	−.17*	26%
Gay political involvement					.18**	39%
Years of education						16.9

*$p < .05$ **$p < .01$

median change was zero. There was a mean increase of $1224, but because this figure mixes shifting values of the dollar over time, and because the cost of living in the Bay Area is higher than most other locales, this number is not readily interpretable.[31] A quarter reported earning less in their first San Francisco job than in the one they had preceding migration; 57 percent reported earning more. These data do not seem to be to be consistent with the view that migration to a gay center necessarily, or even usually, involves a sacrifice of job/career.[32] They show that migration did not lead to any substantial immediate economic betterment.[33] With a national data set, Tienda and Wilson (1992:668) found that in the short run, migration had a negative effect (a 1–4% decrease) on earnings for Anglos and two of three Latino groups (those of Puerto Rican and Mexican descent, but not those of Cuban descent), so there seems to be less economic sacrifice for gay migration to

to those who reported decreased earnings than on the numbers reported, even if these were converted to constant dollars (an exercise in misplaced concreteness I have not undertaken). Harvey Molotch reminded me that the cost of living in the Bay Area is exceptionally high, so that, depending on the place from which one migrated, as well as when, a higher salary may not indicate any real upward mobility, and the same salary might indicate real/net downward mobility.

31. Those who judged their first San Francisco job worse than their pre-immigration job reported a salary decrease (mean $571).

32. Four of the 21 who reported less satisfying first Bay Area jobs moved to the Bay Area with a lover, apparently subordinating their careers. Another 3 moved with their families. This leaves only 14 (6.5% of the 216 who supplied information about migration) who might fit with the stereotype of sacrificing careers to move to the Gay Mecca of San Francisco.

33. The payoffs gay men expected from moving to "Gay Mecca" differed from those 19th-century Chinese anticipated for going to "Gold Mountain."

San Francisco than there is for Anglo or Latino interurban migration within the United States.[34]

I certainly do not mean to imply that no individuals had a hard time getting established in San Francisco; I did myself.[35] For those of us who left little or nothing behind (e.g., moving after finishing some level of school, or being laid off a job, or divorced), the "in San Francisco" was not necessarily the most important part of "I had a hard time getting established in San Francisco." Many of us did not have much to throw away by migrating— as I noted, more than half of us did not have a full-time job in the place from which we emigrated, for instance.

One recurrent problem for migrants to a place where many people wish to live is finding a job. Whether or not we had local networks we could try to mobilize to find out about job possibilities, less than half of us received the information that led to our first Bay Area job from personal contacts. Fifty-eight percent of the San Francisco gay immigrants in my sample found out about the possibility of what became their first full-time San Francisco job through formal channels (want ads or employment agencies). Of those told about a job possibility by a person, 53% of the persons supplying what turned out to be salient information were gay or lesbian; 69% were strong ties (friends or relatives), 31% weak ties (friends of friends or acquaintances).[36]

Contrary to claims that gay chain migration does not occur,[37] Table 9.4 shows that a third of the gay men queried moved to San Francisco with or to live with someone they knew before moving.[38] This someone was a gay man in 78.4 percent of these cases. Nearly half stayed with someone they previously knew when they first moved to San Francisco; 81.5 percent of the persons with whom they stayed were gay, and 83.0 percent were strong ties. Thus, combining these two measures, nearly half the gay male émigrés to San Francisco mobilized a preexisting network upon initial arrival. Presumably, not everyone who knew people in San Francisco well enough to stay with them actually did so. Some had arranged housing before arrival. Some

34. Tienda and Wilson (1992:672) also found that the Hispanic migrations were predominantly to existing ethnic concentration rather than dispersion from ethnic enclaves.

35. Murray 1989b and Knopp 1990b challenge the view of privileged builders of gay ghettoes. It also bears stressing again that those who tried to but failed to establish themselves in the Bay Area and moved back or moved on were not available to be sampled. Out-migration from gay centers would be an interesting research topic.

36. Marsden and Campbell (1985) compare various measures and make a case for this straightforward categorization of tie strength.

37. E.g., Murray 1979b:171.

38. Chauncey (1994:271) also notes help for prewar gay men who moved to Manhattan.

TABLE 9.4 Percentage of gay male immigrants to San Francisco who moved with or stayed with someone at the time of immigration by ethnicity

Ethnicity	Moved and stayed with someone	Stayed with someone	Moved with someone	Alone	N
White/Anglo	21.3	28.4	14.2	36.2	141
Hispanic	7.1	35.7	21.4	37.7	14
Black	14.3	7.1	35.7	42.9	14
Asian	8.3	29.2	4.2	58.3	24
Total	18.7	28.0	14.5	38.9	193

had lodging provided by employers as part of moving expenses. Still others chose not to impose on friends. A third of those who did not stay with anyone when they first moved knew one or more San Franciscans before moving. Half, thus, would be an underestimate of preexisting ties.

Of the 35 men who migrated to San Francisco before 1960, only 2 reported their first San Francisco job being better than the one left behind when they moved. Thirty percent of later gay male immigrants reported that their first Bay Area job was better than the job they left when they migrated. Less than half as many of the pre-1960 immigrants as those who migrated later (35% compared to 78%) report their overall satisfaction with their lives in San Francisco as being greater than in the places from which they moved.[39] Moving to a promised land did not resolve the dissatisfactions that propelled them to migrate alone to San Francisco.

It is certainly likely that the pioneers had a harder time than those who followed, since they lacked not only the access to a visible gay community, but also the social support enjoyed by many later immigrants. Another possible interpretation is that a comparison between their present life in San Francisco and their life before pre-1960 migrations involved comparing their youth elsewhere with their middle or old age in San Francisco in the age of AIDS. Still another possible interpretation is that earlier immigrants were more negativist personalities. Comparing decade cohorts of gay male immigrants to San Francisco shows that the reason is not command of economic resources. From Table 9.5, it is obvious that there are some very affluent

39. None of those who migrated before 1963 or between 1966 and 1983, and 5.5% of the post-1983 immigrants, judged living in the Bay Area less satisfying overall than where they lived before moving. Two of these three men moved to the Bay Area at the impetus of a lover. None had jobs arranged before moving to the Bay Area, and two of the three had jobs in the place from which they moved.

TABLE 9.5 Mean Current Household and Per Capita Income by Year of Arrival
in Bay Area

Year of immigration	Household income	Per capita income	Percent living alone	N
Natives	$38,611	$23,500	44	18
Before 1960	$85,909	$46,227	32	22
1960–69	$49,769	$28,192	31	26
1970–79	$57,742	$35,742	35	66
1980–89	$54,662	$29,868	25	68
After 1989	$65,941	$30,765	18	17

immigrants from long ago. Almost as obviously, natives are less affluent than immigrants. They are also more likely to live alone.[40]

Gay Asian men who moved to San Francisco as adults moved alone more than gay men of other ethnicities. They were only half as likely to have jobs before moving as white gay men (16.7% compared to 34.0%), and were less likely to have had full-time jobs before moving (33.3% in contrast to 55.3%).

Those who stayed with someone when first moving were somewhat more likely to find housing better than that from which they moved (72% vs. 47%). Those who already had jobs before moving found housing they judged to be better than what they left more often (73% to 51%) and judged their Bay Area jobs better than the ones they left behind more often (44% to 22%). More (70%) of those moving during the 1970s reported improving their housing thereby than did either their predecessors (47%) or followers (63%). Similarly, the 70s immigrants were more likely to report securing a better job (39%) than their predecessors (12%) or followers (26%).

CONCLUSION

These results challenge the widespread view that gay men abandoned careers to move to San Francisco, taking any available job just to live there. The East Coast stereotype of a professional throwing away his career elsewhere to subsist as a waiter or security guard in San Francisco in order either to be gay in relative peace or to increase sexual opportunities does not seem to be the norm, if this sample's experiences are at all typical. Although there is some indication of lower wages for workers within the gay ghetto,[41] these were not men trained as professionals. Those who were downwardly mobile in job satisfaction and/or income were mostly those who moved with a partner and

40. From Martin, García, and Beatrice 1989:274, one might extrapolate that 85% of those living with someone else are living with a lover.
41. Murray 1992c:131–34; appendix to chapter 8.

subordinated their career to the partner's, not those who moved alone to "the sexual frontier."

Respondents who migrated before 1960 mostly lacked any social supports in the destination city to buffer the stress of migration. In subsequent decades, more than half the gay immigrants received information about jobs and places to live through strong ties. Many of the Asian/Pacific gay men had moved to the San Francisco Bay Area as children, or to complete school, or immediately after completing it. They generally were not part of gay networks before migrating, often coming out only after moving to the Bay Area.

Temporal and ethnic differences exist in conception of who is a part of "gay community," in the process of moving to a "gay capital city," in finding a place to live, and in finding a way to make a living. Nonetheless, in the experiences of an admittedly nonrandom sample of gay male San Franciscans, gay networks cushioned these events more than has been supposed. A diversity of personal paths leads to the San Francisco gay community. This chapter has mapped some of the patterning, but should close by acknowledging considerable individual differences in experiences and in the meanings derived from experiences by those categorized as "gay" of this or that "ethnicity" and of one or another age cohort.

Ten

Absent Laiuses
PSYCHIATRIC FANTASIES
IN BLACK AND GAY

If the psychoanalytic fantasy of intimate, seductive, controlling mothers and absent or remote fathers causing homosexuality were true, urban African American households should be mass-producing homosexuals. The widespread impression[1] that there are fewer African American than white men who are *exclusively* homosexual would be anomalous to a scientific theory, if psychoanalysis were one. However, from the very birth of the movement, psychoanalysis was a faith within which dissent was severely curtailed. Usually, if reality contradicts the prediction of psychoanalytic "theory," reality is regarded as being in error, whether such error is labeled "delusion" or "resistance."

In a rare acknowledgment that empirical evidence might be of some interest, the psychiatrist Herbert Hendin (1969) elicited life histories from a sample of four gay African American men who had attempted suicide. This sample of attempted suicides seemed large and typical enough to serve as the basis for generalization about the etiology of African American homosexuality, so that there is now a separate (and equal?) psychoanalytic theory of the family patterns that cause homosexuality (and suicide as a final stage) among African Americans. It is almost the obverse of the classic (white) homosexual-genic family with its sex-denying but seductive and domineering mother and emotionally withdrawn father. Rather, "The black homosexual's family pattern consisted of a sexually promiscuous mother and a father who was violent to both mother and child. Homosexuality was an escape from the destructive heterosexuality associated with the brutality of the father" (Day 1972:328).

---

1. E.g., Day 1972:327; Binson et al. 1994.

That four African American cases occasioned a theoretical revision is rather surprising when contrasted to the well-documented finding that single mothers (a category that is very common in African American communities) can raise resolutely heterosexual children. Mother fear is so pervasive in the heterosexual circles from which psychiatrists come that classic Oedipal theory dies hard. The African American homosexual-genic family "theory" preserves a place for this cherished fear.

Over the course of the past few decades, the pioneering work of Evelyn Hooker (and other null hypothesis finders using projective tests followed by ethnographic study) exploded the view of homosexuality built on generalizations from populations imprisoned or under psychiatric treatment. Social science understanding of gay African Americans now is analogous to the understanding of gay whites circa the mid 1960s.

This includes the almost total invisibility of women. Bass-Haas (1968), the only study in M. Weinberg and Bell's (1972) wide-ranging bibliography that dealt with African American women, claimed later initial experience for nonwhites than for whites, and the latter's greater satisfaction with both present and pre-"marital" partners. Arthur Hoffman (1960) contended that in prisons, "Unlike whites, Negroes practice homosexuality in a primitive way and without emotion." This indicates the standards of scientific reporting in this area![2]

When Martin Levine organized his 1979 anthology *Gay Men*, he could find no methodologically sophisticated work on gay African Americans. Dank (1980) vehemently criticized Levine's decision to use a folk assessment from the popular press (Soares 1979), but could not suggest any scholarly work that should have been included instead.

The Institute for Sex Research's large-scale 1969–70 survey of diversity of homosexuality in the San Francisco Bay Area (A. P. Bell and Weinberg 1978) paid no attention to African American or Latino cultural differences (and excluded Asian Americans altogether). Moreover, as Carrier (1979) demonstrated, Bell and Weinberg's African American sample was quite atypical in education and occupation from the demographic profile of San Francisco Bay Area African Americans. Carrier suggested that Bell and Weinberg tapped a select group integrated into middle-class white American culture and missed those African Americans involved with other African Americans and regarding their African Americanness as more salient to identity than sexual orientation. In other words, they sampled only those who identified as *gay*. The same is true of Lockman's sample (1984) of 27 black–

2. See also Otis 1913 on "perversion" among imprisoned black women.

white couples who were members of Black and White Men Together,[3] my own sample of gay San Franciscans (Murray 1992c and this volume), and Kennedy and Davis's sample (1993) of Buffalo, New York, black women. In his ethnography of "Southern Town," Whittier (1995) suggested that even among the gay-identified black men, only those who were interested sexually in white men were willing to be interviewed by him.

Faderman (1991a:55) recalled that whites who sought out Harlem homosexual nightlife in the 1920s Harlem vogue "felt they were not just being tolerated in Harlem for economic reasons, but rather that black people understood them." A character in Blair Niles's 1931 novel *Strange Brother* says, "In Harlem . . . they know all about me and I don't have to lie."[4] Although there was surely considerable wish fulfillment in this belief, and, as in other sites of sexual colonialism, "it was easier for white interlopers to be openly gay during their brief visits to Harlem than for the black men who lived there round the clock,"[5] the image does not derive just from white writers such as Carl Van Vechten and John Dos Passos, but also from African American writers such as Bruce Nugent, Chester Himes, and Claude McKay. Faderman supplemented the fictional representations by including the lyrics and cover photos of Ma Rainey and Bessie Smith blues songs, along with interviews of some survivors.[6] Bruce Nugent recalled, "People did what they

3. Being in an interracial couple is not prima facie evidence of gay identity being more salient than race. Similarly, that 24 of 27 reported racism being no hindrance in their relationship does not mean that they considered racism unimportant in their lives. Indeed, combating racism is the raison d'être for BWMT (now extended to MACT "Men of All Colors Together").

4. Quoted by Faderman 1991b:68. Middle-class forays into the lower class (and/or south from Europe and North America) have often led to the belief that homosexuality is more accepted elsewhere than in one's native society: see Weeks 1977:40; Manalansan 1991, 1993; Aldrich 1993; Murray 1995b.

5. Chauncey (1994:244), who added, "Although they were casually accepted by many poor Harlemites and managed to earn a degree of grudging respect from others, they were excoriated by the district's moral guardians" (p. 253), notably Adam Clayton Powell, Sr. Faderman (1991b:68) similarly cautioned that despite the need for tourist dollars inhibiting explicit condemnation of carryings-on, visitors "believed Harlem gave them permission—or they simply took permission there—to explore what was forbidden in the white world." They did in Harlem what they dared not to anywhere else, and didn't investigate too closely what the natives thought or felt about their enthusiasms. Grave Digger and Coffin Ed, the Harlem detectives in most of Chester Himes's later work, exemplify a probably typical contemptuous laissez-faire attitude: "They had no use for pansies, but as long as they didn't hurt anyone, they could pansy all they pleased. They weren't arbiters of sex habits. There was no accounting for the sexual tastes of people" (1986:33). In the novel from which this quotation is taken, they lead on a young black queen and accompany him to a downtown bathhouse (in the line of duty, of course). Himes distanced himself from his experience of prison homosexuality by making the characters in his prison memoir novel *Cast the First Stone* (1952) white, prefiguring James Baldwin's separation of novels focused on "race problems" from the one *(Giovanni's Room)* focused on same-sex love.

6. De la Croix (1994) provides more on blues singers and blatant lyrics.

wanted to do with whom they wanted to do it. . . . Nobody was in the closet. There wasn't any closet."[7]

In the absence of much credible social science study of gay African American experience, those seeking realistic accounts of gay African Americans in African American communities are likely to turn to novels. While fiction often vividly exemplifies abstract social science concepts and sometimes provides usable data about which the authors are unlikely to have conscious theories,[8] fiction must be treated cautiously as a source of data for matters about which authors have theories of their own to push.[9] Enshrouded in controversy, the structure and adequate functioning of the African American family is something about which an ideologist such as James Baldwin—preoccupied for more than the last decade of his life with fostering African American families as havens in a heartless, racist world—is bound to have opinions, and these opinions are bound to be embedded in his fiction.[10]

The homosexual characters in Baldwin's late fiction are not a part of any African American or gay community—not even imagined utopian ones. I do

7. From Kisseloff 1989:288–89. Cf. Avi-Ram 1990 and Woods 1993 on the need to decode Harlem Renaissance poetry. See also Garber 1982; C. Smith 1986; Pinckney 1987; Faderman 1991a, 1991b:67–79; Reimoneng 1993; Chauncey 1994 on the era. Rosse 1892 and C. Hughes 1893, 1907 provide early contemptuous psychiatric notice of African American drag balls and "miscegenation."

8. E.g. Brown and Gilman 1960; Friedrich 1978; Phillips 1987.

9. Unfortunately, a lack of literary portraits of gay African Americans parallels the dearth of social science work. Other than some mysteries by Joseph Hansen—especially two novels written under the pseudonym James Colter ca. 1970, Richard Hall's *The Butterscotch Prince* (1975) and stories (notably "The language animal"), Merle Miller's *Something Happened* (1972), and Tony Kushner's *Angels in America,* African Americans don't exist in gay literature: "Look at mainstream post-Stonewall gay fiction—the work of White, Ferro, Holleran, Pintauro, Virga, Aldyne[, Chabon, Cunningham, Feinberg, Indiana, Kramer, Leavitt, McCauley, Maupin, Monette, Picano, Rechy, Torchia]—and you'll find it's as segregated as any 'Christian academy' in Hattiesburg or Tuscaloosa" (Jurrist 1987:34). Outside the mainstream is Coleman Dowell's *White on Black on White* (1983), dealing with a male and female who are sexually obsessed with black men. From inside the Violet Quill circle, there is Michael Grumley's posthumously published *Life Drawing* (1991). The main two characters in the major British novel about the "clone" era, Alan Hollinghurst's *The Swimming Pool Library* (1988), prefer blacks (the elder says all his real friends were black; the younger, who says he has no friends, objectifies his sex partners regardless of color). Gay African American writing also has a quite limited palette—that is, it is not notable for including Latino, or Native, or Asian Americans—while often objectifying blond as the only other recognized hue.

10. Baldwin's own biography (Eckerman 1967; Leeming 1994) can be considered a source of data about one person, which is only slightly smaller (three less) than Hendin's sample upon which the current orthodox psychoanalytic theory rests. Claude McKay, a Harlem Renaissance figure who was almost surely kept by an older British man in Jamaica, also had a stern Baptist deacon father (see Cooper 1987 and Pinckney 1987). This is not the place to enter the controversy about whether Langston Hughes had sexual relations with men in general, or with Wallace Thurman in particular.

not think that his novels provide acceptable descriptive data from which one can draw reliable generalizations about etiology, or typical family or subcultural dynamics.[11] The agitprop families in Baldwin's novels after *Another Country* (1962) are prescriptions about what kind of African American families Baldwin thought were needed, not descriptions of his own or anyone else's family. In contrast, Baldwin's seemingly autobiographical first novel, *Go Tell It on the Mountain* (1953), contains a very much present and quite authoritarian father, like the father of Johnny Ray in Larry Duplechan's novels. Similarly, the strict father of another, far more flamboyant "sissy" was alive and raising other, straight sons until Little Richard was twenty.[12]

Etiology is not a concern of the writings collected in Cornwell (1983) or in the works in Roberts's bibliography (1981) of writings by and about African American lesbians, nor of the men (especially Ron Vern) in M. J. Smith 1983. These works are sources of other data about African American gay and lesbian experiences. In addition, some beginning graduate student social science work on African American lesbians and gay men exists.[13] The only moderately large sample of African American men engaged in homosexuality is that from San Francisco described in the dissertation of Julius Johnson (1981).

Johnson's research focused on differences in attitude and interaction patterns between homosexual African American men who identified primarily as African American (31 of his 61 respondents) or as gay (21). (The other 9 refused to choose one or the other as primary; unfortunately Johnson dropped them from his analysis.) Although it would be incautious to generalize the rates of primary identification to the population of all African American men significantly involved in homosexuality, the sampling bias

11. In a 1984 interview, Baldwin said, "I feel a stranger in America from almost every conceivable angle except, oddly enough, as a black person. The word 'gay' has always rubbed me the wrong way. . . . Even in my early years in the Village, what I saw of that world absolutely frightened me" (quoted by Drewes 1989:E-9), as the portraits of gay couples thriving only away from the vortex of other gay people from his 1957 novel *Giovanni's Room* onward show. Even in *Another Country* (1962), in which Baldwin prescribed sexual freedom (Eric's bisexuality in particular) as the road to redemption of racism-scarred America, Eric must rescue Yves (a male Eve for a Garden of Eden in a utopia free of sexual or racial hatreds) from any possibility of corruption by a homosexual underground (see Margolies 1986:68–70; more generally see Soneschein 1968:83). As early as in a 1949 essay, Baldwin (reprinted 1989) was already resisting labels with a rhetoric of "full human complexity." In contrast, Audre Lorde (1982 and elsewhere) accepted (even multiplied) labels.

12. See Slim 1969. C. White (1984) provides a rich source on African American folk/Christian conceptions of homosexuality. Slater (1992) and Corbin (1994) recall abusive, emotionally distant fathers.

13. Cauthern 1979; Sawyer 1965; Lockman 1982, 1984; Loiacano 1988, 1989; Hawkeswood 1990; Whittier 1995.

would seem to have been toward gay identification, because Johnson's quest for subjects was more visible in the gay community than in the African American community, and because in the African American gay subculture, "heavier emphasis is based on home-based entertainment, where participation is complicated by the relatively closed nature of the social network and the relative invisibility of such support groups to newcomers" (p. 22).

It is likely the case that race generally is a more important basis of self-identification than sexual orientation for African American gay men. As some told Johnson, being African American is immediately visible, as being gay is not: "I have this skin every moment of my life" and "It's the first thing people see [whereas] I can hide being gay." [14] Consciousness of race would seem to occur earlier than sexual orientation, and in that sense to be more primordial, except, perhaps, for those who grow up in an all-black environment.

Somewhat surprisingly, more of the primarily gay-identified African American men than the primarily black-identified ones in Johnson's sample were in the lowest income group (less than $5,000 in 1978 dollars): 35 percent in contrast to 26 percent, although 10 percent of the predominantly gay-identified black men earned more than $20,000 (1980 dollars) in contrast to 6 percent of the predominantly black-identified. More of the black-identified than gay-identified respondents were college-educated (45% to 35%), also. The differences in education and income are anomalous to the view that African Americans who have assimilated to middle-class lifestyles are the ones who identify with the gay community more than with the black community. [15]

Also surprising Johnson's expectations, there were no statistically significant differences in self-acceptance between those identifying more as gay and those identifying more as African American. Nor were there significant dif-

14. Johnson 1981:102, 87–88. Baldwin expressed this view during the late 1970s: "Blacks don't have the choice of being invisible. I don't advocate invisibility for gay people, but historically they have not been shut out in the same absolute terms that blacks have been. My black family needs me more than my gay family, and there's only so much of me to go around." He also noted, "I was too queer and too pacific to be easily accepted by movement blacks—too black and too radical to be embraced by movement gays" (quoted by Reh 1987:30; see Nelson 1991). Bayard Rustin, a long-time black activist without Baldwin's qualms about gay African Americans coming out, asserted, "There is no question in my mind that there was considerable prejudice amongst a number of people I worked with, but, of course, they would never admit they were prejudiced. They would say they were afraid it might hurt the movement" (quoted by Lightweaver 1987:13). Hemphill (1991a:182–83) criticized black leaders and media for consciously and cynically keeping sexual diversity within the black community invisible and inaudible.

15. Explicitly following Carrier in criticizing the black samples of A. P. Bell and Weinberg (1978), Johnson suggested that their data do not show a relationship between higher class and primary identification as gay rather than black.

ferences in indices of acceptance of homosexuality, psychosomatic complaints, loneliness, depression, paranoia, tension or suicidal feelings, or in
racial self-esteem. More of the predominantly gay-identified than of the predominantly black-identified men reported having no gay male friends (10%:
3%). In contrast, 60% of the more gay-identified men and 68% of the more
African American–identified men reported that most or all of their friends
were gay men.[16]

Those identifying primarily as gay were (unsurprisingly) more open
about being gay than those identifying more as being black: 75% of the former, in contrast to 42.5% of the latter, reported most or all of their heterosexual friends knew they were gay; 40% in contrast to 32% reported that
most or all of their neighbors knew they were gay.[17]

Those identifying primarily as black were more likely to have African
American sexual partners: 58% in contrast to 25% reported that half or more
of their sexual partners in the previous twelve months had been black; 10%
in contrast to 35% reported no black sexual partners in the previous year;
19% of the former and 15% of the latter reported no white sexual partners.
The black-identified gay men were more likely to believe that a black partner
offered the strongest chance of happiness (64.5% to 25%; 23% vs. 70%
thought a white partner a more likely route), were more comfortable in all-
black settings (45% to 35%, with none feeling uncomfortable in contrast to
15% of the gay-identified men), felt less isolated from the black community
(10% felt very isolated and an additional 26% somewhat isolated; in contrast
to 35% and 30% respectively of predominantly gay-identified black men),
had more black gay friends (57% of their best friends in contrast to 25% of
the predominantly gay-identified black men). Those identifying more as
black than gay spent less leisure time with whites (10% in contrast to 60%
estimated they spent more than 80% of their time away from work with
whites), and were more likely to have a generally negative view of whites
(10% to 0%, with 6.5% positive in contrast to 35%, the remainder neutral).
All in all, those who identified more as black than as gay spent more time
in black settings and were more comfortable with other blacks in and out
of bed.[18]

16. Johnson 1981:81. Cf. the 78% found by A. P. Bell and Weinberg (1978) in the Bay Area,
ca. 1970.

17. Johnson 1981:73. Considering the primarily gay-identified black men were more likely
to live in "gay neighborhoods," this difference is trivial: 61% of the more gay-identified black
men reported that half or more of their neighbors were gay, in contrast to 37% of the more
black-identified gay men (Johnson 1981:81).

18. Johnson 1981:71–73.

In using gay/black self-identification as his only independent variable, and various indicators of social and sexual involvement as dependent variables, Johnson (1981) treated identity as prior to interaction, rather than forged through interactions. The qualitative data (comments written on his questionnaires) he reported suggest that experiences—especially negative experiences in either the black or gay community—strongly influence relative preference for black or gay self-identification.

Johnson's study is such a vast improvement over Hendin's in conception and in sampling that it is perhaps caviling to fault it for psychologism, especially since it is not mired in etiologic speculation, as even too much sociological writing about homosexuality is. Johnson (1981) provides by far the best available data on patterns of interaction and of identification among gay blacks. Even apart from the effects of AIDS on gay blacks, there is much that remains unknown about differential enculturation in black and gay worlds.

Icard (1986) mostly rehashed Johnson's data with an emphasis on dual oppression, a theme Loiacano (1989) also picked up in three interviews with African American lesbians and three African American gay men in Philadelphia. Both women and men reported considerable pain in reaction to perceived rejection by lesbigay or black communities.[19] Loiacano interpreted the political activism of his rather special sample as evidencing a need to integrate lesbigay with African American identities. One of the men he interviewed asserted that he "found more overt racism among White gays than I did among just whites period" (p. 23), and Loiacano reported that "none of the individuals who were interviewed stated that he or she thought the Black community as a whole was less accepting of gay men and lesbian women than the White community as a whole" (p. 24).[20]

One of the nine or ten San Francisco Bay Area African Americans interviewed by Weston (1991:59) said, "There's things you can be that are worse than gay. I don't think it's regarded as the most horrible thing, overall" (compared to thieves, drug dealers, and drug users). Even this less-than-ringing endorsement was "refuted" by others, "citing experiences of being 'kicked out' by relatives, or an initial apprehension that rejection could have followed disclosure" (with an example of an African American lesbian who only much later realized she wouldn't have been rejected by her family).[21]

19. Ernst et al. (1991) presented data on gender differences among African Americans in condemnation of homosexuality.

20. See also Faderman (1991b:240), although she suggested that this did apply to the 1930s–1950s (p. 184).

21. In gay black representations (e.g., Dixon 1989; Corbin 1993), female kin seem readier not to judge homosexuality (especially male homosexuality) than male kin. Although this

Audre Lorde (1984:99), who refused "to be more vulnerable by putting weapons of silence in my enemies' hands,"[22] recalled that in the early 1970s "the idea of open lesbianism in the Black community was totally horrible." Writing of the late 1960s, Lorde (1984:137) recalled: "Either I denied or chose between various aspects of my identity, or my work and my Blackness would be unacceptable"[23] Much of her writing addresses her embrace of her multiple stigmatized identities, her refusal to deny any one of them. Her family "only allowed themselves to know whatever it was they cared to know, and I did not push them as long as they left me alone."[24] The sister closer in age to her told her: "I am not interested in understanding whatever you're trying to say—I don't care to hear it."[25]

In their interviews with survivors of Buffalo gay female settings of the 1940s and 1950s, Kennedy and Davis (1993:61) judged that the family of one black butch treated her lesbianism more positively than the families of the other women (black and white) they interviewed.[26] Debra's sister told her: "You're not interested in men at all, you seem to be more interested in women." Debra demanded: "No more conversation concerning women or me or my private life. I live my life to suit myself, you live yours to suit you." That they continued to see each other and not talk further about preferring women, Kennedy and Davis treat as "acceptance."

Although (as Kennedy and Davis recognized on pp. 17 and 24) their sample is biased against those women who primarily identified as black rather than gay, they still found that "for most Black lesbians their roots were firmly established in their Black communities and, in the 1950s, their social lives were led within these communities" (p. 114) more than in the bars that were the locus of working-class white woman-loving women. Even

once the bars were desegregated, the Black lesbian community continued to maintain its relative autonomy just adding the bars as one more place to so-

---

parallels the experience of white gay men, it seems to me that in East Asian/West Pacific families female kin enforce the obligations of traditional sex and gender roles more than male kin do (e.g., in the 1992 films *Okoge* and *The Wedding Banquet*).

22. "Nothing I accept about myself can be used against me to diminish me" (p. 147).

23. See also Lorde 1984:47–48, 120–22, 143 on lesbian-bating by black men, and on black invisibility to white lesbians, including feminists (1984:67–70; 1982:181, 203, 224).

24. Lorde 1982:216.

25. Lorde 1984:155.

26. At age thirteen in 1934 in Virginia, she began an affair with a white woman three years her senior (p. 33). The relationship lasted about three years, and Debra accepted her orientation by the time she was 18 (p. 34). After moving to Buffalo in 1938, she met lesbians through her racially mixed church (p. 36). Despite her concern with discretion (pp. 42, 62), she was the only woman who lost a job (two jobs) for being gay (p. 56).

cialize. By giving parties in their own neighborhoods, Black lesbians could escape the restrictions of white bar owners and remove themselves temporarily from the racial tensions that accompanied desegregation.

House parties remained the major milieu,[27] and when black women did venture into gay bars, they preferred to go in groups for mutual protection and support (p. 117).

Lorde (1982:224), who thought that she "wasn't cute or passive enough to be a 'femme'" or "mean or tough enough to be a 'butch'" was frightened by the heavy role dichotomization she saw among the few black women in gay bars during the 1950s.

> During the fifties in the Village [New York's Greenwich Village], I didn't know the few other Black women who were visibly gay at all well. Too often we found ourselves sleeping with the same white women. We recognized ourselves as exotic sister-outsiders who might gain little from banding together. Perhaps our strength might lie in our fewness, our rarity. That was the way it was Downtown. And Uptown, meaning the land of Black people, seemed very far away and hostile territory. (P. 177)

In discussing how black lesbians' greater allegiance to their "parent culture" led to joining black mobilizations rather than to forging a "Lesbian Nation" during the 1970s, Faderman (1991b:240) asserted that "lesbians and gay men were generally more outcast in [minority] communities than in many white communities, because the minority racial and ethnic communities tended to be working class and particularly rigid about machismo and sexuality," referring to Shockley's (1979) explanation that "the woman-identified-woman, the black lesbian, was a threat not only to the projection of black male macho, but a sexual threat, too—the utmost danger to the black man's institutionally designated role as 'King of the Lovers.'"[28] Somewhat more generally, Faderman (1991b:242) continued: "The few minority women who became part of visible lesbian-feminist life in the 1970s were usually able to do so only at the cost of alienation from their ethnic communities. Often they were women who had a love relationship with a white woman and maintained few ties back in the ghetto."

27. House parties were also the locus of middle-class white woman–woman socializing, but working-class blacks and middle-class whites did not mix (p. 122), although gay men came to the black lesbian house parties (p. 125). On black lesbian house (or apartment) parties, see also Joseph 1981:182–86 and Garber 1982. On the continued importance of house parties rather than public gay places for African American gay men in a small Southern city, see Whittier 1995.

28. See also Lorde 1982:121, 181–82, 1984:47–48, 60–64; B. Freeman 1991:62. Kennedy and Davis (1993:127), drawing on hooks (1988), denied that black men physically attacked black or white lesbians. That is, they "hit on" rather than "hit." Faderman (1991b:184) contrasted something of a homosexuality vogue in Harlem during the 1920s with later increased intolerance by black men (through at least the 1950s).

Among the 530 disproportionately middle-class black lesbians in a national survey reported by Mays and Cochran (1988a), a third had given birth to one or more children. Nearly two thirds were in a committed relationship. The median length of the longest (lifetime-to-date) relationship was 42 months and the median number of serious/committed relationships was three; 83 percent of the women reported at least one committed relationship with a black woman, 40 percent with an Anglo woman, and 17 percent with other (than black) women of color. Ninety-three percent reported at least one sexual relationship with a black woman, 65 percent with an Anglo, and 38 percent with other women of color (with a median of 9 lifetime sexual partners). Mays and Cochran did not report data on degree of identification with black, lesbian, or gay communities, or multivariate analyses of these data.

Instead, Mays, Cochran, and Rhue (1993) reported conceptions of discrimination by eight African American women in relationships with other African American women. Five felt discrimination as women, four as black, and one for sexual orientation (seemingly the only one who was out of the closet at work; "the true nature of their relationships was not openly discussed" in families of origin, either). Two did not have sufficient contact with other African Americans to have opinions about negative African American community views of homosexuality. The others agreed that this is not accepted and that the focus of hatred is male homosexuality. Half participated in mostly white lesbian events. Of the other half, one was "not a joiner," another too "in the closet," and two did not want to socialize with predominantly white women. In a national sample of 605 black lesbians, Mays (1995) found slightly more reporting both perceived and experienced discrimination as black than as woman, and slightly more reporting more discrimination as women than as lesbians. She also noted that black gay men reported more discrimination as gay than as black.

Acceptance by and identification with gay and with black communities continues to be problematic for African Americans sexually/romantically involved with persons of the same sex.[29] Although Herdt and Boxer (1993)

29. I believe that higher rates of unsafe sex and HIV infection among gay African Americans are at least in part due to anomie (in particular, lack of peer support for safe sex). Lemp et al. (1994) found that young (17–22) San Francisco Bay Area African Americans who have sex with men were substantially more likely to be HIV-antibody positive (21.2%) than Latinos (9.5%), Anglos (8%), or Asian/Pacific Americans (4%). The young African Americans were also more likely to have engaged in unprotected intercourse in the previous six months (38.5%) than Anglos (28%) and Asian/Pacific-Americans (27%), though slightly less likely than were Latinos (40%). In a study by Peterson et al. (1992) of 250 gay and bisexual African American men (with a mean education of 13 years; all but three were between 20 and 39 years of age) recruited in

provide no racial/ethnic breakdowns of the data on young Chicagoans they studied, that lesbian or gay identity is more problematic for African Americans of the generation coming out in the late 1980s is suggested by their greater reluctance to join in the Gay Pride Parade (p. 164) and one young African American woman's distaste for the word "lesbian" (p. 117).

1990 from San Francisco Bay Area bars, bathhouses, and erotic bookstores, and through African American gay organizations, street outreach, advertisements in gay mainstream and African American newspapers, health clinics, and personal referral from other participants, more than 50% reported having had unprotected anal intercourse in the past 6 months, in contrast to 21% of white gay men in San Francisco in comparable studies. The African American men who practiced unprotected anal intercourse were more likely to be poorer, to have used injection drugs, or to have been paid for sex, and to have a higher perceived risk of HIV infection.

Eleven

Some Gay African American Self-Representations from the 1980s and 1990s

Although the dearth of social science research on gay African Americans has continued since Johnson (1981), some other African American writers continue to address the central problematics he explored: primary identification as gay or as African American, and the relation of this identification to choice of sexual partners. This chapter reviews some of these. For instance, Reginald Shepherd (1986:52) described himself as someone who had "spent years proudly and often militantly defining myself as a gay man; [but] I am still tentatively moving toward the point at which I may accept myself as a black man." He recognized that, "In my growing up I knew what black people were like and I knew I wasn't one of them" (p. 51), and castigated as "obsessive" his attraction to white men (p. 47), "the ultimate prize and ensign of validation" (p. 53):

> If I in particular am seen with a beautiful man, whiteness being intrinsic to my definition of beauty, then in my own mind and in the minds of those around me, around us, I am thereby one worthy of whiteness. By being seen with him, I am made an honorary white man for so long as I am with him. Suddenly I am part of the [gay] community. . . . The circle is vicious and the stereotypes are not all on one side. (P. 54)

For Shepherd, there are a gay community to which he can belong only as the partner of a white man, and hence as "an honorary white man"; and the world of the African American lumpen proletariat, which scares him as much as it does middle-class whites. Uneasy about being attracted to white men, angry about white men who reject him because he is African American, he also exhibits unease about those attracted to him because he is African

246

American. A white man who might want to be "an honorary African American" in an African American community could, in his view, only be using him for validation.[1] Moreover, Shepherd does not seem to believe there is any African American gay community of which he could be a part.

After recalling growing up in black Philadelphia "with practically no self-esteem, a desperate need to love and be loved, and an ingrained sense that I was unlovable," Harpe (1991:54) notes that "the community of black gay men is very diverse," and suggests that "what we have in common is the fact that we do not always treat ourselves and each other very well." In a winter 1992 *Out/Look* symposium, Ken Dixon focused on hierarchy in black–black relationships:

> When I've been involved with Black men there's a lot more power issues; who's going to be on top and who's going to be on the bottom. I think it has to do with growing up in a matriarchal society and Black men having less power in their own social structure. So when two Black men come together you just complicate that because they have both come out of a matriarchal society. Somebody's going to have to vie for position on top. But I haven't been that kind of person, so my relationships with Black men have suffered in some ways because I don't play the power game.

He did not have the sense of "coming home" to unproblematic shared assumptions in an intra-ethnic relationship that Chicanos and Chicanas described in the same issue. Essex Hemphill (1991a:xix, 1992:40) wrote, "There was no 'gay' community for Black men to come home to in the 1980s." While suspecting black–white sexual relations, Wayne Corbitt noted,

> In the black community it's OK to be gay, just don't say it out loud. . . . You're already an outcast in the eyes of mainstream society by being black, and yet among blacks you won't be acceptable because you're queer. It's the same thing only one step further out. It's being doubly marginalized. And if you're the kind of queer I am, who sticks out and who identifies himself that way, it can get pretty rocky. Which sometimes makes me want to hide. (Quoted by Knapper 1995:42)

Hemphill believed that he no more could rely upon acceptance (in contrast to tolerance) of gay men in African American circles than upon acceptance (in contrast to tolerance) of African Americans in gay circles. There is also no acceptable erotic response from whites: one or another African American will interpret as "racist" a nonblack man either desiring or not desiring

---

1. See Reid-Pharr 1993 or the more complex explanation in Mitchell 1980:193–95, 243–44. A Boston-born African American man resident in Atlanta suggested regional differences, telling E. White (1980:241), "In Boston all the blacks want a white lover. . . . Here there's less mixing—you seldom see mixed couples—so blacks go with each other. Blacks here are much friendlier than back home; their social isolation, however, has made them very clannish."

a particular black man or finding black men as a category desirable or undesirable.[2]

Film director Marlon Riggs, who took "Black men loving black men is a revolutionary act" as the main text of his film *Tongues Untied,* considered the question of primacy/hierarchy of racial or sexual identity absurd.[3] In that film, a gay African American retorted that such a question is like asking "Is your left nut more important to you than your right nut?" In his 1990 film *Affirmations,* one says, "I want to be both black and gay and not have to be divided." In an interview distinguishing "loving black men" from intragroup exclusivity in partners, Riggs said,

> Many of us trying to divide ourselves up into part black and part gay and then to arrange these parts in some formal kind of hierarchy and decide "which am I first?" I think is a very silly thing to do, because one cannot divide up one's character just so. Also it's a very dangerous and self-defeating thing to do.[4]

In regard to separatist organizations, Riggs continued,

> When you're asking in terms of "should there be black gay organization?" I give a resounding "yes" to that. I think there are many issues that we as black people need to deal with each other on first, before attempting to coalition-build and to build bridges across racial and multi-cultural boundaries. There are so many issues between us that we have not deal with adequately, all kinds of hostilities among ourselves that we have not in any way resolved. . . . What tends to happen with all kinds of organizations, not just black gay organizations, is that they themselves tend to forget the lessons of oppression and become just as chauvinistic as the organizations that they were set up to be an alternative to rather than embracing notions of diversity, multiculturalism and respect for difference.[5]

In particular, even those who challenge a gay/straight dichotomy tend to dichotomize race as black or white, ignoring both differences within those two categories and other peoples who live in North America.

In analyzing life history materials from 57 gay African American men in Harlem, Hawkeswood (1990) challenged many common assumptions about

2. See Preston 1993a:207–8 on the related matter of black images, Hemphill's focus— Mapplethorpe's "Man in a Polyester Suit"—in particular. Some gay Asian Americans (e.g., Justin Chin and others associated with the Gay Asian Pacific Alliance) repeat this "damned if you do, damned if you don't" pattern.

3. Lockman (1984) also reported a survey of African American men in lover relationships with Anglo/white men who did not find interracial relationships very problematic.

4. From Banneker 1990:18. That homosexuality does not make one less black is a major theme in his film *Black Is, Black Ain't,* completed after his death in 1994.

5. From Banneker (1990:18–19). This was well exemplified by an attack on Riggs in a letter to the editor in the next issue of *BLK.*

continuities of gender and sexuality.[6] Louis, the one informant whose views on the primacy of race over sexual orientation Hawkeswood quoted, stressed the inseparability of these attributes of self: "I'm a man who is Black and gay. That's how I describe myself. In that order: man, Black, gay. But it's all one person. I'm all o' those together" (p.12).

Hooks (1988:25, see also 1992) noted that "for some people there are concrete situations in which they are compelled to choose one identification over another," while stressing that many individuals feel isolated from both identities and both communities. Loiacano (1989), who regarded the need to integrate the two identities as a paramount concern, also found this.

Tinney (1986:73) took the existence of an African American gay community as inevitable, "because of the uniqueness in talents, gifts, sensitivity, experience, dress, and behavior that is inherently a part of being both black and gay," but in his ministry refused to "affirm and 'baptize' everything black and everything gay" and had "to come to grips with the fact that much within our communities is, indeed, pathological. . . . A black gay church exists, among other reasons, to 'free ourselves up' to deal with negativities in our lives that we would resent others approaching us about" (pp. 84, 83).[7]

Others, such as Cornwell (1978:468–69), reject the black church as itself pathological:

> Even unto this very day, all too many black womyn are still so hung up on Jesus Christ and the Bible, they may as well be living in the time of Moses and the Burning Bush. During the time of our great oppression in America, the Bible

6. Hawkeswood (1990:7, 9) asserted that "the 'sissies' are often the active partner sexually, and the 'men' are almost always the passive partners," and that "most of the 'butch' hustlers assumed a passive role sexually . . . [and] call themselves 'gay.'" He explained the blatant effeminacy of those men seeking masculine sexual partners as, "if you want a man, then this is the way that you must behave to entice him, irrespective of what you may actually want to do with him sexually" (p. 8), an explanation discussed in chapter 6.

7. In an earlier discussion of the overt condemnation of and covert reliance on homosexuals in black pentecostal churches, Tinney (1983:170) recalled, "I could not grow up in a religious environment wherein a majority of my spiritual teachers and preachers and shouters and other liturgical actors were known to me to be gay (sometimes also being my own bedmates) without feeling that, despite their disclaimers, homosexuality could not be altogether wrong. Despite the anti-sexual theme which characterizes much of Pentecostal preaching, a certain practical tolerance of variant sexual activity (including both hetero- and homosexual acts) exuded itself. The conscious way in which the presence of homosexuality was recognized (whether approved or not) contributed to a feeling that it was really no worse than women wearing open-toe shoes or saints missing a mid-week prayer meeting."

Wayne Corbitt, who described himself as "the jaded son of a preacher woman" (to Knapper 1995:33), also complained that closetry was the price of participation in the African American "sanctified church."

was about the only source of comfort for most black womyn. . . . It apparently became the only framework that sustained them. And if there is any document anywhere that is more anti-female and pro-male than the Bible, I simply do not want to hear about it. In retrospect, I believe that's why so many black lesbians feel so guilty about being gay.

And some seek to recover West African religious roots.[8]

Acceptance by the African American community of African American gay churches, social service agencies, and publications seemed impossible to Dais (1986:61), who related concerns that he would not be allowed to serve the African American community, because he is not suitably straight.[9] The value of masculinity is certainly central to this. A gay non-sissy is not a traditional category (to African Americans or to whites). Masculine deportment may not be enough to establish masculinity: "The thinking of many African American brothers and sisters is that being gay is somehow the opposite of being a man, and that fathering a child is somehow the proof of one's manhood."[10]

Even some flamboyant black queens marry and have children.[11] Such an affirmation of masculinity "proves" (in the social view) that one is not "queer," so does nothing to establish the (social) possibility of being a masculine gay man. That is, behavior does not affect the social logic, which remains dichotomous. Men who impregnate women are masculine adults, whatever their other "crazy notions" and sexual behavioral patterns may be.[12]

As Samuel Delaney explained, "When you talk about something openly for the first time, for better or worse, you use the public language you've been given."[13] More specifically, as Fuller wrote,

> Since the only homosexual role models I was aware of at that point were whispered about over back fences, I suppressed what was natural in me and retreated into my writing, music, and books. . . . At seventeen, I already knew that in desiring a special male friend I did not want to replace women in any straight man's life. I wanted a man who wanted a man—nothing less. Even so, clear as that concept was to me in 1972, I had no experience, personal or otherwise on which the build my defense. . . . I waffled. I bullshitted, I tried to change the subject. (1992:235–36)

Realizing that the public language betrays one's own experience does not instantly change that language. That language's equation of homosexuality

---

8. E. g., Blackberri 1990; Somé 1994.
9. See also Harris (1986) on the rejection by the family of his lover who has died of AIDS.
10. A. Jones 1986:144. See also Delaney and Beam 1986:196–97.
11. See C. Smith 1986:217.
12. See Hemphill 1992:102–4; L. Jones 1966:138–48. Cf. C. Smith 1986:217–18.
13. Delaney and Beam 1986:197.

and effeminacy was (and is) reinforced by masculine-appearing men passing as straight and by effeminate-appearing or -acting men being the only ones who are openly gay. Samuel Delaney recalled one particularly flamboyant African American queen he knew growing up in the 1940s.

[Then,] some blacks were more open about being gay than many whites. My own explanation was, I suppose, that because we had less to begin with, in the end we had less to lose. Still, the openness Herman showed, as did a number of other gay men, black or white, never seemed an option for me. . . . At the time I would have analyzed my own "lack of options" in this way: I wasn't personally attracted to effeminate men. Therefore I couldn't imagine the men I would be attracted to would be attracted in turn to someone who was effeminate. (Delaney and Beam 1986:191)[14]

Fisher (1983:32), who came out at age fifteen in 1971 in his own world, the streets of Harlem and the South Bronx, recalled that in black bars then and there, "the queens and drags were respected. . . . They were no slouches these queens. They carried blades and guns filled with lead. Go off wrong with them—you were dead!" Similarly, the narrator in Steven Corbin's novel *A Hundred Days From Now* (1994) recalled as "his premiere gay role models—openly effeminate gay men and drag queens whom people feared and respected." Growing up in Jersey City's black ghetto during the 1960s, "flamboyant, effeminate homosexuals and drag queens were known to parade up and down the streets without being bashed or harassed. The fact that most of them were ex-convicts and not to be messed with had plenty to do with it" (pp. 80–81).

In a 1986 discussion with a black woman from Suriname who did not want to be "labeled" *lesbian*, Audre Lorde insisted that calling herself a *black lesbian* was important.[15] She recalled that

in the sixties we could do anything we wanted to as long as we did not talk about it. If you speak your name, you represent a threat to the powers that be, the patriarchate. That [a black lesbian] is what I want to be, too. The price I pay for that and the vulnerability it makes me aware of are no greater than what I feel if I keep it a secret and let others decide what they want to call me. That also perpetuates the position of inferiority we occupy in society. (Quoted in Wekker 1993:153)

14. Cf. Clark 1983; Hemphill 1991b; R. Jackson 1991.

15. She made clear that, in what she meant by *lesbian*, "it is not having genital intercourse with a woman that is the criterion. There are lesbian women who have never had genital or any other form of sexual contact with other women, while there are also women who have had sex with other women but who are not lesbian. A lesbian is a woman who identifies fundamentally with women. . . . It is not my behavior that determines whether I am lesbian, but the very core of my being" (quoted in Wekker 1993:153–54).

Bell hooks wrote that homophobia was even more acute toward women:

> In the particular black community where I grew up, . . . black male homosexu-
> als were often known, talked about, and seen positively; they played important
> roles in community life. Lesbians, however, were talked about solely in nega-
> tive terms. . . . In those days, homophobia directed at lesbians was rooted in a
> deep religious and moral belief that defined womanness through bearing chil-
> dren. The prevailing assumption was that to be a lesbian was "unnatural." . . .
> There were no identified lesbian parents . . . [although] there were men known
> to be gay who were caretakers of other folk's children. (1988:22–23)

Cornwell recalled a colloquium in which she felt she was the only one to
notice that

> black men were just as sexist as other men. Then I eventually realized that
> most of the vocal members in the room were holding fast to the idea that black
> womyn only had one of two choices: either they had to join the womyn's lib-
> eration movement and be led by white womyn, or become part of the civil
> rights movement and be led by black men. Finally, I put my question to this
> young black dude: "You seems to be saying that I have to be led either by white
> womyn or by black men. Why can't I lead myself?" He hemmed and hawed
> but never came out with any clearcut reply. (1978:475)

As Simmons (1991:214, 217) observed, "In the black community a male is
often forced to denounce homosexuality in order to avoid suspicion. . . . To
prove their manhood, they often attack what they fear in themselves. . . . It's
easy to prove your manhood by putting down 'faggots.'" Or, in Riggs's words,

> Because of my sexuality, I cannot be black. A strong, proud, "Afrocentric"
> black man is resolutely heterosexual. . . . I am consigned, by these tenets, to
> remain a Negro faggot. And as such I am game for play, to be used, joked about,
> put down, beaten, slapped, and bashed, not just by illiterate homophobic thugs
> in the night, but by black American culture's best and brightest. (1991a:254)

Perhaps it is the last who most need to reassure themselves they are macho
enough. Riggs continued with an analysis paralleling Simmons's:

> What lies at the heart, I believe, of black America's pervasive cultural homo-
> phobia is the desperate need for a convenient Other within the community, yet
> not truly of the community, an Other to which blame for the chronic identity
> crises afflicting the black male psyche can be readily displaced, an indispens-
> able Other which functions as the lowest common denominator of the abject,
> the base line of transgression beyond which a Black Man is no longer a man, no
> longer black, an essential Other against which black men and boys maturing,
> struggling with self-doubt, anxiety, feelings of political, economic, social, and
> sexual inadequacy—even impotence—can always measure themselves and by
> comparison seem strong, adept, empowered, superior. (Ibid.)

African American men and women express similar frustrations at the
racism, sexism, and heterosexism of supposed "brothers" and "sisters," re-

gardless of whether the basis for the supposition is race, sex, or sexual orientation.[16] Those who "view our racial heritage as primary, frequently live 'bisexual front lives' within black neighborhoods," while "those who identify first as gay usually live outside the closet in predominantly white gay communities," explained Max Smith (1986:226). He estimated there are nine of the former for every one of the latter.

African American leaders and intellectuals have sought to keep the existence of lesbigay blacks, past and present, invisible.[17] This seems to me to be true even of those pressing gay rights issues as part of "rainbow coalition" politics, such as Jesse Jackson nationally, and Willie Brown in California, i.e., their coalitions seem to be between African Americans and white gay men, without acknowledging and lesbigay African Americans. Similarly, "Afrocentric" intellectuals such as Molefi Kete Asante deny indigenous African homosexuality,[18] while work in "black studies" ignores African and African American homosexualities. For instance, Nelson (1991:128) noted that "among black scholars of the Harlem Renaissance there is a remarkable reticence about the [homo]sexualities of these pioneering artists and a determined unwillingness to explore the impact of their gayness"; Román (1993: 215) reported that the pathbreaking Pomo Afro Homo performance piece *Fierce Love*[19] was almost totally ignored by the black press and blocked from African American venues. Reflecting on censorship by the Langston Hughes Estate of homosexual implications in Isaac Julien's 1989 film *Waiting for Langston*, Essex Hemphill (1991a:183) wrote: "It was common at one time to openly silence and intimidate outspoken black people. Now black people practice these tactics against each other."[20] Perhaps as Barbara Smith said of the African American community's "tolerance" of homosexual sex, "you can play it, but don't say it. . . . If you're a lesbian, you can have as many women as you want; if you're a gay man, you can have all the men you want; but just don't say anything about it or make it political."[21] This closely resembles the "tolerance" of sex and preoccupation with respectability of family honor in

16. See also Beame 1983:59; Clayborne 1978; Goldsby 1990; hooks 1988; R. Jackson 1991: 210; Omosupe 1991; Riggs 1991b:200; Simmons 1991; Corbin 1993:98.

17. A notable exception is Henry Louis Gates, Jr., for instance in recalling Bayard Rustin, the real organizer of the 1963 March on Washington (1993:44).

18. Cf. Murray 1990a; Murray and Roscoe 1997.

19. See B. Freeman 1991.

20. See also Julien's later film, *The Darker Side of Black*, which focuses on how rap music incites fag-bashing.

21. In Gomez and Smith 1990:33. In a gay rather than an African American magazine, Hemphill (1991c) refuted the crypto-Freudian black homophobe psychiatrist Frances Cress Welsing.

Latin American countries, or of maintaining face and invisibilizing lesbian relations in Thailand.[22]

Conservativeness of self-presentation and concern to not "rock the boat" are not confined to straight African American organizations. J. C. Roberts (1986) recounted and excoriated the cliquishness and timidity of a Philadelphia African American gay organization, as well.

Several contributors to Beam (1986)—Branner, Delaney and Beam, A. Jones, and C. Smith—discuss the conflictedness of accepting gayness within African American milieux. In his memoir of the East Village of 1957– 65, Delaney (1988) elaborates on this. Hemphill (1992:10) celebrates his "natural tendencies," while wondering whether the black men to whom he is sexually receptive can view him as a "brother," recalling the violent challenge to a glimpse of his adolescent desires (pp. 96–101) and the continued physical and emotional dangers to him as an adult from black men (pp. 63– 64, 79–90, 159–60).[23] Alexandre (1983:80) expressed regrets about the seeming impossibility of finding a black partner, since "only another Black man could show me off properly," while dancer/choreographer Bill T. Jones, acknowledging to Gates (1994:116) the attraction, viewed sleeping with black men as "incestuous." The seemingly autobiographical narrator of Jack Slater's "New Year" (1992) had a black partner as an adolescent (berated by the narrator's father for making his son a "faggot": "He spat the word like he was some white man saying the word nigger," p. 236).

Steven Corbin (1993) showed the conflict (in Delaney's generation) between the protagonist's mother's homosexual (but "no punk") brother and the father who exclaims with contempt that his brother-in-law "got the nerve to be proud of being a freak" (p. 277), and Corbin also portrayed high school verbal hazing of the coterie of boys of his own generation who recognized their homosexual desire and had it recognized by classmates (pp. 139–50), concluding with a new generation's realization that "faggots and punks weren't necessarily synonymous."[24] Melvin Dixon (1992:98–99) included Jesse's rejection by the blacks at a mostly white college, once they find out he

22. See Murray 1987b:124–27; Morris 1994. Kenan's "The foundations of the earth" (1992:49–72) contains at least one representation of acceptance by a pious and ultrarespectable rural African-American matriarch. As usual, the plot kills off one member of the long-term interracial male couple. Unusually, in this instance, it is not the white one, who instead goes south to be with his dead black lover's grandmother.

23. See also Hemphill 1991c; R. Jackson 1991:207; 1991:37.

24. Cf. the late Glenn Burke, a former professional baseball player, in M. J. Smith 1983: 123, 126, and Rudy in Corbin's 1989 novel about 1920s Harlem.

is studying dance, even without any evidence of the seeming corollary of homosexuality.[25]

Larry Duplechan's (1985) fictional protagonist across several novels, singer Johnnie Ray, grew up in a predominantly white small city in San Bernardino County, inland from Los Angeles. His primary identification is gay, not African American. I take the character in his story "Presently in the past" to be autobiographical in recalling that before 1964 "I had never thought of myself or my family as Negroes. . . . As far as I know, I was just me, we were just us. I had of course noticed that some people—myself included were brown and some people were of a more pale-pink-and-orange, and so what?" (1991b:192–93).

In telling of his adolescence, Johnnie Ray, is not colorblind; neither is he blind to discrimination against him (specifically, in the casting of a school play). Although candidly attracted to white men, he does not seem to need them to gain legitimacy or entrée to the Los Angeles gay community (once he goes off to UCLA). Although guilt-tripped into having sex with one African American "brother" (1985:189), Johnnie Ray never feels that his desires for white men are strange. He accepts his desires as natural, although his parents in *Blackbird* are so upset by his coming out that they have a formal exorcism.[26] He humors them, as he humors his friend Cherie by having sex with her, confident that neither experience is going to change who he is, and that who he is is just fine. In *Eight Days a Week*, his affluent white lover's possessiveness and bisexuality, not his color, concern him.[27]

Although, as in Baldwin's fiction, Duplechan's plots are contrived and overly melodramatic, his books show that despite all the obsessive societal concern about race and sexuality exhibited by some adults, including his own

25. Dixon also included quasi-rapes of black males by black males (adult on pp. 114–15, child on p. 163; with *nigger* and *punk* as the terms of endearment used)—and the murder by white teenagers of Jesse's white lover. Similarly, Larry Duplechan has the white lover killed off more obliquely, leaving him no less dead . . .

26. In a collection also containing a story by Duplechan, Tinney (1983:170–71) attested that exorcisms of homosexuality happen (see also Gevisser and Cameron 1995:122). Duplechan's own experience of a modicum of tolerance without approval was less melodramatic. He recounted that "it was during my first year at UCLA that my mother found out I was gay. I'd told my father about a year earlier, but he had simply prayed over me, asking God to remove these wild ideas from my mind, and considered the case closed" (1992:49).

27. The problems of loving a bisexual man recur in Duplechan's third novel, *Tangled Up in Blue* (1989), one in which black characters are not quite incidental, although none of the central tetrad is black. The gay leads in his first three novels are exceedingly perky and resilient. In his fourth, *Captain Swing* (1993), a wise young cousin and a former teacher take up these attributes to cure a grieving Johnnie Ray and enable him to sing again.

parents, for at least some gay African Americans neither may be particularly problematic. Johnnie Ray doesn't need to work through loathing either being gay or being African American.[28]

As for many gay white men,[29] accepting his gayness frees Johnnie Ray from being a scrawny ugly duckling hating team sports. He can then transform himself into a beautiful gay swan by lifting weights. He discovers that he can have a masculine body like the ones he wants and still retain his interest (and talent) in the arts, have a masculine lover, and live happily ever after in a geographically dispersed L.A. gay network.[30] Random violence truncates the ever-after, and in his latest tale, Johnnie Ray's desires are more politically correct—i.e., black, though too incestuous (too "down home"!) and intergenerational enough not to be p.c. except on the homoracial criterion.[31]

In Steven Corbin's novel *Fragments That Remain* (1993), Skylar is almost as ambivalent about his white lover Evan's racial specialization in partners as he is about his black father's self-loathing and jealousy of his gay son.

> Like most black gay men, I stand on the periphery of the gay community, something Evan can't understand. I don't see myself represented in Gay Pride Week, during the parades, in the bars, in the press. . . . The gay community only minimally represents me. Some of the most bigoted people I've met are gay. While the gay liberation and pride movement has its important function in society, it's the result of millions of white, male, often blond and blue-eyed people who never before had to deal with bigotry, feeling appalled that they could be denied a civil right—or denied anything in this country. (P. 311)

African Americans seem unable to comprehend that the—at least in Corbin's case, fetishistic—reduction of white men to blonds with blue eyes might strike European Americans with other colorations as racist,[32] as might the invisibility of any but black and blond men in gay African American discourse, leaving aside the not wholly positive valuation of blond(e)s in American culture and representations—and the outright use of blue eyes as a metaphor of male effeminacy by the recurrently homophobic, Nobel Prize–winning African American novelist Toni Morrison (1970). At a black–white

---

28. Alan Miller (1988:14) recalls similar self-affirmation as black and as gay in the very white schools (the Chicago Latin School and Amherst College) he attended. See also Lockman 1984 and Parker 1992. Cf. B. Freeman 1991.

29. See Harry 1982b.

30. Duplechan 1991a.

31. Duplechan 1993. See also Hardy 1994.

32. Sergio, the Mexico City–born lover of the black writer Dexter, in *A Hundred Days From Now* (Corbin 1994), has a Mexican father but an Anglo mother, so that he too has blue eyes, although culturally he is very Latino elite (indeed, too Latino elite, to have been raised by his Anglo mother struggling to make ends meet in Seattle). Early in the novel and their relationship, "Dexter was proud to be seen with" his blue-eyed trophy (p. 27).

gay rap group Skylar and Evan attend, one African American complains that "when white people see me, they don't see a gay man. They see a black man,"[33] and another spits out, "White faggots don't like niggers any more than white America!" (p. 175). It is hard to sort out self-conception from how and as what a self is regarded by significant others, and projections run both ways across racial divides in contemporary America (as vividly, if melodramatically, represented by Corbin 1993:175–76 and Dixon 1992:103, 113, 210), especially around sexual desires for otherness.

33. Those who are "dark like us, despised like us" (Hemphill 1992:13; Riggs 1991b:202, 205) who choose blonds make substituting "black" for "white" and "white" for "black" in this assertion at least conceivable.

Twelve

Mexican American Homosexuality

The extent to which sexual socialization during adolescence was mostly with Mexican Americans or with Anglo Americans is the best predictor of whether a Mexican American's homosexual conduct tilts toward Anglo or Mexican patterns of homosexuality.[1] Socializing mostly with Anglos—at school or in childhood play—increases the likelihood that Mexican Americans will select Anglos as sex partners and will be affected by and/or emulate their sexual styles.[2]

A major difference of particular relevance to the spread of HIV is that the available data suggest that Mexican men generally prefer and more consistently play one sexual role (either *pasivo* 'receptive' or *activo* 'insertive'), and prefer anal intercourse over fellatio, whereas Anglos tend to be more versatile in sexual role, to have more non–steady sexual partners, and to be less focused on anal intercourse.[3] If it exists, the stronger commitment to a single role among less acculturated Mexican Americans may explain some of the

1. Although I think that there are cultural similarities between southwestern U.S. Mexican American culture and East Coast Caribbean (Cuban and Puerto Rican) American cultures, both my own observations and the bulk of the social science literature on homosexuality among Latinos in the United States focus on the former. (A pioneering exception is the article on Puerto Rican lesbians by Hidalgo and Christensen 1976.) Some of those of Mexican ancestry born before 1940 and/or in Texas and New Mexico reject the label *Chicano. Mexican American* includes Mexican-born and U.S.-born, whereas *Chicano* usually refers only to the U.S.-born (stretched to include those who attended grade school in the U.S.).

2. As noted in chapter 9, gay-identified Latinos in San Francisco tend to have their first homosexual experience at an earlier age than Anglos or those of Asian/Pacific Islander origin/ancestry (median 15 in contrast to 17 and 19). No one knows the extent of ethnic endogamy or exogamy in partners, either for initial homosexual encounters or for enduring relationships, for Mexican Americans or those of other ethnicities.

3. Carrier 1989, 1995; Carrier and Magaña 1992. Murray 1995a:145–49 reviews some data showing middle-class urban Mexican role versatility and cautions against generalizing very much from these data.

differences in AIDS rates between urban northern and southern California (472 per 100,000 in San Francisco in contrast to 48 per 100,000 in Los Angeles as of 1990), although differences in the rates of infection among available non-Mexican partners must also account for some of the differences.[4]

The less Americanized, especially the Mexican-born, Mexican Americans tend not to identify themselves as *lesbian* or *gay;* and they tend to find Spanish-speaking sexual partners in the neighborhood (barrio) straight bars and clubs, and in certain parks, very much as in Mexico, rather than at multiethnic gay institutions in which English is the lingua franca. U.S.-born Mexican Americans are more likely to identify themselves as *gay*, to find sexual partners in gay institutions, and to engage in a wider repertoire of sexual acts and roles. Generally, the first generation born in a country are more able and more eager to adopt the lifeways and worldviews of the country than are their foreign-born and -socialized parents. Even if Mexican-born parents convey some of the strong gender-deviant conception of homosexuality to their American-born children, an alternative conception is more readily available to the children as they grow up in a country in which a visible gay culture rejects any "natural" link between effeminacy and homosexual receptivity. The ethnic composition of adolescent friendship networks, and especially the ethnicity of early sexual partners, seems to best predict identification as *gay*, later participation primarily in gay or in Latino worlds, and the ethnicity of later sexual partners.

Scattered evidence[5] shows that Mexican American men who have sex with men report having fewer sexual partners, fewer anonymous sexual encounters, being less likely to use condoms, and being less comfortable with nudity than Anglo or African American men who have sex with men.[6]

As in Latin America,[7] those stigmatized as unmasculine may opt for the label *gay* in preference to pejoratives such as *joto* and *maricón*. In turn, this borrowing makes *gay* seem to others to be a term for effeminate men rather than a term for those rejecting the linkage and endeavoring to obliterate the stigma. The influence of the dominant cultural definition of everyone who has homosexual intercourse as *gay*, along with a readier availability of female sexual outlets and an earlier age of male marriage, probably result in less bisexual behavior than in Mexico and points south of it.

4. California AIDS Office 1990. On assessing risks in populations with different rates of infection see Koopman et al. 1991.

5. Reviewed in Murray 1995a:170–79; see especially Doll et al. 1990.

6. Alcoholism is prominent in representations of gay Mexican Americans, though I know of no attempt to assess ethnic differences in its prevalence.

7. See Murray 1987b:129–38, 1992b, 1995d.

The importance of early sexual socialization also predicts later participation in Mexican institutions or in multi-ethnic lesbian ones. Given the simplistic cultural conception of women as either saintly mothers or dissolute whores, and the pressure to avoid expression of personal feelings—especially any sexual desires—Mexican American lesbians seem more likely than Anglo lesbians to bear children.[8] The general dependence of lesbian mothers on their natal families[9] reinforces a primary identification by Mexican American women with *la familia* rather than with lesbians who do not share language, cultural traditions, and experience of class and ethnic devaluation.

Prominent lesbian Mexican-American writers such as Gloria Anzaldúa and Cherríe Moraga describe the dilemmas of identity, family, and sexuality for Mexican-American women.[10] John Rechy has frequently described masculinist sex with little focus on identities (gay or Mexican American), while the lawyer and mystery writer Michael Nava's autobiographical hero Henry Rios embraces them (though, like Nava himself, Rios is ambivalent about his lower-class background).[11]

My impression that gay male Latinos are less likely to live far away from their families than gay male Anglos is supported by my finding that the Latinos were 3.5 times more likely to be natives of the San Francisco Bay Area than were Anglos, and that nonnative Latinos were somewhat (though only 5%) more likely to have moved to the Bay Area with family members than were nonnative Anglos. Even if it is neither necessary nor sufficient, geographical distance makes psychological distance from family constraints easier. While gay Anglos often view Latinos as excessively closeted and uptight, gay Latinos often view Anglos as excessively loose and shockingly cut off from their natal families. For instance, Castillo (1991:38) wrote that Latina lesbians "do not want to lose the love and sense of place they feel within their families and immediate communities. In light of intense Anglo alienation, this is a crucial aspect to their sense of identity." These stereotypes are, I think, grounded in some real interethnic differences.[12]

8. See Trujillo 1991:190 on the greater pressure to do so.

9. Illustrated by Lewin (1993).

10. See, e.g., Anzaldúa 1987; Moraga and Anzaldúa 1981. See also the materials collected by Trujillo (1991).

11. See Ortiz 1993; Murray 1995a:161–67.

12. On a structural basis in the lack of state provision of disability and unemployment insurance in Latin America, see Murray 1987a:118–28; 1995a:33–48. Dependence on familiy is not only a product of such insecurity (attenuated for those born in the U.S.). Child-rearing practices also enhance family orientation, and differences may become markers of ethnic pride (e.g., "We're not cold-hearted like Anglos who don't love their mothers," etc.).

Thirteen

Gay Asian/Pacific Americans

The category "Asian/Pacific" has only slightly more specific cultural content than "people of color," "non-white," or "the Other."[1] "Chinese" or "Indian" or "Filipino" each encompasses immense, linguistically and culturally variegated populations with long histories. The white American majority in North America uses such blunt categories and through indiscriminate lumping of a "them," promotes some solidarity of resistance, sometimes overcoming deeply rooted antipathies for others lumped together.[2] As Craig Fong put it,

> Asian/Pacific-Americans are a community because the mainstream says we are. You know as well as I do that people from Singapore haven't much in common with people from Korea, or Koreans from Indians. The reality is that mainstream America, because of its numbers, looks at us as one group. And frankly, I think that we must accept it that way. It's a function of living in a predominantly white America. (1993:16)

I respect attempts to mobilize around discrimination (including violence) that does not make fine distinctions among different cultural backgrounds. While more specific ethnicities are salient for most of the persons of Asian or Pacific ancestries that I know, I have met people whose "master identity" is "Asian/Pacific."[3] I have also met others who call themselves "Orientals." Exoticism can be marketed, on the sexual as on other markets, and it is

---

1. As used in mobilization (among blacks and whites) against brown-skinned competitors recently in California, "illegal alien" includes legal immigrants.

2. See Glick 1942; Shibutani and Kwan 1965.

3. See the testimony "What GAPA means to me" in *Lavender Godzilla* 3,3 (June 1990). One of the gay Japanese Americans in Wooden, Kawasaki, and Mayeda (1983:242) expressed his view that "it's unnecessary to categorize and label every little group of people within groups." Malaysian-born critic Lawrence Chua (in various venues) goes further, embracing "black" as well as "queer" as generic labels.

tempting to extend the explanation from chapter 6 about enacting gender-variant roles to get the attention of partners by feigning stereotypical Asian exoticism, geisha-like complaisance, domesticity, drag queen flamboyance, or Bruce Lee–like machismo. Others, especially many of those raised in the U.S. or Canada (or Hong Kong or Singapore), are horrified to be considered "exotic." Playwright Chay Yew told S. Warren (1993:28) that in his experience, "African Americans and Latinos know they're different and forge their own identities. Asians assimilate and hate other Asians," especially those who act "fresh off the boat."[4] His play *Porcelain* analogizes some gay diaspora Asians to a gawky crow that leaves its "own kind" to try to join higher flying, melodious sparrows, ending up with no support either from the sparrows or from the other crows spurned in the attempted ascension.[5]

It seems to me that, like "Latino" and "Native"/"Indian," "Asian/Pacific" presents a sort of test for labeling theory. Such categories are officially assigned, and in various applications (to schools, for jobs, for social services) persons are pressed to choose from a small number of the imaginable categories. An interesting analog from the largest remaining communist state, the People's Republic of China, may be illuminating. "Hui" is a sort of residual category for Muslims not distinguished from "Han" by language or location. Being one of the official classes of "peoples" within the P.R.C. has a practical advantage: special treatment. "Hui" in the P.R.C. do "not so much believe that they have common ancestors as believe that they all have foreign ancestors who themselves have no common ancestry" (Bowen 1994: 990). While there are Chinese ethnic enclaves in various Chinatowns; Flushing, New York; and Monterey Park, California; and a substantial Filipino population in Daly City, California (just south of San Francisco) large enough to make networks of gay Filipinos or gay Chinese possible, the relatively small numbers and geographical dispersion of others (e.g., Sinhalese, Taiwanese, Guamanian) makes the consolidation of an intra-ethnic lesbigay organization and/or identity unlikely. I would think that lesbigay persons from such smaller immigrant pools and those with more than one Asian/Pacific derivation would be more likely than lesbigay Chinese and Filipinos to socialize with and identify as Gay Asian/Pacific Islanders

---

4. Clearly some African Americans are similarly embarrassed by others who act "too black" (sometimes applying the "N-word" and being considered "Oreos" or white-worshipping in return). Traditional ranking by lightness of skin has not altogether disappeared with assertions of Black Pride.

5. A seeming alternation between being ignored and being exoticized by gay white men rightly annoys many gay Asian/Pacific Islanders, although some (such as performance artist Justin Chin) suspect any kind of interest from gay white men, while also complaining bitterly when interest is not evidenced, and show little or no interest in Asian or Pacific sexual partners.

(GAPIs).[6] Not knowing what the denominators are, comparison of rates is impossible.[7] Lesbigay Chinese and Filipinos are most visible in GAPI organizations, but surely there are also more lesbigay Chinese and Filipinos than other kinds of GAPIs.

There is very little written about gay Asian/Pacific pan-ethnicity in America, and practically no social science research. Hom and Ma (1993:44) assert that GAPI men pair with Anglos, GAPI women pair with each other. I have heard of some of the same comfort in "coming home" to partners who "really understand where I'm coming from" along with some of the same skepticism about whether there is any acceptance at home (among whatever "my people" is) that exercise lesbian and gay African Americans (see chapter 11).

Given the general ignorance about the history of homosexualities in ancient Asian, medieval Japanese, and traditional Pacific Island (or African) cultures, American ethnic community activists and parents of lesbigays often consider homosexuality "a Western concept, a product of losing touch with one's Asian [or Pacific] heritage, of becoming too assimilated" (Hom and Ma 1993:41). Not just elders, but ethnically similar peers retain such notions. This probably accounts for Chan's finding (1989) that of 19 lesbians and 16 gay men belonging to lesbigay Asian organizations, 27 reported it harder to come out to other Asian Americans, in contrast to four who found it easier. A majority reported greater comfort and identification with gay or lesbian than with Asian American (20% were unwilling to divide themselves).[8] Duazo's survey (1989:7) of 28 mostly Chinese American gay men (16 of whom were born in the U.S., 19 raised in the U.S.) found 9 in frequent contact with their families, 12 moderate, 6 low, with one having no contact. Ten had not come out to family members. Eleven felt completely, 12 highly, and 5 somewhat acculturated.[9]

Surina Khan (1995:28–29) quoted two South Asian-American lesbians recalling, "I didn't identify as a lesbian because I didn't know what a lesbian was" and "I saw myself as straight because I wasn't aware of such a thing as

6. I know a number of men of Chinese or Japanese descent who grew up in Latin America and identify as Latino. Leonard's study (1992) of Punjabi Mexican Californians shows some of the complexity and historical influences on ethnogenesis.

7. I do not believe that the rate of gay or of lesbian identification is constant from ethnic group to group (or from place to place), so that estimates of the total ethnic group's numbers cannot be used.

8. I would think the sampling bias (within a GAPI organization) would be toward being more comfortable with "Asians" than with lesbigays.

9. His article lists the reasons respondents gave for coming out (or not) to family members. He did not cross-classify contact frequency and having come out.

a lesbian identity." Khan generalized: "For those of us living in the West, many have assimilated into the white culture, making it difficult to connect with other South Asian lesbians," and she quoted one South Asian lesbian saying "I can count on one hand the South Asian lesbians that I have met in the eight years since I've come out."

At the same winter 1992 *Out/Look* panel "Sleeping with the enemy?" from which I quoted Ken Dixon in chapter 11, Hong Kong native Ming-Yeung Lu said:

> For me there was no gay Asian community, and so there was a lot of alienation from my own community. When I came out, not knowing other gay Asians, I naturally dated from the majority of the "gay community," which was white. And until there was a gay Asian community, I didn't have choices. . . . When I think about my fear of other gay Asian men before I got used to interacting with them, I think it had something to do with my internalized stuff. I could deal with white men because they are not like me, at least racially. But when I would see someone who is like myself, I'd get uncomfortable.[10]

Similarly, Michael, the second-generation Chinese "snow queen" growing up in Hawaii in Norman Wong's *Cultural Revolution* (1994), finds "a preference for Chinese men odd because he himself had never been attracted to them. They would have been too much like his father" (p. 161).[11]

Joel Tan, a Filipino emigrant, recalled, "I was not only invisible to others but also to myself" (1992:35). Nicholas Shi (1993:9), who grew up in El Salvador, recalled that before going to college in the U.S., "I knew I was Chinese and I knew I was gay, but not having any contact with other gay people, I never had a chance to explore the implications of being a minority within a minority." Takagi (1994:6) generalized that gay and lesbian Asian Americans strive to keep their gay world separate from their family/community world more than do other kinds of gay and lesbian Americans. I would interpret the data from chapter 9 on later GAPI first homosexual experience as consistent with this. More GAPI men than men of other ancestries have told me that they knew they were gay long before they had any

---

10. Exoticizing goes both ways, and I have seen as many GAPI treating white boy- or girl-friends as pets (rather than equal, sentient human beings) as whites treating GAPI lovers that way. And for regarding blacks as subhuman, it would be difficult to compete with some Asians and Pacific Islanders. For a candid discussion of GAPI racism, interethnic stereotyping, and native-born vs. immigrant animosity, see Mattos 1991.

11. Others recall childhood sleeping in the same bed with their father, brothers, or other male relatives as having been intriguing or exciting. My impression (hypothesis) is that these men are more likely to have intraracial sexual relationships as adults than those who recall such childhood bed-sharing as unpleasant.

sexual experience. Once they stopped holding back from the same-sex sex that they had desired for a long time, these men moved quickly to being out. My less than systematic observation is that Chinese, Japanese, and South Asian lesbians and gay men endeavor to compartmentalize gay and family worlds more than Anglos, while descendants of Austronesians (notably Filipinos) try to bring everyone they love together, coming out sooner to parents and celebrating holidays with their gay and natal families mixed together. This leaves Southeast Asians somewhere in between (with Latinos). I throw this out as a hypothesis, not as an established fact.[12]

In closing, I want to mention three studies of gay men from particular Pacific and Southeast Asian heritages. Wooden, Kawasaki, and Mayeda (1983) asked thirteen Los Angeles–area gay Japanese American men about their "double minority" experiences. They reported widespread belief in the Japanese American community that gay Japanese Americans don't exist. Although one thought that "as long as nothing is said, there is no problem," another expressed the majority view from this sample: "The Japanese-American community tolerates homosexuality in other communities, but in their own community? No way! It is looked upon as being dishonorable and disgraceful. I do not feel these ideas are changing at all" (p. 239).[13]

Their most interesting finding was that "five of the seven who were 'out' to family members were somewhat involved in Asian political activity, compared to none of those who were not open about their homosexuality" (p. 237). Similarly, 57 percent of those who were out to family members (mostly, sisters) were "involved in the gay community" in contrast to only 17 percent of those who were not out to family.[14] Readers are left to guess

12. Its plausibility is enhanced by the correlation with ancestor worship in the cultures of GAPI ancestors. Pressure to marry and reproduce seems strongest on Chinese American men. There seem to be alternative ways for Filipinos to be good sons, but not for Chinese or Japanese. Another probably important factor is the high rate of family businesses among Chinese Americans, in contrast to low Filipino American entrepreneurship.

13. Even San Jose Congressman Norman Minetta—in a 6 August 1994 speech at the Japanese American Citizen's League in Salt Lake City that helped pass a resolution in support of gay rights—argued that gay rights are a Japanese American issue from coalition obligations without acknowledging that there are gay and lesbian Japanese Americans.

14. All but one respondent had more than five gay friends who were not Japanese American (77% reported having 15 or more). The one who did not also did not have Japanese American gay friends. Of the two respondents (out of four quoted in the fuller conference version of their report) who saw no "double minority" problems, one was not out to his family, the other reported his family was supportive. The former, incidentally, was the same one quoted above on not needing to categorize "every little group."

whether the same individuals were active in both communities, or whether involvement was specialized.[15]

In a preliminary report from his dissertation research, Manalansan (1994) reported that gay Filipino American men (in New York) do not identify as Asian or even Pacific Islander. He sees little likelihood of pan-ethnicity becoming salient. Analogously to the pattern among Mexican Americans discussed in chapter 12, Filipinos who are socialized into gay culture in the U.S. tend to reject idioms of effeminacy (traditional, gender-stratified *bakla'* homosexuality) as archaic and/or lower class, while those whose early homosexual experience was in the Philippines tend to retain it (emulating women to get men, as discussed in chapter 6).[16]

Doing fieldwork and interviews in southern California, Carrier, Nguyen, and Su (1992) located Vietnamese gay networks and learned something about Vietnamese men who have sex with men but are not integrated into those networks. They found "one 'large' network of recently arrived homosexual Vietnamese men who socialize in a cafe located in the major Little Saigon mall" in Garden Grove. This network "makes possible the sharing of information by newcomers about the homosexual world of Little Saigon and provides its members access to relatively well-off older Vietnamese men who prefer younger Vietnamese men as sex partners" (p. 556). Such "patrons" throw parties and may provide jobs that are contingent on sexual complaisance. In addition to this homosexual scene, there are two groups of "moderately acculturated young men," one gathering at the central Los Angeles house of two men in their late 20s who had gone through a marriage ceremony together, and another gathering at the house in southern Orange County of a Vietnamese gay man in his late 40s. Those involved in this gay Vietnamese network mostly arrived in the U.S. before or around puberty. Most of their sexual partners have been and continue to be Anglo or Latino,[17] though they gather to socialize where they can speak Vietnamese with gay

15. In their conference version, Wooden et al. reported contrasts with three San Francisco gay Japanese Americans, who came out to their families sooner and were more politically involved in the gay community than their Los Angeles sample, and with two gay Japanese Americans in Hawaii who were neither out to their families nor politically active.

16. He also found class and language differences at home in the Philippines to be less salient to gay Filipinos in the United States than in the homeland. But when they revisit the Philippines, their sexual adventures seem to be distinguished from American sex tourism only in their fluency with the native language (see Silva 1992 and some other less blatant "returning to the homeland" accounts in *Lavender Godzilla*).

17. Sexual socialization in the U.S., especially with Latinos, has made them more likely to engage in anal sex, whereas those whose sexual socialization was in Vietnam, or with relatively unacculturated fellow immigrants, tend to focus on oral and manual sex.

Vietnamese friends. Some spoke of moving from a "White phase" to a "Vietnamese phase" in their sexual relationships, but the network "is more social in its orientation than sexual" (p. 554) . In contrast to those involved in homosexual relations that are ethnically endogamous (though stratified by age, class, and/or gender), these men "want gay liberation but also want to retain their Vietnamese heritage" (p. 554). Additionally, some "highly acculturated Vietnamese men tend not to have many homosexual Vietnamese friends and to find their sexual partners mostly through the institutions of the Anglo gay world," and there are also "loners" who have Anglo male sexual partners but who do not participate in friendship circles or institutions of the gay world or of the Vietnamese American enclave in Orange County.

The gay Vietnamese interviewed by Carrier et al. reported the Vietnamese American community as unable to conceive that Vietnamese could be gay and as believing that Vietnamese men could be involved in homosexual activity only if seduced by white perverts or if they are *lai ca* (half-man, half-woman). A county that elects representatives who have made careers of gay-baiting, such as William Dannemyer and Robert Dornan, is not very accepting of homosexuality, so that the dominant culture of Orange County reinforces the rejection and invisibility of homosexuality by residents of Vietnamese background. Formation of a Vietnamese chapter of Parents and Friends of Lesbians and Gays in 1991 and its subsequent visibility at the annual Tet Fairs in Little Saigon have begun to challenge this invisibility, however.

The ratio of what is known to what is unknown about GAPIs is even lower than for lesbigays of other American ethnicities.[18] A great deal more research is needed to sort out differences among GAPI ethnicities and between GAPIs and other Americans, or between those involved in homosexuality in their ancestors' countries and between men and women. I think that lesbigays of every ethnic group overestimate the ease of acceptance of living and loving the same sex in other groups. The fear of losing families is general, though it has a special edge for those working in family businesses and/or in ethnic enclaves. Across ethnicities, sisters are most likely to be the first ones to be told.[19] Whereas black and white and Filipino gay men and

18. Autobiographical works in various media by GAPIs and Manalansan's research are remedying this. Ratti (1993) collects materials from lesbigay South Asians in England and North America.
19. Six of the seven in Wooden, Kawasaki, and Mayeda 1983.

lesbians are more likely to come out to mothers than to fathers, it seems to me that Chinese and Japanese (American) lesbians and gay men are as reluctant to come out to their mothers as to their fathers. This, too, is a hypothesis. Due to the smallness and likely unrepresentativeness of GAPI samples in research published so far, none of the findings discussed in this chapter should be considered well-established facts—even about GAPI men.

Valediction

The preceding chapters obviously do not constitute a single narrative. Nor do they employ a single master trope to order the world (or even North American homosexualities).[1] Trying to tie everything together in either a single logical model or one master narrative seems as impossibly old-fashioned as trying to produce an integrated holistic ethnography. It's very tempting to leave it at saying "The social world is complicated: there's a lot of variability out there," and possibly enumerating some of the factors and phenomena I have not considered,[2] or writing only about my experiences in the world(s) I tried to examine as postmodernist ethnographers do.

I certainly do think that there is much variability, but also (as should be obvious from the preceding chapters—and books), I think that there are some recurrent patterns. The world, desire, and self are not an entirely inchoate, unnamable, unpredictable flux from which behavior and identities are negotiated anew in every instance of human encounters each day. Negotiations in particular encounters rest on considerable preexisting structure, experience, and swiftly presumed and applied categories.

In some ways, the scariest of the patterns out there in the world is de-assimilation. As stultifying as Weber and Frankfurt School social theorists found the iron cage of formal rationality divorced from substantive rationality, the genocide and gang warfare in Meso-Africa, the Balkans, Cambo-

---

1. Although I think that I valiantly resist the currently dominant one, i.e., gender, Joel Brodsky complained that I gave it way too much weight in chapter 3 and err in considering urban North American homosexuality as primarily gender-stratified as late as during the 1960s.

2. Some of the major ones about which there is substantial published material are causation ("etiology"); hate crimes and other violence against those thought to be gay or lesbian, including initiatives to authorize discrimination; "homophobia"; identity; lesbian mothers and gay fathers; "pornography"; "prostitution"; risk-prevention "education"; and, perhaps most surprisingly, given my particular interests, language use and sexual conduct.

dia, or North American cities can make one nostalgic for the orderliness that was supposed to be coming to the planet—or even for the bad old days of colonialism in Africa and communism in southeastern Europe. Not that all such violence is rationalized with primordial loyalties: some of the "tribes" are pretty ad hoc.

I do not think that de-assimilation necessarily leads to violence against other groups. In the instance discussed in this volume, despite the on-going history of violence against gay men and lesbians, there have been no cases of straight couples being pulled from their cars in the Castro, Chelsea, or West Hollywood and beaten by rampaging queers. The violence against men by "the Lesbian Avengers" has been entirely symbolic.[3] Similarly, those asserting a Taiwanese identity have not called for reprisals for the 1947 massacre by Chinese troops, and the Taiwanese nationalists I know seek to build a society with respect for all cultures and languages there. That is, the examples of previously invisibilized and still stigmatized groups asserting themselves do not always and everywhere involve violence or calls for violence against their historical oppressors.

Clearly, differences and identities are not going to disappear. I fervently hope that retribalization ("identity politics") can lead to respecting and even valuing differences and to living together rather than trying to dominate or kill those who aren't like a particular "us." I cannot say that the new, allegedly "inclusive" *queers* have exemplified acceptance of difference, having mostly defined themselves by derogating older lesbian-feminists and gay male *clones*.[4] Especially since I regard the rapidity of human population increase as very ominous,[5] I find it difficult to be optimistic, or to see human history as progress toward any good or goal. Despite my qualms about where de-assimilation might lead, I think that it is real. Not unlike Durkheim, I hope that interdependence and mutual respect rather than endemic intergroup violence will result from on-going differentiation—i.e., that the telos

3. Outside North America, "identity politics" are more than semantic skirmishes and "symbolic politics." The relationship between "symbolic politics" and all-too-real violence is another important task for social theory and research to sort out. Herek and Berrill (1992) begin this task in regard to hate crimes against lesbigays.

4. Similarly, I have noticed on e-mail networks and in lesbigay periodicals and organizations that lesbians may make sweeping derogations about gay men (or all men), but that gay men may not make any critical statements even about particular women without being trashed (flamed) as "sexist," and that any statement of gay pride by men is regarded as necessarily "white supremacist."

5. In my view, anti-natal policies should include valuing homosexuality. I would like to see better care taken of fewer children (in North America and elsewhere) and for population growth to be reversed (while remembering that economic development is more efficient than is coercion at lowering birth rates).

of a postmodernist world is complex cooperation, not increasingly efficient attempts to slaughter this or that "Other."

As argued in chapter 1, mobilization requires a sense by a critical mass of people that some pattern is both intolerable and changeable.[6] Stigmatization of *homosexuals* and neglect of people dying of AIDS are instances of patterns believed by some not to be inevitable. On-going challenges to these intolerable realities instance a more general social model of a recurrent process, just as de-assimilation does.

Gay, etc., people are marginal to the ever more rational single moral community that various classical social theorists imagined they saw coming. The ways we have mobilized and challenged our place as monsters to be pitied or exterminated are central to the project of theorizing the present and the seeming direction into the multicultural future in which differences are revalued.

Understanding mobilizations, lesbigay among others, requires careful comparison of data that have not been gathered about social movements and about those whose involvement in pressing for lesbigay rights and spaces have not included membership in formal organizations. Chapter 1 merely sketched some of what needs to be compared.[7]

Chapters 3 to 5 deal with some of the curves history threw at gay liberationists and lesbian-feminists. The venerable Mertonian locution "unanticipated consequences of social change" seems at once too grandiose for the resurgence of gender stereotyping and too inadequate for the carnage of AIDS.[8]

I would say that the whole book endeavors to sort out what happened from various myths—most of which have been advanced by some lesbians and gay men rather than by external enemies. (The latter continue to distribute other falsehoods than the ones I address in this book.) The chapters in part 1 endeavor to sort out a relatively macro-level history of cultural patterns and, especially, protests.

Those who see themselves or who are seen by others as members/instances of stigmatized(/dominated) groups thrash around a lot. Is this a theoretical generalization? I think so. Adam (1978c) provided a very elegant

6. We remain vague about how many it takes to reach "a critical mass" and about what it takes to succeed (in contrast to what it takes to have a movement).

7. As I noted in the introduction, forgotten (erased?) research on lesbigay lives, networks, and institutions of the 1970s and earlier needs to be recovered and used as historical documentation (though this is not the use that those doing the research had in mind for it).

8. Increased and rapid movement around the globe is the "social change" of relevance for this. The structure of sexual conduct of the gay clone world only provided a site for maximal distribution of a virus such as HIV once it reached North America.

and detailed comparison of how stigmatized peoples persist and cope, how they challenge and perpetuate their stigmas, often doing both at the same time. Adam's Frankfurt-suffused social psychology of dominated peoples underlies my attempts to make sense of the recurrent surrenders of autonomy to supposedly friendly experts who "know better" than we could what should be done to or about us, and to the surprising directions that rebellions not orchestrated by Leninist vanguards sometimes take.

I hope that the rest of the book does not appear to have abandoned—or even to have bracketed—the knowledge that gay life and institutions have changed and continue to change. My aim in looking more closely at the contested categories of *role, community,* and *enclave economy* and at the surprisingly little contested category *couple* is not synchronic. I argue that the way to understand and to deploy *community* is as a process, not as an entity fixed in space or time—while also cautioning against considering gay (or lesbian or lesbigay) community in a vacuum of disappointed longings rather than in comparison to other communities. At a more micro (individual) level, I contend that *un*learning "the homosexual role" (in the singular) is more important for those who live in lesbigay worlds than learning it is. I also endeavor to show why some people, especially in some places, continue to play the part of "the bogeyman-woman" that is "the homosexual role." In the intermediate chapter of part 2 (and level), I mostly synthesize existing research, while suggesting that the dynamics of same-sex couples provide insight into the realities of devalued domestic work and much more highly valued external careers that increasingly are also faced by heterosexual couples.

While focusing on ethnic differences in the last part of the book, I document significant temporal differences in the experiences of coming out and in migration to a gay metropolis. The contrast between the two chapters focused on lesbigay African Americans is mostly between external scientistic accounts and self-representations. The former were also earlier, but considerable caution should be exercised in interpreting the differences between these chapters as documenting changes in the organization of experiences of African American sexualities. The final short chapters on Mexican Americans and Asian/Pacific Islander Americans entirely lack historical depth: there are few synchronic data and no longitudinal data upon which to draw.[9]

Greater fragmentation is where I think we are heading—or perhaps, what

9. Although barely reaching into the U.S., my 1995a book focuses on the change from gender-stratified to gay male homosexuality in Latin America. A need to define selves against Anglo models within the U.S. (i.e., in antagonistic acculturation) may impede the influence of gay Anglo homosexuality north of the Mexico–U.S. border, so I have not felt that I could extrapolate across it.

is happening among American intellectuals is greater recognition of how fragmented we already are. Collective and individual experiences are considerably more nonlinear and complex than the organization of this book. And we know little more than social scientists did in the years between the world wars when Edward Sapir advocated (without exemplifying) the study of individual integrations of culture(s).[10] I think that we should try to learn much more about how individuals put together sexualities (homo- and other), as well as about the diversity of meanings of some of the same acts.[11] While waiting for more nuanced data about diverse human beings, I hope that some of the ideas stimulated in me by looking at aspects of contemporary gay and lesbian experience are useful to others—and that some of the bad ideas I criticize that are already around will wither.

10. See Murray 1986:251–60.

11. I do not mean just sexual acts—which have rarely been the focus in this book. It is how people have been gay or lesbian in the wide world, not in the bedrooms, bushes, or back rooms, that I have discussed. This does not betoken a lack of interest in the phenomenology of sexual conduct. My attempts to illuminate that (notably Murray 1980a) are unpublished, and appear to be unpublishable.

Acknowledgments

So anti- (not just non-) linear a text, based on two decades of gathering data and thinking about a variegated non-unitary phenomenon in two very complex societies (Canada and the United States), primarily in the very multi-ethnic metropolises of Toronto and San Francisco, has to have a complicated genealogy and is almost certain to have had a difficult gestation. In the introduction I mentioned that my thinking about the place and meaning of homosexuality in an industrial capitalist world began in the utopian conception of Herbert Marcuse (1955). Already as an undergraduate, I was immersed in the writings of his friends in the Frankfurt School, and their earlier associates such as Georg Lukacs and Karl Mannheim. I remember discussing some of their ideas, and how they might make sense of our lives, with Walteen Grady, Nell Hennessy, and Michael Betzold, but I do not know who introduced me to the tradition of critical theory. Peter Lyman introduced me to serious study of Nietzche, Mannheim, and other pre–World War II sociology of knowledge, as well as to the earlier European classical tradition of social and political theory.

Along with a very unwieldy label (Justice, Morality, and Constitutional Democracy) that fits in no space I have ever seen in which to list one's college major, I received a firm grounding in social/political theory from classes taught by Peter Lyman, Richard Zinman, and the late Lewis Zerby at James Madison College within Michigan State University. In graduate school I had the good fortune to study "the grand tradition" of social theory with Robert Nisbet, Phillip Hammond, Irving Zeitlin, and Gregory Baum. Each of them encouraged me to pursue my own interests, which included French social thought from Montesquieu to Lévi-Strauss, structuralism(s) and language,[1] as well as the Germanic pessimistic, historic critiques of the social-

1. I discussed the genealogy and methods of my social historical research in Murray 1994c: 491–502. Preferences for quoting what natives say at length, for recording dissent from my

275

psychological roots of modern dystopia(s). Astonishingly, I had discovered Freud and Goffman and Foucault in the hyper-behaviorist psychology department in which I earned a second undergraduate major.[2]

It was in Arizona that I was disappointed to realize that there was no necessary connection between homosexuality and opposing oppression[3]—even, alas, to the oppression of homosexuality/homosexuals. The trauma of discovering that (contra Marcuse) there is, after all, a "performance principle" involved in homosexual encounters was cushioned by positive evaluation but still forced me to curtail my faith that homosexuality necessarily challenges the status quo and transcends the instrumental rationality of capitalism. I continue to think that my *own* oppositional temperament (at least) is part of my gay identity.[4] Sexual dissidence (in contrast to hidden participation in "deviance") seems to me related to a distrust of other authoritative/received knowledge. Nonetheless, in subsequent observation I have not been able to avoid noticing that not only "homosexuals" but open gays and lesbians may be generally conformist, avid apologists for oppressive social conditions—including racial injustice and carnage in Southeast Asia: the prime concerns of American (New) leftists, including me, during the late 1960s and early 1970s—and even apologists for discrimination on the basis of sexual orientation. Recognizing that the category I had found my way into was less socially than culturally avant garde (and less culturally avant garde

conclusions (prototypically, noting that "Two Crows denies this"), and for what some consider bibliographical overkill are as apparent in my research on gay men as in that on social scientists.

2. Much later, at Berkeley, I was able to talk to Michel Foucault about premedicalization categories of homosexual persons and to attend the last seminar course that he gave (see Murray 1985).

3. For a recent general romanticization of all women who sought erotic satisfaction from other women during the 1930s, 1940s, and 1950s as "radicals," see Kennedy and Davis (1993: 414 n. 15). It is possible to be gay and contrarian in quite different directions, as conservatives like Andrew Sullivan and David Brock show (Shumante 1995:59).

4. My sense of being "different" from the time of puberty until finding reciprocated love was not based on labeling (self- or by others) of gender or sexuality variance. I was intensely alienated in high school, but I didn't know that two males could have sex, let alone that two males could love each other! Indeed, I was 21 and had been in a relationship for two years before it dawned on me that this intense, long-term relationship might suggest application of the frightening category *homosexual* to us. I still didn't know that there were *gay people* or where they were. Even after I concluded that I was *gay*, found MSU's Gay Liberation Front, visited gay bars in Lansing and Tucson, participated in founding several gay organizations, and began to do gay research, many of my more sexually conventional friends continued not to make the connection between their pair of friends and the category *homosexual*. We continued not to be labeled, even having lived together for years and moved back and forth across the continent several times. This personal experience guaranteed that I would understand that males and females whose emotional and sexual orientations and careers are same-sex may not label themselves or be labeled by others with even readily available, widely known categories. "You just can't be *that* way!" some respond.

than many suppose!), I tried to make sense of it across space and time (in that order). I spent considerable time in Mesoamerica between 1974 and 1982, and read everything I could find about homosexuality—without defining what I was doing as fieldwork in the first instance or as entering the then-nonexistent specialty of gay/lesbian studies in the second.[5]

Both at the University of Arizona and the University of Toronto, fellow students unequivocally supported my incipient research on gay men and my tentative activism in support of gay rights. I appreciated such solid support all the more, because teachers at Arizona made clear that research about gay men was somewhere between unwelcome and illegitimate. In one class, the best paper I wrote—a testable functionalist theory about sexual orientation and belief in reincarnation—was the only one that dealt with homosexuality and the only one that did not receive an "A." In another, what I now am certain was a very good research proposal on gay men and mental health received the lowest grade in the class. The professor returned it with a note saying, "No one is interested in your lifestyle." I was particularly shocked by this comment, because I didn't know that I had a lifestyle. (Insofar as I did, it was enmeshed with my straight graduate student peers, not a "gay lifestyle" about which I then knew anything only from reading.) Although I moved on to what were in several senses the greener pastures of Toronto, I did not even think of doing gay research for my dissertation.

I doubt that I would have survived my second graduate school without the practical guidance of Barry Adam and Dennis Magill, both of whom I met at the formation meeting of the Sociologists' Gay[6] Caucus (SGC) in Montreal in 1974. Along with John Alan Lee, who became my Toronto landlord and friend, Barry and Dennis eased my entrée into what still seems to me the especially unfriendly-to-outsiders gay community of Toronto. The kind of sponsorship John Grube has written about was still important in the mid 1970s (and perhaps still is). Half the founders of the Toronto Gay Academic Union in 1974 were sociologists (John, Barry, and I, along with the late Michael Lynch, who was an English professor, and librarians Bob Wallace and the late Jim Quixley). In those days the study of gay people, insofar as it was a research specialty, was empirical. My dissertation research, supervised and protected by Dennis Magill, was not on a gay topic; but, encouraged by friends in SGC and the Gay Academic Union, I began research on gay speech and on gay residential concentration in Toronto.[7] Two Toronton-

---

5. I discuss this at length in Murray 1995b.

6. "Lesbian" was added to the name later (SLGC).

7. I presented this research at professional association meetings in 1977 and published them in Murray 1979a,b. John Lee and Dennis Magill were the Canadianization committee of the

ians with whom I collaborated, Lucille Covelli and John Firth, had important influences both on what I studied and how I went about it.

In marked contrast to my experience of being taught in the Arizona sociology department not to do gay research, during my very pleasant tenure as a post-doctoral fellow in the Language Behavior Research Laboratory at the University of California, Berkeley, and afterward, my gay research was encouraged by John Gumperz, Paul Kay, Niyi Akinnaso, Jim Boster, Linda Coleman, the late Jay Hayes, Wendy Leeds-Hurwitz, Danny Maltz, and Amparo Tusón; as well as by Keith Basso, who had earlier introduced me to anthropology; and by Dell Hymes and Regna Darnell, who were mentors acting mostly at considerable geographical distances.

My informal and formal mentors in Toronto and a continent-wide network of those involved in pressing for recognition of gay concerns in the American Sociological Association through SLGC enhanced my understanding of North American homosexualities. Those who particularly influenced (and/or encouraged) me were Barry Adam, the late Phil Blumstein, Mike Gorman, Meredith Gould, the late Laud Humphreys, the late Marty Levine, Stuart Michaels, Brian Miller, Peter Nardi, Larry Ross, Wag Thielens, and Wayne Wooden. After I moved to Berkeley, Wayne Dynes and Deborah Wolf took an interest in clarifying and communicating my thoughts, especially in *Social Theory, Homosexual Realties* (Murray 1984), which was edited by the former and prefaced by the latter. Since settling in the San Francisco Bay Area in 1978, I have also received reassurance about the value of my work and comparative insights at various times (and, in most cases, over the course of many years) from Eric Allyn, Deb Amory, Manuel Arboleda, Diane Beeson, David Bergman, Evie Blackwood, Ralph Bolton, the late Joel Brodsky, Roger Brown, Gary Bukovnik, Joe Carrier, Chris Carrington, Lawrence Cohen, Lou Crompton, Norman Dale, Peter T. Daniels, John DeCecco, Millie Dickemann, Alan Dishman, Steve Epstein, Manuel Fernandez, Kent Gerard, Peter Goldblum, David Greenberg, John Grube, Gil Herdt, Richard Herrell, Ross Higgins, John Hollister, Keelung Hong, William Horstman, Lee Jenkins, Badruddin Khan, Joe Kao, Clay Lane, Bill Leap, Theresa Montini, Nii Narh Noye, the late Kenneth Payne, the late Arnold Pilling, Ken Plummer, Frank Proschan, Will Roscoe, Gayle Rubin, the late Jesse Sawyer, Bill Simon, Gerard Sullivan, the late Jean Swallow, the late Russ Tabtab, Clark Taylor, Theo van der Meer, Unni Wikan, and Walter Williams. Most of those named in this paragraph (along with John Lee) have

---

Canadian Sociology and Anthropology Association, but Bob Wallace was more responsible than they for teaching me about Canadian identity and literature (preparing me better to appreciate Benedict Anderson's writing on print capitalism as the motor for nationalist consciousness).

read and commented on drafts of parts of this book.[8] Ralph Bolton, Peter T. Daniels, David Greenberg, Gilbert Herdt, and Douglas Mitchell commented on the whole of it. I am grateful for both criticism and encouragement from all the above-mentioned readers.

I am also very grateful to my nonacademic friends who have shared their perspectives on contemporary gay life, tolerated with good grace various interrogations, and secured the cooperation of their friends in answering my often seemingly peculiar questions.

Not just this book, but my life have been improved by knowing these scholars, most especially my life partner and sometimes co-author Keelung Hong. Among many other gifts, he has helped me to attain a comparative perspective on the insidious maintenance of invisibilities.[9]

Last but not least, I would like to acknowledge Frederic Santiago and Lawrence Goldyn, the physicians who have helped ensure that I could finish this book. By showing that they are on my side (in genuine therapeutic alliances), they have also helped me see that biomedicine is not a monolith.

Although I have had the intensely unpleasant experiences of occupational marginality for doing gay research (which is far more stigmatized than being openly gay or lesbian) and of seeing empirical and genuinely cross-cultural research and theory in gay/lesbian studies ignored and supplanted by queer "theory" that is opposed in principle to the possibility that facts exist or that there could be any external standards by which to evaluate often ingenious interpretations of a slightly expanded canon of literary and pop-culture texts, I feel that the mists of what has misappropriated the label "theory" will at some point dissipate, and history outside medical discourse and popular representations will again be of interest. Since it seems unlikely that I will live so long, this book is what Adorno recurrently likened to a message in a bottle to those somewhere or at some time who are interested in how people live, not just how they appear on screens or in novels. I even have some hope that interest in how people involved in homosexuality live their lives will rekindle. If this happens quickly, perhaps my work will attain some recognition during my lifetime. Again as in the Frankfurt tradition, pessimism does not

---

8. Others who commented helpfully on earlier drafts of particular chapters or parts of chapters include Edward Albert, the late John Boswell, Andy Boxer, Linda Coleman, Paul Farmer, John Gagnon, Joe Harry, John Hart, Sue-Ellen Jacobs, Robert F. Jones, Philip Kayal, John Kitsuse, Mary McIntosh, Harvey Molotch, Steven Nachman, Barrie Thorne, Vera Whisman, Fred Whitam, and a few (a very few from among many ignorant, hostile to me, to gay men, and/or to lesbigay studies) anonymous journal referees. Both for helping secure informants and for rescuing data files, I owe special thanks to Brett Turner.

9. Specifically, how "Taiwanese" is as unthinkable as "gay/lesbian" to social scientists and to the powers they too often serve. See Hong 1994; Murray and Hong 1994.

entirely preclude hope for changes in systems of domination (including dominant discourses—though the fascination of intellectuals in these does not make them the most important facet of any social system).

PREVIOUS INCARNATIONS OF PORTIONS OF THIS VOLUME

The first three chapters elaborate and update my Gai Saber Monograph *Social Theory, Homosexual Realities* (© 1984).

Parts of chapter 4 were presented at the 1985 meeting of the Society for the Study of Social Problems in New York City and published as "Medical policy without scientific evidence: The promiscuity paradigm and AIDS" in a special issue, "Perspectives on the social effects of AIDS," of the *California Sociologist* 11, edited by Peter Nardi (© 1988).

I presented an early version of chapter 6 at the 1987 meeting of the American Sociological Association in Chicago. It was the basis for my "role" entry in the *Encyclopedia of Homosexuality* edited by Wayne Dynes (© 1990). An earlier version of the appendix appeared as " Subordinating native cosmologies to the Empire of Gender" in *Current Anthropology* 35 (© 1994 by The Wenner-Gren Foundation for Anthropological Research. All rights reserved).

Chapter 7 elaborates my "couples" entry in the *Encyclopedia of Homosexuality* (© 1990). The appendix to it is a revision of a note that originally appeared in *Sociologists' Gay Caucus Newsletter* 17 in 1979.

Chapter 8 includes data and ideas I presented at the 1978 meeting of the Canadian Sociology and Anthropology Association in London, Ontario; the 1981 meeting of the Kroeber Anthropological Society in Berkeley; and the 1988 meeting of the American Anthropological Association in Phoenix. I published some preliminary parts of this chapter in a special issue, "Homosexuality in international perspective," of the *International Review of Modern Sociology* 9, edited by Joseph Harry (© 1979; also published separately, New Delhi: Vikas, 1980); in my "community" entry in the *Encyclopedia of Homosexuality* (© 1990); and in my "Components of *gay community* in San Francisco" chapter in *Gay Culture in America,* edited by Gilbert Herdt (© Beacon Press 1992).

I presented preliminary results for the analyses in the appendix of chapter 8 and in chapter 9 at the 1989 meeting of the American Sociological Association in San Francisco and in my chapter in *Gay Culture in America* (© Beacon Press 1992).

I am grateful to these copyright holders for their permission to rework materials here.

Bibliography

ABBREVIATIONS

AA	*American Anthropologist*
AAA	American Anthropological Association
AE	*American Ethnologist*
AJS	*American Journal of Sociology*
ASA	American Sociological Association
ASB	*Archives of Sexual Behavior*
ASR	*American Sociological Review*
JH	*Journal of Homosexuality*
JSR	*Journal of Sex Research*
LG	*Lavender Godzilla*
SGCN, SLGCN	*Sociologists' (Lesbian and) Gay Caucus Newsletter*
SOLGAN	*Society of Lesbian and Gay Anthropologists' Newsletter*
SP	*Social Problems*

Only the first author is listed for publications with more than four authors.

Abramson, Paul E. 1992. "Sex, lies, and ethnography." In Herdt and Lindenbaum 1992:101–23.

Achilles, Nancy. 1967. "The development of the homosexual bar as an institution." In Gagnon and Simon 1967:228–44. Repr. in Dynes and Donaldson 1992: 159–76.

Adair, Nancy, and Casey Adair. 1978. *Word Is Out*. New York: Delta.

Adam, Barry D. 1978a. "Capitalism, the family, and gay people." *SGC Working Paper* 1.

———. 1978b. "Inferiorization and 'self esteem.'" *Sociometry* 41:47–53. Repr. in Dynes and Donaldson 1992:33–39.

———. 1978c. *The Survival of Domination*. New York: Elsevier.

———. 1979. "Reply." *SGCN* 18:8.

———. 1981. "Stigma and employability." *Canadian Review of Sociology and Anthropology* 18:216–21.

———. 1982. "Where did gay people come from?" *Christopher Street* 64:50–53.

———. 1985. "Age, structure and sexuality." *JH* 11:19–33.

———. 1987. *The Rise of a Gay and Lesbian Movement.* Boston: Twayne. 2d ed., 1995.

———. 1992. "Sex and caring among men: Impacts of AIDS on gay people." In Plummer 1992:175–83.

Adelman, Marcy. 1986. *Long Time Passing: Lives of Older Lesbians.* Boston: Alyson.

Albert, Edward H. 1984. "AIDS and the press." Presented at the Society for the Study of Social Problems annual meeting, San Antonio.

Aldrich, Robert. 1993. *The Seduction of the Mediterranean: Writing, Art and Homosexual Fantasy.* New York: Routledge.

Alexandre, Wayne. 1983. "Black homosexual masochist." In Smith 1983:77–83.

Alonzo, D. 1983. "Stories out of school." *Los Angeles Edge* 7,13:20–21.

Altman, Dennis. 1971. *Homosexual: Oppression and Liberation.* New York: Avon.

———. 1982. *The Americanization of the Homosexual, The Homosexualization of America.* New York: St. Martin's.

———. 1986. *AIDS in the Mind of America.* Garden City, N.J.: Doubleday.

———. 1988. "Legitimation through disaster: AIDS and the gay movement." In Fee and Fox 1988:301–316.

Anderson, Nels. 1923. *The Hobo.* Chicago: University of Chicago Press.

Anderson, Benedict R. O'Gorman. 1983, 1992. *Imagined Communities: Reflections on the Origin and Spread of Nationalism.* London: Verso.

A. Nolder Gay. 1978. *The View from the Closet.* Boston: Union Park.

Anzaldúa, Gloria. 1987. *Borderlands/La Frontera.* San Francisco: Spinsters' Ink.

Arenas, Reinaldo. 1993. *Before Night Falls.* New York: Viking.

Arno, Peter S., and Karyn L. Feiden. 1992. *Against the Odds: The Story of AIDS Drug Development, Politics, and Profits.* New York: Harper Collins.

Asch, Solomon. 1958. "Group pressure upon the modification and distortion of judgments." In *Readings in Social Psychology,* ed. E. Macoby et al., pp. 174–83. New York: Holt.

Ashworth, A. E., and W. M. Walker. 1972. "Social structure and homosexuality." *British Journal of Sociology* 23:146–58. Repr. in Dynes and Donaldson 1992: 40–52.

Astor, Gerald. 1983. *The Disease Detectives.* New York: New American Library.

Ault. Amber. 1994. "Hegemonic discourse in an oppositional community: Lesbian feminists and bisexuality." *Critical Sociology* 20, 3:107–22.

Avi-Ram, Amitai F. 1990. "The unreadable black body: 'Conventional' poetic form in the Harlem Renaissance." *Genders* 7:32–45.

Baldwin, James. 1953. *Go Tell It on the Mountain.* New York: Knopf.

———. 1956. *Giovanni's Room.* New York: Dial.

———. 1962. *Another Country.* New York: Dial.

Banneker, Revon Kyle. 1990. "Marlon Riggs untied." *BLK* 2,4 (April):10–19.

Barker, Virginia. 1982. "Dangerous shoes, or what's a nice dyke like me doing in a get-up like this?" In *Coming to Power,* pp. 101–4. Boston: Alyson.

Barnhart, Elizabeth. 1975. "Friends and lovers in a lesbian counterculture community." In *Old Family/New Family,* ed. N. Glazer-Lalbin, pp. 90–115. New York: Van Norstrand.

Barth, Fredrik. 1969. *Ethnic Groups as Boundaries.* Boston: Little Brown.

Bass-Haas, Rita. 1968. "The lesbian dyad." *JSR* 4:108–26.

Basso, Keith. H. 1976. "'Wise words' of the Western Apache: Metaphor and semantic theory." In *Meaning in Anthropology*, ed. Keith Basso and Henry Selby, pp. 93–122. Albuquerque: University of New Mexico Press.

———. 1981. *Portraits of the "Whiteman."* Cambridge: Cambridge University Press.

Baumeister, Roy F. 1988. "Gender differences in masochistic scripts." *JSR* 25:478–99.

Bayer, Ronald. 1981. *Homosexuality and American Psychiatry*. New York: Basic Books.

———. 1989. *Private Acts, Social Consequences*. New York: Free Press.

Beam, Joseph F., ed. 1986. *In the Life*. Boston: Alyson.

Beame, Thom. 1983. "Racism from a black perspective." In Smith 1983:57–63.

Becker, Howard S. 1963. *Outsiders*. New York: Free Press.

Becker, Howard S., Blanche Geer, Everett C. Hughes, and Anselm Strauss. 1961. *Boys in White*. Chicago: University of Chicago Press.

Becker, Marshall H., and Jill G. Joseph. 1988. "AIDS and behavioral change to reduce risk." *American Journal of Public Health* 78:394–410.

Beer, William. 1980. *The Unexpected Rebellion*. New York: New York University Press.

Bell, Alan P., and Martin S. Weinberg. 1978. *Homosexualities*. New York: Simon and Schuster.

Bell, Arthur. 1971. *Dancing the Gay Lib Blues*. New York: Simon and Schuster.

Bell, Daniel. 1960. *The End of Ideology*. New York: Macmillan.

Bellah Robert N., Richard Madsen, William M. Sullivan, Ann Swidler, and Steven T. Tipton. 1985. *Habits of the Heart*. Berkeley and Los Angeles: University of California Press.

Beniger, James R. 1986. *The Control Revolution*. Cambridge: Harvard University Press.

Bennett, Garrett, Simon Chapman, and Fiona Bray. 1989. "Sexual practices and 'beats': AIDS-related sexual practices in a sample of homosexual and bisexual men in the western area of Sydney." *Medical Journal of Australia* 151:309–14.

Berger, Raymond M. 1981. *Gay and Gray*. Urbana: University of Illinois Press.

Bergesen, Albert. 1978. "Durkheimian theory of with hunts." *Journal of the Scientific Study of Religion* 17:19–29.

Bergman, David. 1991. *Gaiety Transfigured*. Madison: University of Wiesconsin Press.

Berlandt, Konstantin. 1970. "My soul vanished from sight: A California saga of gay liberation." In Jay and Young 1972:38–55.

Berlin, Brent. 1992. *Ethnobiological Classification*. Princeton, N.J.: Princeton University Press.

Berlin, Brent, and Paul Kay. 1969, 1991. *Basic Color Terms*. Berkeley and Los Angeles: University of California Press.

Bernard, Jessie. 1981. *The Female World*. New York: Free Press.

Bérubé, Alan. 1981. "Marching to a different drummer." *Advocate* (15 October):20–24.

———. 1984. "The history of gay bathouses." *Coming Up!* 6,3:15–19.

———. 1990. *Coming Out Under Fire*. New York: Macmillan.

Binson, Diane. 1994. "Ethnic–racial differences in behavioral and self-identified sexual orientation in men who have sex with men." Presented at the ASA annual meeting in Los Angeles.

Blackberri. 1990. "Searching for my gay spiritual roots." *BLK* 2,6 (June) 11.

Block, Adam. 1990. "Bad rap." *San Francisco Examiner Image* (26 August) 6–8.

Blumer, Herbert. 1973. "Reflections on theory of race relations." In *Race Relations in World Perspective*, ed. A. Lind, pp. 217–27. Westport, Conn.: Greenwood.

Blumstein, Philip W. 1973. "Audience, Machiavellianism, and tactics of identity bargaining." *Sociometry* 36:346–65.

Blumstein, Philip W., and Pepper Schwartz. 1983. *American Couples*. New York: Morrow.

Boas, Franz. 1912. *Changes in Bodily Form of Descendants of Immigrants*. Washington: 61st Congress, Senate Document 208.

Bolton, Ralph. 1992a. "AIDS and promiscuity: Muddles in the models of HIV prevention." *Medical Anthropology* 14:145–223.

———. 1992b. "Mapping terra incognita: Sex research for AIDS prevention." In Herdt and Lindenbaum 1992:124–58.

———. 1994. "Sex, science, and social responsibility: Cross-cultural research on same-sex eroticism and sexual intolerance." *Cross-Cultural Research* 28:134–90.

Bolton, Ralph, John Vincke, and Rudolf Mak. 1994. "Gay baths revisited: An empirical analysis." *GLQ* 1:255–73.

Bolton, Ralph, John Vincke, Rudolf Mak, and Ellen Dennehy. 1992. "Alcohol and risky sex: In search of an elusive connection." *Medical Anthropology* 14:323–63.

Bonaparte, Marie. 1973 [1951]. "Some biophysical aspects of sadomasochism." In *The First Freudians*, ed. H. Ruitenbeek, pp. 164–93. New York: Jason Aronson.

Bosco, Joseph. 1992. "Taiwan factions: *guanxi*, patronage and the state in local politics." *Ethnology* 31:157–83.

Bosk, Charles L. 1979. *Forgive and Remember: Managing Medical Failure*. Chicago: University of Chicago Press.

Boswell, John. 1980. *Christianity, Social Tolerance and Homosexuality*. Chicago: University of Chicago Press.

———. 1982. "Revolutions, universals, categories." *Salmagundi* 58:89–113.

Bottomore, Tom, and Robert Nisbet. 1978. *A History of Sociological Analysis*. New York: Basic Books.

Bowen, John. 1994. Review of *Muslim Chinese* by D. Gladney. *AE* 21:989–90.

Bowman, Chris. 1990. "Dianne Feinstein's record on gay/lesbian concerns." *San Francisco Sentinel* (1 November) 11,16.

Bradburn, Norman M., Lance J. Rips, and Steven K. Shevell. 1987. "Answering autobiographical questions." *Science* 236:157–61.

Brandt, Allen M. 1988. "AIDS: From social history to social policy." In Fee and Fox 1988:146–70.

Branner, Bernard. 1986. "Blackberri." In Beam 1986:170–84.

Bray, Alan. 1982. *Homosexuality in Renaissance England*. London: Gay Men's Press.

Breines, Wini. 1992. *Young, White, and Miserable: Growing Up Female in the Fifties*. Boston: Beacon.

Breton, Raymond. 1964. "Institutional completeness of ethnic communities." *AJS* 70:195–205.

Brodsky, Joel I. 1989. "Controlling sickness: The political economy of gay men's health care." Ph.D. dissertation, University of Nebraska.

———. 1993a [1987]. "The Mineshaft: A retrospective ethnography." *JH* 24: 233–51.

———. 1993b. Review of Kayal 1993. *SOLGAN* 15,3:34–37; also *SLGCN* 76: 9–10.

Bronski, Michael. 1988. "Death and the erotic imagination." In Preston 1988: 133–44.

———. 1993. "How sweet and sticky it was." In Preston 1993b:73–84.

Brown, Roger. 1976. "Reference." *Cognition* 4:125–33.

Brown, Roger, and Albert Gilman. 1960. "The pronouns of power and solidarity." In *Style in Language,* ed. Thomas A. Sebeok, pp. 253–76. Cambridge, Mass.: Technologist Press.

Brym, Robert J. 1980. *Intellectuals and Politics.* London: Allen and Underwin.

Bullough, Vern L., and Bonnie Bullough. 1977. "Lesbianism in the 1920s and 1930s." *Signs* 2:895–904.

Burgess, Ernest W., and Harvey J. Locke. 1945. *The Family: From Institution to Companionship.* New York: American Book Co.

Burnham, John C. 1973. "Early references to homosexual communities in American medical writings." *Medical Aspects of Human Sexuality* 7:40–49.

Burns, John Horne. 1947. *The Gallery.* New York: Harper & Row.

Butler, Judith. 1990. *Gender Trouble: Feminism and the Subversion of Identity.* New York: Routledge.

Califia, Pat. 1982. "A personal view of the history of the lesbian S/M community and movement in San Francisco." in *Coming to Power,* pp. 243–87. Boston: Alyson.

California AIDS Office. 1990. *Monthly Surveillance Reports for State and for Counties of Orange, Los Angeles and San Diego and a Special Breakdown of Latino PWAs.* Sacramento: California AIDS Office.

Callendar, Charles, and Lee M. Kochems. 1985. "Men and not-men: male gender-mixing statuses and homosexuality." *JH* 11:165–78.

Camus, Renaud. 1981. *Tricks.* New York: St. Martin's Press.

Carrier, Joseph M. 1972. "Urban Mexican Male Homosexual Encounters." Ph.D. dissertation, University of California, Irvine.

———. 1979. Review of Bell and Weinberg 1978. *JH* 5:296–98.

———. 1989. "Sexual behavior and the spread of AIDS in México." *Medical Anthropology* 10:37–50.

———. 1995. *"De los otros": Mexican Male Homosexual Encounters.* New York: Columbia University Press.

Carrier, Joseph M., and J. Raúl Magaña. 1992. "Use of ethnosexual data on men of Mexican origins for HIV/AIDS prevention programs." In Herdt and Lindenbaum 1992:243–58.

Carrier, Joseph M., Bang Nguyen, and Sammy Su. 1992. "Vietnamese American sexual behaviors and HIV infection." *JSR* 29:547–560.

Carrington, Christopher. 1995. "Lesbian and gay couples' domestic and emotional labor." Ph.D. dissertation, University of Massachusetts, Amherst.

Cass, Vivienne C. 1978. "Homosexual identity formation." *JH* 4:219–36.

Castells, Manuel. 1983. *The City and the Grassroots*. Berkeley and Los Angeles: University of California Press.

Castells, Manuel, and Karen Murphy. 1982. "Cultural identity and urban structure: The spatial organization of San Francisco's gay community." *Urban Affairs Annual Reviews* 22:237–59.

Castillo, Ana. 1991. "La macha: Toward a beautiful whole self." In Trujillo 1991: 24–48.

Cauthern, Cynthia R. 1979. "900 African-American lesbians speak." *Off Our Backs* 9,6:12.

Cavan, Sherri. 1963. "Interaction in home territories." *Berkeley Journal of Sociology* 7:17–32.

———. 1966. *Liquor License*. Chicago: Aldine.

Centers for Disease Control. 1981a. "Pneumocystis pneumonia—Los Angeles.: *Morbidity and Mortality Weekly Reports* 30:250–52.

———. 1981b. "Kaposi's sarcoma and pheumocystis pneumonia among homosexual men—New York City." *Morbidity and Mortality Weekly Reports* 30:305–9.

Champagne, John. 1990. *When the Parrot Boy Sings*. Secaucus, N.J.: Meadowlands.

Chan, Connie S. 1989. "Issue of identity development among Asian-American lesbians and gay men." *Journal of Counseling and Development* 68:16–20.

Chauncey, George. 1982. "From sexual inversion to homosexuality." *Salmagundi* 58: 114–46.

———. 1985. "Christian brotherhood or sexual perversion? Homosexual identities and the construction of sexual boundaries in the World War One era." *Journal of Social History* 19:198–211.

———. 1993. "The postwar sex crime panic." In *True Stories from the American Past*, ed. W. Graebner, pp. 160–78. New York: McGraw-Hill.

———. 1994. *Gay New York*. New York: Basic Books.

Cheever, John. 1982. *Oh What A Paradise It Seems*. New York: Knopf.

———.1991. *The Journals*. New York: Knopf.

Chen Bou-See, and Stephen O. Murray. 1984. Review of Wolf 1979. *Urban Life* 12: 113–15.

Chesebro, James, ed. 1981. *Gayspeak*. New York: Pilgrim.

Chin, Justin. 1991. "Doing it on the *Oriental*." *LG* 4,2:22–24.

Chiñas, Berverly Newbold. 1995. "Isthmus Zapotec attitudes toward sex and gender anomalies." In Murray 1995a:293–302.

Choi, K.-H., et al. 1995. "High HIV risk among gay Asian and Pacific Islander men in San Francisco." *AIDS* 9:306–9.

Clark, Cheryl. 1983. "The failure to transform: Homophobia in the black community." In *Home Girls: A Black Feminist Anthology*, ed. Barbara Smith, pp. 197–208. New York: Kitchen Table Press.

Clayborne, John L. 1978. "Blacks and gay liberation." In Jay and Young 1978: 458–65.

Cohen, Albert K. 1965. "The sociology of the deviant act." *ASR* 30:5–14.

Cohen, Anthony P. 1985. *The Symbolic Construction of Community*. New York: Tavistock.

Coleman, James S. 1993. "The rational reconstruction of society." *ASR* 58:1–15.

Collins, Randall. 1986. "Is 1980s sociology in the doldrums?" *AJS* 91:1336–55.

Comstock, Gary D. 1989. "Victims of anti-gay/lesbian violence." *Journal of Interpersonal Violence* 4:101–6.

———. 1991. *Violence against Lesbians and Gay Men.* New York: Columbia University Press.

Concorde Coordinating Committee. 1994. "Concorde: MRC/ANRS randomised double-blind controlled trial of immediate and deferred zidovudine in symptom-free HIV infection." *Lancet* 343:871–81.

Connell, R. W. 1992. "A very straight gay: masculinity, homosexual experience, and the dynamics of gender." *ASR* 57:735–51.

Conrad, Peter, and Joseph Schneider. 1980. *Medicalization and Deviance.* New York: Mosby.

Cooper, Wayne F. 1987. *Claude McKay: Rebel Sojourner in the Harlem Renaissance.* Baton Rouge: Louisiana State University Press.

Corbin, Steven. 1989. *No Easy Place to Be.* New York: Simon and Schuster.

———. 1993. *Fragments That Remain.* Boston: Alyson.

———. 1994. *A Hundred Days from Now.* Boston: Alyson.

Cornwell, Anita. 1978. "Three for the price of one: Notes from a gay black feminist." In Jay and Young 1978:466–76.

———. 1979, 1983. *African-American Lesbian in White America.* Tallahassee, Fla.: Naiad Press.

Cory, Donald Webster [Edward Sagarin]. 1951. *The Homosexual in America.* New York: Greenberg.

Cotton, Wayne L. 1972. "Role-playing substitutions among homosexuals." *JSR* 8:310–23.

———. 1975. "Social and sexual relationships of lesbians." *JSR* 11:139–48.

Cottrell, Leonard S., Jr. 1942. "The adjustment of the individual to his age and sex roles." *ASR* 7:67–70.

Coxon, Tony. 1988. "'Something sensational': The sexual diary as a tool for mapping detailed sexual behavior." *Sociological Review* 36:353–67.

Crimp, Douglas, ed. 1988. *AIDS: Cultural Analysis, Cultural Activism.* Cambridge: MIT Press.

Crompton, Louis. 1985. *Byron and Greek Love.* Berkeley and Los Angeles: University of California Press.

Cronin, Denise M. 1974. "Coming out among lesbians." In Goode and Troiden 1974:268–77.

Culliton, Barbara J. 1976. "Legion fever: Postmortem of an investigation that failed." *Science* 194:1025–27.

Dais, Stephan Lee. 1986. "Don't turn your back on me." In Beam 1986:60–62.

Dalby, Liza Chrifield. 1983. *Geisha.* Berkeley and Los Angeles: University of California Press.

Dall'Orto, Giovanni. 1988. "'Socratic love' as a disguise for same-sex love in the Italian Renaissance." *JH* 16:33–65.

Dalton, Susan. 1995. "Privatization of public space: How we lost the debate on 'gays in the military.'" Presented at the Pacific Sociological Association meeting in San Francisco.

Dank, Barry M. 1971. "Coming out in the gay world." *Psychiatry* 34:180–97. Repr. in Dynes and Donaldson 1992:60–78.

———. 1980. Review of Levine 1979c. *Contemporary Sociology* 9:441–42.

Darnell, Regna D. 1981. "Taciturnity in Native American etiquette: A Cree case." *Culture* 1:55–60.

Darty, Trudy, and Sandee Potter, eds. 1984. *Women-identified Women*. Palo Alto, Calif.: Mayfield.

D'Augelli, A. R., and M. M. Hart. 1987. "Gay women, men and families in rural settings." *American Journal of Community Psychology* 15:79–93.

Day, Beth. 1972. *Sexual Life between African-Americans and Whites*. New York: World.

De Cecco, John. 1987. "Scrutinizing the sissies: Homophobia as 'science." *Advocate* (7 July) 9.

———. 1988. *Gay Couples*. New York: Harrington Park Press.

de la Croix, Sukie. 1994. "Sissy man blues." *perversions* 1,2:77–91.

Delaney, Samuel R. 1988. *The Motion of Light in Water*. New York: Arbor.

Delaney, Samuel R., and Joseph Beam. 1986. "The possibility of possibilities." In Beam 1986:185–208.

Delph, Edward William. 1978. *The Silent Community: Public Homosexual Encounters*. Beverly Hills, Calif.: Sage.

D'Emilio, John. 1983. *Sexual Politics, Sexual Communities*. Chicago: University of Chicago Press.

———. 1992. *Making Trouble: Essays on Gay History, Politics, and the University*. New York: Routledge.

Denneny, Michael. 1979. *Lovers*. New York: Avon.

Desroches, Frederick J. 1990. "Tearoom trade: A research update." *Qualitative Sociology* 13:39–61. Repr. in Dynes and Donaldson 1992:79–101.

DeVault, Marjorie L. 1991. *Feeding the Family: The Social Organization of Caring as Gendered Work*. Chicago: University of Chicago Press.

Devereux, George. 1937. "Institutionalized homosexuality of the Mohave." *Human Biology* 9:498–527.

Dickemann, Mildred. 1993. "Reproductive strategies and gender construction: An evolutionary view of homosexuality." *JH* 24:55–71.

Dillard, Gavin Geoffrey. 1993. "Race." In Preston 1993b:301–6.

Dixon, Melvin. 1989. "Aunt Ida pieces a quilt." In Hemphill 1991a:145–47.

———. 1992. *Vanishing Rooms*. New York: Plume.

Doll, Lynda S., et al. 1990. "Sexual behavior before AIDS: The hepatitis B studies of homosexual and bisexual men." *AIDS* 4:1067–73.

Donoghue, Emma. 1994. *Passions between Women: British Lesbian Culture 1668–1801*. London: Scarlet Press.

Dorsey, J. Owen. 1890. "A study of Siouan cults." *Bureau of American Ethnology Annual Report* 11:378–517.

Douglas, Mary. 1966. *Purity and Danger*. Baltimore: Penguin.

Dowell, Coleman. 1983. *White on African-American on White*. New York: Wiedenfeld and Nicolson.

Drewes, Caroline. 1989. "Baldwin: A legacy." *San Francisco Examiner* (9 July) E1, E9.

Duazo, Dino. 1989. "Coming out to family." *LG* 2,6:6–7.

DuBois, Cora. 1944. *The People of Alor*. Minneapolis: University of Minnesota Press.

Duberman, Martin Bauml. 1993. *Stonewall*. New York: Penguin.

Duplechan, Larry. 1985. *Eight Days a Week*. Boston: Alyson

———. 1986. *Blackbird.* New York: St. Martin's Press.

———. 1989. *Tangled Up in Blue.* New York: St. Martin's Press.

———. 1991a. "Mar Vista, California." In Preston 1991:245–56.

———. 1991b. "Presently in the past." In *Certain Voices,* ed. Darryl Pilcher, pp. 190–97. Boston: Alyson.

———. 1992. "She's my mother." In Preston 1992b:41–52.

———. 1993. *Captain Swing.* Boston: Alyson.

Durkheim, Émile. 1893. *De la division du travail social.* Paris: Alcan.

———. 1895. *Les règles de la methode sociologique.* Paris: Alcan.

Duster, Troy. 1990. *Backdoor to Eugenics.* New York: Routledge.

Dykstra, Dirk. 1989. "A little off the top." *Advocate* 520 (14 March) 7.

Dynes, Wayne R. 1979. "Purity and status politics." *Gay Books Bulletin* 3:21ff.

———. 1981. "Privacy, sexual orientation and self-sovereignty of the individual." *Gay Books Bulletin* 6:20–23.

———. 1990a. "Bathhouses." *Encyclopedia of Homosexuality,* 1:113–15. New York: Garland.

———. 1990b. "Wrestling with the social boa constructor." In *Forms of Desire,* ed. Edward Stein, pp. 209–38. New York: Garland.

Dynes, Wayne R., and Stephen Donaldson, eds. 1992. *Sociology of Homosexuality.* New York: Garland.

Eckerman, Fern M. 1967. *The Furious Passage of James Baldwin.* New York: Signet.

Edgerton, Robert B. 1964. "Pokot intersexuality." *AA* 66:1288–99.

Edwards, Tim. 1992. "The AIDS dialectic." In Plummer 1992:151–59.

Ehrlich, Gretel. 1985. *The Solace of Open Spaces.* New York: Viking.

Ekstrand, Maria L., and Thomas J. Coates. 1990. "Maintenance of safer sexual behaviors and predictors of risky sex." *American Journal of Public Health* 80:973–77.

Embree, John. 1950. "Thailand: A loosely-structured social system." *AA* 52:1–12.

Enloe, Cynthia. 1993. *The Morning After: Sexual Politics at the End of the Cold War.* Berkeley and Los Angeles: University of California Press.

Epstein, Edward Jay. 1973. *News from Nowhere* New York: Vintage.

Epstein, Steven G. 1987. "Gay politics, ethnic identity: The limits of social constructionism." *Socialist Review* 93/94:9–54.

———. 1988. "Nature vs. nurture and the politics of AIDS organizing." *Outlook* 1,3:46–53.

———. 1993. "Impure science: AIDS, activism, and the politics of knowledge." Ph.D. dissertation, University of California, Berkeley.

———. 1994. "A queer encounter: Sociology and the study of sexuality." *Sociological Theory* 12:188–202.

Erikson, Kai T. 1962. "Notes on the sociology of deviance." *SP* 9:307–14.

———. 1966. *Wayward Puritans.* New York: Wiley.

Ernst, Frederick A., Rupert A. Francis, Harold Nevbels, and Carol A. Lemeh. 1991. "Condemnation of homosexuality in the black community: A gender-specific phenomenon?" *ASB* 20:579–85.

Esterberg, K. G. 1994. "From accommodation to liberation: A social movement analysis of lesbians in the homophile movement." *Gender and Society* 8:424–43.

Ettorre, E. M. 1980. *Lesbians, Women and Society.* Boston: Routledge and Kegan Paul.

Evans, Arthur. 1988. *The God of Ecstasy*. New York: St. Martin's.

Evers, Hans D., ed. 1969. *Loosely Structured Social Systems: Thailand in Comparative Perspective*. Yale University Southeast Asia Cultural Report 17.

Ewing, Katherine P. 1990. "The dream of spiritual initiation and the organization of self representations among Pakistani Sufis." *AE* 17:56–74.

Fabrega, Horacio. 1971. "Begging in a Southeastern Mexican city." *Human Organization* 30:277–87.

Faderman, Lillian. 1978. "The morbidification of love between women by 19th-century sexologists." *JH* 4:73–98.

———. 1981. *Surpassing the Love of Men*. New York: Morrow.

———. 1991a. "Harlem nights." *Advocate* 573 (26 March):54–55.

———. 1991b. *Odd Girls and Twilight Lovers: A History of Lesbian Life in Twentieth-Century America*. New York: Columbia University Press.

———. 1992. "The return of butch and femme." *Journal of the History of Sexuality* 2:578–96.

Fee, Elizabeth, and Daniel Fox, eds. 1988. *AIDS: The Burdens of History*. Berkeley and Los Angeles: University of California Press.

———. 1992. *AIDS: The Makings of a Chronic Disease*. Berkeley and Los Angeles: University of California Press.

Fein, Sara Beck, and Elaine M. Nuehring. 1981. "Intrapsychic effects of stigma." *JH* 7:3–13.

Feinberg, David. 1990. *Eighty-sixed*. New York: Penguin.

Fettner, Ann G. 1986. "A place to die and a drink of water." *New York Native* 157 (21 April) 22–26.

Fine, Gary Alan. 1987. *With the Boys: Little League Baseball and Preadolescent Culture*. Chicago: University of Chicago Press.

Fine, Gary Alan, and Sherryl Kleinman. 1979. "Rethinking subculture." *AJS* 84:1–20.

———. 1983. "Network and meaning." *Symbolic Interaction* 6:97–110.

Fischer, Claude S. 1975. "Toward a subcultural theory of urbanism." *AJS* 80:1319–41.

———. 1976. *The Urban Experience*. New York: Harcourt, Brace, Jovanovich.

———. 1982. *To Dwell among Friends*. Chicago: University of Chicago Press.

Fisher, Bernice, M., and Anselm L. Strauss. 1978. "Interactionism." In Bottomore and Nisbet 1978:499–576.

Fisher, Salih Michael. 1983. "Assumptions about the Harlem brown baby." In Smith 1983:31–32.

Fishman, Mark. 1978. "Crime waves as ideology." *SP* 25:531–43.

Fitzgerald, Frances. 1986. *Cities on a Hill*. New York: Simon and Schuster.

Fleck, Ludwig. 1979 [1935]. *The Genesis of a Scientific Fact*. Chicago: University of Chicago Press.

Fleming, Thomas. 1983. "Criminalizing a marginal community: The bawdy house raids." In *Deviant Designations*, ed. T. Fleming and L. Visano, pp. 37–60. Toronto: Butterworth.

Fong, J. Craig. 1993. "Thin air: Nurturing national leaders." *LG* "Families" issue, 16–19.

Foster, George M. 1965. "Peasant society and the idea of the limited good." *AA* 67: 293–315.

Foucault, Michel. 1961. *Folie et déraison: Histoire de la folie à l'âge classique.* Paris: Plon.

———. 1980 [1976]. *The History of Sexuality.* New York: Pantheon.

Fox, Renée C., and Judith P. Swazey. 1978. *The Courage to Fail.* Chicago: University of Chicago Press.

Freeman, Brian. 1991. "Pomo Afro Homos presents *Fierce Love.*" *Out/Look* 14: 58–62.

Freeman, David L. [Chuck Rowland]. 1953. "The homosexual culture." *One* 1,5 (May):8–11.

Freud, Sigmund. 1939. *Civilization and Its Discontents.* Boston: Norton.

Fried, Suzanne R. 1989. "Boon for the burbs." *San Francisco Sentinel* (13 July) 8–9.

Friedman, Edward. 1993. "A failed Chinese modernity." *Daedalus* 122,2:1–17.

Friedman, Mike. 1993. "Missing in action: AIDS, the military ban and the 1993 march." *Radical America* 25,1:32–38.

Friedrich, Paul. 1978. *Language, Context and Imagination.* Stanford, Calif.: Stanford University Press.

Fugita, Stephen S., and David J. O'Brien. 1991. *Japanese American Ethnicity.* Seattle: University of Washington Press.

Fulton, Robert, and Steven W. Anderson. 1992. "The Amerindian 'man-woman.'" *Current Anthropology* 33: 603–10.

Fuss, Diana. 1989. *Essentially Speaking: Feminism, Nature and Difference.* New York: Routledge.

Gagnon, John. 1975. "Sex research and social change." *ASB* 4:111–41.

Gagnon, John, and William Simon. 1973. *Sexual Conduct.* Chicago: Aldine.

Gagnon, John, and William Simon, eds. 1967. *Sexual Deviance.* New York: Harper & Row.

Galliher, John F., and John H. Cross. 1983. *Moral Legislation Without Morality.* New Brunswick, N.J.: Rutgers University Press.

Gallin, Bernard. 1968. "Political factionalism and its impact on Chinese village social organization in Taiwan." In *Local-Level Politics,* ed. Marc Swartz, pp. 377–400. Chicago: Aldine.

Gamson, Joshua. 1989. "Silence, death, and the invisible enemy." *SP* 36:351–367. Repr. with an afterword in *Ethnography Unbound,* ed. M. Burawoy et al., pp. 35–57. Berkeley and Los Angeles: University of California Press, 1991.

———. 1994. "Must identity movements self-destruct? A queer dilemma." Presented at the ASA annual meeting in Los Angeles.

Gans, Herbert J. 1962. "Urbanism and suburbanism as ways of life." In *Human Behavior and Social Process,* ed. Arnold Rose, pp. 625–48. Boston: Houghton-Mifflin.

Garber, Eric. 1982. "'Tain't nobody's business': homosexuality in Harlem in the 1920s." *Advocate* 341 (13 April) 39–43. Repr. in Smith 1983:7–16.

Gates, Henry Louis, Jr. 1993. "Backlash?" *New Yorker* (17 May) 42–44.

———. 1994. "The body politic." *New Yorker* (28 November) 112–24.

Geertz, Clifford. 1959. "Form and variation in Balinese village structure." *AA* 61: 991–1012.

Gerard, Kent. 1981. "The tulip and the sodomite." Presented at the Kroeber Anthropological Society annual meeting.

———. 1982. "The erection of the sodomite." Presented at the Kroeber Anthropological Society annual meeting.

———. 1988. Review of Murray 1984. *JH* 16:492–99.

Gevisser, Mark, and Edwin Cameron, eds. 1995. *Defiant Desire: Gay and Lesbian Lives in South Africa*. New York: Routledge.

Gilman, Sander L. 1986. *Jewish Self-Hatred: Anti-Semitism and the Hidden Language of the Jews*. Baltimore: Johns Hopkins University Press.

———. 1988. *Disease and Representation: Images of Illness from Madness to AIDS*. Ithaca, N.Y.: Cornell University Press.

Gilmore, David D. 1990. *Manhood in the Making: Cultural Concepts of Masculinity*. New Haven: Yale University Press.

Gitlin, Todd. 1980. *The Whole World Is Watching*. Berkeley and Los Angeles: University of California Press.

———. 1987. *The Sixties*. New York: Bantam.

Glick, Clarence. 1942. "The relation between position and status in the assimilation of the Chinese in Hawaii." *AJS* 47:667–79.

Godfrey, Brian J. 1988. *Neighborhoods in Transition*. Berkeley nd Los Angeles: University of California Press.

Goffman, Erving. 1959. *The Presentation of Self in Everyday Life*. Toronto: Doubleday.

———. 1961. *Encounters*. Indianapolis: Bobbs-Merrill.

———. 1963. *Stigma*. Toronto: Prentice-Hall.

Goldsby, Jackie. 1990. "What it means to be colored me." *Out/Look* 9:7–17.

Gomez, Jewelle, and Barbara Smith. 1990. "Taking the home out of homophobia: Black lesbians look in their own backyards." *Out/Look* 8:32–37.

Good, Byron J. 1977. "'The heart of what's the matter': the semantics of illness in Iran." *Culture, Medicine and Psychiatry* 1:25–58.

Goode, Erich. 1981. Comment on Whitam 1977. *JSR* 17:54–65, 76–83.

Goode, Erich, and Richard Troiden, eds. 1974. *Sexual Deviance*. New York: Morrow.

Goode, William J. 1960. "A theory of role strain." *ASR* 25:483–96.

Goodenough, Ward. H. 1965. "Rethinking 'status' and 'role.'" in *Cognitive Anthropology*, ed. Stephen Tyler, pp. 311–30. New York: Holt.

———. 1990. "Evolution of the human capacity for beliefs." *AA* 92:597–612.

Goodfield, June. 1982. *Science and the Public*. Washington: National Academy of Science.

Goodich, Michael. 1979. *The Unmentionable Vice*. Santa Barbara: Ross-Erikson.

Goodwin, Joseph P. 1989. *More Man Than You'll Ever Be: Gay Folklore and Acculturation in Middle America*. Bloomington: Indiana University Press.

Goodwin, Marjorie Harness. 1990. *He Said, She Said*. Bloomington: Indiana University Press.

Gorman, E. Michael. 1980. "A new light on Zion." Ph.D. dissertation, University of Chicago.

———. 1992. "The pursuit of the wish: An anthropological perspective on gay male subculture in Los Angeles." In Herdt 1992:87–106.

Gottlieb, Michael S., et al. 1982. "GRID." *Clinical Research* 30:349A.

Gramsci, Antonio. 1971 [1937]. *Prison Notebooks*. New York: World.

Granovetter, Mark. 1974. *Getting a Job*. Cambridge: Harvard University Press.

Gray, Jane K. 1988. "The tearoom revisited." Ph.D. dissertation, Ohio State University.

Green, Richard. 1986. *Sissy Boys Grow Up*. New Haven: Yale University Press.

Greenberg, David F. 1988. *The Construction of Homosexuality*. Chicago: University of Chicago Press.

———. 1990. "The socio-sexual milieu of *The Love Letters*." *JH* 19,2:93–103.

———. 1993. *Crime and Capitalism*. Palo Alto, Calif.: Mayfield.

Greenblatt, Stephen. 1982. "Filthy rites." *Daedalus* 111,3:1–15.

Grube, John. 1986. "Queens and flaming virgins." *Rites* 2,9:14–17.

———. 1987. "Have you ever been an essentialist?" Paper presented at the "Homosexuality/Which Homosexuality?" conference in Amsterdam.

———. 1990. "Natives and settlers: An ethnographic note on early interaction of older homosexual men with younger gay liberationists." *JH* 20:119–35.

Grumley, Michael. 1991. *Life Drawing*. New York: Grove Weidenfeld.

Gumperz, John J. 1982a. *Discourse Strategies*. New York: Cambridge University Press.

———, ed. 1982b. *Language and Social Identity*. New York: Cambridge University Press.

Gusfield, Joseph R. 1963. *Symbolic Crusade*. Urbana: University of Illinois Press.

———. 1975. *Community*. Oxford: Blackwell.

Hall, Richard. 1975, 1983. *The Butterscotch Prince*. Boston: Alyson.

Halperin, David. 1990. *One Hundred Years of Homosexuality*. New York: Routledge.

Hamilton, Richard. 1982. *Who Voted for Hitler?* Princeton, N.J.: Princeton University Press.

Handler, Richard. 1984. "On sociocultural discontinuity: Nationalism and cultural objectification in Québec." *Current Anthropology* 25:55–71.

Hardy, James Earl. 1994. *B-Boy Blues*. Boston: Alyson.

Harpe, Charles. 1991. "At 36." In Hemphill 1991a:52–56.

Harper, Phillip Brian. 1993. "Eloquence and epitaph: Black nationalism and the homophobic impulse in responses to the death of Max Robinson." In *Writing AIDS*, ed. T. Murphy and S. Poirier, pp. 117–39. New York: Columbia University Press.

Harrington, Mark. 1990. "Let my people in." *Outweek* (8 August) 34–37.

Harris, Craig G. 1986. "Cut off among their people." In Beam 1986:63–69.

Harry, Joseph. 1974. "Urbanization and gay life." *JSR* 10:238–47.

———. 1982a. "Derivative deviance: The cases of fag-bashing, blackmail, and shakedown of gay men." *Criminology* 19:546–64.

———. 1982b. *Gay Children Grow Up*. New York: Praeger.

———. 1984. *Gay Couples*. New York: Praeger.

———. 1985. "Defeminization and social class." *ASB* 14:1–12.

———. 1987. "Gender schemas and gender deviance." Paper presented at the Society for the Study of Social Problems annual meeting in Chicago.

———. 1993. "Being out." *JH* 26,1:25–39.

Harry, Joseph, and William Devall. 1978a. "Age and sexual culture among gay males." *ASB* 7:199–208. Repr. in Dynes and Donaldson 1992:123–34.

———. 1978b. *The Social Organization of Gay Males*. New York: Praeger.

Harry, Joseph, and Robert Lovely. 1977. "Gay marriages and communities of sexual orientation." *Alternative Lifestyles* 2:177–200. Repr. in Dynes and Donaldson 1992:135–58.

Hart, C. W. M. 1954. "The Sons of Turimpi." *AA* 54:242–61.

Hart, John, and Diane Richardson. 1981. *The Theory and Practice of Homosexuality.* London: Routledge and Kegan Paul.

Hatfield, Larry D. 1989. "Gays say life is getting better." *San Francisco Examiner* (6 June) A15–19.

Haverkos, Harry W., William J. Bukoski, Jr., and Zili Amsel. 1989. "Initiation of male homosexual behavior." *Journal of the American Medical Association* 262:501.

Hawkeswood, William G. 1990. "I'm a Black man who just happens to be gay." Paper presented at the AAA annual meeting in New Orleans.

Hayes, Joseph J. 1976. "Gayspeak." *Quarterly Journal of Speech* 62:256–66.

———. 1981. "Lesbians, gay men and their 'languages.'" In Chesebro 1981:28–42.

Hechter, Michael. 1975. *Internal Colonialism.* Berkeley and Los Angeles: University of California Press.

Heiss, Jerome. 1981. "Social roles." In *Social Psychology,* ed. Morris Rosenberg and Ralph Turner, pp. 94–132. New York: Basic Books.

Hemphill, Essex. 1991b. "Washington, D.C." In Preston 1991:211–15. Partially repr. as "Without comment" in Hemphill 1992:74–77.

———. 1991c. "If Freud had been a neurotic colored woman: Reading Dr. Frances Cress Welsing." *Out/Look* 13:50–55.

———. 1992. *Ceremonies.* New York: Plume.

Hemphill, Essex, ed. 1991a. *Brother to Brother: New Writings by Black Gay Men.* Boston: Alyson.

Hencken, Joel D. 1984. "Conceptualization of homosexual behavior which preclude homosexual self-labeling." *JH* 9:53–63.

Hendin, Herbert. 1969. *African-American Suicide.* New York: Harper and Row.

Henry, George W. 1941. *Sex Variants.* New York: Hoeber.

Henry, George W., and Alfred A. Gross. 1938. "Social factors in the case histories of one hundred underprivileged homosexuals." *Mental Hygiene* 22:591–611.

Herdt, Gilbert H., ed. 1982. *Rituals of Manhood: Male Initiation in Papua New Guinea.* Berkeley and Los Angeles: University of California Press.

———. 1984. *Ritualized Homosexuality in Melanesia.* Berkeley and Los Angeles: University of California Press.

———. 1992. *Gay Culture in America.* Boston: Beacon.

———. 1994. *Third Sex, Third Gender.* New York: Zone.

Herdt, Gilbert H., and Andrew M. Boxer. 1993. *Children of Horizons.* Boston: Beacon.

Herdt, Gilbert H., and Shirley Lindenbaum, eds. 1992. *The Time of AIDS.* London: Sage.

Herek, Gregory M., and Kevin Berrill, eds. 1992. *Hate Crimes: Confronting Violence against Lesbians and Gay Men.* London: Sage

Herrell, Richard K. 1992. "The symbolic strategies of Chicago's Gay and Lesbian Pride Day Parade." In Herdt 1992:225–52.

———. 1993. "Sin, sickness, crime: Queer desire and the American state." Presented at the AAA annual meeting in Washington, D.C.

Herrell, Richard K., and Gilbert H. Herdt. 1993. "From homosexual to gay in Chicago." In Herdt and Boxer 1993:25–69.

Hessoll, Nancy A., et al. 1987. "The natural history of HIV-infection in a cohort of homosexual and bisexual men." Paper presented at the International AIDS Congress in Washington, D.C.

Hidalgo, Hilda A., and Elia Hidalgo Christensen. 1976. "The Puerto Rican lesbian and the Puerto Rican community." *JH* 2:109–21.

Hilbert, Richard A. 1981. "Toward an improved understanding of 'role.'" *Theory and Society* 10:207–25.

Hillery, George A., Jr. 1959. "A critique of selected community concepts." *Social Forces* 37:237–42.

Himes, Chester. 1952. *Cast the First Stone.* New York: Coward-McCann.

———. 1986. *Blind Man with a Pistol.* London: Allison and Busby.

Hippler, Mike. 1989. *Matlovich.* Boston: Alyson.

———. 1990. *. . . So Little Time: Essays on Gay Life.* Berkeley: Celestial Arts.

Hocquenghem, Guy. 1978 [1972]. *Homosexual Desire.* London: Allison and Busby.

Hoffman, Arthur V. 1960. "Sex deviation in a prison community." *Journal of Social Therapy* 6:170–81.

Hoffman, Martin. 1968. *The Gay World.* New York: Basic Books.

Holleran, Andrew. 1978. *Dancer from the Dance.* New York: Morrow.

———. 1988. *Ground Zero.* New York: Morrow.

Hollinghurst, Alan. 1988. *The Swimming-Pool Library.* New York: Random House.

Hom, Alice Y., and Ming-Yuen S. Ma. 1993. "Premature gestures: A speculative dialogue on Asian Pacific Islander lesbian and gay writing." *JH* 26,2/3:21–51.

Hong, Keelung. 1994. "Experiences of being a 'native' observing anthropologists." *Anthropology Today* 10,3:6–9.

Hong, Keelung, and Stephen O. Murray. 1995. "A Taiwanese woman who became a spirit medium." Manuscript.

Hooker, Evelyn. 1957. "Adjustment of male overt homosexuals." *Journal of Projective Techniques* 21:18–31.

———. 1961. "The homosexual community." In *Perspectives in Psychopathology,* ed. J. Plamer and M. Goldstein, pp. 354–64. New York: Oxford University Press, 1966. Repr. in Gagnon and Simon 1967:176–94.

———. 1965. "Male homosexuals and their 'worlds.' " in *Sexual Inversion,* ed. Judd Marmor, pp. 83–107. New York: Basic Books.

———. 1993. "A scientific view on homosexuality: Reflections of a 40-year exploration." *American Psychologist* 48:450–53.

hooks, bell. 1988. "Reflections on homophobia and black communities." *Out/Look* 1,2:22–25.

———. 1992. *Black Looks: Race and Representations.* Boston: South End Press.

Huber, Joan. 1995. "Institutional perspectives on sociology." *AJS* 101:194–216.

Hudson, James R. 1987. *The Unanticipated City.* Amherst: University of Massachusetts Press.

Hughes, Charles H. 1893. "An organization of colored erotopaths." *Alienist and Neurologist* 14:731–32.

———. 1907. "Homo sexual complexion perverts in St. Louis." *Alienist and Neurologist* 28:487–88.

Hughes, Everett C. 1945. "Dilemmas and contradictions of status." *AJS* 51: 353–59.

———. 1963. "Race relations and the sociological imagination." *ASR* 28:879–90.

Humphreys, Laud. 1970, 1975. *Tearoom Trade*. Chicago: Aldine.

———. 1971. "New styles of homosexual manliness." *Transaction* (March) 38–65.

———. 1972. *Out of the Closets*. Toronto: Prentice-Hall.

———. 1979. "Exodus and identity: The emerging gay culture." In Levine 1979c: 134–47.

Humphreys, Laud, and Brian Miller. 1980. "Identities in the emerging gay culture." In *Homosexual Behavior*, ed. Judd Marmor, pp. 142–56. New York: Basic Books.

Humphries, Martin. 1985. "Gay machismo." In *The Sexuality of Men*, ed. A. Metcalf and M. Humphries, pp. 70–85. London: Pluto.

Hyde, Louis. 1978. *Rat and the Devil: Journal Letters of F. O. Matthiessen and Russell Cheney*. Boston: Alyson.

Icard, L. 1986. "Black gay men and conflicting social identities: Sexual orientation versus racial identity." *Journal of Social Work and Human Sexuality* 4:83–93.

Isaacs, Gordon, and Brian McKendrick. 1992. *Male Homosexuality in South Africa*. Cape Town: Oxford University Press.

Isherwood, Christopher. 1976. *Christopher and His Kind*. New York: Farrar Strauss Giroux.

———. 1980. *My Guru and His Disciple*. New York: Farrar Strauss Giroux.

Jackson, Jean. 1989. "Is there a way to talk about making culture without making enemies?" *Dialectical Anthropology* 14:127–43.

———. 1995. "Culture, genuine and spurious: The politics of Indianness in the Vaupés, Colombia." *AE* 22:3–27.

Jackson, Peter A. 1989. *Male Homosexuality in Thailand*. Amsterdam: Global Academic Publishers.

Jackson, Reginald T. 1991. "The absence of fear." In Hemphill 1991a:206–10.

Jacobs, Sue-Ellen, and Jason Cromwell. 1992. "Visions and revisions of reality: Reflections on sex, sexuality, gender, and gender variance." *JH* 23,4:43–69.

Jay, Karla, and Allen Young, eds. 1972. *Out of the Closets*. New York: Douglas.

———. 1979. *Lavender Culture*. New York: Jove.

Jeffreys, Sheila. 1985. *The Spinster and Her Enemies: Feminism and Sexuality, 1880–1930*. Boston: Pandora Press.

Jennes, Valerie. 1995. "Social movement growth, domain expansion, and framing processes: The gay/lesbian movement and violence against gays and lesbians as a social problem." *Social Problems* 42:145–70.

Johansson, Warren. 1984. "London's medieval sodomites." *Cabirion* 10:5–7.

Johnson, Julius M. 1981. "The influence of assimilation on the psychosocial adjustment of black homosexual men." Ph.D. dissertation, California School of Professional Psychology, Berkeley.

Jones, A. Billy S. 1986. "A father's need; a parent's desire." In Beam 1986:143–51.

Jones, Brian. 1984. "The doctor and the gay pols." *Bay Area Reporter* 14,15: 6.

Jones, Leroi. 1966. *The System of Dante's Hell*. London: MacGibbon and Kee.

Joseph, Gloria. 1981. "Styling, profiling and pretending: The games before the fall." In *Common Differences: Conflicts in Black and White Feminist Perspectives*, ed. G. Joseph and J. Lewis, pp. 181–94. Garden City, N.Y.: Doubleday.

Jurrist, Charles. 1987. "In search of African-American images." *Stallion* 6,7:34–39.

Kando, Thomas. 1974. "Males, females, and transsexuals." *JH* 1:64–69.

Kahn, Marla J. 1991. "Factors affecting the coming out process in lesbians." *Journal of Homosexuality* 21:47–70.

Khan, Surina. 1995. "India and Pakistan: sexual politics and oppression." *Harvard Gay & Lesbian Review* 2,4:27–29.

Kamel, G. W. Levi. 1983. "The leather career." In *S&M*, ed. Thomas Weinberg and Levi Kamel, pp. 73–79. Buffalo, N.Y.: Prometheus.

Kane, Stephanie, and Theresa Mason. 1992. "IV drug users' and 'sex partners': The limits of epidemiological categories and the ethnography of risk." In Herdt and Lindenbaum 1992:199–222.

Kanouse, David E., et al. 1991. *Response to the AIDS Epidemic: A Survey of Homosexual and Bisexual Men in Los Angeles County*. Santa Monica: RAND Corporation.

Kantrowitz, Arnie. 1977. *Under the Rainbow*. New York: Morrow.

———. 1986. "Friends gone with the wind." *Advocate* 454 (2 September). Repr. in Preston 1988:13–26.

Kaslow, Richard A., et al. 1987. "The Multi-Center AIDS Cohort Study." *American Journal of Epidemiology* 126:310–18.

Kay, Paul. 1978. "Tahitian words for 'race' and 'class.'" *Publications de la Société des Océanistes* 39:81–91.

Kayal, Philip. 1992. "Healing homophobia: 'The sacred' in AIDS volunteerism." *Journal of Religion and Health* 31:113–28.

———. 1993. *Bearing Witness: Gay Men's Health Crisis and the Politics of AIDS*. Boulder, Colo.: Westview.

Keene, John, Jr. 1991. "Adelphus King." In Hemphill 1991a:31–46.

Kehoe, Monika. 1988. *Lesbians over 60 Speak for Themselves*. New York: Harrington Press.

Kenan, Randall. 1989. *A Visitation of Spirits*. New York: Grove Press.

———. 1992. *Let the Dead Bury Their Dead*. New York: Harcourt, Brace, Jovanovich.

Kennedy, Elizabeth Lapovsky, and Madeline D. Davis. 1993. *Boots of Leather, Slippers of Gold: The History of a Lesbian Community*. New York: Routledge.

Kessler, Ronald C., et al. 1988. "Effects of HIV infection, perceived health and clinical status on a cohort at risk for AIDS." *Social Science and Medicine* 27:56–78.

King, Edward. 1994. *Safety in Numbers: Safer Sex and Gay Men*. New York: Routledge.

King, Samantha. 1993. "The politics of the body and the body politic: Magic Johnson and the ideology of AIDS." *Sociology of Sport Journal* 10:270–85.

King, Thomas A. 1994. "Performing 'akimbo.'" In *The Politics and Poetics of Camp*, ed. Moe Meyer, pp. 23–50. New York: Routledge.

Kinsey, Alfred C., Wardell B. Pomeroy, and Clyde E. Martin. 1948. *Sexual Behavior in the Human Male*. Philadelphia: Saunders.

———. 1953. *Sexual Behavior in the Human Female*. Philadelphia: Saunders

Kisseloff, Jeff. 1989. *You Must Remember This*. New York: Harcourt, Brace, Jovanovich.

Kitsuse, John I. 1962. "Societal reactions to deviant behavior." *SP* 9:247–56.

———. 1980. "Coming out all over: Deviants and the politics of social problems." *SP* 28:1–13.

Kitsuse, John I., and Malcolm Spector. 1973. "Toward a sociology of social problems." *SP* 20:407–19.

Klein, Alan M. 1989. "Managing deviance: Hustling, homophobia, and the body-building subculture." *Deviant Behavior* 10:11–27. Repr. in Dynes and Donaldson 1992:159–76.

Kleinman, Arthur. 1980. *Patients and Healers in the Context of Culture.* Berkeley and Los Angeles: University of California Press.

Knapper, Karl Bruce. 1995. "Wayne Corbitt's 'A fish with frog's eyes.'" *Bay Area Reporter* 25,8 (23 February) 33,42.

Knopp, Lawrence M., Jr. 1986. "Gentrification and gay community development: A case study of Minneapolis." Association of American Geographers annual meeting in Minneapolis.

———. 1990a. "Social consequences of homosexuality." *Geographical* 62,5:20–25.

———. 1990b. "Some theoretical implications of gay involvement in an urban land market." *Political Geography Quarterly* 9:337–52.

———. 1992. "Sexuality and the spatial dynamics of capitalism." *Environment and Planning D—Society and Space* 10:651–69.

Kollock, Peter, Philip Blumstein, and Pepper Schwartz. 1985. "Sex and power in interaction." *ASR* 50:34–46.

Komarovsky, Mirra. 1946. "Cultural contradictions and sex roles." *AJS* 51:193–203.

Koopman, J. S., et al. 1991. "Assessing risk factors for transmission of infection." *American Journal of Epidemiology* 133:1199–1209.

Kramer, Jerry Lee. 1995. "Bachelor farmers and spinsters: Gay and lesbian identities and communities in rural North Dakota." In *Mapping Desire,* ed. David Bell and Gill Valentine, pp. 200–213. London: Routledge.

Kramer, Larry. 1978. *Faggots.* New York: Random House.

Krieger, Lisa M. 1993. "S.F. remains a mecca for gay couples: Census data reveal same-sex households abound in The City." *San Francisco Examiner* (12 September) A1, A10.

Krieger, Susan. 1983. *The Mirror Dance.* Philadelphia: Temple University Press.

Kroeber, Alfred L. 1909. "Classificatory systems of relationship." *Journal of the Royal Anthropological Institute* 39:81–84.

Kronhausen, Phyllis, and Eberhard Kronhausen. 1970. *Erotic Fantasies: A Study of the Sexual Imagination.* New York: Grove Press.

Krouse, Mary Beth. 1994. "The AIDS Memorial Quilt as cultural resistance for gay communities." *Critical Sociology* 20,3:65–80.

Kuhn, Thomas S. 1962. *The Structure of Scientific Revolutions.* Chicago: University of Chicago Press.

———. 1977. *The Essential Tension.* Chicago: University of Chicago Press.

Laner, Mary R., and Roy Laner. 1979. "Personal style or sexual preference: Why gay men are disliked." *International Review of Modern Sociology* 9:214–28.

———. 1980. "Sexual preference or personal style? Why lesbians are disliked." *JH* 5:339–56.

Lansing, J. Stephen. 1987. "Balinese 'water temples' and the management of irrigation." *AA* 89:326–41.

Laumann, Edward O., Robert T. Michael, John H. Gagnon, and Stuart Michaels. 1994. *The Social Organization of Sexuality.* Chicago: University of Chicago Press.

Lauria, Mickey, and Lawrence Knopp. 1985. "Toward an analysis of the role of gay communities in the urban renaissance." *Urban Geography* 6:152–69.

Lauritsen, John. 1985. "CDC's tables obscure AIDS/drug connection. *Coming Up!* 6,7:6–18.

Leap, William L. 1995a. *Gay Men's English.* Minneapolis: University of Minnesota Press.

————, ed. 1995b. *Beyond the Lavender Lexicon: Gay and Lesbian Language.* New York: Gordon and Breach.

Lee, John Alan. 1976a. "Forbidden colors of love: Patterns of gay love and gay liberation." *JH* 1:401–17.

————. 1976b. *Lovestyles.* London: Dent.

————. 1977. "The romantic heresy." *Canadian Review of Sociology and Anthropology* 12:514–28.

————. 1978a. *Getting Sex.* Toronto: General.

————. 1978b. "Going public." *JH* 3:49–78.

————. 1978c. "Meeting males by mail." In *The Gay Academic,* ed. Louie Crew, pp. 415–27. Palm Springs, Calif.: ETC.

————. 1978d. "The social organization of sexual risk." Canadian Sociology and Anthropological Association meetings, London, Ontario.

————. 1979a. "Comment." *SGCN* 17:9.

————. 1979b. "The gay connection." *Urban Life* 8:175–98.

————. 1979c. "The social organization of sexual risk." *Alternative Lifestyles* 2:69–100. Repr. in Dynes and Donaldson 1992:177–95.

Leeming, David Adams. 1994. *James Baldwin.* New York: Knopf.

Leger, Mark. 1989. "The boy look." *Out/Look* 1,4:44–45.

Lemp, George F., et al. 1990. "Projections of AIDS morbidity and mortality in San Francisco." *Journal of the American Medical Association* 263:1497–1501.

————. 1994. "Seroprevalence of HIV and risk behaviors among young homosexual and bisexual men: The San Francisco/Berkeley Young Men's Survey." *Journal of the American Medical Association* 272:449–54.

Leonard, Karen I. 1992. *Making Ethnic Choices: California's Punjabi Mexican Americans.* Philadelphia: Temple University Press.

Lessor, Roberta, and Katarin Jurich. 1985. "Ideology and politics in the control of contagion: The social organization of AIDS care." Presented at the Society for the Study of Social Problems annual meeting, Washington, D.C.

Levin, Jim. 1981. "The homosexual rights movement in the US to 1979." *Gay Books Bulletin* 7:19–22, 30.

Levine, Martin P. 1979a. "Employment discrimination against gay men." *International Review of Modern Sociology* 9:151–63.

————. 1979b. "Gay ghetto." *JH* 4:363–77. Repr. in Levine 1979c:182–204 and in Dynes and Donaldson 1992:196–218.

————. 1986. "Gay macho." Ph.D. dissertation, New York University.

Levine, Martin P., ed. 1979c. *Gay Men.* New York: Harper and Row.

Levine, Martin P., and Robin Leonard. 1984. "Discrimination against lesbians in the workplace." *Signs* 8:700–710.

Levine, Martin P., and Richard R. Troiden. 1988. "The myth of sexual compulsivity." *JSR* 25:347–63.

Levy, Robert I. 1973. *The Tahitians.* Chicago: University of Chicago Press.

Lewin, Ellen. 1993. *Lesbian Mothers.* Ithaca, N.Y.: Cornell University Press.

Leyland, Winston, ed. 1978. *Gay Sunshine Interviews.* San Francisco: Gay Sunshine Press.

Leznoff, Maurice. 1954. "The homosexual in urban society." M.A. thesis, McGill University.

Leznoff, Maurice, and William A. Westley. 1956. "The homosexual community." *SP* 2:257–63. Repr. in Dynes and Donaldson 1992:219–25.

Licata, Salvatore J. 1981. "The homosexual rights movement in the United States." *JH* 6:161–89.

Lieberson, Jonathan. 1986. "The reality of AIDS." *New York Review of Books* (16 January) 43–48.

Lightweaver, Corinne. 1987. "Bayard Rustin leaves legacy." *San Francisco Sentinel* 15,35 (28 August) 1,13.

Lindenbaum, Joyce P. 1985. "The shattering of an illusion: The problem of competition in lesbian relationships." *Feminist Studies* 11:85–103.

Lindenbaum, Shirley. 1995. "Culture, structure, and change." In *Conceiving Sexuality,* ed. R. Parker and J. Gagnon, pp. 273–78. New York: Routledge.

Linton, Ralph. 1936. *The Study of Man.* New York: Appleton.

Lipton, Jack P., and Alan M. Hershaft. 1985. "On the widespread acceptance of dubious medical findings." *Journal of Health and Social Behavior* 26:336–51.

Lockman, Paul T., Jr. 1982. "African-American gay men." Pacific Sociological Association annual meeting in San Diego.

———. 1984. "Ebony and ivory: The interracial gay male couple." *Lifestyles* 7:44–55.

Loiacano, Darryl. K. 1988. "Gay identity acquisition and the black American experience." M.A. thesis, University of Pennsylvania.

———. 1989. "Gay identity issues among black Americans." *Journal of Counseling and Development* 68:21–25.

Lorde, Audre. 1982. *Zami: A New Spelling of My Name.* Trumansburg, N.Y.: Crossing Press.

———. 1984. *Sister Outsider.* Trumansburg, N.Y.: Crossing Press.

Louganis, Greg. 1995. *Breaking the Surface.* New York: Random House.

Lukes, Steven. 1974. *Power.* New York: MacMillan.

Luo Zhufeng. 1991. *Religion under Socialism in China.* Armonk, N.Y.: M. E. Sharpe.

Lyman, Stanford M. 1984. "Interactionism and the study of race relations at the macro-sociological level." *Symbolic Interaction* 7:107–20.

———. 1988. "Le Conte, Royce, Teggart, Blumer." *Symbolic Interaction* 11:125–43.

Lynch, Frederick. 1992. "Non-ghetto gays: An ethnography of suburban homosexuals." In Herdt 1992:165–201.

Lynch, Michael. 1985. "'Here is adhesiveness': From friendship to homosexuality." *Victorian Studies* 29:67–96.

Mains, Geoff. 1984. *Urban Aborigines.* San Francisco: Gay Sunshine.

Maltz, Daniel, and Ruth Borker. 1982. "A cultural approach to male–female miscommunication." In Gumperz 1982b:195–216.

Manalansan, Martin F., IV. 1991. "Neo-colonial desire." *SOLGAN* 13:37–40.

———. 1993. "(Re)locating the gay Filipino: Resistance, postcolonialism, and identity." *JH* 26,2/3:53–72.

———. 1994. "Searching for community: Gay Filipinos in New York City." *Amerasia* 20:59–73.

March, Andrew L. 1974. *The Idea of China*. New York: Praeger.

Marcus, Eric. 1992. *Making History: The Struggle for Gay and Lesbian Equal Rights*. New York: Harper Collins.

Marcuse, Herbert. 1955. *Eros and Civilization*. Boston: Beacon.

Margolies, Edward. 1986 [1968]. "The Negro church." In *James Baldwin*, ed. Harold Bloom, pp. 59–76. New York: Chelsea House.

Marks, Stephen R. 1987. "Multiple roles and role strain." *ASR* 42:921–36.

Marotta, Toby. 1981. *The Politics of Homosexuality*. New York: Houghton Mifflin.

Marsden, Peter V., and Karen E. Campbell. 1985. "Measuring tie strength." *Social Forces* 63:482–501.

Martin, Biddy. 1988. "Lesbian identity and autobiographical difference[s]." In *Life/Lines: Theorizing Women's Autobiography*, ed. B. Brodzki and C. Schrenck, pp. 77–103. Ithaca, N.Y.: Cornell University Press.

Martin, Del, and Phyllis Lyon. 1972. *Lesbian/Woman*. New York: Bantam.

Martin, John L. 1987. "The impact of AIDS on gay male sexual behavior patterns in New York City." *American Journal of Public Health* 77:578–81.

Martin, John L., and Laura Dean. 1990. "Developing a community sample of gay men for an epidemiological study of AIDS." *American Behavioral Scientist* 33:546–61.

Martin John L., M. A. García, and S. T. Beatrice. 1989. "Sexual behavior changes and HIV antibody in a cohort of New York City gay men." *American Journal of Public Health* 79:501–3.

Massey, Douglas S. 1989. "Social structure, household strategies, and the cumulative causes of migration." Presented at the ASA annual meeting in San Francisco.

Massey, Douglas S., Rafael Alarcón, Jorge Durand, and Humberto González. 1987. *Return to Aztlán: The Social Process of International Migration from Western Mexico*. Berkeley and Los Angeles: University of California Press.

Mattos, Francisco. 1991. "Yellow trash: Racism among GAPIs: A round-table talk." *LG* 4,2:13–20.

Mays, Vickie M. 1995. "Health care concerns of African-American gay men and lesbians." Presented at the Health Sciences, Heterosexism and Homophobia conference at the University of California, San Francisco.

Mays, Vickie M., and Susan D. Cochran. 1988a. "The black women's relationships project: A national survey of black lesbians." In *A Sourcebook of Gay/Lesbian Health Care*, ed. M. Shernoff and W. Scott, pp. 54–62. Washington: National Gay and Lesbian Health Foundation.

———. 1988b. "AIDS and Black Americans." *Public Health Reports* 102:224–31.

Mays, Vickie M., Susan D. Cochran, and Sylvia Rhue. 1993. "The impact of perceived discrimination on the intimate relationships of black lesbians." *JH* 25,4:1–14.

McAdam, Doug. 1982. *Political Process and the Development of Black Insurgency, 1930–1970*. Chicago: University of Chicago Press.

McCombie, Susan C. 1986. "The cultural impact of the 'AIDS test.'" *Social Science and Medicine* 23:455–59.

McIntosh, Mary. 1968. "The homosexual role." *SP* 16:182–92. Repr. in Dynes and Donaldson 1992:226–36.

———. 1993. "Queer theory and the war of the sexes." In *Activating Theory: Lesbian, Gay and Bisexual Politics,* ed. J. Bristow and A. Wilson, pp. 30–52. London: Lawrence and Wishort.

McKay, Claude. 1973 [1928]. *Home to Harlem.* Chatham, N.J.: Chatham.

McKirnan, David J., and Peggy L. Peterson. 1989. "Alcohol and drug use among homosexual men and women." *Addictive Behaviors* 14:545–53.

McKusick Leon, Thomas J. Coates, Stephen F. Morin, L. Pollack, and C. Hoff. 1990. "Longitudinal predictors of reductions in unprotected anal intercourse among gay men in San Francisco: The AIDS Behavioral Research Project." *American Journal of Public Health* 80:978–83.

McKusick, Leon, William Horstman, and Arthur Carfagni. 1983. *Report On Community Reactions to AIDS Survey.* San Francisco: Department of Public Health.

———. 1984. *Reactions to the AIDS Epidemic in Four Groups of San Francisco Gay Men.* San Francisco: Department of Public Health.

———. 1985. "AIDS and sexual behavior reported by gay men in San Francisco." *American Journal of Public Health* 75:493–96.

McNee, Bob. 1983. "It takes one to know one." *Transitions* 14:12–15.

———. 1984. "If you are squeamish . . ." *East Lakes Geographer* 19:16–27.

Mead, George Herbert. 1934. *Mind, Self, and Society.* Chicago: University of Chicago Press.

Melucci, Alberto. 1989. *Nomads of the Present.* Philadelphia: Temple University Press.

Merton, Robert K. 1968. *Social Theory, Social Structure.* New York: Free Press.

Miles, Sara. 1995. "Don't ask, it's hell." *Out* 19:61–5, 108–10.

Miller, Alan. 1988. "Community shaker." *San Francisco Sentinel* 16,26 (24 June) 14.

Miller, Brian. 1978. "Adult sexual resocialization." *Alternative Lifestyles* 1:207–34. Repr. in Dynes and Donaldson 1992:237–64.

———. 1979. "Unpromised paternity: Life styles of gay fathers." In Levine 1979: 239–52.

———. 1983. "Identity conflict and resolution." Ph.D. dissertation, University of Alberta.

———. 1987. "Counseling gay husbands and fathers." In *Gay and Lesbian Parents,* ed. F. Bozett, pp. 175–87. New York: Praeger.

Miller, Brian, and Laud Humphreys. 1980. "Lifestyles and violence." *Qualitative Sociology* 3:169–85.

Miller, Merle. 1972. *What Happened.* New York: Harper & Row.

Mills, C. Wright. 1968. "Comment on Criticism." in *C. Wright Mills and the Power Elite,* ed. G. W. Domhoff and H. B. Ballard, pp. 229–50. Boston: Beacon.

Mishima, Yukio. 1958 [1949]. *Confessions of a Mask.* New York: New Directions.

Mitchell, Lionel. 1980 [1973]. *Traveling Light.* New York: Seaview Books.

Miyamoto, S. Frank. 1963. "The impact on research of different conceptions of role." *Sociological Inquiry* 33:114–23.

———. 1964 [1950]. "The process of intergroup tension and conflict." In *Contribu-*

tions to Urban Sociology, ed. Ernest Burgess and Donald Bogue, pp. 389–403. Chicago: University of Chicago Press.

————. 1973. "Self, motivation, and symbolic interactionist theory." In *Human Nature and Collective Behavior*, ed. Tamotsu Shibutani, pp. 271–85. Toronto: Prentice-Hall.

Moerman, Michael. 1965. "Ethnic identification in complex civilization: Who are the Lue?" *AA* 66:1215–30.

Mohr, Richard. 1988. *Gays/Justice*. New York: Columbia University Press.

Monette, Paul. 1992. *Becoming a Man*. New York: Harcourt Brace Jovanovich.

Monteagudo, Jesse. 1986. "Books and gay identity—a personal look." In *Gay Life: Leisure, Love, and Living for the Contemporary Gay Male*, ed. Eric Rofes, pp. 210–18. Garden City, New York: Doubleday.

Montini, Theresa. 1995. "Foreclosure of disclosure." Presented at the Pacific Sociological Association meeting in San Francisco.

Moore, Wilbert E. 1978. "Functionalism." In Bottomore and Nisbet 1978:321–61.

Moraga, Cherríe. 1984. *Giving Up the Ghost*. Los Angeles: West End Press.

Moraga, Cherríe, and Gloria Anzaldúa, eds. 1981. *The Bridge Called My Back: Writings by Radical Women of Color*. Watertown, Mass.: Persephone Press.

Morris, Rosalind C. 1994. "Three sexes and four sexualities: Redressing the discourses on gender and sexuality in contemporary Thailand." *Positions* 2:15–43.

Morrison, Toni. 1970. *Bluest Eye*. New York: Holt, Rinehart and Winston.

Moses, Alice E. 1978. *Identity Management in Lesbian Women*. New York: Praeger.

Mott, Luiz, and Aroldo Assunção. 1988. "Loves labors lost: Five letters from a seventeenth-century Portuguese sodomite." *JH* 16:91–101.

Mount, Douglas. 1972. Foreword to *The Queens' Vernacular: A Gay Lexicon* by Bruce Rodgers. San Francisco: Straight Arrow Books.

Murray, Stephen O. 1979a. "The art of gay insulting." *Anthropological Linguistics* 21:211–23.

————. 1979b. "Institutional elaboration of a quasi-ethnic community." *International Review of Modern Sociology* 9:165–78.

————. 1979c. "Screening information: The social psychology of 'my type.'" *SGCN* 17:6–8.

————. 1979d. "The 'species homosexual' as an aberration of late capitalism?" *SGCN* 18:7–8.

————. 1979e. "The uniqueness of San Francisco." *SGCN* 17:8–10.

————. 1980a. "Cloning." Manuscript.

————. 1980b. "Gatekeepers and the 'Chomskian revolution.'" *Journal of the History of the Behavioral Sciences* 16:73–88.

————. 1980c. "The invisibility of scientific scorn." In *The Don Juan Papers*, ed. Richard de Mille, pp. 188–202. Santa Barbara, Calif.: Ross-Erikson.

————. 1981. "Labels and labeling: The prototype semantics of 'gay community.'" *Working Papers of the Language Behavior Research Laboratory* [Berkeley] 50.

————. 1983a. "Fuzzy sets and abominations." *Man* 19:396–99.

————. 1983b. "Mother Camp, Father Camp, concentration camp?" Manuscript.

————. 1983c. "Ritual insults in stigmatized subcultures." *Maledicta* 7:189–211.

————. 1984. *Social Theory Homosexual Realities*. New York: Gay Academic Union.

———. 1985. "Remembering Michel Foucault." *SGCN* 43: 9–12.

———. 1986. "Edward Sapir in the 'Chicago School of Sociology.'" In *New Perspectives on Language, Culture and Personality,* ed. W. Cowan, M. Fox, and K. Koerner, pp. 241–91. Amsterdam: Benjamins.

———. 1987a. "A loaded gun: Some thoughts on American concentration camps and the AIDS epidemic." *New York Native* (27 July) 15–17.

———. 1987b. *Male Homosexuality in Central and South America.* New York: Gay Academic Union.

———. 1988a. "Homosexual acts and selves in early modern Europe." *JH* 16: 421–39.

———. 1988b. "The reception of anthropological work in sociology journals, 1922–1951. *Journal of the History of the Behavioral Sciences* 24: 135–51.

———. 1988c. Review of Weeks 1985. *JH* 16: 183–86.

———. 1988d. "W. I. Thomas, behaviorist ethnologist." *Journal of the History of the Behavioral Sciences* 24: 381–91.

———. 1989a. "AIDS, gay men and their invisible sociology." *ASA Footnotes* 17,3: 8.

———. 1989b. "Urban land values, public safety, and visible gay cultures." *SLGCN* 59: 7–8.

———. 1990a. "Africa, Sub-Saharan." *The Encyclopedia of Homosexuality,* 1: 22–24. New York: Garland.

———. 1990b. "Sociology." *The Encyclopedia of Homosexuality,* 2: 1219–27. New York: Garland.

———. 1991a. "Ethnic differences in interpretive conventions and the reproduction of inequality in everyday life." *Symbolic Interaction* 14: 187–204.

———. 1991b. "Social constructionism and ancient Greek homosexuality." *SOLGAN* 16: 19–26.

———. 1991c. "'Homosexual occupations' in Mesoamerica?" *JH* 21: 57–64. (Revised version in Murray 1995a: 71–79.)

———. 1992a. *Oceanic Homosexualities.* New York: Garland.

———. 1992b. "The 'underdevelopment' of gay homosexuality in Mesoamerica, Peru and Thailand." In Plummer 1992: 28–38.

———. 1992c. "Components of *gay community* in San Francisco." In Herdt 1992: 107–46.

———. 1993. "Writing with others." Presented at the annual AAA meeting in Washington, D.C.

———. 1994a. "The obdurateness of AIDS-risk-group categories." *Contemporary Sociology* 23: 751–53.

———. 1994b. "Subordinating native cosmologies to the empire of gender." *Current Anthropology* 35: 59–61.

———. 1994c. *Theory Groups and the Study of Language in North America.* Amsterdam: John Benjamins.

———. 1995a. *Latin American Male Homosexualities.* Albuquerque: University of New Mexico Press.

———. 1995b. "Male homosexuality in Guatemala: Possible insights and certain confusions of sleeping with natives." In *Lesbian and Gay Ethnography,* ed. Ellen Lewin and William Leap. Urbana: University of Illinois Press, forthcoming.

―――. 1995c. "Some Southwest Asian and North African terms for homosexual roles." *ASB* 23:623–29.

―――. 1995d. "Stigma transformation and relexification in the international diffusion of *gay*." In Leap 1995b:236–60.

―――. 1996. "The Sohari *khanith*." In Murray and Roscoe 1996. Forthcoming.

―――. 1997. "Kamau, a 26-year-old Kikuyu." In Murray and Roscoe 1997. Forthcoming.

Murray, Stephen O., and Kent Gerard. 1981. "Renaissance sodomite subcultures?" *Onder Vrouwen, Onder Mannen* 1:182–96.

Murray, Stephen O., and Keelung Hong. 1994. *Taiwanese Culture, Taiwanese Society.* Lanham, Md.: University Press of America.

Murray, Stephen O., and Theresa Montini. 1994. "The social implications of the search for 'the gay gene.'" Manuscript.

Murray, Stephen O., and Peter M. Nardi. 1979. "The second face of power in micro perspective." Presented at the ASA annual meeting in Boston.

Murray, Stephen O., and Kenneth W. Payne. 1985. "The remedicalization of homophobia: 'Scientific evidence' and the San Francisco bathhouse closure decision." Presented at the Society for the Study of Social Problems meeting in Washington, D.C.

―――. 1988. "AIDS and the promiscuity paradigm." *California Sociologist* 11:13–54. Repr. in Dynes and Donaldson 1992:119–60.

―――. 1989. "The social classification of AIDS in American epidemiology." *Medical Anthropology* 10:115–28.

Murray, Stephen O., Joseph H. Rankin, and Dennis W. Magill. 1981. "Strong ties and academic jobs." *Sociology of Work and Occupations* 8:119–36.

Murray, Stephen O., and Will Roscoe. 1996. *Islamic Homosexualities.* New York: New York University Press.

―――. 1997. *African Homosexualities.* New York: New York University Press.

Mutchler, Matt. 1995. "The Pride Mission: AIDS, community building, and safer sex among a micro-cohort of the AIDS generation." Presented at the Pacific Sociological Association meetings in San Francisco.

Myrdal, Gunnar. 1944. *An American Dilemma.* New York: Carnegie.

Myslik, Wayne D. 1995. "Renegotiating the social/sexual identities of places: Gay communities as safe havens or sites of resistance." To appear in *(Re)placing: Destablising Geographies of Gender and Sexuality,* ed. Nancy Duncan. New York: Routledge.

Nanda, Serena. 1990. *Neither Man Nor Woman: The Hijra of India.* Belmont, Calif.: Wadsworth.

Nardi, Peter M. 1982. "Alcoholism and homosexuality." *JH* 7:9–25.

―――. 1992a. *Men's Friendships.* London: Sage.

―――. 1992b. "That's what friends are for: Friends as family in the gay and lesbian community." In Plummer 1992:108–20.

―――. 1994. "Friendship in the lives of gay men and lesbians." *Journal of Social and Personal Relationships* 11:185–99.

Nardi, Peter M., and Ralph Bolton. 1991. "Gay-bashing: Violence and aggression against gay men and lesbians." In *Targets of Violence and Aggression,* ed. R. Baenninger, pp. 349–400. New York: Elsevier.

Nardi, Peter M., David Sanders, and Judd Marmor, eds. 1994. *Growing Up before Stonewall: Life Stories of some Gay Men.* New York: Routledge.

Nelson, Emmanuel S. 1991. "Critical deviance: Homophobia and the reception of James Baldwin's fiction." *Journal of American Culture* 14,3:91–96.

Nestle, Joan. 1987. *A Restricted Country.* Ithaca, N.Y.: Firebrand Books.

Newton, Esther. 1978 [1972]. *Mother Camp.* Chicago: University of Chicago Press.

———. 1984. "The mythic mannish lesbian." *Signs* 9:557–75.

———. 1993. *Cherry Grove.* Boston: Beacon.

Nielson, François. 1980. "The Flemish movement in Belgium after World War II." *ASR* 45:76–94.

Niles, Blair. 1992 [1931]. *Strange Brother.* Boston: Alyson.

Nisbet, Robert A. 1966. *The Sociological Tradition.* New York: Basic Books.

Noel, Thomas J. 1978. "Gay bars and the emergence of the Denver homosexual community." *Social Science Journal* 15:59–74.

Norman, Colin. 1986. "Sex and needles, not insects and pigs, spread AIDS in Florida town." *Science* 234:415–17.

Novick, Alvin. 1985. "Quarantine and AIDS." *Connecticut Medicine* 49:81–83.

Noye, Nii Narh. 1997. "West African men who have sex with men." Forthcoming in Murray and Roscoe 1997.

Nugent, Bruce. 1983 [1926]. "Smoke, lilies and jade." In Smith 1983:17–30.

Nungesser, Lon G. 1983. *Homosexual Acts, Actions, and Identities.* New York: Praeger.

Oakley, Ann. 1974. *The Sociology of Housework.* New York: Pantheon.

Oberschall, Anthony. 1973. *Social Conflicts and Social Movements.* Toronto: Prentice-Hall.

Ogburn, William F. 1928. *Family Life Today.* Boston: Houghton-Mifflin.

———. 1933. "Changing functions of the family." *Journal of Home Economics* 25:660.

Ogburn, William F., and M. F. Nimkoff. 1955. *Technology and the Changing Family.* Boston: Houghton-Mifflin.

Oliver, Pamela E., and Gerald Marwell. 1988. "The paradox of group size in collective action: A theory of critical mass II." *ASR* 53:1–8.

Omark, Richard C. 1978. "A comment on the homosexual role." *JSR* 14:273–74.

Omosupe, Ekua. 1991. "Black/Lesbian/Bulldagger." *Differences* 3:101–11.

Opler, Morris E. 1967. "Franz Boas: Religion and theory." *AA* 69.171–75.

Opp, Karl-Dieter. 1988. "Grievances and participation in social movements." *American Sociological Review* 53:853–64.

Oppenheimer, Gerald M. 1988. "In the eye of the storm." In Fee and Fox 1988:267–300.

Oresko, Robert. 1988. "Homosexuality and the court elites of early modern France." *JH* 16,1:105–28.

Ortiz, Ricardo L. 1993. "Sexuality degree zero: Pleasure and power in the novels of John Rechy, Arturo Islas, and Michael Nava." *JH* 26,2/3:111–26.

Otis, Margaret. 1913. "A perversion not commonly noted." *Journal of Abnormal Psychology* 8:113–16.

Parker, Canaan. 1992. *The Color of Trees.* Boston: Alyson.

Parkin, David. 1978. "Social stratification." In Bottomore and Nisbet 1978:599–632.

Parsons, Talcott. 1951. *The Social System.* Glencoe, Ill.: Free Press.

————. 1960. *Structure and Process in Modern Society*. New York: Free Press.

————. 1967. "Full citizenship for the Negro American?" In *Sociological Theory and Modern Society*, pp. 422–65. New York: Free Press.

Parsons, Talcott, and Robert F. Bales. 1955. *Family, Socialization and Interaction Process*. Glencoe, Ill.: Free Press.

Partridge, Edward B. 1958. *The Broken Compass: A Study of the Major Comedies of Ben Jonson*. New York: Columbia University Press.

Perlstadt, Harry, and Russell E. Holmes. 1987. "The role of public opinion polling in health legislation." *American Journal of Public Health* 77:612–14.

Perry, M. J., et al. 1994. "High risk sexual behavior and alcohol consumption among bar-going gay men." *AIDS* 8:1321–24.

Perry, Mary E. 1980. *Crime and Society in Early Modern Seville*. Hanover, N.H.: University Press of New England.

Peterson John L., et al. 1992. "High-risk sexual behavior and condom use among gay and bisexual African-American men." *American Journal of Public Health* 82: 1490–94.

Phillips, Herbert P, ed. 1987. *Modern Thai Literature with an Ethnographic Interpretation*. Honolulu: University of Hawaii Press.

Pinard, Maurice, and Richard Hamilton. 1988. "Intellectuals and the leadership of social movements." *McGill Working Paper on Social Behavior.*

Pinckney, Darryl. 1987. "The outsider." *New York Review of Books* (17 Dec.) 15–21.

Pitt-Rivers, Julian. 1973. "Race in Latin America." *Archives Européenees de Sociologie* 14:3–31.

Piven, Frances Fox, and Richard A. Cloward. 1971. *Regulating the Poor: The Functions of Public Welfare*. New York: Pantheon.

Plummer, Kenneth. 1975. *Sexual Stigma*. Boston: Routledge and Kegan Paul.

————. 1981a. "Social change, personal change and the life history method: researching the social construction of sexuality." In *Open University, An Introduction to Sociology*, pp. 15–27.

————. 1988. "Organizing AIDS." In *Social Aspects of AIDS*, ed. P. Aggleton and H. Homan, pp. 20–52. London: Falmer.

————. 1989. "Lesbian and gay youth in England." *JH* 17:195–224.

————. 1995. *Telling Sexual Stories*. New York: Routledge.

Plummer, Kenneth, ed. 1981b. *The Makings of the Modern Homosexual*. London: Hutchinson.

————. 1992. *Modern Homosexualities*. New York: Routledge.

Ponse, Barbara. 1978. *Identity in the Lesbian World*. Westport, Conn.: Greenwood.

Preston, John. 1983. *Franny, the Queen of Provincetown*. Boston: Alyson.

————. 1993a. *My Life as a Pornographer and Other Indecent Acts*. New York: Masquerade Books.

————. 1993c. "John Preston on himself, his work, and S/M in the '90s." *Bay Area Reporter* 23,44 (4 November) 33, 41.

Preston, John, ed. 1988. *Personal Dispatches: Writers Confront AIDS*. New York: St. Martin's Press.

————. 1991. *Hometowns: Gay Men Write about Where They Belong*. New York: Dutton.

————. 1992a. *Flesh and the Word*. New York: Plume.

———. 1992b. *A Member of the Family: Gay Men Write About Their Families.* New York: Dutton.

———. 1993b. *Flesh and the Word 2.* New York: Plume.

Rath, R., and R. G. Sircar. 1960. "Inter-caste relations." *Journal of Social Psychology* 51:8–23.

Ratti, Rakesh. 1993. *A Lotus of Another Color: An Unfolding of the South Asian Gay and Lesbian Experience.* Boston: Alyson.

Read, Kenneth E. 1980. *Other Voices.* Novato, Calif: Chandler and Sharp.

Rechy, John. 1961. *City of Night.* New York: Grove Press.

Reckless, Walter C. 1926. "The distribution of commercialized vice in the city." In *The Urban Community*, ed. E. Burgess, pp. 192–205. Chicago: University of Chicago Press.

Redfield, Robert. 1941. *The Folk Culture of Yucatan.* Chicago: University of Chicago Press.

———. 1950. *The Village That Chose Progress.* Chicago: University of Chicago Press.

Redfield, Robert, Ralph Linton, and Melville Herskovits. 1936. "Memorandum on the study of acculturation." *AA* 38:149–52.

Reese, A. 1966. "Information networks in labor markets." *American Economics Review* 57:559–66.

Reh, Lawrence. 1987. "Shouts and whispers: The legacy of James Baldwin." *San Francisco Sentinel* 18 December, 19, 22,30.

Reid-Pharr, Robert F. 1993. "The spectacle of blackness." *Radical America* 24,4: 57–66.

Reimoneng, Alden. 1993. "Countee Cullen's Uranian 'Soul Windows.'" *JH* 26,2/3: 143–65.

Reiss, Albert J. 1961. "The social integration of 'queers' and 'peers.'" *SP* 9:102–20. Repr. in Dynes and Donaldson 1992:296–314.

Rich, Adrienne. 1980. "Compulsive heterosexuality and lesbian existence." *Signs* 5: 631–60.

Richwald, Gary A., et al. 1988. "Sexual activities in bathhouses in Los Angeles County." *JSR* 25:169–80.

Riddle, Dorothy I., and Stephen Morin F. 1977. "Removing the stigma." *American Psychological Association Monitor* (November) 16, 28.

Riggs, Marlon. 1991a. "Black macho revisited: Reflections of a SNAP! queen." In Hemphill 1991a:253–57.

———. 1991b. "Tongues untied." In Hemphill 1991a:200–205.

Rinella, Jack. 1993. "Leather friendship." *San Francisco Sentinel* (22 September) 3.

Rist, Darell Yates. 1989. "AIDS as apocalypse: The deadly cost of an obsession." *The Nation* (13 February) 181–83.

Robert, J. R. 1981. *African-American Lesbians: An Annotated Bibliography.* Tallahassee, Fla.: Naiad Press.

Roberts, James Charles. 1986. "A light that failed." In Beam 1986:87–92.

Robinson, David. 1976. *From Drinking to Alcoholism.* New York: Wiley.

Robinson, Paul A. 1969. *The Freudian Left.* New York: Harper and Row.

Rocke, Michael J. 1988. "Sodomites in fifteenth-century Tuscany." *JH* 16:17–31.

Román, David. 1993. "*Fierce Love* and fierce response." *JH* 26,2:195–219.

Rosaldo, Renato. 1987. *Culture and Truth: The Remaking of Social Analysis.* Boston: Beacon.

Roscoe, Will. 1987. "Bibliography of berdache and alternative gender roles among North American Indians." *JH* 14:81–171.

———. 1988a. "Making history: The challenge of gay and lesbian studies." *JH* 15,3/4:1–40.

———. 1988c. "What child is this?" *San Francisco Jung Institute Library Journal* 8: 41–60.

———. 1991a. *The Zuni Man–Woman.* Albuquerque: University of New Mexico Press.

———. 1991b. Review of Nanda 1990. *JH* 21:117–25.

———. 1994. "How to become a berdache." In Herdt 1994:329–72.

———. 1995a. *Queer Spirits.* Boston: Beacon.

———. 1995b. "'Was We'Wha a homosexual?': Native-American survivance and the two-spirit tradition." *GLQ* 2:193–235.

Roscoe, Will, ed. 1988b. *Living the Spirit: A Gay American Indian Anthology.* New York: St. Martin's Press.

———. 1996. *Radically Queer: The Story of Gay Liberation in the Words of Its Founder, Harry Hay.* Boston: Beacon.

Rosenberg, Morris. 1979. *Conceiving the Self.* New York: Basic Books.

Rosenzweig, Julie M., and Wendy C. Lebow. 1992. "Femme on the streets, butch in the sheets: Lesbian sex-roles, dyadic adjustment, and sexual satisfaction." *JH* 23,3:1–20.

Ross, Michael W. 1984. "Psychosocial factors to admitting to homosexuality in sexually-transmitted disease clinics." *Sexually Transmitted Diseases* 12:83–87.

Rosse, Irving C. 1892. "Sexual hypochondriasis and perversion of the genetic instinct." *Journal of Nervous and Mental Disease* 19:785–811.

Rotenberg, Mordecai. 1974. "Self-labeling." *Sociological Review* 22:335–54.

Roth, Julius. 1957. "Ritual and magic in the control of contagion." *ASR* 22: 10–14.

Rothman, David J., and Harold Edgar. 1992. "Scientific rigor and medical realities: Placebo trials in cancer and AIDS research." In Fee and Fox 1992:194–206.

Rotundo, E. Anthony. 1989. "Romantic friendship: Male intimacy and middle-class youth in the Northern United States, 1800–1900." *Journal of Social History* 21: 1–25.

Rougemont, Denis de. 1955. *Love in the Western World.* New York: Pantheon.

Rubin, Gayle. 1975. "The traffic in women." In *Toward an Anthropology of Women,* ed. Rayna Reiter, pp. 157–210. New York: Monthly Review Press.

———. 1982. "The leather menace: Comments on politics and S/M." In *Coming to Power,* pp. 192–227. Boston: Alyson.

———. 1984. "Thinking sex." In *Pleasure and Danger: Exploring Female Sexuality,* ed. Carol Vance, pp. 300–309. New York: Routledge.

———. 1991. "The Catacombs: A temple of the butthole." In Thompson 1991: 119–41.

Ruggiero, Guido. 1985. *The Boundaries of Eros: Sex, Crime, and Sexuality in Renaissance Venice.* New York: Oxford University Press.

Rust, Paula C. 1992. "The politics of sexual identity: Sexual attraction and behavior among lesbian and bisexual women." *SP* 39:366–86.

———. 1993a. " Coming out in the age of social constructionism: Sexual identity formation among lesbian and bisexual women." *Gender and Society* 71:50–77.

———. 1993b. "Neutralizing the political threat of the marginal woman: Lesbians' beliefs about bisexual women." *JSR* 30:214–28.

Sable, Alan. 1979. "A gay sociologist on the ghetto." *Advocate* (6 September) 16–18.

Sagarin, Edward. 1966. "Strategies and ideology in an association of deviants [New York Mattachine Society]." Ph.D. dissertation, New York University. Pub. New York: Arno, l975.

———. 1969. *Odd Man In.* Chicago: Quadrangle.

Saghir, Michael T., and Eli Robins. 1973. *Male and Female Homosexuality.* Baltimore: William and Wilken.

Saks, Adrien, and Wayne Curtis, eds. 1994. *Revelations: Gay Men's Coming-Out Stories.* Boston: Alyson.

Samois editorial collective. 1981, 1982. *Coming to Power.* Boston: Alyson.

Samuel, Michael, and Warren Winkelstein, Jr. 1987. "Prevalence of HIV in ethnic minority homosexual/bisexual men." *Journal of the American Medical Association* 257:1901–2.

Sanders, Jimy M., and Victor Nee. 1987. "Limits of ethnic solidarity." *ASR* 52: 745–67.

Sandstrom, Kent L. 1990. "Confronting deadly disease: The drama of identity construction among gay men with AIDS." *Journal of Contemporary Ethnography* 19: 271–94.

San Miguel, Christopher L., and Jim Millham. 1976. "The role of cognitive and situational variables in aggression toward homosexuals." *JH* 2:11–27.

Sarbin, Theodore R. 1982. "Role transition as social drama." In *Role Transition,* ed. V. Allen and E. Vilera, pp. 21–37. New York: Plenum.

Sarbin Theodore R., and V. L. Allen. 1968. "Role theory." in *Handbook of Social Psychology,* ed. G. Lindsey and E. Aronson, pp. 448–57. Reading, Mass.: Addison-Wesley.

Sawyer, Ethal. 1965. "A Study of a Public Lesbian Community." M.A. thesis, Washington University, St. Louis, Mo.

Saylor, Steven. 1980. "The blue light." *Malebox* (July). Repr. in Preston 1992a: 125–57.

Schaefer, Sigrid. 1976. "Sexual and social problems of lesbians." *JSR* 12:50–69.

Schiller, Greg. 1982. "S&M: the importance of subculture." Presented at the ASA annual meeting in San Francisco.

Schmitt, Arno. 1992. "Different approaches to male–male sexuality/eroticism from Morocco to Uzbekistan." In *Sexuality and Eroticism among Males in Moslem Societies,* ed. A. Schmitt and J. Sofer, pp. 1–24. New York: Haworth.

Schneider, Beth E. 1984. "Peril and promise: Lesbians' workplace participation." In Darty and Potter 1984:21–30.

———. 1987. "Coming out at work." *Work and Occupations* 13:463–87.

———. 1992. "Lesbian politics and AIDS work." In Plummer 1992:160–74.

Schor, Juliet. 1991. *The Overworked American: The Unexpected Decline of Leisure.* New York: Basic Books.

Schultz, S., S. Friedman, A. Kristal, and D. J. Sencer. 1984. "Declining rates of rectal and pharyngeal gonorrhea among males in New York City." *Morbidity and Mortality Weekly Report* 33:295–97.

Schur, Edwin M. 1965. *Crimes without Victims*. Toronto: Prentice-Hall.

Schwartz, Theodore. 1978. "Where is the Culture?" In *The Making of Psychological Anthropology*, ed. George Spindler, pp. 419–41. Berkeley and Los Angeles: University of California Press.

Sciulli, David. 1988. "Reconsidering Blumer's corrective against the excesses of functionalism." *Symbolic Interaction* 11:69–84.

Scollon, Ronald, and Suzanne Scollon. 1982. *Linguistic Convergence*. San Francisco: Academic Press.

Scott, James C. 1985. *Weapons of the Weak: Everyday Forms of Peasant Resistance*. New Haven: Yale University Press.

———. 1990. *Domination and the Arts of Resistance*. New Haven: Yale University Press.

Seale, John. 1985. "How to turn a disease into VD." *New Scientist* 1461:38–41.

Sears, James T. 1991. *Growing Up Gay in the South*. Binghamton, New York: Haworth.

Sedgwick, Eve Kosofsky. 1991. "How to bring your kids up gay." *Social Text* 29:18–27.

Seidman, Steven. 1992. *Embattled Eros: Sexual Politics and Ethics in Contemporary America*. New York: Routledge.

Selby, Henry A., Jr. 1974. *Zapotec Deviance*. Austin: University of Texas Press.

Shepherd, Reginald. 1986. "On not being white." In Beam 1986:46–57.

Sherman, Suzanne. 1992. *Lesbian and Gay Marriage: Private Commitments, Public Ceremonies*. Philadelphia: Temple University Press.

Shi, Nicholas. 1993. "Footsteps in my father's path." *LG* "Families" issue, 6–9.

Shibutani, Tamotsu. 1955. "Reference groups as perspectives." *AJS* 60:562–69.

———. 1961. *Society and Personality*. Toronto: Prentice-Hall.

Shibutani, Tamotsu, and Kian Kwan. 1965. *Ethnic Stratification*. New York: Macmillan.

Shilts, Randy. 1982. *The Mayor of Castro Street: The Life and Times of Harvey Milk*. New York: St. Martin's Press.

———. 1987. *And the Band Played On*. New York: St. Martin's Press.

Shockley, Ann Allen. 1979. "The black lesbian in American literature." *Conditions* 2,2:133–42.

Shumante, Richard. 1995. "Brock out." *10 Percent* 3,12:56–59, 72–73.

Sieber, Sam D. 1974. "Toward a theory of role accumulation." *ASR* 39:567–78.

Siegel, Karolynn, Laurie Bauman, Grace Christ, and Susan Krown. 1988. "Patterns of change in sexual behavior among gay men in New York City." *ASB* 17:481–97.

Silber, Linda. 1990. "Negotiating sexual identity: Non-lesbians in a lesbian feminist community." *JSR* 27:131–40.

Silva, John. 1992. "The romantic banquero." *LG* "Smut" issue, 10–15.

Silverman, Mervyn F. 1986. "Addressing public health concerns of the city of San Francisco. In *AIDS and Patient Management*, ed. M. Witt., pp. 27–35. Owing Hill, Md.: Rynd.

Simmel, Georg. 1950 [1903]. "The metropolis and mental health." In *The Sociology of Georg Simmel,* ed. K. Wolff, pp. 409–24. New York: Free Press.

Simmons, Ron. 1991. "Some thoughts on the challenges facing black gay intellectuals." In Hemphill 1991a:211–27.

Simon, William. 1994. "Deviance as history: the future of perversion." *ASB* 23:1–20.

Simon, William, and John Gagnon. 1967. "Homosexuality: The formulation of a sociological perspective." *Journal of Health and Social Behavior* 8:177–85. Repr. in Gagnon and Simon 1973:129–75.

———. 1986. "Sexual scripts." *ASB* 15:97–120.

Siu, Helen F. 1993. "Cultural identity and the politics of difference in South China." *Daedalus* 122,2:19–43.

Skinner, G. William. 1964. "Marketing and social structure in rural China." *Journal of Asian Studies* 24:3–23.

Slater, Jack. 1992. "New year." In *Men on Men 4,* ed. G. Stambolian, pp. 216–44. New York: Plume.

Slim, Iceberg. 1969. *Mama African-American Widow.* Los Angeles: Holloway.

Smith, Charles Michael. 1986. "Bruce Nugent: Bohemian of the Harlem Renaissance." In Beam 1986:209–20.

Smith, Max C. 1986. "By the year 2000." In Beam 1986:224–29.

Smith, Michael J., ed. 1983. *Black Men/White Men: A Gay Anthology.* San Francisco: Gay Sunshine Press.

Snow, David A., and Leroy Anderson. 1987. "Identity work among the homeless: The verbal construction and avowal of personal identities." *AJS* 92:1336–71.

Snow, David A., Louis Zurcher, and Sheldon Ekland-Olson. 1980. "Social networks and social movements: A microstructural approach to differential recruitment." *ASR* 45:787–801.

Soares, John V. 1979. "African-American and gay." In Levine 1979c:263–74.

Somé, Malidoma Patrice. 1994. *Of Water and the Spirit.* New York: Tarcher/Putnam.

Soneschein, David. 1968. "The ethnography of male homosexual relationships." *JSR* 4:69–83.

Sontag, Susan. 1964. "Notes on camp." *Partisan Review* 31. Repr. in *Against Method,* pp. 277–93. New York: Dell, 1969.

———. 1980 [1975]. "Fascinating fascism." In *Under the Sign of Saturn,* pp. 73–105. New York: Farrar, Straus, Giroux.

Southern, David. 1981. "An American dilemma." *Journal of the History of Sociology* 3:81–107.

Speare, Alden, Jr. 1971. "A cost–benefit model of rural to urban migration in Taiwan." *Population Studies* 25:117–30.

Spector, Malcolm. 1973. Secrecy in job seeking among government attorneys." *Urban Life and Culture* 2:211–29.

Spiro, Melford E. 1973. "Social change and functional analysis." *Ethos* 1:263–97.

Stall, Ron, and James Wiley. 1988. "A comparison of drug and alcohol use of homosexual and heterosexual men." *Drug and Alcohol Dependence* 22:63–74.

Standing, Hilary. 1992. "AIDS: Conceptual and methodological issues in researching sexual behaviour in sub-Saharan Africa." *Social Science and Medicine* 34:475–83.

Starr, Paul. 1982. *The Social Transformation of American Medicine.* New York: Basic Books.

312

Steakley, James. 1975. *The Homosexual Emancipation Movement in Germany.* New York: Arno.

Stein, Arlene. 1989. "Style wars and the new lesbianism." *Out/Look* 1,4:34–43.

Stelling, Joan, and Rue Bucher. 1973. "Vocabularies of realism in professional socialization." *Social Science and Medicine* 7:661–75.

Stephan, G. Edward, and Douglas R. McMullin. 1982. "Tolerance of sexual nonconformity: City size as a situational and early learning determinant." *ASR* 47:411–15.

Stouffer, Samuel A., et al. 1949. *The American Soldier.* Princeton, N.J.: Princeton University Press.

Strauss, Anselm, Shizuko Fagerhaugh, Barbara Suczek, and Carolyn Wiener. 1985. *Social Organization of Medical Work.* Chicago: University of Chicago Press.

Styles, Joseph. 1979. "Insider/outsider: Researching the gay baths." *Urban Life* 8:135–52.

Sudman, Seymour, and Graham Kalton. 1986. "New developments in the sampling of special populations." *Annual Review of Sociology* 12:401–29.

Sullivan, Gerard. 1990. "Discrimination and self-concept of homosexuals before the gay-liberation movement." *Biography* 13:203–21.

Suttles, Gerald. 1972. *The Social Construction of Communities.* University of Chicago Press.

Sutton, Willis A., and Thomas Munson. 1976. "Definitions of community, 1954–1973." Presented at the ASA annual meeting in New York City.

Swallow, Jean. 1983. *Out from Under: Sober Dykes.* San Francisco: Spinsters Ink.

Sweet, Roxanne Thayer. 1968. "Political and social action in homophile organizations." Ph.D. dissertation, University of California, Berkeley.

Tagaki, Dana. 1994. "Maiden voyage: Excursion into sexuality and identity politics in Asian America." *Amerasia* 20:1–17.

Tan, Joel. 1992. "Memoirs of an invisible man." *LG* "Homelands" issue, 34–37.

Tannen, Deborah. 1990. *You Just Don't Understand!* New York: Morrow.

Tanner, P. M. 1978. *Lesbian Couples.* Lexington, Mass.: Lexington Books.

Tattelman, Ira. 1995. "The rise and fall of the gay bathhouse." *Harvard Gay and Lesbian Review* 2,2:28–30.

Taylor, Clark L. 1978. "*El ambiente:* Homosexual social life in Mexico City." Ph.D. dissertation, University of California, Berkeley.

Taylor, Verta. 1989. "Social movement continuity." *ASR* 54:761–75.

Taylor, Verta, and Nancy Whittier. 1992. "Collective identity in social movements communities: Lesbian feminist mobilization." In *Frontiers in Social Movement Theory,* ed. Aldon Morris and C. Mueller, pp. 104–29. New Haven: Yale University Press.

Teal, Donn. 1971. *Gay Militants.* New York: Stein and Day.

Thomas, W. I., and Florian Znaniecki. 1927. *The Polish Peasant in Europe and America.* New York: Knopf.

Thompson, Mark. 1987. *Gay Spirit.* New York: St. Martin's.

———. 1994. *Gay Soul.* Boston: Beacon.

———, ed. 1991. *Leatherfolks.* Boston: Alyson.

Thongthiraj, Took Took. 1994. "Toward a struggle against invisibility: Love between women in Thailand." *Amerasia* 20:45–58.

Thorne, Barrie. 1993. *Gender Play: Girls and Boys in School*. New Brunswick, N.J.: Rutgers University Press.

Thornton, Russell, and Peter M. Nardi. 1975. "Dynamics of role acquisition." *AJS* 80:870–84.

Thurman, Wallace. 1929. *The Blacker the Berry*. New York: Macaulay.

Tienda, Marta, and Franklin D. Wilson. 1992. "Migration and the earnings of Hispanic men." *ASR* 57:661–78.

Timmons, Stuart. 1990. *The Trouble with Harry Hay*. Boston: Alyson.

Tinney, James S. 1983. "Struggles of a Black Pentecostal." In Smith 1983:167–71.

———. 1986. "Why a black gay church?" In Beam 1986:70–86.

Tobin Kay, and Randy Wicker. 1972. *Gay Crusaders*. New York: Paperback Library.

Toch, Hans. 1965. *The Social Psychology of Social Movements*. Indianapolis: Bobbs-Merrill.

Tocqueville, Alexis de. 1856. *L'ancien régime et la révolution*. Paris: Michel Levy Frères.

Touraine, Alain. 1985. "An introduction to the study of social movements." *Social Research* 52:747–87.

Townsend, Larry. 1972. *The Leatherman's Handbook*. San Francisco: Le Salon.

———. 1983. *The Leatherman's Handbook II*. San Francisco: Le Salon.

Tracy, Steve. 1989. "Straights to hell: Gay-only issue clouds Gay Softball World Series." *The Advocate* 535:50–51.

Tremble, Bob, Margaret Schneider, and Carol Appathurai. 1989. "Growing up gay or lesbian in a multicultural context." *JH* 17:253–67.

Tripp, C. A. 1975. *The Homosexual Matrix*. New York: McGraw-Hill.

Troiden, Richard R., and Erich Goode. 1980. "Variables relating to the acquisition of a gay identity." *JH* 5:383–92.

Trujillo, Carla, ed. 1991. *Chicana Lesbians: The Girls Our Mother Warned Us About*. Berkeley: Third Woman Press.

Trumbach, Randolph. 1977. "London's sodomites." *Journal of Social History* 11:1–33.

———. 1985. "Sodomitical subcultures, sodomitical roles, and the gender revolution of the 18th century." *Eighteenth Century Studies* 9:109–21.

———. 1988. "Sodomitical assaults, gender role and sexual development in 18th century London." *JH* 16:407–29.

———. 1989. "The birth of the queen." In *Hidden from History*, ed. M. Duberman, M. Vicinus, and G. Chauncey, pp. 129–40. New York: New American Library.

Tucker, Scott. 1987. "Raw hide: The mystery and power of leather." *Advocate* 472 (12 May): 41, 49.

———. 1988. "Well, was it worth it?" In Preston 1988:124–32.

———. 1990. "Gender, fucking, and utopia." *Social Text* 27:3–34.

Turner, Heather A., Joseph A. Catania, and John Gagnon. 1994. "The prevalence of informal caregiving to persons with AIDS in the United States." *Social Science and Medicine* 38:1543–52.

Turner, Jonathan H. 1989. "The disintegration of American sociology." *Sociological Perspectives* 32:419–33.

Turner, Ralph H. 1962. "Role-taking." In *Human Behavior and Social Processes*, ed. A. Rose, pp. 20–40. Boston: Houghton-Mifflin.

————. 1978. "The role and the person. "*AJS* 84:1–23.

————. 1988. "Personality in society." *Social Psychology Journal* 51:1–10.

Umans, Richard. 1982. "On playing games." *Christopher Street* 65:14–17.

Vacha, Keith. 1985. *Quiet Fire: Memoirs of Older Gay Men.* Trumansburg, N.Y.: Crossing Press.

Valdiserri, Ronald O., et al. 1988. "Variables influencing condom use in a cohort of gay and bisexual men." *American Journal of Public Health* 78:801–5.

van der Meer, Theo. 1984. *De wesentlijke sonde van sodomie en andere buyligheeden.* Amsterdam: Tabula.

Vaughan, Diane. 1987. *Uncoupling.* New York: Oxford University Press.

Verdery, Katherine. 1991. *National Ideology under Socialism: Identity and Cultural Politics in Ceausescu's Romania.* Berkeley and Los Angeles: University of California Press.

Verghese, Abraham. 1994. *My Own Country: A Doctor's Story of a Town and Its People in the Age of AIDS.* New York: Simon and Schuster.

Vicinus, Martha. 1992. "'They wonder to which sex I belong': The roots of modern lesbian identity." *Feminist Studies* 18:467–97.

Vincke, John, Ralph Bolton, Rudolf Mak, and Susan Blank. 1993. "Coming out and AIDS-related high-risk sexual behavior." *ASB* 22:559–86.

Vining, Donald. 1979–93. *A Gay Diary.* 5 vols. New York: Pepys Press.

Vollmer, Tim. 1989. "Why gay liberation turned against us." *San Francisco Sentinel* (7 Dec.) 9.

————. 1990. "Drag goes on and beyond." *San Francisco Sentinel* 18,31 (2 August) 9,43.

————. 1995. "Losing San Francisco." *San Francisco Sentinel* 23,15 (12 April) 19.

Wagenhauser, John. 1992. "Safe sex without condoms." In Preston 1992a:272–81.

Wallace, Anthony F. C. 1952a. *The Modal Personality of the Tuscarora Indians* (Bureau of American Ethnology Bulletin 150). Washington, D.C.: GPO.

————.1952b. "Individual differences and cultural uniformities." *ASR* 17:747–50.

————.1956. "Mazeway resynthesis." *Transactions of the New York Academy of Sciences* 18:626–38.

————.1961. *Culture and Personality.* New York: Random House.

Wallis, Roy. 1977. "A critique of the theory of moral crusaders as status defense." *Scottish Journal of Sociology* 1:195–203.

Ward, David. 1989. *Poverty, Ethnicity and the American City.* Cambridge: Cambridge University Press.

Warner, Michael. 1991. "Fear of a queer planet." *Social Text* 29:3–17.

Warren, Carol A. B. 1972. "Observing the gay community." In *Research on Deviance,* ed. Jack Douglas, pp. 139–63. New York: Random House.

————. 1974. *Identity and Community in the Gay World.* New York: Wiley.

Warren, Carol A. B., and John Johnson. 1972. "A critique of labeling theory from a phenomenological perspective." In *Theoretical Perspectives on Deviance,* ed. R. Scott and J. Douglas, pp. 69–92. New York: Basic Books.

Warren, Steve. 1993. "Porcelain marks Rhino's sweet sixteen." *San Francisco Sentinel* (8 September) 25, 28.

Watney, Simon. 1987. *Policing Desire: Pornography, AIDS and the Media.* Minneapolis: University of Minnesota Press.

Weatherburn, Peter, et al. 1993. "No connection between alcohol use and unsafe sex among gay and bisexual men." *AIDS* 7:115–19.

Webber, Melvin M. 1964. *Explorations into Urban Studies.* Philadelphia: University of Pennsylvania Press.

Weber, Max. 1947. "Class, status, party." in *From Max Weber,* ed. Hans Gerth and C. Wright Mills, pp. 180–95. New York: Oxford University Press.

———. 1978. *Economy and Society.* Berkeley and Los Angeles: University of California Press.

Weeks, Jeffrey. 1977. *Coming Out.* London: Quartet.

———. 1981. "Discourse, desire and sexual deviance." In Plummer 1981:76–111. Repr. in Weeks 1991:10–45.

———. 1985. *Sexuality and Its Discontents.* New York: Routledge.

———. 1991. *Against Nature.* Concord, Mass.: Paul.

Wegener, Bernd. 1989. "Soziale Verwandtschaften im Karriereprogress." *Kölner Zeitschrift für Soziologie* 41:270–97.

———. 1991. "Job mobility and social ties." *ASR* 56:60–71.

Weightman, Barbara. 1980. "Gay bars as private places." *Landscape* 24:9–16.

Weinberg, Martin S., and Alan P. Bell. 1972. *Homosexuality: An Annotated Bibliography.* New York: Harper and Row.

Weinberg, Martin S., and Colin J. Williams. 1974. *Male Homosexuals.* New York: Oxford University Press.

———. 1975. "Gay baths and the social organization of impersonal sex." *SP* 23:124–36. Repr. in Dynes and Donaldson 1992:350–62.

Weinberg, Thomas S. 1978a. "On 'doing' and 'being' gay." *JH* 4:143–56.

———. 1978b. "Social and political issues and strategy in gay communities." *SGCN* 15:5–8.

———. 1983. *Gay Men, Gay Selves.* New York: Irvington.

Weiser, Jay. 1986. "Gay Identity." In *Gay Life: Leisure, Love, and Living for the Contemporary Gay Male,* ed. Eric Rofes, pp. 283–93. Garden City, N.Y.: Doubleday.

Weitz, Rose. 1984. "From accommodation to rebellion: The politicalization of lesbianism." In Darty and Potter 1984:233–49.

———. 1991. *Life with AIDS.* New Brunswick, N.J.: Rutgers University Press

Wekker, Gloria. 1993. "Mati-ism and black lesbianism: Two ideal typical expressions of female homosexuality in black communities of the diaspora [US and Suriname]." *JH* 24:145–58.

Wentworth, William M. 1980. *Context and Understanding.* New York: Elsevier.

Werdegar, David et al. 1987. "Self-reported changes in sexual behaviors among homosexual and bisexual men from the San Francisco City Clinic cohort." *Morbidity and Mortality Weekly Report* 36:171–73.

Wermuth, Laurie. 1995. "Heterosexual women and HIV risk." Paper presented at the Pacific Sociological Association annual meetings in San Francisco.

Werner, Dennis. 1979. "A cross-cultural perspective on theory and research on male homosexuality." *JH* 4:345–62.

Wescott, Glenway. 1990. *Continual Lessons: The Journals of Glenway Wescott.* New York: Farrar Straus Giroux.

Weston, Kath. 1991. *Families We Choose: Gays, Lesbians and Kinship.* New York: Columbia University Press.

————. 1993a. "Do clothes make the woman? Gender, performance theory and lesbian eroticism." *Genders* 17:1–21.

————. 1993b. "Lesbian and gay studies in the house of anthropology." *Annual Review of Anthropology* 22:339–67.

Whisman, Vera. 1993. "Lesbians, gay men and difference." Ph.D. dissertation, New York University. Revision pub. New York: Routledge, 1995.

————. 1997. "The seams in our constructions: AIDS in the history of lesbian self-definition." In *A Plague of Our Own: The Impact of the AIDS Epidemic on Gay Men and Lesbians*, ed. M. Levine, J. Gagnon, and P. Nardi. Chicago: University of Chicago Press, forthcoming.

Whitam, Frederick L. 1977. "The homosexual role reconsidered." *JSR* 13:1–11. Repr. in Dynes and Donaldson 1992:363–74.

————. 1980. "The pre-homosexual male child in three societies." *ASB* 9:87–99.

————. 1983. "Culturally invariable properties of male homosexuals." *ASB* 12: 207–22.

Whitam, Frederick L., and Mary Jo Dizon. 1979. "Occupational choice and sexual orientation." *International Review of Modern Sociology* 9:137–49.

Whitam, Frederick L., and Robin M. Mathy. 1986. *Male Homosexuality in Four Societies*. New York: Praeger.

White, Charles. 1984. *The Life and Times of Little Richard*. New York: Harmony Press.

White, Edmund. 1980. *States of Desire*. New York: Dutton.

Whitehead, Harriet. 1981. "The bow and the burden strap." In *Sexual Meaning*, ed. S. Ortner and H.Whitehead, pp. 80–115. New York: Cambridge University Press.

Whittier, David Knapp. 1995. "Life outside the gay ghetto: The social organization of male homosexualities in a southern town." Ph.D. dissertation, State Univeristy of New York, Stony Brook.

Wikan, Unni. 1977. "Man becomes woman: Transsexuals in Oman as a key to gender roles." *Man* 13:304–19.

————. 1978. "The Omani *xanith*: A third gender role?" *Man* 13:473–75.

————. 1982. *Behind the Veil in Arabia: Women in Oman*. Baltimore: Johns Hopkins University Press.

Williams, Andrea M. 1994. "In your face and just out of reach: The 'queer' social movement in San Francisco." Manuscript.

Williams, Colin J., and Martin S. Weinberg. 1971. *Homosexuals and the Military*. New York: Harper and Row.

Williams, Walter. 1986. *The Spirit and the Flesh*. Boston: Beacon.

Wilson, Doric. 1994. "Stonewall." *Gay Times* 189 (May) 20–21.

Winkelstein, Warren, et al. 1987a. "Reduction in Human Immunodeficiency Virus transmission among homosexual/bisexual men, 1982–86." *American Journal of Public Health* 76:685–89.

————. 1987b. "Sexual practices and risk of infection by the Human Immunodeficiency Virus." *Journal of the American Medical Association* 257:321–25.

————. 1988. "Continued decline in HIV seroconversion rates among homosexual/bisexual men." *American Journal of Public Health* 78:1472–74.

Winkin, Yves. 1988. "Erving Goffman: Portrait du sociologue en jeune homme." In *Les moments et leurs hommes*, pp. 13–92. Paris: Minuit.

Winkler, John J. 1990. *The Constraints of Desire: The Anthropology of Sex and Gender in Ancient Greece.* New York: Routledge.

Winters, Christopher. 1979. "The social identity of evolving neighborhoods." *Landscape* 23:8–14.

Wirth, Louis. 1928. *The Ghetto.* Chicago: University of Chicago Press.

———. 1938. "Urbanism as a way of life." *AJS* 44:3–24.

Wittman, Carl. 1970. "A gay manifesto." In Jay and Young 1972:330–45.

Wolf, Deborah Goleman. 1979. *The Lesbian Community.* Berkeley and Los Angeles: University of California Press.

———. 1982. "Lesbian mothers and artificial insemination." In *Anthropology of Human Birth,* ed. Margarita Artschwager Kay, pp. 321–39. Philadelphia: F. A. Davis.

———. 1984a. "Growing older: Lesbians and gay men." Manuscript.

———. 1984b. "Lesbian childbirth and woman-controlled conception." In Darty and Potter 1984.

———. 1984c. Preface to Murray 1984.

Wong, Norman. 1994. *Cultural Revolution.* New York: Persea Books.

Wood, Michael, and Michael Hughes. 1984. "The moral basis of moral reform." *American Sociological Review* 49:86–99.

Wooden, Wayne S., Harvey Kawasaki, and Raymond Mayeda. 1983. "Identity maintenance of Japanese-American gays." *Alternative Lifestyle* 6:236–43.

Woods, Gregory. 1993. "Gay re-readings of the Harlem Renaissance poets." *JH* 26,2:127–42.

Wright, Louis. 1935. *Middle-Class Culture in Elizabethan England.* Chapel Hill: University of North Carolina Press.

Wrong, Dennis. 1961. "The oversocialized conception of man in modern sociology." *ASR* 26:183–93.

Yearwood, Lennox, and Thomas S. Weinberg. 1979. "Black organizations, gay organizations: Sociological parallels." In Levine 1979c:301–16.

Zadeh, Lofti. 1965. "Fuzzy sets." *Information and Control* 8:338–53.

Zeeland, Steven. 1993. *Barrack Buddies and Soldier Lovers: Dialogues with Gay Young Men in the U.S. Military.* New York: Haworth.

Zhou, Min, and John R. Logan. 1989. "Returns on human capital in ethnic enclaves." *ASR* 54:809–20.

Ziebold, Thomas. 1978. *Alcoholism and the Gay Community.* Washington: Blade.

Zimmerman, Bonnie. 1990. *The Safe Sea of Women: Lesbian Fiction, 1969–1989.* Boston: Beacon.

Zita, Jacquelyn N. 1981. "Historical amnesia and the lesbian continuum." *Signs* 7:172–87.

Zola, Irving K. 1972. "Medicine as an institution of social control." *Sociological Review* 20:487–504.

Zurcher, Louis A. 1970. "The friendly poker game: A study of an ephemeral role." *Social Forces* 49:173–86.

———. 1977. *The Mutable Self.* Beverly Hills, Calif.: Sage.

Zurcher, Louis A., and R. George Kirkpatrick. 1976. *Citizens for Decency.* Austin: University of Texas Press.

Index